THE SUICIDAL PATIENT

Clinical and Legal Standards of Care

Bruce Bongar

Eric Harris
Legal Consultant

American Psychological Association
Washington, DC 20002

First Printing July 1991
Second Printing September 1992
Third Printing August 1994

Published by
American Psychological Association
750 First Street, NE
Washington, DC 20002

Copies may be ordered from
APA Order Department
P.O. Box 2710
Hyattsville, MD 20784

In the United Kingdom and Europe, copies may be ordered from
American Psychological Association
3 Henrietta Street
Covent Garden, London
WC2E 8LU England

Cover designed by Debra Riffe
Typeset by Harper Graphics, Waldorf, MD
Printed by Braun-Brumfield, Inc., Ann Arbor, MI
Technical editing and production coordinated by
Linda J. Beverly

Library of Congress Cataloging-in-Publication Data

Bongar, Bruce Michael.
    The suicidal patient : clinical and legal standards of care /
Bruce Bongar ; Eric Harris, legal consultant. — 1st ed.
        p.   cm.
    Includes bibliographical references and index.
    ISBN 1-55798-109-4 (acid-free paper)
    1. Suicidal behavior. 2. Suicidal behavior—Treatment. 3. Forensic psychiatry.
I. Title.
    [DNLM: 1. Defensive Medicine. 2. Physician-Patient Relations.
3. Psychotherapy—standards. 4. Suicide—prevention & control.
5. Suicide—psychology.   WM 33.1 B713s]
RC569.B66   1991
616.85'8445—dc20

                                                            91-4568
                                                            CIP

Printed in the United States of America

CONTENTS

Appendices

Foreword

About two millennia before Durkheim and Freud, a Jewish scholar and sage named Hillel voiced a number of questions for times of crisis: If not now, when? If not here, where? If I am not for myself, who will be for me? If I am only for myself, what am I? A formidable set of ringing rhetoricals that are, more than ever, pertinent. This book, *The Suicidal Patient: Clinical and Legal Standards of Care*, by Bruce Bongar, satisfies Hillel's implicit criteria for action. It is timely, it is pertinent to the needs we face as professionals, and it reflects both the mutual dependence and responsibility we share with our colleagues, our patients, and their families.

If not now, when? Some years ago, this book might have been premature; a few years from now, we would suffer for its absence. The fact is that we as psychologists and suicidologists (the two are not mutually exclusive) now possess sufficient and voluminous literature that can be of direct help in determining how to identify and treat suicidal patients. It *is* possible to develop standards for caring for and monitoring the patient, guidelines for consultation, models of treatment, and models for involving significant others. It *is* also possible to develop a thorough understanding of the uniqueness of the therapist–patient relationship that exists specifically when the patient is highly lethal.

If not here, where? This book provides a nexus for the essential clinical and legal ingredients of suicide. It offers a practical and multidimensional approach to the challenge of working with the suicidal patient, and in this it is perhaps unique. Although no book is indispensable (and one can always make blunders on one's own), this book will be welcomed and treasured as an important resource for it has *substance*. Our attention is drawn to the fact that in treating suicidal persons, the clinical and legal aspects are almost constantly intertwined. This book emphasizes the fact that one should not take one's eye off either aspect for more than a moment, if at all.

If I am only for myself, what am I? The sages of old tell us not to permit a fellow creature to be pushed to desperation or dreadful alternatives, that it is one's moral duty to anticipate cruel perturbation by preventing its root causes.

In the case of suicide, prevention means mollifying overwhelming psychological pain, and, prevention is always better than rescue. In either case, one must act. These key principles—prevention, rescue, and appropriate action within the existing social and legal nexus—are clearly put forth in this volume for us to read, to digest, and to apply.

The Suicidal Patient is philosophically in accord with a consultative model and clinical stance in which I firmly believe and which I have tried to emulate in my own work. This approach recognizes the difference between "perturbation" and "lethality." It propounds the concept that if one wishes to effectively decrease an individual's perturbation, one must do what is necessary to decrease that individual's perturbation, to relieve the intolerable psychological pain—which is, by definition, the extreme of perturbation. Take away the pain and the suicidality will lose its reason for being. The author of this volume has a profound understanding that the goal is to prevent suicidal deaths. He has grasped the fundamental idea that the management of suicidal patients borrows heavily from the goals of crisis intervention. First, one cannot attempt to ameliorate the suicidal individual's entire personality. The primary goal is to keep the person alive. Second, acceptance of this single concept—that one must be alive to change—is the *sine qua non* without which all other psychotherapy and efforts to help the suicidal person cannot function and, indeed, would be pointless.

If I am not for myself, who will be for me? Finally, *The Suicidal Patient* has personal focus. It addresses *us*, the readers, the individuals who must provide the therapy, the advice, and the nurturance needed by suicidal persons. This book grew out of profoundly felt, personal experiences of the author. The experiences that those who live with, work with, and support suicidal individuals come to know so well are reflected within. This volume has a quality of direct involvement and demands that we, too, become involved. At the same time, it supports our efforts to improve our skills and increases our capacity to uphold the best in our professions.

I am proud to be associated with this book, not only because I have had the opportunity to write this foreword, but even more so because I find my own work, pieces of myself, in its content and message. In the preface to my book, *Definition of Suicide*, I indicated that it was not an empirical book and that there were relatively few findings or new data in it; nor did it contain a comprehensive review of the literature on suicide. In *The Suicidal Patient*, Bruce Bongar has filled in those lacunae with solid facts and new data. He has also erected numerous signposts that will lead the rest of us further along the road to successful intervention with suicidal patients.

Edwin S. Shneidman
University of California
at Los Angeles

Preface

In the practice of psychology, there are dangerous intersections—crossings where both patient and psychologist run the risk of injury. For our patients, their physical and emotional well-being at this juncture depends in no small part on the clinical wisdom and skill of their psychologists. For psychologists, their personal and professional well-being depends on their possessing a fund of solid clinical information, experience, and training to ensure that the approach to this hazardous intersection is well-charted and understood. One of the most common and poorly marked of these dangerous intersections is the treatment of the suicidal patient.

This book is, in essence, a series of signposts created to provide the clinician with more prominent markings at such intersections. Its creation originated in our concern that there is no single source available to professionals, or those who are becoming professionals, in the field of psychology that summarizes the overarching concerns related to treating the suicidal patient or to the legal implications inherent in providing such treatment.

Completed and attempted suicide represents a very serious public health problem in the United States today. Each year almost 30,000 individuals take their own lives, making suicide the eighth leading cause of death in this country (Alcohol, Drug Abuse, and Mental Health Administration, 1989; Hirschfeld & Davidson, 1988). The data on completed suicide become all the more disturbing when one considers that completed suicides arguably represent only a small percentage of the number of attempts; that suicide may be statistically underreported; and that the rates of suicide in most industrialized countries are increasing, particularly among the age group 15 to 24 and among persons over the age of 65 (Maris, 1988).

The Emotional Effects of Patient Suicide on the Clinician

Suicide has been found to be the emergency situation most frequently encountered by mental health professionals (Schein, 1976), with clinicians consistently ranking work with suicidal patients as the most stressful of all clinical endeavors (Deutsch, 1984). One national survey found that psychologists who had lost a patient to suicide responded to the loss in a manner similar to persons who had experienced the death of a family member (Chemtob, Hamada, Bauer, Torigoe & Kinney 1988).

Patient suicide has a significant impact on the professional lives of a substantial number of therapists (Chemtob, Bauer, Hamada, Pelowski, & Muraoka, 1989), and it is alarmingly clear from recent empirical findings that the average professional psychologist involved in direct patient care has better than a 1 in 5 chance of losing a patient to suicide at some time during his or her professional career, with the odds climbing to better than 50/50 for psychiatrists (Chemtob, Hamada, Bauer, Torigoe & Kinney 1988; Chemtob, Hamada, Bauer, Kinney & Torigoe, 1988). Even a psychologist in training, according to one study, has a 1 in 7 chance of losing a patient to suicide (Brown, 1987).

Another more recent study (Kleespies, Smith, & Becker, 1990), investigating the incidence, impact, and methods of coping with patient suicide by psychology graduate students, found that 1 in 6 students had experienced a patient's suicide at some time during their training. Trainees with patient suicides reported levels of stress that were equivalent to those found in "patient samples with bereavement and higher than that found with professional clinicians who had patient suicides" (Kleespies et al., 1990, p. 257). This study also found that trainees who had lost a patient to suicide responded (in order of frequency) with feelings of shock, guilt or shame, denial or disbelief, feelings of incompetence, anger, depression, and a sense of being blamed. After the suicide, trainees frequently turned to their supervisors, both for emotional support and for help in understanding the suicide.

Therefore, it is particularly important that training programs in psychology and psychiatry "not convey, either explicitly or implicitly, the impression that patient suicides are an unlikely event (Brown, 1987). . . . It may be time that psychiatrists and psychologists explicitly acknowledge patient suicide as an important occupational hazard" (Chemtob, Bauer, Hamada, Pelowski, & Muraoka, 1989, p. 299).

The Legal Effects of Patient Suicide on the Clinician

The most common legal action involving psychiatric care is the failure to "reasonably" protect patients from harming themselves (Simon, 1987, 1988). Harris (1988) wrote that as professional psychology seeks parity with psychiatry in the area of professional privileges (such as voting membership on hospital staffs and full admitting privileges), the profession will expose itself to many of the same clinical risks and liabilities to which psychiatry is exposed. Gutheil and Appelbaum (1982) stated that "to the extent that psychologists, social workers, and nurses assume primary responsibility for patient care, they can be said to establish the same duty of care, within the context of a fiduciary relationship, that exists for psychiatrists" (p. 175).

Why *Patient* Rather Than *Client?*

Before proceeding in our discussion of the suicidal patient, we wish to state an important stylistic point, namely that throughout the course of this work we will be using the word *patient* rather than *client* to describe the populations with whom psychologists work in their professional practice activities. We have tried to use the word *patient* consistently throughout the book, not because we feel that its use is ideologically superior or preferable to the word *client*, but because, in any discussion of the legal system, the word *client* has another and special meaning.

Strickland (1987) makes this point clear in writing about the outcome of the 1987 Conference on Graduate Education and Training in Psychology. Psychology, she stated, is an autonomous and independent health profession, wherein psychologists assume responsibility for psychological health service delivery and are accountable to the profession and to the public for their assessment, evaluation, and treatment activities. If psychologists present themselves as independent health service providers, the word *patient* may better fit the expectations of attorneys, judges, and juries who will be likely to regard the deceased individual as having been in this role. Rachlin (1984) noted that, from a legal perspective, the simple fact that an individual is receiving psychological treatment indicates that a *legal* duty of care exists along the lines of a medical patient–physician relationship.

What This Book Does

The following chapters will present a number of suggestions for optimal psychological practice in the assessment, management, and treatment of the suicidal patient. In stating these recommendations, the author will be using "we" stylistically to reflect the author's own position and the concordance of the book's legal consultant.

The reader may wish to note that we have chosen to take an integrated approach to the voluminous literature on these subjects. We have used examples drawn from case law, opinions by noted clinical and legal scholars, malpractice insurance data, and state and federal statutes on suicide to support our various clinical teaching points. Through this process, we hope to illustrate precisely the dynamically changing array of clinical and legal opinions on the management of suicidal patients and to integrate this knowledge into a set of specific recommendations for clinical assessment, treatment, hospitalization, consultation, supervision, and so forth. The ultimate goal of this endeavor is to blend pragmatically (Halgin, 1985) the clinical and legal wisdom on suicide risk factors and clinical management into a set of sensible guidelines.

However, before beginning our discussion of problems in establishing clinical and legal standards for professional psychological practice in matters of suicide, it is necessary to state emphatically what the present book is *not*. This book is not a source of legal advice, nor a substitute for consultation with a competent attorney, a psychologist, or both. Nor is it an attempt to impose standards of care on our colleagues. Instead, we hope that the information in this book will help psychologists to decide when they need to seek a clinical consultation or when they need to contact an attorney. Furthermore, because of practical considerations, we will not be giving specific details of all the mental health laws and regulations that apply in the 51 state jurisdictions. (Here, readers are directed to their own state psychological association and to their respective state licensing/certification boards.) Instead, we will try to provide the underlying broad legal and clinical principles that often shape specific statutes and case law.

A Training Tool for Students and Professionals

Despite these obvious and grim realities in our field, it appears that we may not be training psychologists adequately to manage suicidal patients. For the most part, no routine formal training in suicide management is conducted in United States clinical psychology graduate training programs, psychiatric residencies, social work schools, or nursing programs (Berman, 1986a). In addition, a recent and comprehensive study (Bongar & Harmatz, 1989) found that although training directors of the traditional programs in clinical psychology (i.e., member programs of the Council of University Directors of Clinical Psychology) rated the study of suicide as very important to the graduate education of psychologists, and indicated that graduate training was the most appropriate place for this training to occur, only 35% of the programs offered any formal training in the management of suicidal patients as part of their curriculum. Even when all the efforts of the traditional scientist–practitioner and professional school training programs are combined, only 40% of all graduate programs in clinical psychology offer formal training in the study of suicide (Bongar & Harmatz, 1990).

As we have already discussed, patient suicide is not a rare event in psychological practice and should be considered a very real personal and occupational hazard by those psychologists involved in direct patient care (Chemtob, Hamada, Bauer, Torigoe, & Kinney, 1988). In order to meet the challenge of the suicidal patient, psychologists need to approach this population with confidence and not with fear (Berman & Cohen-Sandler, 1983). Confidence building begins with demanding professional standards aimed at moving clinical practice beyond merely defensive care. Of course, higher standards also stand to reduce the threat of a malpractice action (Berman & Cohen-Sandler, 1983).

An essential step in the direction of higher standards is the explication of clinical and legal management issues, focusing on standards for professional practice with the suicidal patient. The main goal of this book is to review the voluminous theoretical and empirical literature on this high-risk patient population and then to combine it with information on the necessary legal and statutory duties imposed on professional psychologists who see suicidal patients as part of their professional practice. We hope that the result for the reader will be a praxis-oriented distillation of the essentials for sound clinical work with these patients, combined with clear explanations of the legal and statutory demands that seeing such patients impose on the practitioner. For at its heart, this book seeks to provide usable recommendations designed to facilitate high-quality professional practice in working with suicidal individuals.

Most practicing psychologists will see patients in their professional practice activities who meet the profile of an elevated risk for attempted or completed suicide. Clinical wisdom among mental health practitioners "admonishes that it is not a matter of whether one of their clients will someday commit suicide, but of when" (Fremouw, de Perczel, & Ellis, 1990, p. 129). Patient suicide is not a tragedy that exclusively confronts the mental health professions, but "the incidence of its occurrence is such a frequent issue, both professionally and sometimes legally, that it demands special consideration" from mental health professionals (Smith, 1986, p. 62).

Further complicating the clinical situation is the fact that, although investigators have identified many clinical indicators of suicide risk, there are "no pathognomic predictors of suicide" (Simon, 1988, p. 89). Authorities who investigate suicidal phenomena have not reached consensus on the key risk factors, both short-term and long-term, that distinguish suicide completers. Ironically, for the practicing clinician, this lack of consensus is somewhat protective from a legal perspective. Courts and juries have often held that when it comes to suicide, there is no single correct or perfect solution in the management of the suicidal patient; the clinician's actions tend to be judged in comparison to what seemed reasonable compliance with the accepted standards of their profession (Simon, 1988).

Because professionals face the potential for a malpractice suit to be brought against them daily, it is important not only to provide the most effective clinical care possible, but to do so in the context of providing an increased level of legal protection. Therefore, many authorities consider the key to successful clinical practice with suicidal patients to be the use of risk management practices that adequately follow and document clinical practices that are in accord with the behavior of the average, reasonable and prudent practitioner of similar training and experience.

In addition, the practitioner, by consistently providing a reasonable standard of care in assessing and managing suicidal patients, preempts the very problematic issue of prediction of suicide for which standards do not exist (Simon, 1988). Therefore, our purpose is to present a list of fundamental, detectable risk factors that should alert the psychologist (in outpatient and inpatient settings) to engage in appropriate risk management behavior using a sound, well-documented management plan based on a thorough evaluation of the patient for the detection of an elevated risk for suicide.

Of course, despite such diligence, a patient may still commit suicide, and, if so, there is a high risk of a malpractice action being brought (Gutheil, 1990). However, the author and the legal consultant for this book believe that, if psychologists follow the basic risk management steps outlined herein (the guidelines for optimal levels of clinical care, careful documentation and consultation, etc.), it is likely that such an action will be abandoned at an early stage in the proceedings or be settled quickly out of court.

Most important, following sound clinical and risk management guidelines may save patients' lives, through the provision of a higher overall standard of patient care.

The Structure of the Volume

The essential factors and gray areas in the clinical knowledge base are presented in chapter 1. This chapter seeks to give the reader a basic understanding of the complexities and controversies in our understanding of suicide, and how these affect clinical practice.

In chapter 2, we convey how the suicide or attempted suicide of a patient under one's care may result in litigation or complaints to licensing boards and ethics committees (or both). Underlying this discussion is the understanding that, although the prevention of every suicide in clinical practice may never be possible, it is possible to protect oneself through sound risk management strategies and a basic knowledge of how the legal system operates should a suit or complaint be brought. (The basic message of this chapter is how high-quality clinical care is always the best protection.)

In chapter 3, we explore the complexities of the difficult clinical task of assessing elevated risk. In chapters 4 and 5, we discuss the implementation and clinical care strategies of outpatient and inpatient management and treatment, respectively. The principles of risk management in the context of both suicide prevention and postvention are distilled in chapter 6. Chapter 6 is followed by a comprehensive bibliography on suicide, clinical practice, and the law, and a series of appendices containing selected examples of suicide risk estimators and lethality scales.

In developing this brief and, to the best of our knowledge, unique volume, we drew on a large number of clinical and legal sources, on the skills and experience of numerous experts in suicidology, and on our own clinical and consultative experience. It is our hope that this distillation of knowledge will provide psychologists (whether psychologists-in-training, new professionals, or broadly experienced senior members of the field) with a useful compendium.

Acknowledgments

In the writing of *The Suicidal Patient: Clinical and Legal Standards of Care*, there were a large number of people who contributed their time, advice, and support in each stage of the book's gestation.

Firstly, I would like to thank my colleague and the book's legal consultant Eric Harris for his wise and authoritative counsel with regard to the complexities of the forensic realm. Eric's consultative expertise, his own original and fundamental writings on general theories of risk management in psychological practice—based on his many years of practical experience as both psychologist and attorney—and his wide-ranging knowledge of psychology and the law, were an invaluable asset as I worked on the development of this book. The lively debates that Eric and I had over the pros and cons for the various suggested standards of care in the suicidal scenario were of great value in fine-tuning and strengthening these guidelines, and are reflected in the reasonable and prudent nature of the suggestions for optimal levels of professional practice contained in this book.

Next, I would like to gratefully acknowledge the faith and support that Professor Edwin Shneidman has had for this project since its inception. While writing this book, his clinical wisdom and theoretical acumen often served as a model for optimal levels of clinical practice, and his seminal work on suicide continues to serve and inspire each new generation of psychologist-practitioners.

I would also like specifically to acknowledge and thank the many authorities in the areas of clinical psychology, psychiatry, and suicide and life threatening behaviors with whom I periodically consulted. A number of these authorities were kind enough to give permission for the reproduction of various scales and materials, to send along preprints and "in progress" copies of important recent studies, and to listen patiently, and sometimes at great length, as I struggled to sort out what might constitute optimal levels of clinical practice and risk management. While I accept full responsibility for all of the suggested guidelines and recommendations contained in this book, it is important to note that their sage counsel and the sharing of their clinical wisdom were of inestimable help in the construction of the guidelines in this book. Specifically, I would like to thank Drs. Aaron Beck, Bruce Bennett, Robert Berchick, Allan Berman, Herbert Brown, James Butcher, Edward Bourg, Claude Chemtob, David Clark, Lewis Cohen, Ronald Davidoff, James Eyman, Norman Farberow, Stuart Golann, Thomas Gutheil, Richard Halgin, Mort Harmatz, Douglas Jacobs, David Jobes, David Lester, Ray William London, Ronald Maris, John McIntosh, Jerome Motto, George Murphy, Charles Neuringer, I. N. Perr, Linda Peterson, Kenneth Pope, Charles Rich, Donna Satterfield, Andrew Slaby, Kim Smith, Robert Steer, Bryan Tanney, Gary VandenBos, Avery Weisman, J. W. Worden, Fred Wright, and Robert Yufit.

I also would like to acknowledge the efforts of my editors at the American Psychological Association (APA), and to mention specifically the superb support, counsel and consultation that Brenda Bryant provided for this work, and to acknowledge the ongoing support and guidance that Julia Frank-McNeil gave to this project. I would like to thank my development editor, Ted Baroody, for his patient and effective comments, and to acknowledge the excellent help that Mary Lynn Skutley, and Patricia Harding-Clark provided for this project.

To my wise and wonderful wife Debbora, how does one ever truly acknowledge so many years of deep love, patience and unqualified support, as well as the authorial inspiration that you model in your own work, except to say thank you for bearing with me during this long project. To our 3-year-old son Brandon, I give a heartfelt promise that the next time we go to France, I will spend more time hiking and swimming, and less time chained to the word processor.

Finally, this book is dedicated to a number of my patients over the years— whether in the hurly-burly of a busy psychiatric emergency room or in the quiet of my consulting room—who helped me to more fully comprehend the suicidal crisis and who shared with me the depths of their terrible pain. Who, in their brave willingness to go forward and attempt to work through their darkest moments of despair in the therapeutic alliance, were always on my mind as I worked on the standards of optimal practice contained within.

I am also grateful to the following sources for permission to reprint previously published material:

Pp. 23, 43, 45–46, 103, 103–104, 106, 116, and 142: W. J. Fremouw, M. de Perczel, and T. E. Ellis, *Suicide Risk: Assessment and Response Guidelines*, © 1990 Pergamon Press. Pp. 169–170, and 170: T. G. Gutheil, *Hospital and Community Psychiatry*, *31*(7), pp. 479–482, 1980. Copyright 1980, the American Psychiatric Association. Reprinted by permission. Pp. 51–52: Reprinted by permission of the publisher from ''Double Jeopardy: Suicide and Malpractice'' by S. Rachlin, *General Hospital Psychiatry 6*, pp. 302–307. Copyright 1984 by

ACKNOWLEDGMENTS

Elsevier Science Publishing Co., Inc. Pp. 2, 36, 48, and 140: J. D. Robertson, *Psychiatric Malpractice: Liability of Mental Health Professionals.* Copyright © 1988 by John Wiley & Sons, Inc. Reprinted by permission of John Wiley & Sons, Inc. Pp. 37, 175–176, 183, 194, and 195: R. L. Sadoff and T. G. Gutheil, "Expert Opinion: Death in Hindsight" in *American Psychiatric Press Review of Clinical Psychiatry and the Law, Vol. 1.* Edited by R. I. Simon. Washington, DC, American Psychiatric Press, 1990, pp. 329–339. Copyright 1990 American Psychiatric Press, Inc. Pp. 38, 42, and 47: L. VandeCreek and S. Knapp, *Psychotherapy: Theory, Research, and Practice, 20*(3). © 1983 American Psychological Association. Reprinted with permission of the editor, *Psychotherapy.* Pp. 41 and 171: From *Tarasoff and Beyond: Legal and Clinical Considerations in the Treatment of Life-Endangering Patients* (pp. 25, 30) by L. VandeCreek and S. Knapp, 1989, Sarasota, FL: Professional Resource Exchange. Copyright 1989 by the Professional Resource Exchange, P.O. Box 15560, Sarasota, FL 34277-1560. Reprinted by permission.

The Knowledge Base

Suicide is one of the few fatal consequences of psychiatric illness; and thus the subject is a source of endless disquiet to the practicing mental health professional (Nemiah, 1982). Among the survivors of a suicide, including the psychotherapist, the reaction is often disbelief, shame, anger, and shock (Goldstein & Buongiorno, 1984).

Suicidal behavior is the most frequently encountered of all mental health emergencies (Schein, 1976), and psychotherapists identify suicidal statements as the most stressful of all client communications (Deutsch, 1984). This is a reflection of the fact that the relationship between psychopathology, suicide attempting, and completed suicide is complex, dynamic, and not yet well understood (Maris, 1981; Peterson & Bongar, 1989; Shneidman, 1989). Recent studies show changes in the identity of high-risk groups (Boyd, 1983; Evans & Farberow, 1988; Maris, 1981, 1989; Roy, 1986; Shneidman, 1989; Weissman, Klerman, Markowitz, & Ouelette, 1989), and follow-up studies demonstrate that risk factors among attempters may be significantly different from those for the general population (Frederick, 1978; Maris, 1981, 1989). Moreover, studies suggest that rates of suicide among the mentally ill (Hirschfeld & Davidson, 1988; Maris, 1981; Pokorny, 1964a, 1964b; Roy, 1986; Simon, 1988), and physically ill (Abram, Moore, & Westervelt, 1971; Hirschfeld & Davidson, 1988; Maris, 1981; Roy, 1986) far exceed that of the population as a whole. However, the estimates of the rate of death by suicide due to psychiatric disorders can vary greatly based on such factors as country of origin (Roy, 1986), regional differences within a single country (Peterson, Bongar, & Netsoki, 1989), and the diagnostic criteria used for the sample (e.g., the number of manic depressives who die by suicide ranges from 15% to 55%; Goldring & Fieve, 1984).

Clearly these variances mitigate against any single explanation of suicidal behavior or any simplistic approach to treatment (Bongar, Peterson, Harris, & Aissis, 1989). Indeed, the diverse explanations for suicide include biological predisposition (Arana & Hyman, 1989; Asberg, Bertillson, & Martensson, 1984; Brown et al., 1982; Mann & Stanley, 1988a; Stanley & Mann, 1988; Van Praag, 1986); reaction to humiliation, helplessness, hopelessness, and guilt (Shneidman, 1986b); manipulation on the part of the patient, an escape from physical or psychological pain, expression of violent rage (Nemiah, 1982); reaction to separation from family or from the loss of a love (Richman, 1986); eroticization of death itself; and an aesthetic completion of patriotic sacrifice (Lifton, Shuichi, & Reich, 1979).

Suicidal phenomena are enormously complex. In order to fully understand the event of suicide, one must attempt to understand the varieties of human behavior, thinking, and reasoning (Shneidman, 1987, 1989). Arguably, the central issue in suicide is not death or killing; rather, it is the stopping of the consciousness of unbearable pain, which, unfortunately, by its very nature, entails the stopping of life. Shneidman (1984, 1989) points out that one of suicide's chief shortcomings is that it unnecessarily answers a remediable challenge with a permanent negative solution. By contrast, living is a long-term set of resolutions with, oftentimes, only fleeting results (Shneidman, 1984).

Impressions From History

Suicide is an ancient behavior; cases from Egypt are documented as early as the third millennium B.C. (Fremouw, de Perczel, & Ellis, 1990), and there are also numerous recorded cases from ancient Greece and Rome (Robertson, 1988; Rosen, 1976). Robertson noted that:

> The Hebrew Torah recorded five acts of self-destruction including the death of the first Israeli king. Aristotle argued that suicide treats a state unjustly. Saint Thomas Aquinas wrote that, since every man is part of a community, he injures that community by killing himself. Blackstone considered suicide to be a form of felonious homicide. It was called the highest crime against the law of nature because it violated the law of self-preservation, infringed upon the King's peace, and deprived him of one of his subjects. (p. 177)

Over the centuries, there have been constantly shifting moral views about the social acceptability of suicidal behavior. These views have ranged from viewing suicide as an appropriate social response (the Japanese code of Bushido in the 17th century, for example, held that the disgrace of failure to one's lord could be expiated by the ritual taking of one's own life) to viewing it as a disgraceful act against nature and society.

Litman (1980) noted that in traditional Western society it was necessary to assign blame for every death either to God or to man (i.e., homicide, suicide);

that if God was responsible for the death, nothing more needed to be done, but if a human being was to blame, then there must be a punishment for the guilty. "Thus for centuries, English law designated suicide as a special crime, punished by mutilation of the body, sanctions on the place and manner of burial, forfeiture of property, and censure of family" (p. 841). He also pointed out that the trend in modern times is to regard suicide less as being a sin or a crime, and more as being an unfortunate consequence of mental illness and social disorganization.

Social-demographic theories of suicide have been historically prominent in effecting an empirical understanding of suicidal phenomena (Jacobs, 1988). The most cogent exponent of the sociological view was the French sociologist, E. Durkheim (Maris, 1976). *Le Suicide*, first published in 1897, was Durkheim's comparative study of suicide in postindustrial society (Durkheim, 1951). This work continues to generate extensive research and discussion. Durkheim's general thesis states that the suicide rate varies inversely with external constraint and that external societal constraint has two dimensions—what Durkheim called *integration* and *regulation* (Maris, 1976). Roy (1988) spoke of the three categories that Durkheim used to demonstrate this relationship: *egoistic* (lack of meaningful family ties or social integrations); *anomic* (the relationship between the person and society is broken by economic or social adversity); and *altruistic* (excessive integration, e.g., hari kiri, suttee).

An additional element in the sociological approach to understanding suicide is the concept of status integration: namely, that the suicide rate is inversely related to the stability and duration of social relationships (Gibbs & Martin, 1964). There are important social meanings in the way we calculate the rate of suicide; for example, the reported suicide rates and specific criteria for reporting have as many meanings and variations as there are coroners and medical examiners (Douglas, 1967). Another example of an important social element in assessing risk is that of status loss, especially the loss of occupational status (Maris, 1976).

Even though attitudes in Western societies have become more tolerant toward suicide, there are still undercurrents of ambivalence and social condemnation (Litman, 1980). Judicial attitudes toward suicide have moved away from assessing "guilt and enforcing punishment toward protecting suicidal persons when possible, and toward efforts to care for or compensate the surviving victims of suicide deaths" (Litman, 1980, pp. 841–842). Litman also noted that because of this undercurrent of social condemnation, the friends and relatives of the completed suicide feel themselves to be not only bereaved, but also stigmatized. These significant others often attempt to persuade, coerce, or otherwise influence the certifying authorities against a verdict of suicide (e.g., suicide notes may be hidden or destroyed).

Shneidman (1986a) pointed out that Freud—eschewing both the notions of sin and crime—gave suicide back to the individual, but put the locus of action in the unconscious mind. Shneidman stated that diagnosis of suicide depends on an unambiguous definition (Shneidman, 1985), and he pointed out that, historically, *suicide* is a word that seems to have both a core and a periphery. The unambiguous core is the simple formula that *suicide is the act of taking one's own life*. Shneidman continues:

> There is something more to the human act of self-destruction than is contained in this simple view of it. And that something more is the periphery of any satisfactory definition. Are totally lethal intended acts which fail (e.g., shooting oneself in the head and surviving) suicide? Are nonlethal attempts on the life (e.g., ingesting a possibly lethal dose of barbituates) suicidal? Are deleterious and inimical patterns of behavior (e.g., continued smoking by a person with acute emphysema) suicidal? Are deaths which have been ordered by others or deaths under desperation (e.g., Cato's response to Caligula's requesting his death, or the deaths on Masada or in Jonestown) suicide? All of these questions constitute the indispensable periphery of the definition of suicide. (p. 6)

Definition and Theories of Suicide

Shneidman (1985, 1989) proposed that an operational definition of suicide must limit the term *suicide* to acts of committed suicide (or efforts or attempts to be dead by suicide). This definition would follow the British tradition of separating self-inflicted, sublethal acts from suicide. An individual who has made a nonlethal, self-inflicted, injurious suicide-like act is said to have committed *parasuicide*. Shneidman added that each suicidal event should be evaluated on a continuum of lethality, for example, Weisman and Worden's (1974) risk-to-rescue ratio assessment, where in a suicide attempt "the risk of death is extremely high and probability of rescue is extremely low" (Shneidman, 1985, p. 20).

The boundaries between self-mutilation, sensation seeking, and suicidal behavior are murky (Peterson & Bongar, 1989). Historically, there is a lack of clarity about whether consciously expressed suicidal desire accompanying the behavior should be requisite in order to classify the behavior as suicidal. However, in the heat of the emergent clinical moment, psychologists who must evaluate and triage acts of suicidal or life-threatening behavior might do well to adopt a definition of attempted suicide such as Stengel's (1965):

> A suicidal attempt is any act of self-damage inflicted with self-destructive intention, however vague and ambiguous. . . . For the clinician, it is safer still to regard all cases of potentially dangerous self-poisoning or self-inflicted injury as suicidal attempts, whatever the victim's explanation, unless there is clear evidence to the contrary. Potentially dangerous means in this context: believed by the attempter possibly to endanger life. (p. 74)

With regard to the actual danger of eventual completed suicide for the suicide attempter, Maris (1981) stated that there is a body of evidence to indicate that, in general, suicide completers are likely to make one lethal attempt, whereas most suicide attempters make multiple low-lethality attempts. This is in accord with Stengel's observation that those who attempt suicide and those who complete suicide may constitute two distinct, yet overlapping populations (Stengel, 1965).

Maris (1981) further noted that nonfatal suicide attempts occur approximately 6 to 8 times more often than completed suicide, and that the risk of eventual completed suicide among attempters is roughly 15%. Other estimates of the ratio of attempters to completers place their risk at 8:1, or approximately 12.5% (Cross & Hirschfeld, 1985; Hirschfeld & Davidson, 1988). Finally, although estimates place the percentage at 10% to 20% of attempters who eventually go on to complete suicide, Hirschfeld and Davidson (1988) emphasized that a history of suicide attempts significantly increases the likelihood of subsequent suicide.

Such fine discriminations between suicide, attempted suicide, parasuicide, suicidal gestures, suicidal manipulations, and so forth are both necessary and important from a heuristic and research perspective. However, from a clinical *and* legal perspective any time a patient uses—or threatens to use—even a superficially suicidal or suicidal-like behavior to demonstrate their psychological pain, that communication initiates a situation of elevated risk that calls upon the psychologist to ascertain, in a timely and systematic manner, whether this situation is indeed a true emergency (e.g., during the course of a therapy session, a depressed patient mentions a desire to drive a car into a concrete highway abutment). In support of this position, Shneidman (1985) wrote that, although attempting suicide with less than total lethality might be called parasuicide (or even quasisuicide), such events are still psychological crises and warrant a full professional and sympathetic response on the part of the psychologist. (The thorny issue of repetitive low-lethality, self-destructive acts will be addressed in chapter 3.)

Research in Suicidology

The research on understanding suicide has focused on a number of different approaches (Shneidman 1985, 1989) including the following:

- psychological—identifying psychological states in suicide victims as well as the examination of cognitive, behavioral, and emotional components of suicidal acts (e.g., Beck, 1967; Beck, Kovacs, & Weissman, 1975; Ellis, 1986; Shneidman, 1984);
- psychodynamic—the turning against oneself of angry and destructive impulses, unconscious hostility, the splitting of ego states, self-destructive instincts, and so on (e.g., Freud, 1917; Jacobs,

1989b; Litman, 1967, 1968, 1989; Maltsberger, 1986; Menninger, 1938; Shneidman, 1989);

- sociocultural—assessing the impact of social and cross-cultural factors, or the correlation of social change with suicide (e.g., Douglas, 1967; Durkheim, 1951; Gibbs & Martin, 1964; Henry & Short, 1954; Maris, 1976, 1981, 1989a);
- biological, biochemical, and constitutional—looking at the relationship of genetics, neurotransmitters, biochemistry, and so forth to suicide (e.g., Arana & Hyman, 1989; Maris, 1986; Motto, 1986);
- psychiatric and mental illness (e.g., American Psychiatric Association, 1987; Fawcett et al., 1987; Klerman, 1989; Perlin & Schmidt, 1976);
- epidemiological and demographic—population identifying (Cross & Hirschfeld, 1985; Hirschfeld & Davidson, 1988; Klerman, 1987; Maris, 1981; Roy, 1986; Sainsbury, 1986);
- prevention, intervention, and postvention (e.g., Litman, 1971; Murphy, 1984, 1986, 1988a, 1988b; Shneidman, 1985; Shneidman, Farberow, & Litman, 1970).

Other approaches of note have included the dyadic/familial (Pfeffer, 1986; Richman, 1986); interpersonal (Klerman, Weissman, Rounsaville, & Chevron, 1984); literary and personal document (Alvarez, 1971, 1976; Shneidman, 1989); architectural (Mack, 1989); systems theory (Blaker, 1972); empathic (Jacobs, 1988, 1989b); philosophical and theological (Battin & Mayo, 1980; Camus, 1959); legal and ethical (Battin, 1982; Beyer, 1982; Litman, 1957, 1982; Maris, 1983); global, political, and supranational (Shneidman, 1985, 1989). Public health, economic, and historical perspectives were added to this list by Maris (1988). It is useful to note that the official journal of the American Association of Suicidology has published recommendations for conducting high-quality research in suicidology (Smith & Maris, 1986). More recently, an entire issue of this journal was devoted to strategies for studying suicide and suicidal behavior (Lann & Moscicki, 1989; Maris, 1989a).

Although the focus of the recommendations contained in the present book is primarily on standards of care for the United States, other cross-cultural research data on suicide can illuminate the effects of particular sociocultural differences (see Bohanan, 1943; Malinowski, 1926; Rubinstein, 1983). For example, the United States' suicide rate of approximately 12 per 100,000 places it in the average category for industrialized countries. Higher rates have been reported in Eastern Europe, German-speaking countries, Scandinavia, and Japan (rates often over 25 per 100,000). Lower rates, that is rates below 6 per 100,000, are often seen in countries such as Greece, Ireland, and Italy (Fremouw et al., 1990).

During his studies, Diekstra (1990) found that societies, communities, and social groups that are subject to conditions such as economic instability, deprivation (e.g., unemployment), or the breakdown of traditional "primary or family group structure, interpersonal violence, increases in criminal behavior, secularization, and increasing substance use/abuse, are at high risk for an increase in suicides in youth" (p. 554). He also discovered that many of the developing countries, as a consequence of dramatic growth in urban areas, are "witnessing a disruption of traditional family structure, values, and ways of life . . . . a striking trend is that patterns of mortality in large urban areas in the developing world are beginning to resemble more and more the patterns of mortality in the industrialized world" (p. 554).

The pluralistic nature of contemporary American society necessitates clinical understanding of diverse ethnic groups and subcultures, along with the specific risk factors and diagnostic considerations for each group (Earls, Escobar, & Manson, 1990). The inability to understand a particular language and culture can present a dangerous barrier to correct assessment and treatment. (More information on these specific factors for assessment and management is contained in the Epidemiology of Suicide section of this chapter.)

There also appear to be regional differences in the rates of suicide within the United States (Peterson & Bongar, 1989), with suicide rates being lowest in the northeast, and highest in the west (Fremouw et al., 1990). Some authorities point to the relationship between suicide and urbanization, "with suicide rates increasing more-or-less with the size of cities. A rural exception to this rule might be communities where agriculture is in decline and migration to cities is occurring" (Sainsbury as cited in Fremouw et al., 1990, p. 28).

In his architectural model of suicide, Mack (1989) illustrated the importance of contextual, structural, and systemic information. His approach has a number of implications for treatment, including a particular stress on the current life situation, the evaluation of the dynamics of depression and suicide, a careful assessment of available social supports, and the need to pay attention to the individual's total life context in the prescribing of treatment (Jacobs, 1988).

In 1981, Maris described the study of suicide as a "synergistic" blend of the theories and methods of the social sciences and psychiatry, a notion that Shneidman (1989) extended in his suggestion that suicide can best be understood through multidisciplinary approaches. We would add that psychologists need to understand the complexities that guide the testimony of expert witnesses (often the method used by the courts to establish the retrospective standard of care) to different conclusions in their evaluation of a patient's suicide—that the courts will look to the available research and research methodologies for help in understanding the scientific basis for the experts' diverging opinions. Therefore, as a starting point, it may be helpful to examine the commonalities and differences in the psychological, psychodynamic, biological, and epidemiological approaches to suicide in order to contexualize the case law findings on suicide and to help in the understanding of standards of care.

Psychological Approaches

Shneidman (1989) reported that the psychological approach to suicide does not put forth a set of dynamics or unconscious motives for suicide, but rather emphasizes certain general psychological features that need to be present for a lethal suicide to occur. He listed four such psychological features in completed suicide:

1. acute perturbation, an increase in the person's state of general upset;

2. heightened inimicality, an increase in self-hate, self-loathing, shame, guilt, and self-blame, along with an increase in behaviors that are not in the individual's best interests;

3. a sharp and almost sudden constriction of the person's intellectual focus, in which the patient's thoughts exhibit a tunneling process, a narrowing of the mind's content, a truncating of the capacity to see viable alternatives to their current dilemma;

4. the idea of cessation, the coming into the person's awareness that it is somehow possible to end this terrible and unbearable psychological pain. The patient's idea that cessation, the termination of consciousness by their own hand, is the ''igniting element that explodes the mixture of the previous three components'' (p. 8).

Beck and his colleagues have repeatedly demonstrated the importance of the concept of hopelessness as a predictor of suicide during therapy, as a lead to assessing suicidal ideation, and as a clue to the source and resolution of a clinical impasse (Beck, 1967; Beck et al., 1975; Beck & Steer, 1988). They have been important pioneers in the cognitive approach to the treatment of depression and suicide (for a review of cognitive therapy of depression and suicide, see Rush & Beck, 1989). The importance of feelings of helplessness and hopelessness as precursors of suicide was also stressed by Shneidman (1985). On this point he is clearly in accord with Beck (1967) and Beck, Rush, Shaw, and Emery (1979), who noted that, although there are many types of feelings and affects in a suicidal patient, the common emotion in all patients is hopelessness and helplessness.

An important clinical point here is that depression of all subtypes increases the risk of suicide (Clark, 1988). If a patient speaks of increasing feelings of depression, hopelessness, and helplessness during therapy, the psychotherapist should recognize these psychological signs as major suicidal risk factors for the patient.

In a theoretical paper, Frederick and Resnik (1989) suggested that suicidal

8

behaviors, like many other patterns of behavior, can be learned, and they went so far as to state that "it would be difficult to support any notion that self-destructive behavior could be fully explained without employing learning principles" (p. 21). They then went on to say that, although unconscious conflicts and neurobiochemistry do affect the way in which behavior is motivated and learned, there is no evidence that a complex behavior such as one's own self-destruction resides in the genes. Their premise is of particular interest when one examines patterns of chronic suicidal behavior (e.g., repeated manipulative suicidal ideation or parasuicide).

One of Frederick and Resnik's most provocative ideas is that various behaviors by health care and mental health professionals, as well as by personnel in emergency rooms and crisis intervention centers, may paradoxically reinforce suicidal behaviors via the caretaker's immediate and powerful response to the patient's "cry for help." In an emergency setting, it is not uncommon to see patients making repeated visits to an emergency room for treatment of sublethal self-inflicted harm, or with threats of the same (Bongar, Peterson, Golann, & Hardiman, 1990). Often, these patterns of recidivist behaviors and their reinforcement histories are not acknowledged or examined by emergency room staff. This issue will be discussed further in the chapters on assessment (chapter 3) and on management and treatment (chapters 4 & 5). A central point in Frederick and Resnik's argument is the need for clinicians and clinical facilities to be cognizant of the fact that suicidal behaviors, like many other patterns of behavior, can be learned and that the principles of learning theory must be considered when one develops any assessment or treatment techniques (Frederick & Resnik, 1989).

Liberman and Eckman (1981), using a behavior therapy package, compared behavior therapy with insight-oriented therapy in a clinical trial for repeated suicide attempters. They reported that behavior therapy was the superior intervention, with structured brief hospitalization and assertive follow-up contributing to the main effects.

Fremouw et al. (1990) demonstrated the importance of the cognitive revolution in our understanding of a psychological approach to suicide and cited the seminal contributions of Ellis and Dryden (1987), Beck et al. (1979), Meichenbaum (1977), and Peterson and Seligman (1984). They showed that there are several common threads that tie the cognitive theories together and that there are unique cognitive characteristics of suicidal individuals: that is, cognitive rigidity, dichotomous thinking, impaired problem-solving ability, hopelessness, and irrational beliefs and dysfunctional attitudes.

In his list of psychological risk factors, Schutz (1982) emphasized the potential for manipulativeness in suicidal behavior. This concept suggests that the more aware a suicidal patient is that his or her suicidal action will result in self-destruction, the more likely the patient is to commit suicide. Conversely, if suicidal action is stressed by the patient in terms of the person(s) who will be affected, then the patient is less likely to commit suicide. Other authorities disagree and suggest that fantasies of patients, especially those that involve retrospectives on their own funerals and scenes of life after death, pose a considerable risk (Maris, 1981; Peterson & Bongar, 1989; Shneidman, 1984, 1986a).

There is a substantial body of literature that examines the psychosocial-relational indicators of suicidal intent. Shneidman (1985) pointed to a number of such clues, including the patient putting his or her affairs in order, giving away prized possessions, and behaving in any way that is markedly different from his or her usual pattern of living. Other factors include saying good-bye to friends (or psychotherapists) and settling estates (Beck, 1967). Three risk factors that correlate highly with completed suicide and are primary indicators of suicidal intent are communication of intent, previous suicide attempts, and antecedent circumstances (e.g., a change in family situation, occurrence of a physical illness, drastic financial changes, and substance abuse) (Robins, 1985).

Shneidman (1984, 1986a) warned that extreme caution must be exercised with the patient who is perturbed and who has a lethal means available. This would include patients with poor impulse control who are in crisis and are unable to decrease their level of perturbation in the therapeutic encounter. Shneidman noted that it is important not to minimize the potential suicidality of character disordered patients who are in crisis. On the other hand, patients who are less impulsive, more depressed, or psychotic should be considered at higher risk if their suicidal ideation has been present for more than a few days and if they have articulated any concrete elements of a plan (Shneidman, 1984, 1986a). It is also critical to look at whether the patient has suffered any recent and important losses in his or her life (e.g., job, relationships, residence) or whether the patient has suffered more subtle psychological losses, (e.g., humiliation, shame, or self-hate) (H. Block-Lewis, personal communication, November 15, 1985; Blumenthal, 1990; Lazare, 1987; Peterson & Bongar, 1989; Shneidman, 1986a, 1986b).

Patients with delusional depressions or major depressive episodes who feel that they are a source of shame and humiliation to their family or that they will be letting the family down should be considered a high risk. In a retrospective chart review of cases seen by a major teaching hospital's emergency mental health service from 1984 to 1986 (Peterson & Bongar, 1990), there were two cases where death followed within one week of contact. Both cases were males, age 50 to 60, with major depressive episodes; both had supportive families, but both patients felt nonetheless that they were an inadequate provider for the family. Neither admitted continued suicidal thoughts at the end of their evaluation. In both of these cases, the issues of perceived loss of face, shame, and humiliation were catalytic motivations to suicide (H. Block-Lewis, personal communication, November 15, 1985; Bongar et al., 1989; Lazare, 1987). These findings are in accord with Rangell's observation that a common mechanism behind an acute onset of a suicidal crisis is sudden shame (Rangell, 1988).

Shneidman (1985, 1987, 1989) has repeatedly argued that there are 10 common psychological characteristics of most completed suicides (see Table 1.1). Although the list presented in Table 1.1 certainly addresses the question of what constitutes the relevant common psychological dimensions of completed suicide, in the treatment of suicidal patients, "there are no universals or absolutes . . . . the best that one can reasonably hope to discover are the most frequent (i.e., common) characteristics that accrue to most suicides" (Shneidman, 1987, p. 167).

Psychodynamic Approaches

In a comprehensive review of all of Sigmund Freud's experience with suicide, both personal and professional, Litman (1967, 1989) concluded that Freud never solved the enigma of suicide to his own satisfaction and that the inability to do so had a tremendous influence on his instinct theory. For the last decade of his life, Freud was convinced of the value of his concept of a primary self-destructive instinct that is in conflict with Eros (Litman, 1989).

In refining earlier work by Freud, Zilboorg (1937) wrote that every suicidal case contained not only unconscious hostility, but also an unusual lack of the capacity to love others. Loss of love objects, aggression directed toward an introjected love object, narcissistic injury, overwhelming affect, and a setting of one part of the ego against the others were some of the suicide mechanisms that

Table 1.1
The Ten Commonalities of Suicide

I. The common purpose of suicide is to seek a solution	VII. The common perceptual state in suicide is constriction
II. The common goal of suicide is the cessation of consciousness	VIII. The common action in suicide is egression
III. The common stimulus in suicide is intolerable psychological pain	IX. The common interpersonal act in suicide is communication of intention
IV. The common stressor in suicide is frustrated psychological needs	X. The common consistency in suicide is with life-long coping patterns
V. The common emotion in suicide is hopelessness–helplessness	
VI. The common cognitive state in suicide is ambivalence	

Note. From "A Psychological Approach to Suicide" by E. S. Shneidman, in G. R. VandenBos and B. K. Bryant (Eds.), *Cataclysms, Crises, and Catastrophes: Psychology in Action* (p. 167), 1987, Washington, DC: American Psychological Association. Copyright 1985 by E. S. Shneidman. Adapted from Shneidman (1985) by permission of John Wiley and Sons. Copyright © 1985 by E. S. Shneidman. Reprinted by permission.

Freud conceptualized as involving the breakdown of ego defenses and the release of increased destructive, instinctual energy (Perlin & Schmidt, 1976).

According to Litman (1989), Freud's dictum that suicide begins with a death wish that is directed toward others and then is redirected toward an identification within the self has been overly emphasized among some psychotherapists. In the psychodynamic formulation of suicide risk, Litman believes that there has been an overemphasis on guilt and aggression and an underemphasis on helplessness, the erotic, and paranoia.

Menninger (1938) wrote extensively about the deeper dynamic motives for suicide. He held that suicide must be regarded as a peculiar death that entails three internal elements: the element of dying, the element of killing, and the element of being killed. He also emphasized that people remain alive through the mechanism of a vital balance in the self (Menninger, 1938, 1989). In Menninger's view, the self is composed of component subselves. A weakness in the ability to integrate these subselves and balance them is one measure of a person's vulnerability to suicide (Litman, 1989).

In an important integration of dynamic considerations in the formulation of suicidal risk, Maltsberger (1986) stated that

> to understand the vulnerability to suicide is to understand the psychology of despair . . . . the subjective experience of despair has two parts. First, the patient finds himself in an intolerable affective state, flooded with emotional pain so intense and so unrelenting that it can no longer be endured. Second, the patient recognizes his condition, and gives up on himself. This recognition is not merely a cognitive surrender, even though most hopeless patients probably have thought about their circumstances and reach a conscious, cognitive decision to give up. A more important aspect of the recognition that I am describing is an unconscious, precognitive operation in which the self is abandoned as being unworthy of further concern. (pp. 1–3)

Buie and Maltsberger (1989) went on to discuss how persons who are vulnerable to suicide often have not developed their own internal resources for self-soothing. These vulnerable individuals must look to resources external to themselves for a sense of comfort, and without these external resources they experience *aloneness* (defined as a vacant, cold feeling of isolative and hopeless discomfort). Buie and Maltsberger also elaborated on Kohut's position (Kohut, 1971) that people need to feel valuable, suggesting that immature, narcissistic individuals often use idealized or mirrored external others (self-objects) to feel a sense of value, and that when these self-objects are lost, vulnerable patients "fall prey to dangerous affects of worthlessness or aloneness (sometimes to both at once). Their survival is then in danger" (Buie & Maltsberger, 1989, p. 61).

They also proposed that, at times, suicide is the psychological equivalent of killing someone else and that "this was the circumstance described by Freud in *Mourning and Melancholia* (Freud, 1917). The lost self-object (Freud referred to an object invested with ego libido) may be introjected and felt to reside within the person of the self" (p. 62).

Suicidal patients, according to Buie and Maltsberger's dynamic formulation of risk, need help to work through and understand their sense of murderous rage with a self-object that has disappointed them, to resist primitive conscience or self-contempt, or to recognize the false lure of a fantasized sense of peace through death. Moreover, the prudent clinician will be constantly on the lookout for any losses of external resources for self-worth or soothing by the patient. Overall, Buie and Maltsberger (1989) take the extreme stand that suicide proneness is "primarily a psychodynamic matter; the formal elements of mental illness only secondarily intensify, release, or immobilize it" (p. 66). Going further yet, Rangell (1988) stated that "those patients an analyst knows in depth do not commit suicide. Those who do, the analyst does not know in depth" (p. 37).

In closing this section on psychodynamic approaches to suicide, it is critical to note Litman's (1989) observation that

> Freud, like many other clinicians who deal with suicide regularly in practice, came to adopt a pragmatic treatment attitude. In 1926, in discussing a young patient, Freud wrote, "What weighs on me in his case is my belief that unless the outcome is very good, it will be very bad indeed. What I mean is that he would commit suicide without any hesitation. I shall do everything in my power to avert that eventuality." (p. 148)

Biology of Suicide

From a biological perspective, suicidal behavior has been viewed as the product of genetic predisposition, either related to or separate from hereditary mental illness with high rates of suicide (Egeland & Sussex 1985; Rainer, 1984). In the past 10 years, evidence has accumulated on the biochemical changes in the brain that seem to be highly correlated with aggression, violent suicide attempts, and completed suicide, but not necessarily related to a given psychiatric diagnosis (Arana & Hyman, 1989; Asberg et al., 1984; Brown et al., 1982; Maris, 1986). Maris (1986) reviewed and summarized some of these results as follows:

1. Low levels of hydroxyindoleacetic acid (5-HIAA; a metabolite of the neurotransmitter serotonin, 5-HT) in the cerebrospinal fluid (CSF) were significantly correlated with a history of aggression, violent suicide attempts and other nonviolent attempts (Asberg, Traskman & Thoren, 1976; Van Praag, 1986).

2. Among patients with the lowest levels of 5-HIAA in the CSF

(below 92.5 nmol/liter) there was a 20% incidence of suicide in the following year (Traskman, Asberg, Bertilsson, & Sjostrand, 1981).

3. Blunted thyroid-stimulating hormone (TSH) response to thyrotpropin-releasing hormone (TRH) stimulation has been correlated with low CSF 5-HIAA and violent suicide attempts (Van Praag, 1986).

4. Plasma cortisol level higher than 20 mcg% may be positively related to suicide (Stanley, Stanley, Traskman-Bendz, Mann, & Meyendorff, 1986).

5. Lower levels of serotonin were found in the brains of completed suicides when compared to a control group (Mann, Stanley, McBride, & McEwen, 1986).

In a comprehensive review of the biological and genetic contributions to suicide, Arana and Hyman (1988) concluded that "if genetic predisposition plays a role in determining suicide behavior independent of psychiatric illness . . . . it is plausible that a biological factor independent of psychiatric illness may be identified to serve as a marker for individuals who may be at risk for suicide" (p. 58).[1]

The importance of examining the familial–genetic aspects of suicidality was stressed by Roy (1988). In addition to the issue of genetic transmission of psychiatric illness, Roy emphasized the importance of psychological identification and the possible existence of a genetic link between impulsivity, aggression, and suicidality (for additional information on genetics, family history, and suicide, see Kety, 1990). Buda and Tsuang (1990) stated that the risk of both schizophrenia and affective disorders is significantly higher among relatives of schizophrenic and manic-depressive patients respectively, and that these findings suggest that the rate of suicide in relatives of psychiatric patients is higher than expected.

Mann and Stanley (1988a), two noted biological researchers on suicide, demonstrated that suicide appears to be only poorly correlated with the severity of depressive illness. While constructing a model describing suicide, they found that "it is clear that several causal and facilitatory factors must be considered. No single factor is sufficient alone" (p. 424). They wrote that there are both psychological and biological traits (at least partly inherited) that place certain individuals at risk. "These individuals may never actually experience suicidal ideation or make an attempt unless some other factors come into play" (p. 424). Such other factors can include alcoholism, a depressive illness, schizophrenia,

---

[1]For an additional recent review of the biochemical aspects of suicide, the reader is directed to the work of Winchel, Stanley, and Stanley (1990).

divorce, a physical illness, and so forth. These researchers also stated that mitigating factors such as family support systems, psychiatric intervention, or recognition on the part of the patient of a need for help must also be considered. They proposed a theoretical multifactorial model of suicide that attempts to distinguish between state and trait effects and "emphasizes the multifactorial contribution to the endpoint of the suicidal act" (p. 424).

Winchell and his colleagues (1990) found that the identification of biological factors associated with suicidal behavior holds promise for the development and application of psychopharmacologic interventions for suicide prevention. Although these biological findings are clearly of great significance, the practical meanings and applications of these findings to the daily practice of clinical psychology and psychiatry are not yet clear. Until much more substantiating data are available, these potential biological and genetic markers of suicide risk constitute areas of continuing research rather than established clinical tools (Motto, 1986). As Evans and Farberow pointed out, although some authorities believe that suicides tend to run in families because of innate or genetic predisposition to severe depression, "there has been a substantial effort to reduce the reason for suicide to biological depression . . . . while there may be some basis for this, it is far from the whole story. Suicide and depression are not synonymous" (Shneidman as cited in Evans & Farberow, 1988, p. 135). Perhaps the most useful and cautionary clinical implication that can be drawn from the biological data is that a clinical evaluation for suicide-risk potential would not be complete without a thorough family history examining any attempted or completed suicidal behavior in the patient's close biological relations (e.g., mother, father, siblings, grandparents, etc.)

Epidemiology of Suicide

For all ages, the combined suicide rate in the United States during this century has remained at approximately 12 per 100,000 population (Hirschfeld & Davidson, 1988). However, suicide rates have increased alarmingly for youth (those age 15–24). Although the suicide rates among the young are lower than for the older age groups (especially men over the age of 35), the rates for older persons have decreased during this same time period (Alcohol, Drug Abuse, and Mental Health Administration, 1989; Hirschfeld & Davidson, 1988; National Center for Health Statistics, 1986). Here it is important to note that, although in the United States suicide accounts for roughly 2% of all deaths, it accounts for more than 15% of the deaths among adolescents (Dorwart & Chartock, 1989; see Figure 1.1).

Traditionally, suicide has been considered a mental health problem among older white males. However, since 1980, more than half of all completed suicides occurred among persons under the age of 40 (Alcohol, Drug Abuse, and Mental

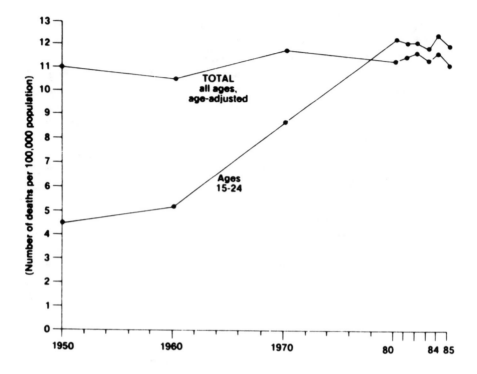

While the overall suicide rate changed little since 1950, rates for young persons 15–24 increased.

Figure 1.1 Trends in suicide rates. From *Report of the Secretary's Task Force on Youth Suicide: Vol. I.* Overview and Recommendations (pp. 1–6) by Alcohol, Drug Abuse, and Mental Health Administration, 1989, Washington, DC: U.S. Government Printing Office.

Health Administration, 1989). The National Conference on Risk Factors for Youth Suicide found that for youths (age 15–24) there were a number of risk factors for suicide, among them the following:

1. substance abuse, both chronic and acute, within the context of the suicidal act (as well as substance abuse as an exacerbating factor in concurrent psychiatric illness);
2. affective disorders, schizophrenia, and borderline personality;
3. familial characteristics, including genetic traits such as a predisposition to affective disorders;

4. low concentrations of the serotonin metabolite 5-hydroxyindole-acetic acid (5-HIAA), and the dopamine metabolite homovanillic acid (HVA) in the cerebrospinal fluid; and

5. parental loss and family disruption, along with being a friend or family member of a suicide victim, a history of previous suicidal behavior, impulsiveness and aggressiveness, media emphasis on suicide, homosexuality, rapid sociocultural change, and ready access to lethal methods (Alcohol, Drug Abuse, and Mental Health Administration, 1989, pp. 1–59).

In a study of "normal" high-school students, Smith and Crawford (1986) found that 62.6% of their subjects reported some degree of suicidal ideation or action and that 8.4% had made an actual attempt. Holinger and Offer (1982) have documented a significant positive correlation between adolescent suicide rates, changes in the adolescent population, and changes in the proportion of adolescents in the population. (For additional information on the issues of assessment, treatment and intervention for suicidal behavior in college students, see Schwartz & Whitaker, 1990).

Leenaars and Balance (1984) examined the suicide notes of 48 completed and 4 attempted suicide victims (age 18–74) in terms of the detection of 25 protocol sentences that reflected important specific aspects of Freud's formulations with regard to suicide. Specific sentences that were found more frequently in the notes of young people showed that they were more self-critical, were harsher toward themselves, perceived themselves as having little worth, and treated themselves as objects.

Although suicide in young children had been thought to be nonexistent, Murphy (1987) reported that a recent study of suicide in children ages 5 to 14 found that their attempts were very grave, with attempted hanging as the most common method, followed by running in front of vehicles, and multiple methods. He concluded that the suicide attempt of a child is a very serious event and that researchers and medical examiners should vigilantly examine any cases of equivocal accidental deaths in this population (see Pfeffer, 1986, for an excellent examination of the specific issue of suicide in children, and Brent & Kolko, 1990, for a review of the important factors in the assessment and treatment of children and adolescents at risk for suicide).

One of the most basic facts about suicide in the United States is that its risk increases as a function of age (Vaillant & Blumenthal, 1990), and although in the past 30 years we have seen a great increase in the rate of suicide in youth, "80-year-olds are still twice as likely to commit suicide as 20-year-olds" (Vaillant & Blumenthal, 1990, p. 1; see Figure 1.2). In addition, Achte (1988) noted that, "although the frequency of attempted suicide decreases as people get older, at the same time, the number of successful suicides increases. Elderly people

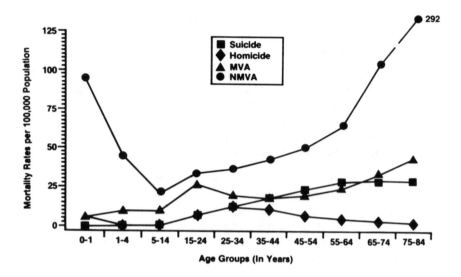

For each type of violent death, the data have been averaged over the years 1900–1980.

MVA = motor vehicle accident

NMVA = nonmotor vehicle accident

Figure 1.2 Age patterns of violent deaths. From "Sociodemographic, Epidemiological, and Individual Attributes" (pp. 2–22) by P. C. Holinger and D. Offer in *Report of the Secretary's Task Force on Youth Suicide: Vol. II* Risk Factors for Youth Suicide, 1989, Washington, DC: U.S. Government Printing Office.

are, in fact, more likely to succeed in taking their own lives than persons belonging to younger age groups" (p. 55). Risk factors for suicide in the elderly specifically include losses and loneliness, injuries to self-esteem in old age, aging and body image, and depression and depressive disorders (Achte, 1988). In confirmation of Achte's observation on the relative importance of social isolation as a risk factor in the elderly, Maris (1981, 1989b) reports that, in one study of the general population, suicide completers generally scored higher in social isolation than nonfatal attempters or than those who died by natural causes. Osgood and Thielman (1990) pointed out that early recognition of depression and other underlying mental disorders is essential for suicide prevention for the elderly.

McIntosh (1988), Morgan (1989), and Osgood (1985) have discussed the special considerations that are necessary when clinicians assess suicide risk in the elderly, including hopelessness as the most common feeling state of older persons who commit suicide. In addition, they observed that diagnostically, depression, alcoholism, and organic brain syndrome are the most common mental disorders of the suicidal elderly. However, Achte (1988), McIntosh (1988), and Morgan (1989) pointed out that, although it is convenient to speak epidemiologically about the elderly as a homogeneous group, the correct assessment of risk must always evaluate the elderly from an individualized perspective, and that the treatment of suicide risk in the elderly does not differ substantially from the treatment of suicide in other age groups. It is also critical to recognize the importance of prevention of suicide in this high-risk group and that

> the prevention of depression and suicide in old age requires a real change of attitude in society toward the elderly—a change that will guarantee every older person the right to work and to love. That was Sigmund Freud's formula for mental health, elegant in its simplicity. Erik Erikson taught us that the theme of old age is the maintenance of integrity. (Achte, 1988, p. 64)

Maris (1988) commented that, although there has been a recent emphasis on the tragedy of youth suicide, suicidologists need to study the entire range of the life cycle, including middle-aged as well as elderly suicide, because

> it is probably true that the longer one lives, the more likely it is that problems will develop. Most suicide tolerance thresholds are gradually breached by accumulated stresses and developmental strain . . . . and youthful suicides often result from relatively few factors acutely overwhelming the young person. (p. xv)

These findings on suicide are all the more disturbing when one considers that it is widely believed that completed suicides probably represent only a small percentage of the number of attempts. Suicide may be statistically underreported, and the rates of suicide in most industrialized countries are increasing, particularly among the age group 15 to 24 and those over age 65 (Maris, 1988).

History of Suicide Attempt and Method of Suicide

As was previously discussed, Maris (1981) found that nonfatal suicide attempts occur approximately 6 to 8 times more often than completed suicide and that the risk of a completed suicide among attempters is roughly 15%. Other estimates of the ratio of attempters to completers place it at 8:1, or approximately 12.5% (Cross & Hirschfeld, 1985; Hirschfeld & Davidson, 1988).

Therefore, a history of suicide attempts may indicate that the likelihood of subsequent suicide is significantly increased. Dorwart and Chartock (1989) unequivocally stated that the best predictor of subsequent suicide attempts and completions is a history of previous attempts. As a dramatic indication of the seriousness of the problem of attempted suicide, Hirschfeld and Davidson (1988) recently estimated that the number of suicide attempts is nearly 300,000 per year, or approximately one person every two minutes.

However, as Maris (1981) noted, in general completers tend to make one high-lethality attempt (using firearms, hanging, jumping, and other violent methods). By far the most common high-lethality method used in the United States is a firearm (particularly handguns; Boyd, 1983). However, use of a particular method can vary by region (Peterson, Bongar, & Netsoki, 1989) and by state. For example, in Massachusetts since the late 1970s, the most common violent method used by suicide completers is hanging/strangulation (B. Blackbourne, personal communication, December 2, 1989).

Maris (1981), in his classic study of self-inflicted deaths in a general population, used multivariate analysis techniques within a more dynamic developmental framework and documented the primary factors in the etiology of completed suicide to be age, negative interactions, drug and alcohol use, hopelessness–depression–dissatisfaction, the number of previous suicide attempts, and the use of lethal methods. Additional factors included sex, religion, early trauma, suicide in the family of origin, sexual deviance, work problems, physical illness, and conceiving of death as an escape. Maris found that suicide completers tend to make just one high-lethality attempt, whereas nonfatal attempters tend to make multiple low-lethality attempts. Suicide completers are more likely to be older males, who are physically ill, disabled or retired, socially isolated, less likely to change their minds after making a decision, and more likely to conceive of death as an escape from pain. The most powerful predictor in this extensive study was the number of previous suicide attempts.

Clinicians should be careful, however, to avoid assuming that a history of previous suicide attempts is an ironclad predictor of completed suicide. It is well known that the male to female ratio for completed suicide is approximately 3:1, whereas women make 3 out of 4 suicide attempts (Robins, 1986). One group of researchers (Kaplan & Klein, 1989) in this area suggested that the existence of such gender-related differences in the nature and causes of suicide strongly suggests the possibility that gender differences in psychological development may underlie key elements in attempted and completed suicide. Furthermore, the suicide rates for women have not approached those for men, and thus the frequency of attempted suicide in the female population is much higher than the frequency of completed suicide (Kaplan & Klein, 1989). (For a more extensive discussion of the issue of women and suicide, see Kaplan & Klein, 1989; Lester, 1988; Weissman & Klerman, 1982; Wilson, 1981.)

Self-poisoning by pill ingestion is the most common method of suicide attempt (70% to 90%) (Jacobs, 1989a). Murphy (1987) found that 80% of recognized suicide attempts are by overdose of medication and that the amount of medication varies widely, but usually poses little or no threat to life (however, exceptions occur and circumstances vary). The self-poisoners who ingested pills were found to have less serious psychiatric disturbances than wrist cutters or those using more violent means, and the catalyst for their attempted suicides was usually interpersonal turmoil, that is a "cry for help," with the ultimate goal of reestablishing the relationship (Jacobs, 1989a).

The second most common presenting problem of suicidal behavior in emergency settings is wrist cutting (Jacobs, 1989a). Murphy (1987) noted that roughly 10% of all suicide attempts are by cutting (90% of these are superficial cuts of the ventral surfaces of the wrist, occasionally of the arm). He also cautioned that systematic studies of wrist cutters as female, single, attractive, and so forth, do not reflect the fact that 40% of wrist cutters are male. (The issue of deliberate self-harm and suicidality is discussed in chapter 4.) Even though pill taking and cutting are usually not fatal, it is important to note Jacobs' (1989a) cautionary dictum that "any suicidal behavior, regardless of severity, places a person at 10 to 100 times more than the normal risk for suicide" (p. 370).

Sex, Race, and Ethnicity

Robins (1986) found that completed suicide is more than three times as likely in males as in females, and that the number of suicides by White males in the United States is 20 times the number of suicides by Black males. Because the population ratio of Whites to Blacks in the United States is approximately 10:1, this places the actual ratio of White male suicide to Black male suicide at 2:1.

Although suicide rates for Blacks are roughly half as great as for Whites, both for men and for women (Alcohol, Drug Abuse, and Mental Health Administration, 1989), Gibbs (1988) noticed that suicide among Blacks is a youthful phenomenon. She pointed out that, at the time when these young people should be exploring job or family possibilities, they are destroying themselves, by suicide, homicide, or fatal accidents. She also showed that, in all other ethnic groups except Native Americans, suicide rates increase with age, whereas the suicide rate for Blacks peaks in the young adult period (age 25–34). Suicide is the third leading cause of death in Black youths, after homicides and fatal accidents, and the suicide rate for Black youths 15 to 24 years of age has more than doubled in the past 25 years, with Black males accounting for most of the increase (Gibbs, 1988).

Suicide is currently the second leading cause of death, after accidents, for young Native Americans. It is important to note that the suicide rates vary considerably among the various tribes; that the age distribution patterns for Native American suicides differ distinctly from the general population; and that Native American suicides are generally much younger, with the rates peaking among those 20–24 years old (Alcohol, Drug Abuse, and Mental Health Administration, 1989).

The data on Hispanic suicides show that the suicide rate is lower than the rates for Whites, but higher than the rates for Blacks in the same geographic locale. Again, the peak age for Hispanic suicide occurs between the ages of 20 to 24 (Alcohol, Drug Abuse, and Mental Health Administration, 1989).

There are few studies that have examined the rates of suicides among Asian Americans. The current available data indicate that Chinese, Filipino, and Japanese male suicide rates are, in general, lower than those of other American males, except in the older age groups (Alcohol, Drug Abuse, and Mental Health Administration, 1989).

Special Populations

Jacobs (1989a) demonstrated that alcoholic patients and chronic suicidal patients make up two of the largest groups seen in the emergency room for suicide attempts. He noted that alcoholic patients constitute a very high-risk group: 15% die by suicide, a rate of 270 per 100,000. Although there is some overlap between alcoholism and depression, the suicide rate for alcoholics does not appear to be inflated by this overlapping of diagnoses, and when suicide does occur, it "tends to occur later in life or as a late complication of alcoholism" (p. 372). Assessment of this population must include factors of intent, lethality, diagnosis, and interpersonal context.

The chronically suicidal patient is defined as a patient for whom suicide has become a way of life (Bongar et al. 1990; Gutheil, 1990; Jacobs, 1989a). Diagnostically, these patients often present with character pathology or schizophrenia (Jacobs, 1989a). An extended discussion of chronicity and suicidality can be found in chapter 5.

Fremouw et al. (1990) found that there are certain special high-risk populations; for example, incarcerated adults in jail have suicide rates (132 per 100,000) that are 10 times higher than those of the general population (an average of 10 to 14 per 100,000). They further noted that the typical jail suicide profile is that of a 22-year-old, single, White male who had been arrested for an alcohol-related offense and who then attempted suicide within 24 hours of the time of his arrest. Compounding the problem of suicide prevention in this population, Maris (1990) found that jail suicides or suicide attempts often occurred within the first few hours after admission to the facility and that the typical method was hanging/strangulation. Maris also noted that it is difficult to determine which particular inmate to put on maximum suicide precautions and that suicide among incarcerated populations may only be preventable at the cost of protective measures that deny essential and basic human freedoms and dignities to all inmates.

The Interpersonal Matrix and Social Factors

Social factors such as unemployment, inflation, and absence of social supports are associated with suicide risk. For example, "nonmarried status represents a risk factor in people who are (in order of decreasing levels of risk) separated, divorced, widowed, or single [Sainsbury, 1986]'' (Fremouw et al. 1990, p. 31). Thus, people who have never been married are twice as likely to commit suicide as married individuals, and the divorced and widowed have even higher rates. Citing the work of Linehan (1981), Fremouw and his colleagues (1990) stated that ''the absence of a spouse, whether due to death, separation, or divorce, increases the probability of suicidal behavior'' (p. 31). They also remarked that the relationship between religion and suicide is unclear, even though Maris' 1981 study found that suicide completers were less likely to participate in religious activities.

Acute versus chronic predictors

Fawcett (1988) made important statements about the differentiation between short-term (acute) and long-term (chronic) predictors. These can be summarized as follows:

Acute
- Acute defensive breakdown (e.g., depressive turmoil, severe panic anxiety, panic attacks, alcohol abuse)
- Negative evaluation (e.g., severe loss of interest and pleasure in life; severe hopelessness)
- Behavioral predictors (e.g., mood cycling, abrupt clinical change, either negative or positive, the negation of help, a suicidal communication to a significant other)

Chronic
- Diagnostic predictors (e.g., suicidal ideation, mood cycling, hopelessness, loss of pleasure/interest, thought insertion, paranoid features, substance abuse, alcoholism)
- Historical predictors (e.g., previous suicidal behavior, psychiatric discharge within 6 to 12 months, no child under 18 years of age to care for, failure to maintain warm and mutually interdependent personal relationships)
- Behavioral predictors (e.g., help negation, social isolation)

In 1988, Fawcett spoke on the importance of the social matrix and the importance of communication of intent, specifically making the following observations:

1. 50% to 70% of suicide completers communicate their intent in advance.
2. Members of high-risk suicide groups often communicate their intent only to a significant other.

3. Members of moderate-risk suicide groups often communicate by frequently threatening suicide to family group members, their physicians, and others.

4. The chronic interpersonal behavior patterns that differentiate patients at high risk for suicide are (a) interpersonal incapacity, (b) marital isolation, (c) help negation, and (d) distorted communication of dependency wishes.

5. The acute interpersonal features of those with increased risk for suicide include (a) communication of intent to significant other only, (b) stated intent to die, and (c) an attempted behavioral change.

Fawcett (1988) concluded that these findings have important implications for assessment and treatment: There should be an increased emphasis on the evaluation of the person's interpersonal relationships through information-gathering activities with significant others.

Perhaps most important for the purposes of the present section on epidemiology, Robins (1986) pointed out that, although age, sex, race, and psychiatric diagnosis are probably the most consistent and accurate predictors of suicide, there is a very high rate of mental illness among those who commit suicide (93% to 100% of samples) and that the percentage of persons who commit suicide who were not diagnosed as having suffered from mental illness was low (0 to 7% of the total samples). Therefore, the remainder of this section will focus on the characteristics of populations who are most likely to be assessed and treated in professional psychological practice and who are most at risk for completed suicide, that is, patients with mental illness, patients with alcohol/substance related problems, and patients with a history of suicide attempts.[2]

Before proceeding to the specifics of the common risk profiles for completed suicide among patients commonly seen in professional psychological practice, it is critical to note Hirschfeld and Davidson's (1988) cautionary dictum to mental health professionals:

> Identifying characteristics of persons at high risk for attempting or committing suicide expands the psychiatrist's reference base for assessing

---

[2]Space limits our ability to discuss specific epidemiological topics and special populations (e.g., children, adolescents, the elderly, women, minorities, suicides in the schools, suicide in the physically ill), rates of suicide in other countries, variations across time, indirect self-destructive behaviors, methodological concerns, the effects of media, contagion, and similar specific topics. Therefore, the reader is directed to the following sources: Achte (1988); Alcohol, Drug Abuse, and Mental Health Administration (1989); Berman (1986b); Dorwart and Chartock (1989); Farberow (1980); Fremouw et al. (1990); Garfinkel (1989); Gibbs (1988); Gould, Shaffer, and Kleinman (1988); Hendin (1989); Klerman (1986); Lester (1988); Maris (1989b); McIntosh (1988); Osgood (1985); Peck, Farberow, and Litman (1985); Pfeffer (1986); Phillips and Carstensen (1988); Robins and Kulbok (1988); Sainsbury (1986); and Shneidman (1985, 1986a, 1989).

suicide potential. The patient who shares characteristics typical of most persons who commit suicide heightens one's estimate of the danger of suicide. On the other hand, one cannot dismiss the possibility of suicide in, say, a thirty-year-old, married Black woman simply because she doesn't fit the epidemiological profile of a high-risk patient. Familiarity with risk factors for suicidal behavior helps the physician register the import of data from the psychiatric interview and make a more cogent appraisal of the possibility of suicide. (p. 307)

In his review of studies of completed suicides, Robins (1986) noticed that two illnesses, affective disorder and alcoholism, accounted for the majority of psychiatric diagnoses among completed suicides (54% to 85%). This finding was supported by Dorwart and Chartock's (1989) statement that depression, either diagnosed or unrecognized, is the most important risk factor for suicide and that 15% of depressed individuals die by suicide.

By one estimate, schizophrenics have approximately a 10% lifetime risk for completed suicide, and 20% of schizophrenic patients make a suicide attempt. The profile of the typical schizophrenic completer is that of a young male, usually in his thirties, who had been ill for 5 to 10 years (Dorwart & Chartock, 1989). Alcohol and polysubstance abuse among patients with a schizophrenic disorder can also greatly increase the risk for suicide (Rich, Motooka, Mitchell, Fowler, & Young, 1988).

In three major studies of completed suicide, 22% of the subjects were diagnosed as having alcoholism (Robins, 1986). In addition, alcohol and substance abuse can often act as a precipitant to the act of suicide (Dorwart & Chartock, 1989). In one study of youth suicide, it was found that substance abuse disorders could well be a major factor in the rising suicide rate for those under 30 years of age (Fowler, Rich, & Young, 1986). In another important study, the researchers examined the relationship between the most common psychiatric illnesses and the most common stressors in 283 suicides in San Diego County and found that interpersonal loss and conflict occurred more frequently near the time of death for substance abusers, with and without depression, than for non-abusers with affective disorder (Rich, Fowler, Fogarty, & Young, 1988).

Murphy (1987) pointed out that other psychiatric illnesses (i.e., illnesses other than depressive illness and alcoholism) do play a role in suicide, "albeit a smaller one, organic brain syndromes contribute 5% to 10% of the total. This includes both delirium and chronic dementia. Epilepsy, general paresis, and a history of serious head injury are encountered more frequently among suicides than one would expect" (p. 3). However, the lifetime risks are not known for any part of this heterogeneous grouping.

Psychiatric patients run a much higher risk for death by suicide than the general population (Clark, Young, Scheftner, Fawcett, & Fogg, 1987). Clark and his colleagues (1987) figured that the annual suicide rate is approximately

15–19/100,000 for the adult general population, 230/100,000 for those with depression, 270/100,000 for those with alcoholism, and 140/100,000 for those with schizophrenia. It is estimated that over a period of 15–20 years, 10%–15% of all patients with depression, alcoholism, or schizophrenia die by suicide. (p. 923)

Whereas Fremouw et al. (1990), after reviewing a number of studies in which suicide rates differed, estimated the suicide rates for major psychiatric diagnoses as being: depression, 230–566/100,000; schizophrenia, 167–750/100,000; alcoholism, 133–270/100,000; personality disorder, 130/100,000; neurosis, 119/100,000; and organic brain disorder, 78/100,000.

Murphy (1987) noted that "retrospective diagnostically oriented studies have shown uniformly that nearly all suicide victims were psychiatrically ill in the time period immediately preceding the suicidal act" (p. 2). Furthermore, two psychiatric illnesses were found to be associated with two-thirds of these suicides, namely depressive disorders (40%–80%) and alcoholism (20%–30%). Murphy concluded that "what this means clinically is that for all of its seeming randomness, suicide is first of all a manifestation of psychiatric illness. Secondly, it is not a manifestation of psychiatric illness in general but rather of certain illnesses in particular" (p. 2).

Recently, Weissman et al. (1989) found that people with a history of panic disorder and panic attacks exhibited a higher rate of suicide ideation and attempts as compared with those with other psychiatric disorders (e.g., people with major depression). These researchers examined data on a random sample of 18,011 adults drawn from five different cities in the United States. They reported that panic disorder and attacks were associated with an increased risk of suicidal ideation and suicide attempts (20% of the subjects with panic disorder and 12% with panic attacks had made suicide attempts). They also noted that the increased risk of suicide attempts "occurs independently of the presence of coexisting depression, alcohol or drug use, or agoraphobia" (p. 1212).

Because this was the first report of its kind, Clark (1990) cautioned that care must be taken in generalizing from these results until the findings have been replicated. The bottom line of this important recent study is that

> whether they present with isolated panic attacks, a full-blown panic disorder, or with a co-existing psychiatric disorder, persons with panic attack symptoms may consider suicide and make suicide attempts more often than patients with illnesses we usually consider to pose a greater suicide risk—those with major depression, alcoholism, drug abuse, or schizophrenia. This is an important new finding, if successfully replicated by other groups. (Clark, 1990, p. 4)

Another important finding was that among completed suicides, there was a high degree of need for medical care within the last year of life and that completers often were under the care of a physician during the last year of their life (Dorpat, Anderson, & Ripley, 1968; Murphy, 1986; Robins, 1986). Dorpat and Ripley (1960) found that 87% of their sample population sought medical attention in the year prior to their suicide; another study found that 100% of the completers sought the care of a physician in the final year of their life (Barraclough, Bunch, Nelson, & Sainsbury, 1974). Robins (1986) concluded that these findings should alert physicians to the need to watch carefully for the signs of clinical depression and suicidality. In addition, various medical and surgical problems place a patient more at risk for completed suicide; for example, patients with respiratory disease are three times more likely to commit suicide than are other medical patients. Patients on hemodialysis are also a high-risk group, as are patients with cancer (Abram et al., 1971; Hirschfeld & Davidson, 1988). It is critical to note that a considerable proportion of all who have died with acquired immune deficiency syndrome (AIDS) were reported to have consulted a psychiatrist or other mental health professional during the last year of their life (Kapantais & Powell-Griner, 1989) and that AIDS patients have a greatly elevated risk for both attempted and completed suicide (estimated to be 36 times the rate of completed suicide in the general population).

Furthermore, more psychiatric patients are treated by primary care physicians than by psychiatrists, "with more than 88% of patients experiencing a first psychiatric crisis seeking medical rather than psychiatric treatment" (Blumenthal, 1990, p. 686). Unfortunately, physicians detect only 1 of 6 patients who later go on to commit suicide, "even though information about warning signs may have been available from others. . . . For many of these patients, the physician has missed the psychiatric diagnosis or, if recognized, has undertreated the illness" (p. 686). Roy (1988) has enumerated a number of physical illnesses that appear to bear examination as contributory causes in completed suicide:

- Gastrointestinal and urogenital disease (e.g., peptic ulcer, cirrhosis, dialysis, prostatism)
- Endocrine disease and other conditions (e.g., Cushing's, anorexia nervosa, Klinefelter's, porphyria)
- Central nervous system disease (e.g., epilepsy, multiple sclerosis, head injury, cerebrovascular disease, Huntington's chorea, dementia, AIDS)
- Cancer

In a recent review on medical illness and suicide, Mackenzie and Popkin (1990) wrote that a medical illness generally increases the risk of suicide and that certain chronic, incurable, and painful conditions seemed to be associated with the greatest risk (specifically, AIDS, cancer, peptic ulcer, spinal cord injury, Huntington's chorea, head injury, and renal dialysis). The relationship of suicide to multiple sclerosis, premenstrual syndrome, pulmonary disease, rheumatoid arthritis, epilepsy, diabetes mellitus, and hypertension was "less clear and requires clarification" (p. 227). Overall, they concluded that a clinical knowledge of the conditions and circumstances that increase the risk for suicide in the medically ill is a "firm foundation for attempts to prevent suicide in this group" (p. 227).

Hirschfeld and Davidson (1988), after an exhaustive review of 11 recent studies of completed suicide among psychiatric patients, summarized the risk factors for suicide in these patients as follows:

1. Rates of suicides in psychiatric patients, particularly inpatients, range from 5 to 6 times to nearly 40 times the comparable rate in the general population. Risk factors for suicide attempts differ from those for suicide completion in some areas, and are quite similar in other areas (see Table 1.2).

2. Men are at higher risk for suicide in psychiatric populations, though the sex ratio is much lower in psychiatric patients than it is in the general population. The ratio in the general population of completed male suicide to completed female suicide is typically about 2.5:1; in all but one study that was reviewed, the male to female ratio among psychiatric patients was 1.5:1.

3. Although in the general population suicide is usually a phenomenon of older White males, this is not necessarily true of psychiatric patients, where the peak suicide rate tends to be in the middle years. Male patients tend to commit suicide between the ages of 25 to 40, whereas female patients tend to be older, between 35 to 50 years old.

Table 1.2

Risk Factors for Suicide Completers Versus Attempters Among Psychiatric Patients

Risk factor	Suicide completion	Suicide attempt
Sex	Males	Females
Age	30s and 40s	Under 30
Marital status	Unmarried	Unmarried
Employment status	Unemployed	Unemployed
Psychiatric diagnosis	Depression and Schizophrenia	Depression

Note. From "Risk Factors for Suicide" by R. M. A. Hirschfeld and L. Davidson, in A. J. Frances and R. E. Hales (Eds.), *American Psychiatric Press Review of Psychiatry: Vol. 7* (p. 327), 1988, Washington, DC: American Psychiatric Press. Copyright 1988 by the American Psychiatric Press. Reprinted by permission.

4. White psychiatric patients kill themselves at a much higher rate than do Blacks and other minority groups.

5. Suicide among alcoholics, in contrast to other psychiatric disorders, is most often a late sequelae of the psychiatric disease process. Therefore, any short-term studies of alcohol-related suicide or suicide attempts, if based on first admission, may grossly underestimate the risk for suicide among alcoholics. Furthermore, alcohol is often used immediately prior to a suicide; 1 in 5 victims of completed suicide are intoxicated at the time of their death. Alcoholics as a group are more likely to communicate suicidal intent, and the risk of completed suicide rises dramatically if there is also a concurrent depressive disorder.

6. A psychiatric history, in general, seems to increase a patient's risk for completed suicide, and a history of previous suicide attempts appears to increase the risk for later completion substantially. The predictive value of a positive history of suicide attempts does not always hold true for psychotic patients, because these individuals are more likely to complete suicide with little or no warning.

7. Depression, schizophrenia, and substance abuse are related to a much higher risk of suicide. Depression, especially psychotic or severely incapacitating depression, is the risk factor that appears to stand out and that places it at the top of the list of all risk factors (see Table 1.3).

Murphy (1988a), as well as Hirschfeld and Davidson (1988), pointed out that methods for identifying those individuals in a clinical population who will later

Table 1.3
Summary of Risk Factors for Suicide in Psychiatric Patients

- Being a psychiatric patient
- Being male: although the gender distinction is less important than among the general population
- Age: middle years, in contrast to the general population
- Race: Whites are at much higher risk than Blacks
- Diagnosis: depression and schizophrenia
- History of suicide attempts, except among psychotic patients
- Undesirable life events, especially humiliating ones or loss of a key person
- Timing: during hospitalization and in the 6–12 months postdischarge

---

Note. From "Risk Factors for Suicide Completers vs. Attemptors Among Psychiatric Patients" by R. Hirschfeld and L. Davidson, in A. J. Frances and R. E. Hales (Eds.), *American Psychiatric Press Review of Psychiatry: Vol. 7* (p. 329), 1988, Washington, DC: American Psychiatric Press. Copyright 1988 by the American Psychiatric Press. Reprinted by permission.

commit suicide inevitably includes large numbers of false positives. This is due to the current lack of unique predictors and the statistical properties of infrequent events.

In one of the most important and ambitious attempts to identify persons who would subsequently commit suicide, Pokorny (1983) examined the records of 4,800 patients who were consecutively admitted to the inpatient service of a Veterans Administration hospital. The patients were followed for a period of 4–6 years and were examined and rated on a range of instruments and measures, including most of those reported in the literature as predictive of suicide. During the 5-year follow-up period, Pokorny identified 67 suicides within the total group of 4,800 patients, as well as 179 suicide attempts. This yielded a rate for the completers of 279 per 100,000, or about 12 times the expected rate for these veterans. "However, all attempts to identify specific subjects were unsuccessful . . . each trial missed many cases and identified far too many false positives to be workable" (p. 249). Pokorny observed that:

> The conclusion is inescapable that we do not possess any item of information or any combination of items to permit us to identify to a useful degree the particular persons who will commit suicide. . . . The negative findings of this study have clear implications. The courts and public opinion seem to expect physicians to be able to pick out the particular persons who will later commit suicide. Although we may reconstruct causal chains and motives after the fact, we do not possess the tools to predict particular suicides before the fact. (p. 257)

Murphy (1988a) continued this train of thought:

> At a clinical level, the focus is on risk detection rather than on specific behavior prediction. Since suicide is intimately related to certain psychiatric illnesses, effective treatment of those illnesses can prevent suicide. . . . Prevention, however, generates no data. If suicide is difficult to predict, its prevention is even more difficult to detect. (p. 57)

Summary

Despite the enormous amount of empirical and clinical research on the subject, completed and attempted suicide are not precisely understood phenomena. Although there is consensus that most completed suicides suffer from a major psychiatric illness in the period immediately prior to their death, there is a lack of consensus on specific casual pathways and on the weight and significance to be given to various psychological, psychodynamic, biological, social-relational, and epidemiological factors (i.e., on how each factor contributes to the completion or attempt and how the factors interact).

Where consensus does exist, suicidality is viewed as a highly complex biopsychosocial phenomenon, with multiple pathways and determiners—all of which must be fitted into the assessment/management equation (Blumenthal, 1990). Many authorities agree that certain psychiatric illnesses, such as depression, alcohol/substance abuse, and schizophrenia, are the most common diagnostic categories among completed suicides. (To demonstrate the rapidly changing and dynamic quality of the knowledge base, an important recent study has reported that those who suffer from panic disorder and attacks exhibited a very high rate of suicide ideation and attempts, see Weissman et al., 1989.) There are also clear differences between the profiles of those who attempt and those who complete suicide (especially with regard to age, sex, race, etc.).

The lack of precision in enumerating what the most salient risk factors are—their interactions and specific pathways (i.e., for a particular patient before the fact)—can of course be a source of great distress to the average practitioner. Most clinicians would prefer a ''by-the-numbers'' set of exact guidelines for the identification and management of suicide risk, particularly when finding themselves at a dangerous suicidal intersection. However (as will be seen in the following chapter on suicide and the law), this lack of consensus among the experts, and the current inability to identify precisely completers (or attempters) before the fact, in the long run may well be a protective factor and mandates a standard of care that rests on a foundation of good clinical judgment, common sense, and a basic knowledge of the ambiguities and uncertainties inherent in this high-risk endeavor.

By understanding these ambiguities and uncertainties, the average practitioner will come to see how expert witnesses will retrospectively examine a clinician's work should a suit be brought following a completed or attempted suicide. More specifically, it will be clear that practitioners who use a simplistic ''cookbook'' approach in their assessment and management of suicide are highly vulnerable should a lawsuit ensue. The reasonable and prudent psychologist must understand the necessity of treating each patient's risk profile and management as a unique set of variables to be addressed comprehensively in their clinical assessment and case management. As will be seen in the chapters on assessment of elevated risk and on clinical management and treatment (chapters 3, 4, and 5, respectively), reasonable and sound clinical practice activities—buttressed by sophisticated risk management behaviors—are the proposed model for both optimizing clinical care (suicide prevention) and for assuaging the common anxieties that occur when clinicians interact with the legal system. Finally, the clinician will come to see that reasonable and prudent practice activities—those grounded in a realistic understanding of the current knowledge base—reflect the reality that each clinical decision point is a probabilistic determination, a decision involving a contemporaneous calculation of risk, rather than a determination of any clinical certainty.

Suicide: Legal Perspectives

An essential element of effective risk management and high-quality clinical care in a professional psychological practice is the possession of a basic working knowledge of the legal system and an understanding of contemporary legal views on the standards of care. This working knowledge is further enhanced by a thorough understanding of what the currently available data on malpractice tell us about specific high-risk clinical scenarios.

Until the 1970s, the incidence of lawsuits against mental health professionals was quite low, especially when compared with what the courts regard as other medical specialties (Robertson, 1988). Furthermore, when there was a lawsuit, the defendant practitioner almost always prevailed (Robertson, 1988). In recent years there has been a steady increase in the number of malpractice actions against mental health professionals; the incidence of claims against psychiatrists and psychologists remains comparatively low, and the majority of claims still result in favorable verdicts for the defendant (Robertson, 1988).

It is important to note, however, that, in a recent analysis of claims against psychiatrists for the years 1980 to 1985, patient suicides resulted in the highest number of lawsuits and the largest cash settlements (see Table 2.1). Suits for suicide accounted for 21% of the claims filed and 42% of the dollars paid in settlement or court awards (Robertson, 1988).

Data from the American Psychological Association's Insurance Trust (APAIT), the malpractice insurance carrier for most psychologists, indicate that the suicide of a patient was the sixth most common category for a claim, but ranked second in the percentage of total costs (5.4% of the claims and 10% of the costs; APAIT Claims Frequency, 5/1/90). Out of a total of 1,892 open and closed claims, there were 102 specifically in the category of suicide. The number one cause for a claim was sexual impropriety ($N = 368$; 19.5% of the claims; 48.8% of the settlement costs). The cost to the insurance trust for claims of sexual impropriety cost on the average about 24% more than the cost of claims for

Table 2.1
Psychiatry Claims Closed 1980–1985

Percentage of Claims	
incarceration/suicide attempts	21%
drugs (overdose or addiction)	20%
miscellaneous (failure to diagnose physical condition,	
breach of contract, and other claims)	18%
psychotherapy/depression	14%
failure to treat psychosis	14%
restraints (paralysis or fracture)	7%
sexual misconduct	6%
Percentage of Dollars	
incarceration/suicide attempts	42%
sexual misconduct	16%
restraints (paralysis or fracture)	16%
drugs (overdose or addiction)	10%
miscellaneous	8%
failure to treat psychosis	5%
psychotherapy/depression	3%

Note. From *Concise Guide to Clinical Psychiatry and the Law* (p. 2) by R. I. Simon, 1988, Washington, DC: American Psychiatric Press. Copyright 1988 by American Psychiatric Press. Reprinted by permission.

suicide based on the current APAIT total loss experience of 51.5 million dollars (M. Bogie, personal communication, December 1990).

Harris (personal communication, May 1990) has speculated that several of the other APAIT claims categories (e.g., incorrect treatment and diagnosis, etc.) may also subsume damage claims for suicide and self-harm. Unfortunately, in the current APAIT database, this information is not distinguishable (M. Bogie, personal communication, April 1990).

Elements of Malpractice Liability

The basic legal standard of care for mental health professionals is that, once a psychotherapist–patient relationship is established, the clinician has a legal duty of ordinary and reasonable care to the patient (Robertson, 1988). (See Table 2.2.) Simon (1988) noted that the most common interjection of the law into health care practice may be the suing of a practitioner by a patient for malpractice. A malpractice lawsuit comes under the heading of a tort action. A *tort* is defined as a civil wrong (a noncriminal or noncontract-related wrong) committed by one person (the defendant) that causes some injury to a second person (the plaintiff). The subsequent lawsuit, or *tort action*, is a request by the plaintiff for compen-

Table 2.2

Actions by Therapists That May Create a Doctor–Patient Relationship

1. Giving advice
2. Making psychological interpretations
3. Writing a prescription
4. Supervising treatment by nonmedical therapist
5. Lengthy phone conversation with a prospective patient
6. Treating an unseen patient by mail
7. Giving a patient an appointment
8. Telling walk-in patients that they will be seen
9. Providing sample medications
10. Acting as a substitute therapist
11. Providing treatment during an evaluation
12. Treatment relationship with patient may create duties ("special relationship") to nonpatient third parties, e.g., *Tarasoff* duty
13. Providing psychiatric opinions to neighbors and friends

Note. From *Concise Guide to Clinical Psychiatry and the Law* (p. 13) by R. I. Simon, 1988, Washington, DC: American Psychiatric Press. Copyright 1988 by American Psychiatric Press. Reprinted by permission.

sation for the damages that have occurred. According to Simon's definition, *malpractice* is "a tort committed as a result of negligence by physicians or other health care professionals that leads to injury to a patient in their care" (p. 1).

Civil suits (tort actions) against mental health professionals are based on the same legal principles as are traditional medical malpractice suits. According to Simon (1988), such an action can be filed against a mental health professional for various reasons, including breach of contract, intentional tort, and violation of civil liberties.

A *breach of contract* might occur, for example, if a patient undertakes treatment on the basis of an agreement with the mental health professional who promises a particular result, but then fails to deliver it. An *intentional tort* is "any act willfully committed that the law has declared as wrong (e.g., treating patients without their consent)" (Simon, 1988, p. 3). Simon goes on to say that a claim may also be based on *violations of a patient's civil rights* "pursuant to federal and/or state law (e.g., discriminatory treatment practices against institutionalized patients)" (p. 3).

A fundamental concept that underlies malpractice actions against mental health professionals is *negligence*. Simon (1988) pointed out that negligence on the part of a mental health professional can be "described as doing something which he or she should not have done [commission] or omitting to do something which he or she should have done [omission]" (p. 3). The fact that a psychologist's or psychiatrist's act that injures a patient is not willful but results instead from carelessness or ignorance does not excuse the clinician from liability

(Robertson, 1988; Simon, 1988). According to Robertson, the law "presumes and holds all practitioners and psychotherapists to a standard of reasonable care when dealing with patients" (p. 7).

Sadoff (cited in Rachlin, 1984) wrote that there are four essential legal elements in establishing negligence. Each of these must be demonstrated by the plaintiff by a preponderance of evidence and "may be remembered by the **4D** mnemonic: **D**ereliction of—**D**uty—**D**irectly causing—**D**amages" (p. 303). Rachlin further noted that in the case of suicide, where damages are readily apparent, there is an "obvious appeal to the sympathies of a jury when the bereaved family claims that the patient was being treated because of suicidal behavior and professional intervention failed to prevent a fatal outcome" (p. 303). The simple fact that the patient was receiving any psychological treatment makes the relationship between the two parties such that a legal duty of care is created.

The question of *direct causality* (i.e., whether the allegedly negligent act is known to be the proximate cause of the patient's injury) is often more complicated. As Rachlin (1984) puts it:

> The terms "but for" and "without which" recur in reported decisions. In other words, if the suicide would not have occurred "but for" the questioned act(s) or omission(s) of the defendant, hospital, or staff member(s), such event(s) are the proximate cause, or alternately, the purportedly wrongful professional behavior is the intervention "without which" the death would not have happened. (p. 303)

Negligence alone, without injury, does not constitute malpractice. "Similarly, negligence accompanied by injury is not actionable unless the plaintiff can cross the all-important bridge of proximate cause" (Robertson, 1988, p. 7). The patient's injury must be the result of a specific departure from the standard of care. As Robertson points out:

> In any medical malpractice action, the plaintiff must prove there was an applicable standard of care that the defendant breached and that the breach was the proximate cause of the injuries. To establish proximate cause, the plaintiff must present evidence from which a reasonable juror could find a substantial and direct causal relationship between the defendant's breach and the plaintiff's injury. (p. 187)

In alleging negligence, expert testimony by other mental health professionals regarding standard of care issues is usually presented. This process generally involves testimony by a clinician with similar expertise on what another reasonably qualified therapist would have done under similar circumstances (Robertson, 1988; Simon, 1988). Robertson has commented that when the alleged substandard "conduct was so outrageous as to constitute gross negligence, the courts have held that no expert testimony is required" (p. 8). He also found that if a patient is successful in suing a therapist, damages are usually awarded "commensurate with the extent of the injury sustained" (p. 7). Both Simon (1988) and Robertson (1988) discuss three types of damages: compensatory, nominal, and punitive.

Compensatory damages are the typical awards in a malpractice action and represent the amount of compensation that "is calculated to replace the loss or injury to the plaintiff" (Robertson, 1988, p. 8). However, Simon (1988) noted that wrongdoers are legally responsible for all of the natural and direct consequences of their actions, and that *punitive damages* will "be awarded when the defendant's conduct is considered willful, wanton, malicious, or reckless" (p. 4). The purpose of punitive damages is to "punish" the wrongdoers rather than to compensate the victim. The finding of mere negligence is insufficient to merit an award of punitive damages. "Punitive damages are usually awarded in addition to compensatory damages as a type of bonus" (Simon, 1988, p. 4).

Nominal damages are rarely awarded in a malpractice action. They are awarded, according to Simon (1988), when the plaintiff suffers no "actual harm or loss but only a technical injury to their legal rights" (p. 4).

Clinicians should be aware that there are court cases in which therapists may not have either deviated from or failed to render reasonable care to a patient, and in which the patient ultimately commits suicide (Perr, 1985a; Simon, 1987). In some cases, regardless of the facts of the case, juries retrospectively have decided in favor of the family of the deceased (Perr, 1985b; Simon, 1987). Simon found that such a finding of strict liability is based on the theory that the defendant is legally responsible for harm done—"even when there is no proof of carelessness or fault on the part of the person who caused the injury" (p. 270).

Robertson (1988) observed that it is more usual that courts understand the imperfections of psychological and psychiatric practice and tend not to hold clinicians liable for "mere mistakes or for failing to effectuate a cure" (p. 8). He further noted that there are hundreds of schools of therapy and that innovations and experimentation are "common requisites in treating certain complex and particularly difficult patients" (p. 8). In other words, courts have been restrained from declaring a therapist's behavior as negligent simply because his or her methods differ from mainstream therapy practices. Gutheil (1990) developed this point for the case of depression:

> When competing views of how to treat a patient with depressive symptoms exists—for example, psychotherapy and medications—decision makers may look to the concept of the "respectable minority." This principle posits that a form of treatment is not inherently outside the standard of care, even though a majority of practitioners may not use it, if it can be demonstrated that a respectable minority of practitioners do use it. (p. 337)

Essentially, what this standard of care dictates to the ordinary practitioner is that he or she make a reasonable attempt to detect elevated risk for suicide. Where the risk is elevated, the standard requires that the psychologist exhibit reasonable clinical management efforts that are based on the detection of this elevated risk. A general practitioner would not be expected to have the level of clinical skill or knowledge found in specialists (Knapp & VandeCreek, 1983). Thus, psychotherapists who claim to be specialists are held to a higher standard than the average practitioner. With regard to the matter of specialization, Vande-Creek and Knapp (1983) commented that:

> Psychotherapists would be evaluated according to their own system of therapy. For example, a behaviorist would be measured according to the accepted practices of behavior therapy, not psychoanalysis. The court is cognizant of, and respectful of, the well-known and important schools of psychotherapy. Generally speaking, the courts will accept any school as legitimate if a substantial minority of psychologists practice it. (p. 275)

However, clinicians should be aware that intense controversy exists over the "respectable minority" issue. (See the current debate between Klerman, 1990, and Stone, 1990.)

What Suicide Case Law and Malpractice Data Tell Us

In recent years, there has been a distinct trend in court decisions toward greater accountability by health care professionals and hospitals (Slawson, Flinn, & Schwartz, 1974). Awards for malpractice and damages have increased dramatically since the mid-1960s (W. Menninger, 1989; Swenson, 1986). Indeed, the overall increase in malpractice dollar awards was greater than could be accounted for by inflation (Slawson & Guggenheim, 1984). Added to the economic effects of this increase in malpractice actions and costs are the effects that such trends have, not only on the health care providers' personal and professional lives, but also on the quality of the health care services that they deliver. For example, one study that assessed the impact of malpractice suits on physicians' personal and professional lives found that significantly more of the physicians who had been sued for malpractice were likely to stop seeing certain types of patients (Charles, Wilbert, & Franke, 1985).

Although, historically, suits for psychiatric malpractice have been less frequent than those for other medical specialities, the frequency of these suits has risen along with those for other medical specialities (Swenson, 1986). Recently the size and number of claims have skyrocketed, claims of $1 million becoming commonplace events (VandeCreek, Knapp, & Herzog, 1987; Waltzer, 1980). Malpractice insurance premiums have increased, and clinicians have become increasingly aware of the malpractice threat (Waltzer, 1980).

Failure to prevent suicide is now one of the leading reasons for malpractice suits against mental health professionals (Szasz, 1986). Indeed, the most common legal action involving psychiatric care is the failure to "reasonably" protect patients from harming themselves (Simon, 1988).

Psychiatric claims are grossly underrepresented in the area of suicide and self-injury, given the number of completed suicides in the United States (Slawson & Guggenheim, 1984). One study found that psychiatric claims accounted for only a small percentage (0.3%) of the total claims against physicians (Slawson & Guggenheim, 1984). The authors of the study speculated that the factor responsible for the more favorable history of claims of psychiatry versus other medical specialities was that psychiatric procedures rarely produce permanent or grave injuries. This study of all malpractice actions brought against psychiatrists between 1974 and 1978 examined the 10 most frequent injuries found in psychiatric care, and found that diagnostic errors made up the largest cluster of injuries (36 claims out of a total of 217, or 17%). Suicide/self-injury was the second highest category (26 claims for suicide or self-injury out of a total of 217 claims, or 12%).

Perr (1985) reported that claims against psychiatrists (i.e., actions against providers that had been reported to an insurance company) were on the rise, with an increase for psychiatrists from 2% to 4% between 1978 and 1983. He noted that "suits involving suicide have increased to 18 to 25 percent of psychiatric malpractice cases" (p. 209). Rachlin (1984), in examining the data on suicide and malpractice, found that, in malpractice cases proceeding beyond the stage of simple notification, 25% of the cases involved a patient's suicide and that there appeared to have been a recent significant increase in the number of claims that involve suicide. (Also, see VandeCreek & Knapp, 1989.)

In 1985, Perr reviewed 32 cases of patient suicide in which he had served as a medico-legal consultant (23 for defense attorneys and 9 for plaintiff attorneys). Perr felt that there had actually been negligence in only 3 out of the 32 cases (10%) and that not all of the claims based on a patient's suicide involved a hospital suicide. None of these cases went to trial with a verdict for the plaintiff and several of the cases were settled out of court. The largest settlement was for $500,000 and involved both a suicide and an injury to another person. In this particular case, although Perr felt that there was no negligence, the almost complete lack of records made the facts of the case a legitimate issue, and, as a result, settlement against the psychiatrist and the hospital was made. Two other cases of injury to the patient from exposure (dangerousness to self) resulted in a settlement of approximately $300,000 in one case, and the other settlement being in the same range. Several other cases were settled in the $30,000 to

$50,000 range. In these cases, the defense attorneys usually felt that their cause was justified, but that the eventual cost of the trial (and risks involved in an adverse decision) justified the settlement. Slawson and Guggenheim (1984), in their review of the national loss experience for psychiatry between 1974 and 1978, found that, with regard to settlements, "suicide indemnity payments averaged $26,000" where "suicide claims usually specified a failure to supervise the patient adequately" (p. 980).

On the basis of the current claims data, the professional practice of psychology, relatively speaking, has been spared this rash of lawsuits for suicide and wrongful death. (The overall rate of malpractice suits against psychologists is relatively low, and, in the past 14 years, only 0.5% of all psychologists insured by the APAIT have been sued for any reason; see Youngstrom, 1990.) In fact, there have been only 102 malpractice claims (open and closed) filed with the APAIT for suicide and wrongful death since the trust began to analyze its loss history (APAIT claims data). However, as professional psychology moves toward models of practice that encourage increased access to full hospital admitting privileges and medical staff memberships, the profession's risk profile will inevitably be heightened.

It is important to note Pope's (1989) finding that 13.2% of the total claims and 8.4% of the total costs of malpractice actions involving psychologists were for claims against psychologists for incorrect treatment. This is often interpreted as psychologists undertaking work in areas for which they are not qualified by reason of training, education, and experience. Slawson and Guggenheim (1985), in their review of the national loss experience for psychiatrists, found that the overall increase for all medical specialities during their study period (1974–1978) was 32%, with the average defense cost increasing 73%. Of the total claims paid for all medical specialities, one third had to do with improperly performed procedures, one third with diagnostic errors, and the remainder with drug reactions, untoward events, and so forth.

Legal Theories of Suicide

Failure to Properly Diagnose

A number of legal theories are brought into play in imposing liability on mental health professionals. One of these is the failure to properly diagnose. That is, if the clinician had taken ordinary and accepted care in making a diagnosis, he or she would have ascertained that the patient was suicidal (see *Dillman v. Hellman*, 1973).

Currently, much of the case law on suicide is based on claims that allege liability for a misdiagnosis or lack of prediction of the risk of suicide (Swenson, 1986; VandeCreek et al., 1987). Most suits brought on this basis are directed against hospitals and institutions for clinical care and involve either inpatients or recently discharged patients (Rachlin, 1984). However, the potential certainly exists for an increase in suits involving outpatient care. For example, a study of completed suicide in Veterans Administration patients found that 65% of the suicides occurred outside the hospital (Farberow, 1981).

In their studies, VandeCreek et al. (1987) found that clinicians and hospitals have not typically been held liable for a patient's suicide if they have taken

> reasonable steps to assess and supervise the patient. . . . On the other hand, liability has frequently been imposed where the hospital should have known or did know about suicidal or escapist tendencies of the patient, but was negligent by placing the patient in a high-risk situation. Some psychiatrists and hospitals also have been negligent in failing to properly supervise the patient (*Fatuck v. Hillside Hospital*, 1974). Hospitals also have been held negligent in releasing a suicidal patient. In *Bell v. New York City Health and Hospitals Corporation* (1982) the physician recommended release of the psychiatric patient even though he had potentially harmful delusions. The physician did not investigate previous psychiatric history of the patient, nor did he investigate the patient's delusions or the incident of the prior evening when the patient had to be restrained. (pp. 150–151)

Failure to Take Adequate Protective Measures

The clinician must take adequate precautions against patient suicide, consistent with accepted psychotherapeutic practices and on the basis of his or her knowledge and assessment of the patient. (See *Bellah v. Greenson*, 1978; *Dimitrijevic v. Chicago Wesley Memorial Hospital*, 1968; *Meier v. Ross General Hospital*, 1968; *Topel v. Long Island Jewish Medical Center*, 1981.) This legal theory is illustrated by the case of *Dinnerstein v. State* (1973), that held that clinicians are liable when a treatment plan overlooks or neglects the patient's suicidal tendencies. VandeCreek and Knapp (1989) commented that the courts will generally not find a psychotherapist liable when the patient's suicide attempt was not foreseeable. They concluded:

> Therefore no liability has been found when cooperative and apparently contented patients suddenly attempted suicide (*Carlino v. State*, 1968; *Dalton v. State*, 1970), or when an aggressive patient failed to reveal suicidal intent (*Paradies v. Benedictine Hospital*, 1980). In contrast, courts have held practitioners or hospitals culpable when the treatment plan overlooked or neglected evidence of suicidal tendencies (*Dinnerstein v. State*, 1973). (p. 25)

That failure to take appropriate precautions was the basis for *Abille v. United States* (1980) was pointed out by Fremouw, et al. (1990). In this case, a psychiatrist was found liable when a patient committed suicide after being transferred from a suicide-watch status to a lower level of precaution without adequate medical notes to explain the rationale for such a critical management decision.

The courts have tended to be less stringent in evaluating cases of outpatient suicide in the absence of clear signs of foreseeability, because of the obvious increased difficulty in controlling the patient's behavior (Simon, 1988). The case law seems to put forward the basic rule that the clinician needs to recognize the risk of suicide and to balance appropriately the risk of suicide with the benefits of greater control through hospitalization (Simon, 1987, 1988).

The principles for establishing liability for outpatient suicide are typically the same as for inpatient cases; that is, clinicians must use reasonable standards of care in making a diagnosis and in developing and implementing a treatment plan (VandeCreek & Knapp, 1989). At least one court has determined that there is no duty to warn relatives of a potential suicide, as was ruled necessary (for dangerousness to others) in *Tarasoff v. Regents of the University of California* (1976) (see *Bellah v. Greenson*, 1978). Knapp and VandeCreek (1983) also noted that, although only a few cases deal with outpatient suicide, the principles are the same as for inpatient cases; namely, clinicians must use reasonable care in the diagnosis of suicidal intent and in the development and implementation of the treatment plan:

> In *Runyon v. Reid* (1973), a psychiatrist and a mental health foundation were sued because their patient had taken a lethal dose of sleeping pills which had been prescribed for him. The court found that the patient's suicidal intent was not foreseeable; hence the psychiatrist and clinic were exonerated. Although this case involved a psychiatrist, it illustrates a principle that applies to nonmedical psychotherapists who treat suicidal outpatients: a psychotherapist using acceptable diagnostic procedures would not be liable for unforeseen suicide attempts. (pp. 277–278)

Because outpatient therapists have much less control over their patients' behavior, outpatient therapists have not been held as responsible for their patients' actions as have the therapists of inpatients (Fremouw et al., 1990). This was demonstrated in the case of *Speer v. United States* (1981), in which the court held that a psychiatrist's duty to outpatients is less than his or her responsibilities to inpatients.

The case of *Bellah v. Greenson* (1978) is of particular interest in this regard, because, unlike so many cases where a lawsuit followed an inpatient's suicide, the *Bellah* case involved the suicide of an outpatient. Specifically, the parents of Tammy Bellah, who died by an overdose of pills, brought a malpractice action for wrongful death against Tammy's psychiatrist, Daniel Greenson. Dr. Greenson, who was treating Tammy as an outpatient at the time of her death, appears to have determined that Tammy was

> disposed to suicide, and he recorded his conclusion in his written notes
> . . . . the plaintiffs instituted the present action for wrongful death alleging
> that defendant had failed to take measures to prevent Tammy's suicide;
> that he failed to warn plaintiffs of the seriousness of Tammy's condition
> and of the circumstances which might cause her to commit suicide; and
> that he failed to inform plaintiffs that Tammy was consorting with heroin
> addicts in the plaintiffs' home. Plaintiffs' complaint purported to state
> two causes of action, one based upon simple negligence, and one based
> upon the defendant's negligent performance of his contract with plaintiffs
> to care for their daughter, which contract allegedly contained the implied
> term that defendant would use reasonable care to prevent Tammy from
> harming herself. (p. 537)

The court in this case refused to mandate a *Tarasoff*-like "duty to warn" (*Tarasoff v. Regents of the University of California*, 1976), although the outpatient was a "danger-to-self." The court held that "a requisite special relationship does exist in the case of a patient under the care of a psychiatrist and that a psychiatrist who knows that his patient is likely to attempt suicide has a duty to take protective measures" (*Bellah v. Greenson*, 1978, p. 538). In their decision, the court clarified the differences between the duty of care for an outpatient and that for inpatients. The court specifically cited the cases of *Vistica v. Presbyterian Hospital* (1967) and *Meier v. Ross General Hospital* (1968). In the *Vistica* case, the cause of action was found to exist against the hospital; in the Meier case, it was found to exist both against the hospital and against the decedent's attending physician.

During the *Meier* case, the court determined that the facts of the case supported a theory of liability that was based on a duty to protect the decedent from his own actions, voluntary or involuntary. The doctor and hospital breached their duty of care when they placed the patient, following an attempted suicide, in a second-floor room with a fully openable window.

Texarkana Memorial Hospital, Inc. v. Firth (1988) had a similar outcome. In this case, the family of a 33-year-old woman

> who was admitted for suicidal risk and psychosis was awarded over
> $950,000 for gross negligence by the hospital. When she was admitted
> the locked ward had no empty beds. To lower her risk of suicide, she
> was sedated but placed in an open ward with no special suicide precau-
> tions. Upon awakening, she jumped to her death. (Fremouw et al., 1990,
> p. 8)

According to the *Bellah* court (*Bellah v. Greenson*, 1978), Tammy Bellah's case is readily distinguishable from the *Vistica* and *Meier* cases because "the duty imposed upon those responsible for the care of a patient in an institutional setting differs from that which may be involved in the case of a psychiatrist treating patients on an out-patient basis'' (p. 538). The court did hold, however, that the facts of this outpatient suicide were sufficient to bring a cause of action for breach of a psychiatrist's duty of care toward his patient. Moreover, the court held that the nature of the precautionary steps that Dr. Greenson could or should have taken presents "purely a factual question to be resolved at trial on the merits, at which time both sides would be afforded an opportunity to produce expert medical testimony on the subject'' (p. 538). That is, resolution of the case would require the testimony of expert witnesses, analyzing Dr. Greenson's performance after the fact, to determine if negligence had occurred.

In refusing to impose a *Tarasoff* duty on Dr. Greenson, the court stated:

> The imposition of a duty upon the psychiatrist to disclose to others vague or even specific manifestations of suicidal tendencies on the part of the patient who is being treated in an out-patient setting could well inhibit psychiatric treatment. . . . that the dynamics of interaction between the psychotherapist and the patient seen in office visits are highly complex and subtle. Intimate privacy is a virtual necessity for successful treatment. Were it not for the assurance of confidentiality in psychotherapist–patient relationships, many in need of treatment would be reluctant to seek help. Even those who do seek help under such circumstances may be deterred from fully disclosing their problems. An element usually assumed essential is the patient's trust that matters disclosed in therapy will be held in strict confidence. (p. 539)

The *Bellah* court held that *Tarasoff v. Regents of the University of California* (1976) requires that a therapist disclose the contents of a confidential communication only "where the risk to be prevented thereby is danger of violent assault, and not where the risk of harm is self-inflicted harm or mere property damage. We decline to further extend the holding of *Tarasoff*" (*Bellah v. Greenson*, 1978, p. 540).

Fremouw et al. (1990) stated that, with outpatients, although a *Tarasoff*-type of duty to warn relatives of potential suicide risk is not the current case law, it remains one of the options that clinicians should consider seriously when a patient presents as at risk. Harris (1988) points out that at least one state (Massachusetts) has imposed a limited statutory "duty to commit" on psychologists seeing patients who are imminently dangerous to themselves (*Massachusetts General Law*, 1988). This statute allows a limited breach of confidentiality (to help safeguard the patient and to help with treatment) by the psychologist when the patient is an imminent danger to himself or herself and when the patient refuses or is unable to follow recommendations for outpatient treatment or voluntary hospitalization. Of course, hospitalization under such circumstances would often involve communication with the family and significant others.

When the suicide attempt is foreseeable, the treatment provided must be consistent with professional standards. The case of *Speer v. United States* (1981) illustrates this. In this case a psychiatric outpatient hoarded pills and then took a lethal overdose of medication. VandeCreek and Knapp (1983) pointed out that the psychiatrist involved was exonerated because he had followed accepted medical standards in prescribing for the patient. They further noted that "although nonmedical psychotherapists would not be treating patients through medication, they would have to follow acceptable procedures in their treatment of suicidal outpatients" (p. 278).

Early Patient Release

A clinician may be found liable for the early release of a patient if the release is negligent and not a valid exercise in professional judgment (Robertson, 1988). For example, in the case of *Bell v. New York City Health & Hospitals Corporation* (1982), the court imposed liability on the grounds that the defendant acknowledged that his decision to release the patient turned on whether the patient was a risk to himself, yet the psychiatrist did not

1. inquire into the nature of patient's auditory hallucinations (even though a nurse had made notes for 3 consecutive days documenting these hallucinations);

2. request prior treatment records;

3. take notice of the patient's chart that showed on the day prior to release, that the patient had to be placed in restraints (an indication of assaultive tendencies); and

4. communicate with the physician and nursing staff.

The court determined that "the decision to release the patient cannot be deemed to have been a professional judgment founded upon careful examination" (Robertson, 1988, p. 190).

When a clinician makes a reasonable assessment of danger and believes that a risk no longer exists, he or she is not held liable for the postdischarge death of a patient:

> For example, in *Johnson v. United States* (1981) and *Paradies v. Benedictine Hospital* (1980), the courts did not find psychiatrists responsible for the postdischarge suicides of their patients because the psychiatrists had assessed the patients and had reasonably concluded that the benefits of release outweighed the potential risks of danger. In *Johnson*, the court observed that "accurate prediction of dangerous behavior, and particular-

ly of suicide and homicide, are almost never possible.'' (Fremouw et al., 1990, p. 8)

Failure to Commit

In making the decision to commit or not to commit a patient, the legal issue is one of whether the clinician took a complete history, made a thorough examination of the patient's status, and then exercised sound judgment in his or her decision to commit or not to commit the patient (Robertson, 1988). The more ''obvious the suicidal intent, the greater will be the practitioner's liability'' for his or her failure to take this elevated risk into account in the treatment plan (VandeCreek & Knapp, 1983, p. 276). For example, in the case of *Dillman v. Hellman* (1973), a patient who had been hospitalized for 9 days was determined by her psychiatrist to be well enough to be transferred to a less secure part of the hospital. The patient jumped out of a window. The plaintiff's only argument was that the psychiatrist erred in her judgment and was thus negligent. According to Robertson (1988), the court in this case ''reinforced the established principle that physicians cannot be held liable for errors in judgment while pursuing methods and practices within the standard of care'' (p. 192). While in the case of *Paradies v. Benedictine Hospital* (1980), the court found that ''if liability were imposed on the physician each time the prediction of the future course of a mental disease was wrong, few releases would ever be made and the recovery of a vast number of patients would be impeded'' (Robertson, 1988, p. 192).

Liability of Hospitals

The malpractice law regarding hospitals is a complex and ever-changing field and a review of the liability of hospitals is beyond the scope of this book.[1] Psychotherapists should know that malpractice actions for inpatient suicides can be directed against the therapist, the hospital, or both. An important point here is that malpractice actions can be brought against psychiatrists or psychologists within the hospital setting, provided they have staff or hospital privileges.

The duty of a hospital can best be defined as the generally accepted standard of using reasonable care in the treatment of the patient (Robertson, 1988). ''If however, the hospital is on notice that a patient has suicidal tendencies, then the hospital also assumes the duty of safeguarding the patient from self-inflicted injury or death'' (p. 193). Thus, as is the case for judging the behavior of the practitioner, the issue of foreseeability is crucial. Even when the patient is under

---

[1]The reader is directed for a complete review of clinical and legal standard in this area to the following sources: Davidson (1969), Friedman (1989), Gutheil and Appelbaum (1982), Jacobs (1989a, 1989b), Litman (1982), Perr (1960, 1965, 1974, 1985a, 1985b, 1988), Robertson (1988), Simon (1987, 1988), Slawson et al. (1974), Smith (1988), VandeCreek and Knapp (1983), and Waltzer (1980).

the care of a private psychotherapist, the hospital staff must still perform the proper evaluations and observations (and take affirmative action if necessary).

Robertson found that hospitals generally have not been held liable when a physician has determined that surveillance was adequate. Nor have hospitals been found liable when proper procedures were followed. He noted, however, that "psychiatric hospitals can be found liable when adequate standards for the protection of patients were not followed," referring practitioners on this point to the Joint Commission on Accreditation of Hospitals (JCAH) guidelines for nursing and safety standards (p. 197).

The courts, in considering malpractice actions against hospitals, have slowly moved the standard of liability away from an earlier "custodial model" to more of an "open door" model (VandeCreek & Knapp, 1983). In the earlier custodial model, the purpose of the hospital was to correctly diagnose suicidal intentions and then to observe the patient so closely that an attempt would be impossible. As VandeCreek and Knapp (1983) said:

> The standard of supervision was so strict that Perr commented that "therapy was imprisonment by a jailor in a white coat" (1965, p. 637). But even when the custodial model was being applied, the courts would find liability only for foreseeable suicide attempts. In *Moore v. United States*, the hospital was not found negligent when the patient pried open the detention screen from the third floor and jumped out. . . . In *Hirsch v. State*, the hospital was absolved of blame when a patient committed suicide with capsules he had hoarded. He had been stripped naked and searched and no one had reason to suspect that he was still concealing barbiturates. (p. 276)

Yet in recent years, hospitals have implemented so-called open door policies, decreasing the level of restrictions and encouraging the patients to assume more responsibility for their behavior. The courts have observed such changes in psychotherapeutic policies, recognizing that "some of the traditional restrictive policies harmed patients because they engendered feelings of helplessness" (VandeCreek & Knapp, 1983, p. 277).

In support of this shift to more liberal policies, the suicide rate decreased in institutions with open door policies (Perr, 1965). VandeCreek and Knapp (1983) wrote that "the open door policy does not deny the risks of suicide. Rather it acknowledges that the effective treatment of suicide may involve some short-term risks (Slawson et al., 1974)"(p. 277). They continued with the observation that the courts no longer require strict observation in all suicide cases: "The law and modern psychiatry have now both come to the conclusion that an overly restrictive environment can be as destructive as an overly permissive one. . . . Now the courts recognize that the therapist must balance the benefits of treatment against the risks of freedom" (p. 277).

Robertson (1988), citing the case of *Krapvika v. Maimonides* (1986), used the words of the court to underscore the issue of such calculated risks:

> The prediction of the future course of a mental illness is a professional judgment of high responsibility and in some instances it involves a measure of calculated risk. . . . Liability cannot be based merely upon the disagreement of another physician with the manner in which treatment is provided. (p. 197)

Yet, as Gutheil (1990) remarks, hospitalization has its drawbacks. Although lay persons may perceive it (and plaintiffs' attorneys may present it) as a panacea, experienced clinicians are aware that a psychiatric hospitalization presents some clear risks as well as benefits, including regression, fostering dependency, loss of time from work or studies, and severe stigma.

In summary, psychologists mindful of maintaining a coherent treatment philosophy with their suicidal patients are protected to the extent that they demonstrate their best professional judgment in assessing the therapeutic risks of freedom. They also must carefully assess decisions (their own and those of others) to reduce the level of supervision of suicidal patients, whether those decisions involve discharge, transfer, decision to commit, or other actions (VandeCreek & Knapp, 1983). It is critical to remember, however, that, when a "patient is dangerously suicidal, hospitalization and close supervision are clearly indicated—an 'open door' policy does not mean an open window policy for highly suicidal patients" (p. 277).

Abandonment

Once a professional relationship has been established, a clinician is required to provide treatment until the relationship is properly terminated. Abandonment can be overt or implied, for example, by a failure to be available or to monitor the patient adequately. The therapeutic relationship may not be terminated by the therapist unless treatment is no longer necessary, the relationship is terminated by the patient, or suitable notice is given by the therapist that gives the patient adequate time to engage another therapist (VandeCreek & Knapp, 1983). Typically, abandonment is based on two theories: (a) If a therapist errs in her or his judgment that treatment is no longer needed, she or he may be liable for negligence under the criteria for malpractice. Usually this is decided by expert witnesses after the fact. (b) If therapists willfully terminate or withhold treatment knowing that further care is needed or that a referral is indicated, she or he may be held liable for intentional abandonment.

The circumstances under which liability could be determined are fairly explicit, especially if a crisis occurs or is foreseeable. Clinicians face charges of abandonment when they fail to provide patients with a way of contacting them after hours, between sessions, when on vacation, on leave, and so forth, with *being on vacation* or *on leave* requiring that the therapist provide adequate coverage. Furthermore, reasonable contact must be maintained with hospitalized patients (Simon, 1988; VandeCreek & Knapp, 1983).

Only if there is no emergency or threatened crisis (e.g., threatened suicide or danger to the public) may a therapist safely terminate a patient by "giving reasonable notice, assisting the patient in finding another therapist, ensuring that appropriate records are transferred to the new therapist, as requested by the patient" (Simon, 1988, pp. 11–12). (We shall return to the clinical dimensions of these procedures in chapter 6.)

Clinical Versus Legal Standards of Care

VandeCreek et al. (1987) have determined that lawsuits over suicide usually fall into one of the three following legal fact patterns: (a) psychotherapists or institutions may be sued when an inpatient commits suicide, with survivors claiming that the facility failed to provide adequate care and supervision; (b) a recently released patient commits suicide; or (c) an outpatient commits suicide. Perr (1979) and Meyer, Landis, and Hays (1988) mentioned that mental health clinicians carry a tremendous legal burden when it comes to a patient's suicide, because, simply stated, the clinician is asked to be responsible for someone else's behavior. Although typically the law does not hold any person responsible for acts of another, suicidal and other self-destructive acts present a clear exception (Meyer et al., 1988):

> The duty of therapists to exercise adequate care and skill in diagnosing suicidality is well established (see *Meier v. Ross General Hospital*, 1968). When the risk of self-injurious behavior is identified an additional duty to take adequate precautions arises (*Abille v. United States*, 1980; *Pisel v. Stamford Hospital*, 1980). When psychotherapists fail to meet these responsibilities, they may be held liable for injuries that result. (p. 38)

Confusing the situation further is a contradiction in clinical and legal philosophies: Psychotherapists "on the one hand are told . . . . not to hospitalize unless the need is blatantly clear; on the other, they are threatened with legal liability if they do not do so and thus minimize a patient's ability to kill himself" (Perr, 1979, p. 91).

Thus, many psychotherapists are reluctant to work with suicidal patients for fear of being sued if the patient takes his or her own life, although decisions by courts have usually maintained that the clinician is not liable if he or she has maintained adequate care for the patient (Kermani, 1982). The attorneys for the family of the deceased patient often argue that a patient's suicide, perhaps the most unfortunate result possible within the context of psychotherapy (as frequently stated by plaintiff lawyers), was the result of the defendant clinician's failure to act reasonably to protect his or her patient from harm (Harris, 1988). More specifically, it is argued that the mental health professional did not correctly diagnose the patient, thus preventing him or her from foreseeing the potential for suicide and that the subsequent lack of proper treatment led directly to the patient's death (Harris, 1988; Simon, 1988). It is hardly surprising that, for the psychologist, suicide is one of the most emotionally dreaded outcomes in clinical work. Regrettably, suicide is also one of the most common clinical outcomes (Brent, Kupfer, Bromet, & Dew, 1988).

The threat of litigation compounds the burden that a patient's death creates for the clinician (Rachlin, 1984). In a general clinical practice setting, the threat of patient suicide is always a possibility. A recent review of risk assessment and treatment procedures for suicidal patients estimates that 10% to 15% of patients with major psychiatric disorders (i.e., affective disorder, substance abuse, and schizophrenia) will die by suicide (Brent et al., 1988). This review states unequivocally that the assessment and diminution of suicide potential among psychiatric patients should be a task of the highest priority for mental health professionals.

If the first concern of the psychologist is to assess and establish whether there is an elevated risk of suicide for a patient (Bongar, et al., 1989), what clinical signs is the clinician legally responsible for recognizing in order to determine if a patient is at risk? To begin with, she or he is likely to come up against statements such as Litman's (1957) in which it is purported that usually all suicidal individuals exhibit specific clinical clues that a competent psychotherapist should recognize as significant. These include complaints of pain, suffering and hopelessness, and physical signs of depression (e.g., sleep disturbance, loss of appetite, and loss of weight). Lesse (1989a) went so far as to state that "almost all suicides are avoidable if patients are properly diagnosed, monitored, and treated in an appropriate and timely manner" (p. ix). Yet suicide, as discussed earlier, is not always preventable and, currently defies predictability, although as Rachlin (1984) commented "these facts offer, of course, little consolation in the courtroom" (p. 305).

Psychologists rely on many clinical observable factors in assessing the potential for suicide in their patients, and some of these variables are vague and difficult to interpret. Furthermore, the clinical value of such risk factors is much greater for short-range assessment of suicide risk in the patient undergoing an acute suicidal crisis (Simon, 1988). It may be safe to state that, at the present time, risk variables identify too many false positives to be of practical use in the *long-term* prediction of suicide (Murphy, 1984, 1986, 1988a, 1988b; Peterson & Bongar, 1989; Robins, 1986; Simon, 1987, 1988).

For example, in one of the most important studies to date, a large-scale prospective study of patients with major affective disorders was undertaken; during the study 25 patients (out of a total of 954) committed suicide. Hopelessness, loss of pleasure or interest, and mood cycling during the index episode differentiated the suicide group (Fawcett et al., 1987). The researchers noted that, although suicide was a relatively frequent event in depressed patients, it still had a statistically low base rate and, therefore, using cross-sectional measures was probably statistically unpredictable on an individual basis.

In his list of clinical considerations that are reasonable from a legal perspective for evaluating suicide risk, Simon (1987, 1988) enumerated a series of specific objective and subjective clinical risk variables that include the following: (a) relationship potential (e.g., lack of a therapeutic alliance or of meaningful supportive relationships); (b) suicidal history (e.g., prior attempts, specific plan, lethality of previous attempts); (c) psychiatric medical factors (e.g., chronic psychiatric disorders, mental incompetence, recent psychiatric discharge); (d) actuarial data (e.g., age 15–24 or advancing age for men, unmarried, a recent personal loss, unemployed); and (e) short-term variables (e.g., within 1 year of the assessment, loss of pleasure, panic attacks, anxiety). As mentioned previously, there is also a substantial body of clinical literature that addresses the psychosocial-relational clues to suicidal intent (see chapter 1).

Nonetheless, in malpractice cases involving suicide, the courts have recognized that the prediction of suicidality in a particular patient is a clinical dilemma fraught with uncertainty (Gutheil, Bursztajn, Hamm, & Brodsky, 1983). For suicidal patients, Gutheil et al. (1983) noted that the standard of due care against which a clinician's diagnosis of risk and subsequent treatment may be measured involves three major traditions of negligence law: (a) community standards (professional customs), (b) maximization of benefits relative to costs, and (c) the notion of the "reasonable and prudent practitioner." Gutheil and colleagues (1983) and Bursztajn, Gutheil, Hamm, and Brodsky (1983) further argued that a sound clinical assessment of suicide risk requires the assessment of both subjective and objective factors.

Rachlin (1984) pointed out that the fulcrum of a malpractice case is usually a dereliction in a duty that is owed to the patient, namely, a failure of the required degree of care (i.e., the treatment is in some way substandard). He also noted that in the absence of such a breach of duty, other questions such as causality are not really relevant. Rachlin (1984) goes on to say that

> The terminology used by various courts in defining the degree of care and skill expected from professional persons includes *requisite, diligent, reasonable, ordinary, proper*, and *as others have and exercise*. One must practice in consonance with accepted principles; thus, more than an honest error of professional judgment is required in order to give rise to liability. It is the role of the expert witness to provide testimony to guide the court

relative to accepted standards of professional practice and any departures therefrom. However, courts have been known to elevate standards and do have the authority to determine what is adequate. In an occasional situation, the breach of duty may be considered so reckless or egregious as to be within the common knowledge of a prudent layman, and no expert testimony would be required. Far more usually, the facts about propriety of treatment are in dispute and so opinion is presented by both the plaintiff and the defendant. In the end, the credibility of the expert testimony may be the determining factor. (p. 303)

Malpractice actions against mental health professionals are also "plagued by such issues as what constitutes an acceptable level of care in suicide treatment and who is qualified as an expert witness to testify to the reasonableness of deviations from that standard" (Berman & Cohen-Sandler, 1983, p. 6). Furthermore, mental health and legal professionals have not yet been able to resolve such basic issues as "who legitimately may decide what constitutes standard or acceptable care in the treatment of suicidal patients, and what level of quality should be considered standard; that is, ought we to demand some minimum degree of care or, instead, more optimal care?" (Berman & Cohen-Sandler, 1982, p. 115).

What seem to be the pivotal elements in most cases of malpractice and suicide, however, are the twin issues of the ability to foresee and causation (Bongar et al., 1989; Perr, 1979, 1988; Rachlin, 1984; Simon, 1988; VandeCreek et al., 1987; VandeCreek & Knapp, 1989).[2] Typically, as the courts have struggled with these two critical issues in cases of suicide, their deliberations have focused specifically on whether the clinician should have predicted the suicide and whether there was sufficient evidence for an identifiable risk of harm—ultimately, that is, whether the psychotherapist or the institution (or both) did enough to protect the patient (VandeCreek et al., 1987). Berman and Cohen-Sandler (1982) have noted that negligence is usually indicated only when, on the basis of expert testimony, treatment, or assessment was found to be deviant, that is, was deemed unreasonable. They stated that, although failures in treatment are often blamed on the patient, mental health professionals often play a significant role in the suicidal deaths of their patients.

Demonstrated negligence requires proof that the patient was clearly identifiable as suicidal on the basis of the recognized criteria used by most clinicians

---

[2]For additional information, the reader is directed to a number of articles and books that have examined recent general trends in malpractice case law on suicidal patients (Berman & Cohen-Sandler, 1982, 1983; Beyer, 1982; Bursztajn et al., 1983; Gutheil & Appelbaum, 1982; Gutheil et al., 1983; Klein & Glover, 1983; Robertson, 1988; Simon, 1987; Slaby, Lieb, & Tancredi, 1986; Slawson et al., 1974; Slovenko, 1985; Smith, 1988; Swartz, 1988; VandeCreek & Knapp, 1983, 1989; Vande-Creek et al., 1987).

of the same training (Meyer et al., 1988). Although the courts have not yet applied a standard of care, through new case law that has found liability when inexperienced or inadequately trained psychologists (especially those practitioners with little or no training and clinical experience with suicidal patients) treat these high-risk patients, we believe that this may be a potential area of increased vulnerability for a malpractice action, especially for neophyte practitioners, practitioners-in-training, and for their supervisors. (This opinion will be discussed in greater detail in chapter 6.)

The Standard of the "Reasonable and Prudent Practitioner"

By now it is clear to the reader that the clinical burdens on psychologists and other mental health professionals who see suicidal patients as part of their professional practice are many and heavy (Maltsberger, 1986). Rachlin (1984) noted that, in the final analysis, instituting a malpractice action is the "ultimate expression of dissatisfaction with our treatment efforts, in this case by the survivors" (p. 305). What, then, are some options for care that are available to the reasonable and prudent psychologist who assesses and treats suicidal patients as part of her or his professional practice?

Up to the present time, the courts have not been consistent in defining a standard of care for the suicidal patient. Perr (1988) noted that studies of legal cases have been of only limited value if one is seeking principle, rationality, and consistency in the application of accumulated knowledge for reasonable legal purposes. He went so far as to state that

> Judicial decisions have become increasingly bizarre as judges make diagnoses, order treatments, reject treatments, and discharge patients, as well as often manifest gross ignorance of the issues about which they make the law, relying on lawyers and doctors who pose as experts—when in reality they are but persuaders, advocates, and propagandists with an economic or other agenda. The applicability of the jury system to evaluation of care also continues to be troublesome. (p. 4)

Gutheil (1984) went so far as to state that "neither the standard of care nor the quality of the clinician's practice has anything to do with malpractice litigation. It is the bad outcome combined with bad feelings that leads to lawsuits. . . . Suicide because it is a classic example of a bad outcome with bad feelings, captures the center stage of the litigation experience" (p. 2).

Rachlin (1984) advocated that outcome in a malpractice case is never assured and that one can never be certain of victory. Liability has been found in circumstances that "would not have seemed to warrant such a conclusion" (p. 305). Yet, as Rachlin further notes,

> it is reassuringly true that, while it is easy to file a claim, proof of negligence is another matter. All of the litigation that has taken place has produced little in the way of concrete guidance, but this may be a benefit in disguise. Strict standards can thwart treatment and lower the quality of care by forcing the adoption of antitherapeutic restrictions. Similarly, little benefit accrues to patients when therapists or administrators engage in obsessive overconcern about legal minutiae to the detriment of the clinical perspective. (p. 305)

Rachlin and Schwartz (1986) described a number of recent court decisions in which judges ignored or distorted acceptable clinical practices, conceivably creating a new liability standard whereby a tragic outcome is seen as the result of a failure to apply appropriate judgment.

Rachlin (1984) also made a number of recommendations designed to minimize the risk of being found negligent as a result of a patient's suicide. These included: careful documentation of decisions to grant patients increased freedom, detailing the specifics of suicide precautions, consultation from supervisors or colleagues, and outreach to survivors. There will always be areas of indecision, gray areas in which clinicians will disagree, resulting in differences of opinion among both treating clinicians and expert witnesses (Sadoff, 1985). "A key element (in the context of the legal system that provides confusing or even contradictory rules) has been attributing to professional people the capacity to predict and control the behavior of the mentally ill" (Perr, 1988, p. 4). Although a patient's suicide is not always preventable, the only course for a clinician is to integrate appropriate guidelines within his or her treatment plans, in good faith that he or she will prevail in convincing the court that no liability need be attached to the patient's demise.

In this belief, we return to Berman and Cohen-Sandler's (1982) position: It is the duty of a clinician or institution to prevent suicide

> through the use of reasonable care and skill. "Reasonable" is considered by law to be the "average standard of the profession"—"the degree of learning, skill, and experience which ordinarily is possessed by others of the same profession" (American Jurisprudence, 1981) . . . . the average standard is essentially defined by the legal system through decisions rendered in malpractice cases, which, in turn, determine completely the liability of the clinician who treats suicidal patients. (p. 116)

We also hold that for *every* patient seen in professional psychological practice, there are a few important steps that can dramatically reduce one's exposure should a malpractice action be brought. More important, these steps may help ensure the highest level of professional treatment for all of the patients under the psychologist's care. (These steps will be detailed in chapter 6.)

In the United States, society has given psychologists and other mental health professionals a special legal status to heal. In turn, society has imposed an expectation on these professionals of a special responsibility to protect their patients from harm, especially harm to self and to others (Harris, 1988). Psychologists have new legal duties that they did not have 15 years ago, and society, through its legal system and through new laws, has begun increasingly to scrutinize the manner in which mental health clinicians exercise appropriate duty of care owed to a suicidal patient.

The issue of what constitutes adequate training is a particularly thorny issue, both for psychology and the other core mental health disciplines (as well as for the growing number of other mental health counselors, marital and family therapists, etc.). A recent and comprehensive study found that little specific formal training in managing suicidal patients was conducted in traditional graduate training programs in clinical psychology (Bongar & Harmatz, 1989). In addition, in an unpublished 1982 study (Berman, 1983, 1986a), it was found that there was little formal training in the management of suicidal patients among the other core mental health disciplines (i.e., psychiatric residency training, clinical social work graduate schools, and psychiatric nursing programs). For example, Berman and Cohen-Sandler (1982) noted that "fewer than one in four psychiatrists and psychologists in the Washington, DC area, who average 11 years in independent practice, have had any postresidency/graduate school training in suicide assessment" (p. 120).

Toward an Integrative Approach

In the preceding pages, we have presented a panoply of expert opinions, theoretical viewpoints, and empirical data in an effort to convey the range of thought that has been brought to bear on the issues of determining reasonable and effective treatments for suicidal patients. Throughout the remainder of this book, we will take an integrative approach to clinical and legal considerations in the management of suicidal patients (Bongar et al., 1989). We do so in the belief that the integration of this voluminous material can best occur in practice, not merely by virtue of integrating theoretical constructs from different schools of thought, but also by providing a more comprehensive framework that would encompass the clinical observables (Goldfried & Wachtel, 1987). Inherent in our approach to the formulation of critically evaluated options for care of the suicidal patient is the acceptance of the biopsychosocial model of assessment and care (Engel, 1977; Rigler, 1982). This approach holds that psychological, biological, and social factors contribute to an individual's experiences of his or her disorder, with the relative contribution of each factor varying with each specific problem (Engel, 1977). Proponents of this biopsychosocial model have, at times, called for an entirely new medical model, one that sees biologic factors as a necessary but not sufficient explanation of the disease process (Rigler, 1982). The bio-psychosocial model sees psychological, biological, and social elements as contributing to the time of onset, to the course of the patient's illness, and to the impact that this problem has on the functioning person (Engel, 1977). We posit, then, that the best approach to the study of suicide is an interdisciplinary approach, in which "domains of discourse must be evaluated by teams of experts trained in the complexities of specific psychosocial, biological, sociocultural, philosophical, and other relevant issues" (Pfeffer, 1988, p. 26).

A note of warning is needed here: Maris (1988) cautioned that one needs to be wary of reduction (biological, psychological, or social) when it comes to the study of the suicidal patient, that suicide is a symptom, not a diagnosis, and that, although the state of being suicidal can be analyzed, the act of suicide cannot. This cautionary note reverberates throughout the suicidology literature. "Suicidal thoughts, like all human thoughts, are experimental actions" (Maris, 1988, p. xii). Shneidman (1988) noted that "study of suicide is multidisciplinary—a never-completed circle, containing many legitimate sectors or fields or approaches" (p. 5). Pfeffer (1988) agreed; "suicidal behavior is a complex, multidetermined phenomenon that can be understood from a variety of key vantage points: psychosocial, sociocultural, constitutional-biological, and many others" (p. 21). Thus, there is no one standard nor is there a static constellation of standards that can be applied in all areas of suicide.

The goal of developing a comprehensive and integrative approach to clinical and legal standards for the care of suicidal patients, when placed within the larger framework of general standards for sound professional practice, is clearly in accord with a goal articulated in a recent paper on the history of the integrative trend in psychotherapy. London and Palmer (1988) see psychotherapy integration as "a commonsensical striving that promotes and sanctions broader, therefore better practice" (pp. 278–279). Berman and Cohen-Sandler (1982) remarked that, if the mental health professions establish norms of practice that demand optimal standards, "we do run the risk of failing to meet them and, consequently, the greater risk of litigation and liability. But clinicians must accept responsibility for providing more than minimum therapeutic response. The risks of litigation seem far outweighed by the potential benefits to our suicidal patients of more optimal care" (p. 121).

Further confounding our understanding of suicide and the law is the realization that it is currently difficult to discern clear legal guidelines for what constitutes an adequate standard of care only on the basis of the reported case law (Harris, 1988). For there are not that many reported cases, and, in most states, court cases are only reported when the decision of a lower court is appealed.

Harris also pointed out that the situation is made even more difficult by the fact that many cases are either settled prior to a trial or are not appealed. Therefore, many experts rely on their own network of professional contacts (other legal and clinical authorities), on their own clinical experience, and on information from empirical studies to define what is (or is not) appropriate care. Thus Rachlin (1984) counsels:

> We cannot afford to be so afraid of litigation as to deny our patients their right to learn to live. Clinical decisions are to be made on a case by case basis, and should represent the most thorough knowledge available. In this way, manageable standards of care will be set by us as mental health professionals and presumably, courts will follow our reasonableness. (p. 306)

Summary

Currently, malpractice actions against psychologists for the death of a patient are relatively rare, although increasing in frequency. According to current APAIT data, there have been only 102 claims for suicide out of a total of 1,892 open and closed claims. As psychology seeks expanded professional privileges, such as hospital staff membership and admission and discharge privileges, the profession will find itself exposed to many of the same malpractice liabilities as our colleagues in psychiatry (the field in which suicide is the number one cause of malpractice action and accounts for the largest dollar amounts in settlements).

Yet, the reported case law gives us a limited view of the total malpractice picture, because most state court cases are only reported when there is an appeal, or when the trial court decision is sufficiently controversial to warrant an appeal. What the current case law does tell us is the following:

- Most of the cases concern inpatients. Hospitals and institutions appear to be held to a higher standard of care, because often the mere fact of hospitalization for suicidal behavior or ideation (two of the most common criteria for a hospital admission) should put the hospital on guard.
- Hospitals are assumed by the courts to have much greater control over the environment and behavior of inpatients, and it is reasonable to expect greater responsibility in effecting a standard of care. It is important to note here that the courts have moved from the older "custodial model" to a more sophisticated acknowledgment of the need to increase a patient's freedom and participation in his or her treatment planning and care.

- In the few outpatient cases that have been reported, the same criteria are used, namely the twin issues of the ability to foresee and causation in the evaluation of negligence in the standard of care. In both inpatient and outpatient cases, the standard of care will most often be decided retrospectively through the testimony of expert witnesses.
- Anecdotal data suggest that many cases of outpatient suicide never reach trial, but instead are settled by the defendant and insurance company (even though the defendant may well have prevailed in a trial). Often, this is done to avoid a costly deposition/trial and possibly also to avoid the stigma of negative publicity.
- It is critical to note that the personal and professional impact of a patient's suicide can be intensely traumatic to the psychologist who loses a patient; thus the psychologist is also a suicide survivor. Adequate postvention consultation with bereaved survivors (i.e., family and significant others) is a crucial and necessary therapeutic intervention, as well as a recommended risk management effort.
- Clinicians should anticipate that there may be a conflict between the clinical and legal standards of care, in which the clinical standard might lean more toward the forensically riskier course of outpatient care and less toward the use of hospitalization.

However, when psychologists can demonstrate that their decision-making process and management efforts were coherent and appropriate and fell within the guidelines of the profession's standard of care, we believe that they are unlikely to be sued successfully, because most suits allege that the psychologist will have failed (a) to detect an elevated risk and (b) to intervene appropriately, or to intervene at all on the basis of this risk. Here, the literature is somewhat confusing. On the one hand, it indicates that psychologists are responsible for foreseeing the patient's ultimate decision to act on suicidal thoughts, which is a kind of prediction. On the other hand, the clinical and empirical data tell us that identification of suicide attempters and completers before the fact is not scientifically possible. We believe that the best response to this conundrum is for psychologists to focus instead on the detection of factors that might lead to any assessment that risk is elevated, and to ensure that their management and treatment efforts adequately demonstrate the probabilistic nature of this risk–benefit analysis.

Claims of negligence are often based on dereliction of duty directly causing damages. Therefore, psychologists in their risk management efforts should:

- make every effort to identify factors that would indicate an elevated risk for suicide;
- make every effort to reduce or eliminate this risk;

- in both their initial evaluation and in ongoing clinical work, record in detail where they identified elevated risk and continually update this assessment, showing clearly how they managed the risk; and
- routinely consider a "second opinion" through consultation, supervision, or both, even at a moderate level of risk.

In the next chapter, we turn to the specifics of how psychologists might accomplish the difficult task of detecting an elevated risk of suicide. Before beginning this task, however, let us offer some words of caution from Menninger (1989), who stated that a sensitive and effective relationship between treaters and patients is still the best safeguard against malpractice litigation.

The Assessment of Elevated Risk

The clinician who must decide how much at risk for suicide a particular patient may be is in a quandary. The enormous amount of information available to clinicians on the psychological, psychodynamic, behavioral, epidemiological, social-relational, and biological risk factors in attempted and completed suicide—as well as psychological tests and sophisticated suicide rating scales—are not adequate to allow one to answer directly the most critical question of all: "Is this patient, sitting here with me now, about to commit suicide?" (Maltsberger, 1988, p. 47).

This problem is not resolved by relying on the two most common methods used to assess suicide danger: the mental status examination and the examiner's intuition about the patient. Drawing a loose analogy between a mental status examination and a physical examination, Maltsberger (1988) wrote, "But what physician would base diagnosis and plan treatment on the physical examination alone? Only a poor one. Good doctors attend to the clinical history as well as to physical signs" (p. 48).

Clinical Assessment and Diagnosis

Because the suicidology literature is voluminous, diverse, and sometimes contradictory, clinicians may have difficulty determining the relative importance of various factors when assessing the individual. Some researchers have emphasized particular charts of variables. Gutheil and Appelbaum (1982), for example, stated that the best approach to gathering data "focuses on previous psychiatric history; recent behavior or behavioral change; significant alteration of circumstances (e.g., loss of job); bizarreness of ideation or action; threats to self or others, or related behavior such as the purchase of poison, rope, or a gun; history of substance abuse and the like" (p. 52). Furthermore, Gutheil and Appelbaum pointed out that the central clinical and legal concerns involve negligence in evaluation and in involuntary interventions (i.e., hospitalization). Brent et al. (1988) noted that an accurate diagnostic assessment is necessary with regard to primary and co-morbid psychiatric disorder, alcohol and drug abuse, personality disorders, and attendant medical disorders. In addition, a proper assessment mobilizes the fa-milies and significant others in order to improve compliance with treatment and decrease the chance of a relapse.

Fremouw et al. (1990; see also Bassuk, 1982) found that the assessment of a patient's potential suicide risk necessitates the gathering and weighing of a variety of information and data. The importance of this particular assessment led these psychologists to construct an impressive decision model that integrates and formalizes the steps for a thorough and reasonable decision about the risk for suicide for a particular patient. Somewhat like Bassuk's 1982 checklist system, their decision model involves seven steps for the psychologist:

1. *The collection of demographic information* (e.g., age, sex, race, marital status, and living situation) to determine whether the patient is in a high-risk or low-risk group.

2. *The examination of clinical and historical indicators* as the more specific information that increases or decreases the patient's risk for suicide (e.g., unique historical, environmental, and psychologi-cal features that a patient presents in the intake interview or during ongoing therapy: (a) questions about general historical–situational factors (which begin to lead the clinician to be concerned about a higher risk); (b) very specific clinical indicators and warning signs that often are the precursors of an imminent attempt (e.g., having a definite plan, strong self-destructive impulses); and (c) psycho-logical indicators such as recent losses, depression–anxiety, isola-tion–withdrawal, hopelessness, disorientation–disorganization, alcohol and drug use, change in clinical features, suicide plan, and final arrangements for his or her own death.

3. *An initial screening for risk*, that is, after examining historical–situational, demographic, and clinical indicators, the clinician must make a decision about whether the potential risk for suicide war-rants any further assessment. If there appears to be no risk, assess-ment and treatment proceed in a routine fashion. However, if there are risk factors in the demographic or clinical–situational–historical matrix, then the clinician should assess the current risk for suicide through two formats initially, through interview and, if indicated, through further assessment by self-report.

4. *Direct assessment of risk* using (a) the *clinical interview* (which includes the patient's reasons for feeling suicidal, as well as his or

her reasons for living), and, where risk appears mild, moderate, or unknown, (b) *assessment by self-report* (e.g., the use of standardized assessment instruments such as the Beck Depression and Hopelessness scales to facilitate a thorough understanding).

5. ***Determination of the level of risk and the implementation of a response*** (e.g., none-to-low, mild, moderate, or high risk).

6. ***Determination of the imminence of risk*** (e.g., assessment and documentation of rationale, consultation).

7. ***Implementation of treatment strategies*** (e.g., intensified outpatient care, voluntary hospitalization, involuntary hospitalization, etc.)

Although, the model shown in Figure 3.1 is a new and important contribution as a systematic decision-making tool for the practicing clinician (and may very well represent the future general shape of standard models of assessment and intervention for suicide potential), Motto (1989), in a review of general problems in suicide risk assessment, made the following observation:

> That the assessment of suicide risk is, indeed, a problem is attested to by the fact that to date we have no established and generally accepted procedure to guide us in this task. Innumerable decisions regarding risk are made and implemented every day—the job gets done—but how it is done is determined primarily by the skills and philosophy of the individual clinician. (p. 245)

Simon (1988) remarked that providing a reasonable standard of care in assessing and diagnosing suicidal patients preempts "the very problematic issue of prediction of suicide for which standards do not exist. Psychiatrists have not been held legally liable for inaccurate predictions of suicide per se. Only when they have failed to collect necessary data and logically assess it in making a prediction of suicide have lawsuits against psychiatrists prevailed" (pp. 86–87). However, as Lewinsohn, Garrison, Langhinrichsen, and Marsteller (1989) pointed out,

> unfortunately, the low base rate of suicide makes it very difficult for screening instruments to predict accurately the degree of suicidal risk for any specific individual. Specifically, the low base rate results in a very large number of false positive assessments relative to the number of true positives, even when the most effective screening instruments are used. (p. 4)

Fawcett and his colleagues (1987), using data from a large-scale prospective study of patients with major affective disorders, found that 25 patients (out of a total of 954) committed suicide; hopelessness, loss of pleasure or interest, and

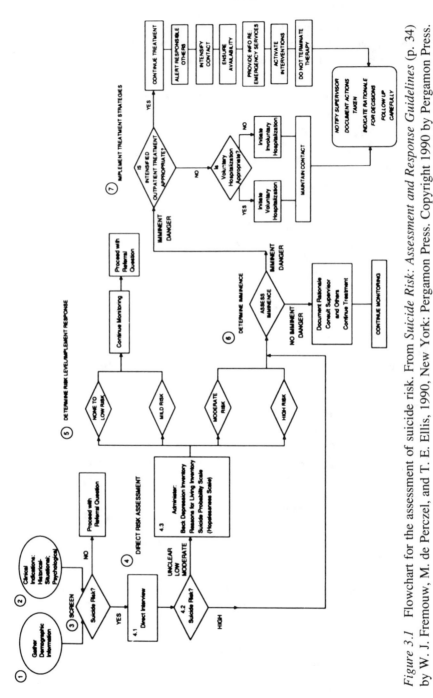

Figure 3.1 Flowchart for the assessment of suicide risk. From *Suicide Risk: Assessment and Response Guidelines* (p. 34) by W. J. Fremouw, M. de Perczel, and T. E. Ellis, 1990, New York: Pergamon Press. Copyright 1990 by Pergamon Press. Reprinted by permission.

mood cycling during the index episode differentiated the suicide group. These researchers noted that, although suicide is a relatively frequent event in depressed patients, it still has a statistically low base rate and, therefore, may be statistically unpredictable on an individual basis using cross-sectional measures. Fawcett (1988) does offer a model, which, although acknowledging the limitations of the current knowledge base, enumerates a variety of both short-term risk features (acute predictors) and long-term suicide risk features (chronic predictors). (This important approach will be discussed in greater detail in the Empirical Data on Acute Versus Chronic Factors section of this chapter.)

In recognition of these methodological and clinical difficulties in predicting suicide, this chapter's focus is on the collection of critical data and decision points in the clinical formulation, detection, and documentation of *imminent and elevated risk* in the usual and customary populations seen in professional psychological practice.[1] In view of publications that focus specifically on the issues of youth suicide and suicide among the elderly (Berman & Jobes, in press; McIntosh et al., forthcoming), the general clinical and legal issues with regard to the formulation of a standard of care for adult clinical populations are emphasized here.

A clinical approach to the assessment of suicidal patients

1. recognizes the probablistic nature of risk detection versus risk prediction;

2. acknowledges the strengths and limitations of the traditional diagnostic categories (e.g., the *Diagnostic and Statistical Manual of Mental Disorders* [*DSM-III-R*], as well as the various theories of psychotherapy and psychopathology);

3. understands epidemiologic and clinical risk factors within specific groups, taking into consideration the data on both acute and chronic predictors of risk;

4. remembers when consultation, supervision, and referral are necessary; and

5. integrates a careful clinical history, mental status examination, ongoing clinical evaluations, consultations, information from sig-

---

[1]For more information on specific methodologies and techniques, see Bongar et al. (1989); Brent et al. (1988); Evans and Farberow (1988); Fawcett (1988); Fremouw et al. (1990); Gutheil and Appelbaum (1982); Hirschfeld and Davidson (1988); Jacobs (1989a, 1989b); Kreitman (1986); Lesse (1988b); Lewinsohn et al. (1989); Litman (1989); Maltsberger (1986 1988); Mann and Stanley (1988a, 1988b); Maris (1981, 1986, 1988, 1989a, 1989b); Motto (1986, 1989); Murphy (1986, 1988a, 1988b); Perr (1985b, 1988); Peterson and Bongar (1989); Pokorny (1983); Pope (1989); Rachlin (1984); Robins (1985, 1986); Robins and Helzer (1986); Roy (1986); Shneidman (1984, 1985, 1986a, 1987, 1989); Simon (1987, 1988); Swartz (1988); Swenson (1986); and VandeCreek and Knapp (1983, 1989).

nificant others, and data from psychological assessment and suicide risk estimators and scales to systematically assess and manage detected risk.

Before proceeding, however, it is essential to emphasize once again that hard and fast actuarial data on the long-term prediction of attempted or completed suicide—predictions that can be directly translated to the emergent clinical moment—do not now exist. Currently, "there are no pathognomic predictors of suicide" (Simon, 1987, p. 259). As Monahan (1981, p. 101) wrote our efforts represent "nothing more (or less) than the professional judgment of persons experienced at the task of prediction," and we suggest that clinicians would do well to follow Meehl's advice that "when actuarial data do not exist, we must use our heads" (Monahan, 1981, p. 108).

Recent Empirical Evidence on Risk Assessment Practices

The Risk Assessment Committee of the American Association of Suicidology (AAS) recently reported the results of their survey on suicide risk assessment procedures among a random sample of practicing psychologists, psychiatrists, and clinical social workers (including members and nonmembers of the AAS). Although the results of this survey should be interpreted with caution because of the small sample size ($N = 414$) and relatively low response rate (38%), they do provide at least an initial glimpse into the assessment practices of practitioners (Jobes, Eyman, & Yufit, 1990). The amount of assessment activity carried out by the respondents, many of whom appeared to be psychologists, is of interest; on the average, 1.9 suicidal adolescents and 2.8 suicidal adults were evaluated per month.

Specifically, Jobes et al. (1990) found that

1. Suicide assessment instruments appear to be used infrequently and are rated as having limited usefulness. For adolescents, the most frequently used were the Beck Hopelessness Scale (BHS; 28%) and the Beck Suicide Intent Scale (SIS; 23%). For adults, the most frequently used were the BHS (34%) and the SIS (28%). These two scales were rated as *somewhat useful* for both adults and adolescents.

2. Although traditional psychological tests are used more frequently, they are not rated as very useful. The most commonly used tests were the Minnesota Multiphasic Personality Inventory (MMPI; 47%), the Beck Depression Inventory (BDI; 46%), the Rorschach (44%), and the Thematic Apperception Test (42%). Of these tests, only the BDI received a rating of *somewhat useful*.

3. With a few exceptions, there are few major differences in the approaches used to assess acute versus chronic risk, and there are limited differences between the assessment of adults compared with adolescents. Instead, most clinicians rely primarily on the clinical interview to assess suicide (specifically, on certain valued questions and observations).

In order to shed some light on these preferences of active practitioners and their primary reliance on interview and observational data, the remainder of this chapter will examine the historical and contemporary literature on the use of psychological tests, suicide scales, and risk estimators, as well as the epidemiological and clinical data on risk factors and the impact of theoretical orientation and *DSM- III-R* diagnosis (American Psychiatric Association, 1987). The importance of formulation of clinical judgment through clinical observations and key elements in the clinical interview that serve as integral components of a model of comprehensive clinical assessment and risk management will also be discussed. At the end of this chapter, a clinical case example will be presented—one that demonstrates a risk-detection and decision-making model for clinical assessment of elevated risk. The purpose of such a model is to incorporate the diverse elements mentioned above into an assessment protocol on which subsequent management and treatment efforts may be based. We will begin by examining the strengths and limitations of traditional psychological testing approaches to the assessment of suicide.

Psychological Testing

The psychological assessment of suicidal risk is a process fraught with personal uneasiness and anxiety on the part of the mental health professional. The burden is awesome, and the responsibility is frightening (Neuringer, 1974a). Yet as Neuringer remarks:

> If all of the methodological problems associated with valid assessment of suicidal risk can be overcome, then the occurrence of false negatives will be severely diminished. The reduction of the number of false negatives (i.e., suicidal people who are erroneously diagnosed as nonsuicidal) is the chief aim of self-destructive risk assessment techniques. It is, in essence, the task of saving lives. (p. 15)

The Rorschach Inkblot Technique

Historically, the Rorschach technique was the most commonly used method for estimating the risk of suicide, although it has been supplanted by more sophisticated psychometric instruments such as the MMPI and various suicide lethality scales (Neuringer, 1974b). Neuringer noted that there certainly does not appear to have been any particular determinant, sign, or set of signs, or content which appears to be associated with suicide under all or even most conditions, that is, there is no pathognomic sign on the Rorschach for suicide which is so strong that it transcends all the various states of suicidality or the differing conditions under which test data were elicited. (p. 88)

However, the Rorschach may still be a potent tool for assessing the risk of suicide, if it is used correctly. Recently, Meyer (1989) argued that Exner's (1978, 1986) research provided an elegant and effective tool for the prediction of suicide potential. He cited a large number of specific factors from Exner's (1978) seminal contribution, *The Rorschach: A Comprehensive System.*[2] Meyer notes that, in general:

A number of authors concur with Exner that the number of responses is low in suicidals, especially when they are depressed, that less integrated color responses are more common, and that the number of popular responses are either very high or low (Swiercinsky, 1985). Also, there is some indication that transparency responses (such as light bulbs) or cross-sectional responses (such as X-rays) are found more commonly in potential suicides than in other persons; and the greater the number of vista and shading responses, the greater the depression-based suicide potential. (p. 319)

Meyer (1989) also points out the importance of content that suggests decay or geographic depression as indicators of suicidal ideation. He notes that "responses that suggest hanging or drowning or other direct means of suicide should obviously alert the examiner to further consideration" (p. 319). Here he is in agreement with Neuringer (1974b), who suggested that the clinician rely most on content from the Rorschach. Neuringer wrote:

If suicidal content appears on the Rorschach, it should be taken very seriously since its manifestation could be an indication that self-destructive behavior is close to the surface, and that the suicidal person may be using the test protocol as a medium of communication to the examiner about his intentions and feelings. (p. 91)

The Rorschach can perhaps be most useful in the assessment of suicide risk if it is combined with appropriate and sound clinical judgment (Eyman & Eyman,

---

[2]For example, "FV + VF + V + FD is greater than 2; occurrence of a color-shading response; Zd greater than or equal to 3.5; 3r + (2)/R is less than 0.30, Experience Potential is greater than Experience Actual; CF + C is greater than FC; S is greater than 3; X + % is less than 0.70; Pure H is less than 2; P is greater than 8, or less than 3; R is less than 17" (Meyer, 1989, p. 319).

in press). Cautioning that suicide is too complex a behavior to be adequately captured by a single sign, Eyman and Eyman suggest that the configurational or constellation approach shows promise for the use of the Rorschach for the assessment of risk.

Neuringer (1974b) further cautioned that the clinician should not make an inference about suicidal intention from the Rorschach by itself and that case history material and data from other psychometric instruments can help to maximize the accuracy of the decision-making process. He concluded that "the clinician should strive to have all the data possible available to him. The presence of previous suicidal attempts and threats should compound the danger associated with the presence of suicidal Rorschach content" (p. 91).[3]

Minnesota Multiphasic Personality Inventory (MMPI)

Clopton (1974), in an extensive review of the MMPI and the assessment of suicide risk, pointed to the findings of Dahlstrom, Welsh, and Dahlstrom (1972)—findings that the degree of the person's depression, that is, an elevated score on Scale 2 (D) of the MMPI, was a mood state frequently associated with a preoccupation with death and suicide. He continued:

> The implication of high scores on Scale 2 depend on other features of the MMPI and upon the behavior of the person taking the test. For instance, it is their conclusion (Dahlstrom et al., 1972) that suicidal risk is greater when a person's MMPI results show a significant elevation on Scale 2 but his behavior does not give any indication of depression, and he denies depressive thought and feelings, than when the depression indicated by a Scale 2 elevation is clearly reflected in the person's behavior. (p. 118)

Clopton also noted that "the one standard MMPI scale found most frequently to differentiate suicidal and nonsuicidal groups is Scale 2" (p. 129). Meyer (1989) agreed and stated that the prototypical pattern for suicidal individuals is the 2–7/7–2 combination on the MMPI. He felt that this code specifically indicates the presence of suicidal ideation, and that whenever "2 is elevated above 80T, the clinician should pursue the question of possible suicidal ideation" (p. 317).

Meyer (1989) pointed out that the critical items on the MMPI concerning suicide should always be carefully checked and that the likelihood of suicidal ideation "being actualized increases as scores on the Scales 4, 8, and 9 rise, reflecting greater loss of control over impulses, a rise in energy available for behavior, and an increasing sense of isolation and resentment toward other

---

[3]For additional information on use of the Rorschach with the suicidal patient, the reader is directed to Exner (1978, 1986), Eyman and Eyman (in press), Meyer (1989), and Neuringer (1974b).

people'' (p. 317), respectively. Specifically, a rise in Scale 8 indicates that suicidal patients may actually kill themselves whether they want to succeed or not, because their impaired judgment may bring about an inadvertent suicide. He also noted that people can become suicidal following a severe loss in their psychosocial world and that a high spike on Scale 2 is characteristic of these circumstances. Meyer believes that the ''2–4/4–2 code is more likely to reflect a manipulative suicide. Where both Scales 4 and 6 are elevated, in addition to at least a moderate elevation on Scales 2 and 7, repressed anger and interpersonal hostility are as basic to a suicide attempt as manipulation'' (p. 318).

Yet, in the absence of more data, Eyman and Eyman (in press) contend that, despite considerable research effort, no MMPI item, scale, or profile configuration has been found to consistently differentiate suicidal and nonsuicidal patients. They do concede that the restandardized MMPI-2 may provide more valid indicators of suicidality.

With the recent release of the MMPI-2, the Koss-Butcher Critical Item Set Revised is now available to practitioners. This is a list of 22 items that are related specifically to depressed suicidal ideation. However, Butcher (1989) noted that these critical items are not designed to operate as scales: ''They are used to highlight item content that might be particularly significant in the individual's case. As sources of clinical hypotheses, the critical items might be used to key the clinician into problem areas or concerns the patient may have'' (p. 17).[4]

After reviewing the use of the MMPI in psychiatric practice, Osborne (1985) argued that the MMPI is best used within the context of other information-gathering techniques and should be viewed as providing the clinician with hypotheses that can be verified using other methods. Such other methods could include the use of other psychological tests, suicide scales and risk estimators, and a comprehensive clinical interview and history (Hendren, 1990).

16 PF

Meyer (1989) noted that on the 16 PF, suicide attempters appear to consistently show themselves more shy, tense, suspicious, expedient, emotionally unstable, apprehensive, self-sufficient, somewhat introverted, and extremely anxious: ''Translated into 16 PF scales, this means high scores on Q_4, O, 1, Q_2 and lower scores on G, H, and C. Furthermore, repeated attempters typically score lower on scales Q_3 and C than do first-time attempters, indicating less stability and more impulsivity'' (p. 318).

Millon Clinical Multiaxial Inventory (MCMI)

McCann and Suess (1988) examined the MCMI profiles of 131 psychiatric inpatients to identify 1–2–3–8 codetypes on the basic personality scales. This

---

[4]For additional information on the specifics of these critical items, the reader is directed to the work of Butcher, Dalhstrom, Graham, Tellegen, & Kaemmer (1989); and Butcher (1989).

profile reflects a schizoid, avoidant, dependent, and passive–aggressive blend of personality traits. Approximately 25% of the subjects obtained the 1–2–3–8 codetype. Their analyses of the diagnoses and clinical records of these patients suggested that this profile reflects an affect/mood disturbance with prominent depressive features and suicidal ideation/attempt prior to admission to the hospital. Summarizing, Meyer (1989) wrote that

> as might be expected, elevation on the MCMI of 85 or higher on D and CC would be indicative of suicide potential. If N begins to increase and a very high D begins to decrease on repeated testing, the patient may be acquiring the necessary resolve and energy to complete the act; thus suicide potential may be high. Those personality patterns most likely to exhibit suicide potential are indicated by elevated scores on 2,8,5, and/or C. These patterns represent the most inconsistent patterns and they are particularly susceptible to poorly developed support systems. High scores on scale 8 are particularly associated with manipulative suicide potential. (pp. 319–320)

Thematic Apperception Test, Bender-Gestalt, and other selected tests

After a review of the literature on the Thematic Apperception Test as a diagnostic instrument for the assessment of suicide risk, McEvoy (1974) concluded that the literature on the use of the Thematic Apperception Test as an estimator of suicide risk is clearly disappointing. He stated that "the literature is sparse and not easily compared for purposes of generalizations. Perhaps the only general conclusion is that the test has not proved to be useful for this purpose" (p. 102).

Eisenthal (1974) evaluated the application of five psychological tests to the task of assessing suicide risk: The Bender-Gestalt, the Rosenzweig Picture-Frustration Study, the Sentence Completion Method, the Hildreth Feeling and Attitude Scale, and the Maslow Social Personality Inventory. He noted that three of these instruments (the Bender-Gestalt, Rosenzweig, and Sentence Completion) are commonly used in clinical assessment. The other two instruments were selected for review because they were directed to two relevant aspects of suicidal behavior: feelings and self-concept. Eisenthal found two unsettling facts after his review: first, there is a sparsity of work on this problem; second, there is a lack of systematic evaluation-centered studies among the published research. He concluded that "the clinician shopping for tests with demonstrated utility in assessing suicidal risk will have to look elsewhere" (p. 146).

Beck Depression Inventory (BDI) and Beck Hopelessness Scale (BHS)

The revised Beck Depression Inventory (BDI) consists of a 21-item instrument designed to assess the severity of depression in adolescents and adults (Beck & Steer, 1987). As Beck and Steer (1987) observed, during the past 26 years, the

71

"BDI has become one of the most widely accepted instruments in clinical psychology and psychiatry for assessing the intensity of depression in psychiatric patients (Piotrowski, Sherry, & Keller, 1985) and for detecting possible depression in normal populations (Steer, Beck, & Garrison, 1985)" (p. 1). A BDI total score can provide an estimate of the severity of the overall depression.

Yet Beck and Steer (1987) stressed that it is also important to attend to specific item content:

> In particular, special attention should be given to those symptoms relevant to suicide ideation (p. 7). Beck, Steer, Kovacs, and Garrison (1985) have pointed out that the BDI's pessimism item (Item 2) was nearly as predictive of eventual suicide in 211 suicide ideators as the 20 item Hopelessness Scale (HS) (Beck, Weissman, Lester, & Trexler, 1974). Patients admitting to suicide ideation (Item 9) and hopelessness (Item 2) with ratings of 3 or 4 should be closely scrutinized for suicide potential. It also is important to observe the overall pattern of the depression symptoms that the patient is describing. The BDI reflects not only cognitive and affective symptoms, but also somatic and vegetative symptoms. For example, some suicidal patients will not express suicide ideation, but have actually stopped eating and sleeping. (pp. 7–8)

Because scores on the Beck Hopelessness Scale (BHS) produce only an estimate of the overall severity of hopelessness (i.e., the severity of an individual's negative attitudes about the future), Beck and Steer (1988) pointed out that it is clinically important to pay attention to other aspects of psychological functioning, in particular the patient's levels of suicidal ideation and depression. They noted the study by Beck et al. (1985) that reported that BHS scores of 9 or more were predictive of eventual suicide in 10 out of 11 depressed suicide ideators who were followed for 5 to 10 years after discharge from the hospital. This pointed to earlier findings that hopelessness has repeatedly been found to be a better predictor of suicidal intention than depression per se (Beck, 1986). Beck and Steer (1988) continued: "Therefore, patients describing moderate to severe levels of hopelessness should be closely scrutinized for suicide potential" (p. 6).

Furthermore, Beck et al. (1985) found that, in a 10-year prospective follow-up of 165 psychiatric patients who had been hospitalized for suicidal ideation, hopelessness was highly predictive of eventual suicide. Of the 11 patients in their study who went on to complete suicide, 10 (90.9%) had BHS scores greater than or equal to 9. Beck and his colleagues recently extended this investigation to an outpatient population and found that in a prospective study of 1,958 outpatients seen at the Center for Cognitive Therapy, hopelessness (as measured on the BHS) was significantly related to completed suicide (Beck, Brown, Berchick, Stewart, & Steer, 1990). Beck et al. specifically found that:

> A BHS cutoff score of 9 or above identified 16 (94.2%) of the 17 eventual suicides, thus replicating a previous study with hospitalized patients. The high-risk group identified by this cutoff score was 11 times more likely to commit suicide than the rest of the outpatients. The BHS thus may be used as a sensitive indicator of suicidal potential. (p. 190)

However, it is important to note that Beck and Steer (1988) also gave several case examples to demonstrate the complexities involved in using the BHS and BDI as predictors of suicide during therapy. They cited the case of a patient who, at the time of the evaluation, showed on the self-report and interview report the signs of severe depression, but no suicidal ideation.

> His BDI score, for example, was 45. He endorsed item 9 as "I don't have thoughts of killing myself." Similarly, the Scale for Suicide Ideation did not indicate current suicidal thoughts or plans. However, his BHS score was 20. He came in for three consecutive sessions, cancelled the fourth, and did not show up for the next scheduled appointment. Scores on the BDI during the three sessions he had kept dropped from 45 at admission to 35, 37, and 37, respectively. During the sessions the patient denied verbally and on self-report forms any suicidal thoughts or plans. However, his BHS remained high (again a score of 20). (p. 22)

The case of this patient, who killed himself three days prior to the next scheduled appointment, demonstrates that, "in the presence of a high BHS and dropping BDI, a psychotherapist should be alert to the possibility of a suicide attempt" (Beck & Steer, 1988, p. 22). Here, Beck and Steer noted that the BHS accurately reflected suicidal risk "whereas the patient's self report of suicidal ideation or suicidal item on the BDI did not" (p. 22). Beck and Steer also emphasized the need to inquire about reasons for any specific hopeless responses to the BHS items, because the clinical exploration of these responses may lead to the patient's acknowledging suicidal wishes. They noted that the BHS is also a

> valuable tool for indicating that the patient is still pessimistic (and possibly suicidal) even though significant improvement in symptoms has occurred. By discussing the specifically endorsed items on the BHS with the patient, the therapist can pinpoint some of the particular situational and psychological factors contributing to a therapeutic impasse. . . . Focusing on specific relevant items on the BHS can help to break up a pervasive hopelessness and foster collaboration. (pp. 24–25)

For the purposes of risk detection, a score of 9 or higher on the BHS is of particular importance, because the BHS attempts to identify the "potential for fatal suicide attempts and not the behavior itself . . . . hopelessness may best be construed as a risk factor, perhaps analogous to a history of smoking or elevated blood pressure as a predispositional factor in heart disease'' (Beck et al., 1990, p. 194).

Assessment of Suicidal Ideation, Intent, and Behavior

Recently, the Suicide and Suicidal Behavior Program of the Mood, Affective, and Personality Disorders Research Branch of the Division of Clinical Research at the National Institute of Mental Health convened a workshop to discuss and address "common problems and issues in research methodology with emphasis on developing a common core of assessment tools and standardized terminology (e.g., suicide versus attempted suicide)" (Alcohol, Drug Abuse, and Mental Health Administration, 1989, pp. 1–81) for use in the study of suicide. In addition, the Child and Adolescent Disorders Research Branch of the Division of Clinical Research commissioned an exhaustive study that reviewed scales suitable for epidemiological and clinical research for the assessment of suicidal behavior in adolescents (Lewinsohn et al., 1989). Although these activities are certainly an important step toward promoting comparative nationwide clinical research for the study of suicide by means of the use of a standardized set of assessment instruments, they have as their purpose the promotion of collaborative and comparative clinical research rather than the setting of standards for frontline clinical practice.

This current ambitious attempt to standardize the assessment of suicide risk for the purposes of clinical research follows a long tradition of efforts at estimating and assessing the risk of attempted and completed suicide. These efforts have included assessment protocols that contain both standardized psychological tests and suicide risk estimator and lethality scales.

Motto (1989) noted that methodological and practical problems have plagued the development of scales of suicide risk "to the point of discouraging even devoted and experienced workers in the field of suicide prevention. . . . These obstacles have been small samples, limited data, a low base rate, nongeneralizability of critical stressors, the individual uniqueness of suicidal persons, unknown and uncontrollable variables that contribute to outcome, ambiguity of outcome (e.g., 'suicidal behavior'), and problems of demonstrating reliability and especially validity'' (p. 133).

Lewinsohn et al. (1989), after comprehensively evaluating all available assessment instruments used to study suicidal behaviors in adolescents and young adults for the National Institute of Mental Health (NIMH) concluded that

> perhaps the most fundamental critique we wish to level at the currently existing instruments is that insufficient attention has been paid to issues of validity. . . . The dearth of this type of information might also explain

why researchers using different instruments to measure suicidal behavior have reported contradictory findings. . . . The success of the various instruments to determine which individuals are at high risk for suicidal behavior or other forms of self-destructive action has not been determined. (pp. 97–98)

As can be seen from the recent efforts of the NIMH, there continues to be an enormous amount of interest in the development of suicide risk scales and estimators. Motto (1989) stated that, historically, the only well-known measure was a little-used suicide risk scale of the MMPI and that contemporary efforts at scale construction began in 1963 when the Los Angeles Suicide Prevention Center developed a special scale for assessing callers to their center (Farberow et al., 1968). Motto noted that this scale has been widely used by suicide prevention and crisis centers.

The Los Angeles Suicide Prevention Center Scale (see Appendix B.2) focuses on demographic and clinical characteristics of patients. Bassuk (1982) noted that, in this regard, it is similar to Tuckman and Youngman's (1986) Scale for Assessing Suicide Risk (SASR). The SASR is a scale used to identify those persons among suicide attempters with a high potential to commit suicide. Citing problems of replication, however, Eyman and Eyman (in press) conclude that the "scale [SASR] is not useful for a psychiatric population and also believe its use is premature in a general population as the original finding has not been replicated" (p. 23).

The Index of Potential Suicide (Zung, 1974), which measures potential suicide risk and includes both clinical and social-demographic variables, has been shown to distinguish adequately between patients with no suicidal behavior and those with a past history of suicidal behavior. However, this scale does not seem to have good predictive validity (Eyman & Eyman, in press).

With regard to the evaluation of an actual suicide attempt, there have been several important developments. One historically important scale is the Risk–Rescue Scale developed by Weisman and Worden (1974), which defines a suicide attempt as an "event where the risk of death is extremely high and probability of rescue is extremely low" (Shneidman, 1985, p. 20). More recently, Smith, Conroy, and Ehler (1984) developed an 11-point scale, the Lethality of Suicide Attempt Rating Scale (LSARS), to measure the degree of lethality of a suicide attempt. Eyman and Eyman (in press), in their review of the assessment of suicide using psychological tests, found that the LSARS was a valuable tool in assessing the lethality of intent and method from a previous suicide attempt. (For the complete Risk–Rescue scale and the LSARS, see Appendices B.3 and B.4.)

Despite the development of a number of alternative instruments (e.g., Beck, Schuyler, & Herman, 1974; Cohen, Motto, & Seiden, 1966; Weisman & Worden, 1972; Yufit & Benzies, 1973; Zung, 1974), such instruments remain primarily useful "as research tools rather than aids for front-line clinicians" (Motto, 1989, p. 133). As Motto (1989) noted, an alternative approach to the search for generalized indicators of risk has been to examine precisely defined populations and settings and to develop scales that would be "situation-specific" (p. 133). For example, Motto (1989) cites the work of Litman (1975), who attempted to provide

> an estimate of risk for nineteen different patient populations, such as suicide attempters seen in the hospital (moderate risk), depressed alcoholic middle-aged male caller to Suicide Prevention Center (high risk), and young female suicide attempters (low risk). Subsequent work continues to focus on "clinical models," defined in terms of personality characteristics or clinical picture; for example, "stable with forced change," "alienated," "nice person," "alcohol abuse," "drug abuse" (Motto, 1977, 1979b), or "suicide attempter" (Pallis, Barraclough, Levey, Jenkins, & Sainsbury, 1982; Pallis, Gibbons, & Pierce, 1984) . . . . as with earlier studies, these reports generated interest among researchers but did not have a demonstrable impact on clinical practice. (p. 133)[5]

One probable explanation for the lack of impact of such scales, collectively or individually, is that, in their development, "little attention was paid to providing clinicians with a simple brief procedure that could be quickly translated into a clear indication of suicide risk" (Motto, 1989, p. 134). However, there have been recent attempts to construct clinically useful screening instruments. The following examples are meant to be representative of this approach to the assessment of suicide, rather than to represent an exhaustive list of all available instruments. (For models of such lists, the reader is directed to Eyman and Eyman, in press and to Lewinsohn et al., 1989.)

Fremouw et al. (1990) noted the usefulness of The Reasons for Living Inventory (Linehan, 1985), a self-report measure with 48 items, including items that reveal the belief systems of a patient that "may serve as mediators of suicidal behaviors" (please note that psychometric properties are still under investigation, and cutoff scores for the scale are currently unavailable). They pointed out that this self-report measure has been found to discriminate between suicidal and nonsuicidal individuals; specifically, Linehan's (1985) findings indicated "the absence of strong positive reasons to live are most indicative of suicidal behavior" (Fremouw et al., 1990, p. 56).

Eyman and Eyman (in press) contend that the Hillson Adolescent Profile (Inwald, Brobst, & Morrissey, 1987), which contains 310 true-or-false items, appears to be a promising tool for distinguishing suicidal and nonsuicidal adoles-

---

[5]To this appraisal Eyman and Eyman (in press) would add the work of Buglass and Horton (1974) and their A Scale for Predicting Subsequent Suicidal Behavior, as well as Miskimins, DeCook, Wilson, and Maley's (1967) Suicide Potential Scale.

opulations. They also note that the Suicidal Ideation
)lds, 1988), which was developed to assess
death and suicide, may be more appropriate and
than for psychiatric ones.
Scale (SPS) is a short self-report measure designed
suicide risk in both adults and adolescents. This
isks patients to rate their present and past behaviors
ll and Gill (1982) state that

sk is reflected in three summary scores: a total
ilized T-score, and a Suicide Probability Score
ited to accommodate different a priori base rates
pulations. . . . The SPS is intended solely as a
should not be used in isolation. Instead other
interview by trained psychiatric professionals
iment, corroborate, and investigate test results.

This instrument, although useful for the development of future assessment instruments, has a number of limitations. The intent of the scale is not particularly disguised, and it assesses an individual's reported feelings and behaviors only at one point in time. However, as the authors themselves recognize, further research on this instrument is needed to establish predictive validity, replicate findings with a wider range of representative samples, and assess its incremental validity "in predicting suicidal behaviors beyond what could be predicted on the basis of commonly available patient demographic and clinical characteristics alone" (Cull & Gill, 1982, p. 61).

Beck and colleagues developed two important scales for the measurement of suicidal ideation and intent. These are the Scale for Suicide Ideation (SSI) and the Suicidal Intent Scale (SIS) (Beck, Kovacs, & Weissman, 1979; Beck, Schuyler, & Herman, 1974, respectively). The SSI has been used in several studies to measure intensity, duration, and specificity of psychiatric patients' wishes to commit suicide (Beck, Steer, & Ranieri, 1988). The SSI is a 19-item instrument that a trained clinician may use to rate the severity of a patient's suicidal thoughts and plans on a 3-point scale that ranges from 0 to 2. Rather than using cutoff scores, a clinician who detects any positive ideation on Item 4 (Active Wish-to-Die) or Item 5 (Passive Wish-to-Die) rates the patient on the remaining 14 items of the scale. The Center for Cognitive Therapy recommends that SSI total scores be used only as measures of suicide ideation in "true" ideators and not in general clinical populations. From a clinical standpoint, the Center for Cognitive Therapy considers an SSI score of 10 or higher as indicating suicidal risk and suggests that patients be followed closely.

The SSI was recognized as a carefully developed, reliable instrument for measuring suicidal ideation by Lewinsohn et al. (1989). Beck et al. (1988)

reported that the SSI, in a self-report version, can be a reliable method for measuring the severity of suicide ideation in outpatients and inpatients. They noted, however, that, "although the present study indicates that the SSI represents a valid and reliable method for rapidly estimating suicide ideation in psychiatric patients, it is not recommended that the self-report version of the SSI replace clinical interviewing as a method for evaluating a patient's suicide plans and thoughts. The self-report version represents another tool for multimethod assessment of suicide ideation" (p. 504).

Lewinsohn et al. (1989) concluded: "given that intentionality is an important construct in the study of suicide, the SIS represents the only rationally derived scale to evaluate suicidal intent" (p. 15). They cited Steer and Beck's (1988) belief that "the information elicited by this test can help clinicians judge how serious the attempt was and might be again, while noting that its use is restricted to people who have made a previous attempt which is a high risk group" (Lewinsohn et al., 1989, p. 15). The SSI and the SIS represent important directions for future clinical research efforts and further the cause of combining clinical interview with clinical assessment protocols so that suicidal ideation and intent may be assessed more systematically. From a general clinical assessment perspective, Bassuk (1982) concluded that "by using the Scale for Suicidal Ideation, the Hopelessness Scale, and the Suicide Intent Scale, the interviewer can assess either directly or indirectly the seriousness of the patient's intent or subjective wish to die" (p. 29).

Motto, Heilbron, and Juster (1985) developed an empirical suicide risk scale for adults hospitalized because of a depressive or suicidal state. Their study of 2,753 suicidal patients prospectively examined 101 psychosocial variables. After a 2-year follow-up, 136 (4.94%) of the subjects had committed suicide. The authors used rigorous statistical analysis, including a validation procedure, to identify 15 variables as significant predictors of suicidal outcome. Their findings were translated into a paper-and-pencil scale that gives an estimated risk of suicide within 2 years. Motto (1989) noted that instruments such as these can provide a valuable supplement to clinical judgment, as well as the kind of quantitative expression of suicide risk that represents to many clinicians "fine tuning" of their judgment. (See Appendix B.1 for the full scale.)

However, Clark, Young, Scheftner, Fawcett, and Fogg (1987) undertook a field test of the Risk Estimator for Suicide (Motto et al., 1985) that "raised questions" about the instrument without invalidating the scale (Clark et al., 1987, p. 926). Clark and colleagues selected a subset of psychiatric patients with major or chronic affective disorders that corresponded to Motto's sample. The subjects in the sample exhibited distinctly lower suicide rates over a 2-year follow-up (2.4%) than the sample reported by Motto (4.9%). What the 1987 study does highlight according to Clark et al. is the critical need to understand the limitations of all such scales, particularly the likelihood that suicide scales derived by multivariate analysis of a large number of clinical, psychosocial, and demographic variables may tend to be arbitrary and sample specific. Our impression is that empirically-derived scales based on a single cross-sectional assessment are always difficult to validate. Repeated assessments over time on a broad array of clinical features may be necessary to develop an adequate and replicable prediction system. We propose that serial assessments which pay attention to the vicissitudes of clinical symptoms, changing life stress, and long-standing character structure in concert (Smith, 1985) would provide a better method of estimating suicide risk. (p. 926)

Assessing Suicide Through Structured Interviews and a Psychological Battery

Yufit (1988) proposed that the assessment of suicidal behavior is best conducted through the use of a Suicide Assessment Team (SAT). Such a team would be composed of a multidisciplinary staff of psychologists, social workers, nurses, and psychology graduate students, specially trained in the use of a focused screening interview format and other assessment techniques for the identification and evaluation of suicide potential. SAT assessment would involve three levels: a focused interview (Level I), the Level I interview plus specialized rating scales (Level II), and an extended psychological assessment (Level III), including the Levels I and II interviews and ratings, in addition to special psychological assessment techniques found in the Suicide Assessment Battery (SAB).

The SAB would be used to make extended evaluation of suicide potential (Level III) beyond interview ratings (Level I) and the scores on the specialized suicide rating scales (Level II). Before proceeding to Level III, the clinician already would have conducted the structured interview (Level I) and used rating scales such as the Beck Depression Inventory, as well as the Risk–Rescue Scale and the Los Angeles SPC Assessment of Suicide Potential (see Appendix B) to evaluate the patient. As Yufit (1988) noted, Level III techniques "would most likely be used with inpatients who make suicidal threats or attempts, or where suicide can be inferred" (p. 26).

One of the most important elements in the SAB is the Time Questionnaire (TQ). The TQ, a semiprojective personality assessment technique, has been found to correlate with suicide potential (Yufit & Benzies, 1979). The TQ has been administered to "over 1,500 persons, including clinical and nonclinical samples, as well as matched sample populations; it has consistently differentiated high lethal suicidal persons from lower levels of suicide lethality and nonsuicidal persons as well as a variety of psychiatric diagnostic groups, on the basis of uniquely different time perspectives . . . the TQ is a key technique in the SAB" (Yufit, 1988, p. 27). More recently, Yufit (personal communication, April 1990)

CHAPTER 3

added the Coping Abilities Questionnaire, a 15-item instrument that measures
the range of coping ability (from *excellent* to *minimal*).

In addition to the Time Questionnaire and Coping Abilities Questionnaire,
other possible key elements in a suicide assessment battery include the following:

1. Q-Sort set, a 22-item set of "descriptive items relating to variables
   often associated with suicidal behavior" (Yufit, 1988, p. 28);

2. Suicide Assessment Checklist, a 36-item checklist to provide a
   supplement to clinical judgment;

3. Experience Inventory, in which the patient is asked to list 10 most
   important experiences (Cottle, 1976);

4. Motto Suicide Risk Assessment, an empirically derived instrument using significant items from a large-scale prospective study
   of a clinic instrument used to assess suicide (Motto et al., 1985);

5. Sentence Completion, a 32-item form with sentence stems especially selected to elicit affect related to morbid thoughts, self-
   destruction, hope, trust, the future, and so on;

6. Draw-A-Person, DAP in the Rain, a variation of the "Draw-a-
   Person in the Rain" projective technique in which rain is an
   ambiguous stimulus ("Scoring is subjective in nature, but the
   work of Machover and other exponents of DAP can be utilized";
   Yufit, 1988, p. 30);

7. Autobiography, in which the patient is asked to write his or her
   life history in any way that he or she wishes;

8. Rorschach, primarily used for associational content;

9. TAT, a quantitative analysis of story themes related to isolation,
   hopelessness, mistrust, morbid content, and future orientation;

10. Object Relations Technique, a variant of the TAT that usually
    gives more elaborate data than the more structured TAT;

11. Erikson Questionnaire, a multiple choice instrument giving scores
    on Erikson's developmental model of stages related to intimacy-
    isolation, trust-mistrust, autonomy-shame, and doubt;

12. Humor Test, a 104-item, objectively scored questionnaire which
    gives polar opposite scores on 13 factor-analytically-determined
    scales; and

13. Hope Scale, a Fawcett-Sussman scale of items relating to the
    evaluation of hope as personality variable.

This list of 13 assessment techniques represents a broad array of available
and useful measures from which a Suicide Assessment Battery can be derived,

usually including 5 or 6 of these measures (e.g., the core SAB battery might include the Suicide Checklist, Coping Questionnaire, Time Questionnaire, and Q-Sort; Yufit, personal communication, August 1990).

Yufit (1988) pointed out that the use of the sample core mentioned in the preceding paragraph includes a number of scales still in experimental form, which "may be questioned, but they are considered very useful in trying to fill the lacunae and tap the nuances in the complex task of identification and assessment of suicide potential" (p. 32). He concluded that

> even in a psychiatric hospital setting, where psychiatric sophistication may be considered deep, there is a need for more *comprehensive* evaluation procedures of the complex behavior of suicide. At this stage of development, these techniques are not necessarily conclusive, nor are they often objective, but they very often do serve as important *guidelines* to assist in the identification and the assessment of the components of suicide potential. They should supplement clinical judgment not substitute for it. (p. 33)

More recently, in an effort to formalize and distill the elements of risk detection (as well as to try to increase the accuracy of diagnosing suicide risk), Yufit (1989) has begun development and field testing of a new integrated instrument, the Suicide Screening Checklist (SSC). The SSC is used by a clinician or interviewer to assess an individual for the "purpose of identification of suicidal potential" with *suicidal potential* (or *suicide risk*) referring to "the likelihood that such a person will engage in behavior that will directly or indirectly lead to self-destruction" (pp. 4–129). The SSC is a screening instrument constructed from empirical data and making use of known and presumed correlates of suicidal behavior, that is designed to complement and improve "the validity of clinical judgment" (pp. 4–139). (See Appendix B.5). In short, instruments such as the SSC (as well as batteries such as the SAB) allow clinicians to supplement their own clinical intuition with a systematized approach to collecting assessment information (Yufit, personal communication, August 1990). An accurate (and widely accepted) model for the assessment of elevated risk in the suicidal patient, however, may require a future research effort that would involve a large-scale collaborative multicenter study designed to evaluate *all* of the existing assessment procedures for both efficacy and significance (Yufit, personal communication, August 1990).

Limitations of Theoretical Orientation and *DSM-III-R* Diagnosis

When clinicians select assessment criteria and then implement an appropriate intervention strategy with suicidal patients, they may find that traditional theories of psychotherapy and traditional psychiatric diagnostic categories are of limited practical value in precisely assessing suicidal risk. As Beutler (1989) pointed out, "the descriptive dimensions embodied in the current diagnostic system bear little relationship to the selection of the mode or frequency of psychosocial interventions . . . . while it would be unthinkable in any practice of medicine for the mode of treatment to be independent of patient diagnosis, this is precisely the case in the assignment of psychotherapy modes and formats" (p. 272).

An integrated perspective on assessment and treatment of the suicidal patient must be maintained (Simon, 1988). For example, psychoanalytic approaches tend to deemphasize discussion of the suicidal patient's condition with family members or deemphasize an evaluation for the efficacy of organic therapies—in which case vital information can be lost. Conversely, biologically based approaches may not place enough emphasis on the need for an ongoing treatment relationship, that is, they might diminish the role of the therapeutic alliance as an essential element of sound psychopharmacologic intervention. There is also the danger of medications being prescribed in lieu of seeing the patient more frequently (Simon, 1988).

Jacobs (1989b) asserted that the clinician must go beyond formal psychiatric diagnosis, because many suicides occur in individuals who have not been labeled as psychiatrically ill. He cited Mack and Hickler's research (1981), in which the following observations were made: the problem of suicide cuts across all diagnoses; many of those who take their own lives are mentally ill, but some are not; some are psychotic, but most are not; and some act impulsively, but most do not. Jacobs (1989b) also found that the next concern for the clinician with regard to assessment relates to an understanding of demographic and clinical risk factors.

Lewinsohn et al. (1989) added that suicide is not a psychopathological entity that is recognized by the *DSM-III-R*. They pointed out that the *DSM-III-R*, instead, includes

> suicidal ideation as a symptom of depression and as a symptom of borderline personality disorder. Although the correlation between suicidal ideation and depression is substantial (Asarnow, Carlson, & Guthrie, 1987), this correlation is far from unity and some suicides occur in people who are not depressed. Suicidal behavior also has important relationships with other psychopathological syndromes such as schizophrenia, personality disorders, and alcohol and drug abuse. As pointed out by Zubin (1974), suicide is the final stage of a very complex *process* which encompasses a heterogeneous set of phenomena and which occurs in people who are anything but homogeneous. (p. 1)

It is clear that the various therapies and procedures from the diverse schools of psychotherapy are applied across diagnostic groupings of patients. Beutler

(1989) pointed out that the recent, rapid development of integrative approaches in mental health treatment "attests to the readiness of therapists to accept comprehensive theories of intervention that cut across disciplines, theoretical systems, and diagnostic labels to provide a comprehensive system for selectively assigning different treatment protocols" (p. 273). He cited the work of Cole and Magnussen (1966) and the more recent work on "operational diagnosis" by Cummings and VandenBos (1979). He also called for basing diagnostic and assessment decisions on a more disposition-focused assessment—that is, for the decisions about patient care to rest on a foundation of empirically derived relationships between patient characteristics, available environmental systems, and therapeutic effects. According to Beutler (1989), focusing on disposition rather than merely symptoms would keep the orientation on the "primary mission of enhancing the efficacy of care" (p. 273). Beutler concluded

> this method of selectively applying treatments to patients represents a compromise between the intense matching of individual patients and therapists and the more global effort to match type of therapy to patient diagnosis. While still in its infancy, this approach to the problem of treatment selection is represented in the so-called "technical eclectic psychotherapy movement" (Lazarus, 1981; Norcross, 1984). . . . Dispositional assessment proposes that diagnosis is a dynamic process that delineates the probability that an identified problem will respond to a given treatment or setting. An assessment procedure such as this will entail a sequential multistepped process of defining treatment propensities, needs, settings, enabling factors, and social contexts through which effective treatment occurs. (pp. 275–276)

In summary, at the level of a diagnostic and initial assessment of the suicidal patient, we believe that the psychologist should concentrate primarily on dispositional assessment and on the formulation and documentation of *risk detection* in the assessment and diagnostic stage, rather than on specific behavior prediction (Murphy, 1988a). However, the mental status examination, clinical interview, and *DSM-III-R* diagnostics are essential and critical elements in a comprehensive clinical assessment process (see also Black & Winokur, 1990; Robins & Helzer, 1986) and, for the purposes of the present chapter, are important tools in the detection of suicide risk.

Deriving Evidence on Risk Factors

Because clinicians may have difficulty determining the relative importance of various risk factors when assessing suicidal patients, Bassuk (1982) proposed a checklist for assessment that includes and integrates both statistical and clinical indicators of risk. Her approach evolved from extensive experience in an emergency setting in an urban general hospital, where approximately one third of the psychiatric patients presented with suicidal ideation and behaviors. In addition, Fremouw et al. (1990) proposed an impressive decision model for assessment and treatment. The recent assessment practices questionnaire data (Jobes et al., 1990), although only the first step in understanding clinical practices with regard to suicide, is of great help in seeing how practicing clinicians actually use interview and observational material.[6] The reader will recognize that in this proposal we have tried to incorporate the important contributions of Beck and his colleagues' empirical model (e.g., hopelessness, helplessness, negative cognitions), Fawcett and colleagues' empirical model (e.g., chronic vs. acute, the social matrix, communication of intent), Hirschfeld and Davidson's epidemiological model, Simon's checklist model, and Shneidman's psychological model.

Therefore, following this decision-checklist tradition, we propose the following steps and detection–decision points. But note well: This is only one possible set of factors, and is not meant to be definitive or exhaustive. Clinicians will almost certainly tailor the assessment to what Motto (1989) has shown to be the uniqueness of every decision on suicide probability.

Obtaining Key Assessment Information

Diagnostic Factors

The goal of this section is to obtain a history of suicidal behavior (previous attempts, impulses, ideation); current suicidal plans, impulses, available methods, ideas and behaviors; history of drug-alcohol use/abuse; hopelessness–helplessness; recent loss, lack of psychosocial supports; and a history of depression or other psychiatric illness.

It is crucial to remember that any suicidal crisis (ideation, threat, gesture, or actual attempt) is a true emergency situation and must be dealt with as a life-threatening issue in clinical practice. Any or all of these should prompt an examination of the lethality potential of present or previous suicidal situations (see Risk–Rescue and LSARS rating scales, Appendices B.3 and B.4). Factors that substantially increase imminent risk include the presence of a specific plan by the patient, accessibility of lethal means, the presence of syntonic or dystonic suicidal impulses, behavior suggestive of a decision to die, and admission of wanting to die.

---

[6]We have drawn significantly on Jobes and colleagues' findings regarding consensual utility.

Accurate DSM-III-R diagnosis

There is high rate of mental illness among those who commit suicide. A psychiatric history places a patient in a still higher risk group, and Simon (1988) noted that patients who have recently been discharged from a psychiatric hospital (that is within 3 months) are in a particularly high-risk pool. Hirschfeld and Davidson (1988) showed that a history of depression, substance or alcohol abuse, schizophrenia, borderline personality, and physical illness increases the general risk profile. Fawcett et al. (1987) found that patients with a history of panic attacks or of mood cycling during an index episode for an affective disorder should also be examined for signs of increased risk. Bassuk (1982) would add paranoid patients to this list, and Simon (1988) would add symptoms of anhedonia and psychosis (with command hallucinations). Black and Winokur (1990) state that accurate psychiatric diagnosis is perhaps the most important signal to alert clinicians to suicidal behavior over the life cycle.

Age

Historically, in the general population completed suicide has been seen as a problem for older White males. However, since 1980, 50% of completed suicides are under the age of 40. Youth 15 to 24 years old and the elderly are especially at risk. For psychiatric patients, males tend to commit suicide between the ages of 25 to 40, whereas females tend to be older, between 35 to 50.

Sex

In the general population men are more at risk for completed suicide (3:1). However, for psychiatric patients, the male–female ratio is smaller (1.5:1).

Ethnicity

The ratio of White male to Black male completed suicide is 2:1. Suicide for Blacks is often a youthful phenomenon, with the peak age for completed suicide among Black males being 25 to 34. Native American and Hispanic suicide is also a youthful problem, with peak ages in the mid-twenties.

The social matrix and communication of intent

Fawcett (1988) has written on the importance of the social matrix and the importance of communication of intent. Specifically, he stated that:

1. From 50% to 70% of suicide completers communicate their intent in advance.
2. High-suicide-risk group members often communicate their intent only to the significant other.

3. Moderate-suicide-risk group members often communicate by frequently threatening suicide to family group members and health care providers.

4. There are *chronic* interpersonal behavior patterns that differentiate patients at high risk for suicide, including: (a) interpersonal incapacity; (b) marital isolation; (c) help negation; and (d) distorted communication of dependency wishes.

5. There are *acute* interpersonal features of those with increased risk for suicide, including: (a) communication of intent to significant other only; (b) stated intent to die; and (c) an attempted behavioral change.

Fawcett concluded that these findings have important implications for assessment and treatment; moreover, there should be an increased emphasis on the evaluation of the person's interpersonal relationships through information-gathering activities with significant others.

Clinicians should make note of other social-relational correlates by asking the following questions: (a) Is the patient single, divorced, widowed, separated, or living alone? (b) Is the patient unemployed or in a high-risk occupation (e.g., police and public safety officials with easy access to weapons, anesthesiologists who are involved in a malpractice suit, health care professional with easy access to lethal amounts of prescription drugs, etc.). There are also a variety of social clues, including the patient's putting his or her affairs in order, giving away prized possessions, behaving in any way that is markedly different from his or her usual pattern of living, saying good-bye to friends or psychotherapists, and settling estates (Beck, 1967; Shneidman, 1985).

Risk Factors

Psychological factors

The presence of one or more of the following psychological variables represents a high risk for completed suicide (Shneidman, 1989):

- Acute perturbation (the person is very upset or agitated).
- The availability of lethal means (e.g., purchasing or having available a gun, rope, poison).
- An increase of self-hatred or self-loathing.
- A constriction in the person's ability to see alternatives to his or her present situation.
- The idea that death may be a way out of terrible psychological pain. (The idea of cessation is a catalytic agent.)

- Intense feelings of depression, helplessness, and hopelessness (see also, Beck, 1967; Beck et al., 1975; Beck & Steer, 1987, 1988; Shneidman, 1985).
- Fantasies of death as an escape, including retrospectives on the patient's own funeral; imagined scenes of life after death increase the risk (Maris, 1981; Peterson & Bongar, 1989; Shneidman, 1984, 1986a).
- A loss of pleasure or interest in life.
- The patient's feeling that he or she is a source of shame to family or significant others, or evidence that the patient has suffered a recent humiliation (Block-Lewis, personal communication, November 15, 1985; see also Blumenthal, 1990; Lazare, 1987; Peterson & Bongar, 1989; Shneidman, 1986a, 1986b).

Psychodynamic factors

These are factors that indicate a breakdown of ego defenses and the release of increased destructive, instinctual energy and that indicate (a) loss of love objects, aggression directed toward an introjected love object, narcissistic injury, overwhelming affect, and a setting of one part of the ego against the rest (Perlin & Schmidt, 1976); (b) an unconscious, precognitive operation in which the self is abandoned as being unworthy of further concern (Maltsberger, 1986); and (c) a lack of internal psychodynamic resources for self-soothing, the inability to feel a sense of value; murderous rage directed toward a self-object that has disappointed the patient (Buie & Maltsberger, 1989).

Patient–clinician interaction variables

- Lack of a therapeutic alliance.
- Communication of intent, previous suicide attempts, and antecedent circumstances (e.g., a change in family situation, occurrence of a physical illness, drastic financial changes, and substance abuse).
- Recent discharge from a psychiatric hospital.
- Chronic suicidality or manipulative suicidality (noting that these may be learned behaviors; Frederick & Resnik, 1989).

Medical care

- Presence of medical problems that place a patient more at risk (e.g., AIDS, cancer, respiratory illness, hemodialysis patients).
- A high-utilization pattern of medical care, noting that many suicide completers often had seen a physician for a medical problem in the months before their death.

Biological–genetic–disposition

- A history of suicide (or attempted suicide) in the patient's close biological relations.
- A family history of affective disorders.
- Physical signs of depression (e.g., loss of appetite, sleep disturbance, change in weight).

Empirical data on acute versus chronic factors

Fawcett (1988) noted the importance of understanding the difference between short-term (acute) and long-term (chronic) factors.

Decision Point

Determine risk level (e.g., none, low, moderate, high). Sort out which risk factors are chronic and which are acute. If risk is moderate to high, immediately consult, consider evaluation for hospitalization, medication evaluation, and other appropriate actions. If the risk is unclear or low to moderate, the clinician may wish to supplement his or her judgment with an awareness of the risk factors shown in Table 3.1. Even if the risk is low, the clinician may still wish to consult.

Acute Factors

- Acute defensive breakdown (e.g., depressive turmoil, severe panic anxiety, panic attacks, alcohol abuse).
- Negative evaluation (e.g., severe loss of interest and pleasure in life; severe hopelessness).
- Behavioral predictors (e.g., mood cycling, abrupt clinical change, either negative or positive, help negation, a suicidal communication to a significant other).

Chronic Factors

- Diagnostic predictors (e.g., suicidal ideation, mood cycling, hopelessness, loss of pleasure/interest, thought insertion, paranoid features, substance abuse, alcoholism).
- Historical predictors (e.g., previous suicidal behavior, psychiatric discharge within 6 to 12 months, no child under 18 years of age to care for, failure to maintain warm and mutually interdependent personal relationships).
- Behavioral predictors (e.g., help negation, social isolation).

Suicide lethality and risk scales

- The Beck Depression Inventory (BDI), Beck Hopelessness Scale (BHS), Beck Scale for Suicide Ideation (SSI), and Beck Scale for Suicide Intent (SIS) are valuable investigative tools in the estimation of risk. BHS scores of 9 or more should be of particular

Table 3.1

Suicide Risk Variables

Relationship potential
  1. Lack of therapeutic alliance with a therapist
  2. Absence or limited meaningful supportive relationships

Suicidal history
  1. Prior suicide attempts, particularly recent
     • high lethality potential of attempt(s)
     • presence of specific plan
  2. Current suicidal ideation
     • presence of specific plan
     • accessibility of lethal means
     • suicidal impulses—syntonic or dystonic
     • behavior suggestive of decision to die (e.g., severing relationships; giving away valued possessions; inappropriate sense of peace, calm, or happiness; verbalizations regarding the utility of death)
     • admission that want to die or considering suicide
     • family history of suicide

Psychiatric medical factors
  1. Chronic psychiatric disorder (e.g., severe depression [with feelings of despair], anhedonia, mood cycling, psychosis [especially with command hallucination], or thought insertion
  2. Mentally incompetent (impacts judgment, impulse control, relationship development)
  3. Recent discharge from psychiatric hospital (within 3 months)
  4. Remission of psychiatric episode but continuance of secondary depression
  5. Impulsivity (violence toward others and self, reckless driving, spending money)
  6. Physically ill, particularly chronic illness
  7. Alcohol abuse
  8. Drug abuse

Actuarial
  1. Age 15–24; advancing age for men
  2. Single, divorced, or widowed
  3. Personal losses; recent or chronic and unresolved
  4. Unemployed
  5. Living alone or in social isolation
  6. Socioeconomic group
  7. Alcohol abuse

Short-term variables (within 1 year of assessment)
  1. Panic attacks
  2. Psychic anxiety
  3. Loss of pleasure and interest
  4. Alcohol or drug abuse
  5. Discharge from psychiatric hospital (within 3 months)

Note. From *Concise Guide to Clinical Psychiatry and the Law* (p. 90) by R. I. Simon, 1988, Washington, DC: American Psychiatric Press. Copyright 1988 by American Psychiatric Press. Reprinted by permission.

concern. Moreover, any increased level of depression on
the BDI, or any indication of
suicide ideation or intent on the
SIS or SSI, should also be alerting signs for heightened level
of risk.

Decision Point

The clinician may now wish to
make a formulation of the probability of risk (see Tables 3.2 and
3.3) and consider using the following specific interview techniques.

- Weisman and Worden's (1974)
  Risk-to-Rescue ratio assess-
  ment is helpful in understanding a suicide attempt "where the risk
  of death is extremely high and probability of rescue is extremely
  low" (Shneidman, 1985, p. 20). Clinicians can also use Smith and
  colleagues' Lethality of Suicide Attempt Rating Scale (LSARS);
  see Appendix B.4 to measure the degree of lethality of a suicide
  attempt.
- The Los Angeles Suicide Prevention Scale (see Appendix B.2) can
  be used to assist in the examination of specific demographic and
  clinical variables. Risk variables from the California Risk Estimator
  for Suicide (see Appendix B.1) can be used as a doublecheck on
  the clinical indicators of risk.
- If logistically possible, the clinician may also consider a specialty
  referral for extended evaluation of risk, for example, the SAT and
  SAB.

Finally, we strongly concur with Clark and his colleagues' position (1987)
that the best estimation of risk comes from repeated assessments over time on a
broad array of clinical variables. Serial assessments allow for the vicissitudes of
clinical symptoms, changing life stress, and long-standing problems in character
structure (Smith, 1985).

Formulation of clinical judgment using the clinical interview

Maltsberger (1988) believes that there are five specific components in the general
formulation of suicide risk:

1. assessing the patient's past responses to stress, especially losses;
2. assessing the patient's vulnerability to three life-threatening affects:
   aloneness, self-contempt, and murderous rage;
3. determining the nature and availability of exterior sustaining resources;
4. assessing the emergence and emotional importance of death fantasies; and

Table 3.2

Assessment of Suicide Risk

Risk variables	Facilitating suicide	Inhibiting suicide
Short-term		
• Panic attacks*		
• Psychic anxiety*		
• Loss of pleasure and interest*		
• Alcohol abuse*		
• Recent discharge from psychiatric hospital (within 3 months)*		
Long-term		
• Therapeutic alliance—ongoing patient		
• Other relationships		
• Psychiatric diagnosis (Axis I & II)		
• Prior attempts		
• Specific plan		
• Living circumstances		
• Employment status		
• Actuarial data (age, sex, race, marital status, socioeconomic group, suicide base rates)		
• Availability of lethal means		
• Suicidal ideation: syntonic or dystonic		
• Family history		
• Impulsivity (violence, driving, money)		
• Drug abuse		
• Physical illness		
• Mental competency		
• Specific situational factors		

1. Rating system: L = low factor
   M = moderate factor
   H = high factor
   O = nonfactor
2. Clinically judge *high, medium,* or *low* the potential for suicide within 24–48 hours from assessment of suicide risk.
3. Short-term* indicators–Risk factors found to be statistically significant within one year of assessment.

Note. From *Concise Guide to Clinical Psychiatry and the Law* (p. 92) by R. I. Simon, 1988, Washington, DC: American Psychiatric Press. Copyright 1988 by American Psychiatric Press. Reprinted by permission.

Table 3.3
Potential for Suicide and Appropriate Intervention

Potential for suicide	Psychiatric interventions
High	Immediate hospitalization
Medium	Hospitalization Frequent outpatient visits Reevaluate treatment plan frequently Remain available to patient
Low	Continue with current treatment plan

Note. Tables 3.2 and 3.3 represent only one method of suicide risk assessment and intervention. The purpose of these tables is heuristic, encouraging a systematic approach to risk assessment. However, the therapist's clinical judgment concerning the patient remains paramount. Given the fact that suicide risk variables will be assigned different weights according to the clinical presentation of the patient, these tables should not be followed rigidly. Adapted from *Concise Guide to Clinical Psychiatry and the Law* (p. 93) by R. I. Simon, 1988, Washington, DC: American Psychiatric Press. Copyright 1988 by American Psychiatric Press. Adapted by permission.

5. assessing the patient's capacity for reality testing. (p. 48)

He adds that "what is sometimes called the 'formulation of suicide risk' offers the clinician a disciplined method for assessing suicide danger that integrates and balances the presenting clinical material from the patient's past history, his present illness, and the present mental status examination" (p. 48).

Another approach to the formulation of clinical judgment and the assessment or risk is a clinical checklist method of conducting an extended assessment of suicide (Bassuk, 1982). In this approach, one uses combinations of structured interviews, checklists, standard psychological instruments and suicide risk scales and estimators to ensure a comprehensive evaluation. (For additional information on comprehensive assessment and interviewing strategies, see Hendren, 1990.)

The assessment of suicide potential will often be accomplished through the initial focused interview (based on either a referral from the emergency room, inpatient service, or outpatient clinician) (Yufit, 1988). The Level I (focused interview) should explore

1. the patient's conscious intent of actually ending his or her own life;
2. risk of rescue or possible interruption during suicide attempt;
3. degree of planning;
4. behavior level (e.g., threats, ideation, gestures, overt attempt);
5. lethality of attempt made;

6. extent of physical injury or toxicity;

7. precipitant factors;

8. intensity of current life stress;

9. history of previous attempts, gestures, threats, and ideation;

10. degree of depression;

11. intense observation of the patient for his or her ability to relate to the examiner during the interview, overt dress and grooming, posture, degree of agitation, ability to discuss their problem, and so - forth;

12. changes in the patient's behavior during the initial contact; and

13. overall psychological status (e.g., the examination of any *DSM-III-R* disorders).

The majority of patients at the Center for Cognitive Therapy at the University of Pennsylvania carry a diagnosis of depression, and therefore hopelessness and suicidal ideation will often be ongoing therapeutic issues. The Center's policy manual indicates that when the patient's suicidal ideation is either continuous or intermittent (i.e., it consists of low-to-moderate levels of purely ideational symptoms), it can be dealt with as with any other depressive symptom—primarily by the treating therapist with regular supervision (R. J. Berchick, personal communication, September 20, 1989; Center for Cognitive Therapy, 1989). However, the Center's special procedure for suicidal patients is as follows:

> The therapist should maintain especially close monitoring of *all* suicidal thoughts as well as concomitant levels of hopelessness and depression. Regular administration of the first five items of the SSI (and the rest of the scale if any of these are positive), the BHS, and BDI at each session is strongly recommended, because these scales will provide a reliable means of monitoring any changes in these variables over time. (Center for Cognitive Therapy Policy Manual, 1989, p. 38)

Richman and Eyman (in press), citing the previous work of Smith (1985), Eyman (1987), and Smith and Eyman (1988), have developed a model for understanding why a person chooses to commit suicide that is based on the data from the Suicide Research Project at Menninger's. This model posits three conditions for suicide:

1. a narrowly defined, unrealistic, and fragile identity;

2. an event that jeopardizes the individual's identity; and

3. deficits in the management of affect and difficulties in problem solving. (Richman & Eyman, in press, p. 2)

Motto (1989) holds that the central clinical task is to "determine and monitor the patient's threshold for pain (either physical or psychological)" (p. 138). This would take into consideration the person's pathology, strengths, and available defensive patterns. If the pain level exceeds the pain threshold (even briefly), Motto sees suicide as imminent. Therefore, the psychologist must carefully assess and monitor the patient's threshold for pain and estimate how close the current level of pain comes to it. "The better we know the patient, the more sensitive we can be to the influences that can alter these two critical determinants of a suicidal act. Treatment aims ideally at both raising the threshold by maturational development, and decreasing the pain level by providing emotional support and by resolution of pain-generating conflicts" (Motto, 1989, p. 254).

Shneidman (1987) likewise believes that the central feature of suicide is pain, and that

> the key to suicide prevention lies in the reduction of that individual's psychological pain. All else—demographic variables, family history, previous suicidal history—is peripheral except as those factors bear on the presently felt pain. Ultimately, suicide occurs when there is the co-existence of intolerable pain, intense negative press, and extreme perturbation with perceptual constriction and an irresistible penchant for life-ending action. (pp. 176–177)

Clinicians must also, according to Shneidman (1984, 1986a), exercise extreme caution with any patient who is perturbed and who has a lethal means available. This would include clinical work with patients with poor impulse control who are in crisis and are unable to decrease their level of perturbation in the therapeutic encounter. Shneidman (1987) presented a theoretical cubic model of suicide that includes the combined effects of psychological pain, perturbation, lethality, and what he terms *press* to attempt to identify those individuals most at risk for suicide. Here *press* is similar to what Murray (1938) called pressure—that is, those aspects of the inner or outer world or environment that touch, move, impinge on, or affect an individual, and to which he or she reacts. Press can be either positive or negative (see Figure 3.2).

Practically speaking, Pokorny (1983) noted that the identification and care of the suicidal patient in clinical practice is made up of a *sequence of small decisions*, a point we wish to underscore. Murphy (1988a) expanded on this dictum by noting that

> the first decision might be based on some alerting sign or clinical configuration, and the decision would be to investigate further. After further

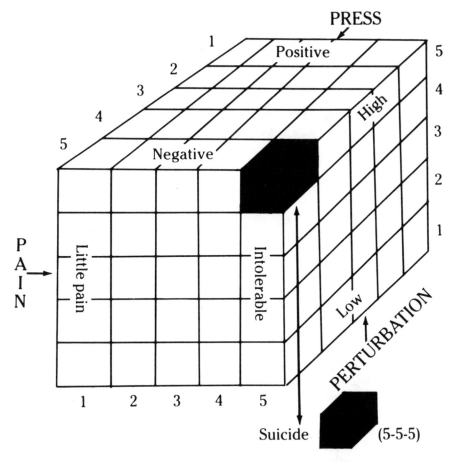

Figure 3.2 A theoretical cubic model of suicide. From "A Psychological Approach to Suicide" (p. 175) by E. S. Shneidman in *Cataclysms, Crises, and Catastrophes: Psychology in Action* edited by G. R. VandenBos and B. K. Bryant, 1987, Washington, DC: American Psychological Association. Copyright 1987 by American Psychological Association and E. S. Shneidman. Reprinted by permission.

investigation, one might stop, if no additional alerting or confirming indicator were found. Or one might decide to explore the situation even further; perhaps even to hospitalize, for example. In each case, the decision is not what to do for all time, but rather what to do next, for the near future (Pokorny, 1983) . . . . there is continuing opportunity for feedback, and thus for modification of risk assessment and intervention. (p. 53)

From the standpoint of any potential malpractice action, the most crucial element in the formulation of clinical judgment is that the psychologist's professional behavior does not significantly deviate from what is usual and customary for the care of patients with these particular signs and symptoms. That is, the psychologist will have demonstrated the behavior of a reasonable and prudent practitioner and not made any significant omissions in assessment, as well as have taken appropriate precautions to minimize the risk of a patient suicide (Berman and Cohen-Sandler, 1982, 1983).

A Clinical Case Example

John Smith was a 48-year-old Caucasian. He was a middle manager for a small manufacturing concern in a large urban center. John was recently divorced, ending a marriage of 22 years, and had 4 children ranging in age from 7 to 18. He was referred for outpatient psychotherapy by his family physician, as well as by his lawyer who was handling the custody case for John's children. Both professionals were concerned about John's increasing anger and despondency over the divorce and the ongoing and bitter child-custody battle. These pressures also had affected John's work, and recently his supervisors had been critical of his performance. He was worried about losing his job.

John's previous psychological treatment included therapy at a Veterans Administration outpatient clinic 24 years ago, following his discharge after military service in Vietnam. At that time, he stated he was treated for "drinking too much and being down in the dumps." John and his wife also saw a marriage counselor for 3 months before the breakup of their marriage, but John stated that "the son of a bitch was always on my wife's side." John reported in the initial interview that he was having trouble eating (he had lost 15 pounds in the past 2 months) and sleeping (however, his family physician had given him a supply of sleeping medication and "some sort of pill that will make me less depressed"). He was drinking a good deal, but only "after work and on the weekends." His history also revealed that as a 17-year-old adolescent, John had made an impulsive suicide attempt (by slashing his wrists) after being jilted by a girlfriend, but he denied subsequent suicidal behavior. Moreover, when John was 11, his paternal grandfather committed suicide using a pistol.

The psychologist decided that John was depressed as a result of his recent losses and current extreme life stress. She also decided to postpone an extended evaluation of suicidal ideation and behavior because she felt that it might terrify and anger John or even suggest to him that she feared he might consider harming himself. (Because he was still so angry with the previous marital therapist, the therapist decided to wait until she had a better ongoing relationship with him to bring up the subject.) She recommended psychotherapy on a weekly basis.

During the next 2 sessions, over a 10-day period, she explored with John his feelings about his recent divorce, ongoing child custody battle, and his problems at work. She also gave him homework assignments and a record-keeping diary to keep track of levels of anger and any drops in self-esteem. In Session 2, John mentioned that at times "the pain is just too much . . . but then I drink until the pain stops." As he was standing up to leave at the end of the fourth session, John profusely thanked the psychologist for all the help she had provided, and told her that he might not be able to make next week's appointment, but would call to reschedule.

The following week, John did not call for a therapy appointment. When the psychologist called John's home and, then (after being unable to reach him for several days) his office, she discovered that John had committed suicide by shooting himself in the head, the evening after his last therapy appointment.

Summary

Using John Smith's case history as a basis for discussion, we will now summarize what constitutes a good clinical assessment model. First, however, it should be stressed that the assessment of suicide risk is a clinical procedure that should *always* be carefully documented in a timely manner. Such a written record serves not only to provide a good clinical chart, but also attests to the care and attention the psychologist has paid to this high-risk clinical dilemma (Bongar et al., 1989; Gutheil & Appelbaum, 1982; Motto, 1989; Simon, 1988). When the psychologist has adequately documented general assessments, special assessments, and specific measures (e.g., obtaining a consultation), as well as how the results of these assessments and specific measures led to a particular course of intervention, the clinician can feel that he or she has made an important step toward doing "all that can be done regarding legal vulnerability, and all available energy can then be directed into the process of therapy" (Motto, 1989, p. 140). (We will present the specifics of model charting and documentation procedures in chapter 6.)

It is important to note that the problem of suicide risk assessment is basically the same as other evaluative procedures in medicine and psychology. As Motto (1989) points out

> data are gathered from the patient, from the family, and other collaterals, from the history, from specific tests, and from direct observation. All information is tinged with intuitive elaboration of a nature and degree that is unique to each clinician. Though the available information at any given time may be incomplete, ambiguous, contradictory, or of questionable validity, a decision is made, primarily on intuitive grounds, as to estimated level of risk. As new data become available, and circumstances change, the estimate of risk is modified accordingly. (p. 140)

What then would be the model clinical assessment procedure for John Smith—or perhaps, more constructively, what mistakes were made—and what actions would be necessary to ensure that the psychologist provided optimal levels of assessment and adequate care on the basis of that assessment? In arriving at such a decision, the clinician usually applies the available information to a personal theoretical model and her or his own training as it applies to self-destructive behaviors (Bongar et al., 1989; Bongar & Harmatz, 1989; Motto, 1989). The problem of assessment is also compounded by the "specters of social stigma, professional embarrassment, and legal liability in the event of a suicide" (Motto, 1989, p. 140). Motto cautioned that these pressures can be such that the clinician adopts defensive maneuvers, such as denying risk, clinging to a rigid and doctrinaire approach, or regressing to emotional states that further compromise his or her effectiveness. Using the checklist model previously discussed, one can review the case example and identify aspects of the case that were either overlooked by the therapist or at least were not documented by her.

Diagnostic Information

Background sources

In our clinical case example, John Smith was referred by his family physician. The referral was by telephone. In order to ascertain whether the psychologist acquired a complete history for John, the following questions must be asked

- Did the psychologist ask for releases from John to contact this physician and to obtain the records from John's previous treatment?
- Has the psychologist talked to the patient's physician about any medical problems, and about why particular medications and particular doses were prescribed (i.e., could John use these medications to harm himself)?
- Has the psychologist talked to the marriage counselor and, in particular, obtained information about John's ability to control impulses, show insight, and form a therapeutic alliance?
- Were the Veterans Administration records available? What can be inferred from them?
- Has the psychologist talked to the lawyer who is handling John's custody battle?
- Has the issue of confidentiality been considered with regard to the issue of child custody?
- Has the psychologist explored avenues other than the wife (because of the custody battle, she may be lost as a valuable source) to obtain collateral information while maintaining John's confidentiality? (Such alternative avenues would include releases to talk to

members of John's side of the family about his current condition, and exploring with them his adolescent suicide attempt.)

- Has the psychologist considered a referral for a psychiatric consultation with regard to John's use of psychotropic medications and sleeping pills concurrently (unless the internist or family physician is also a specialist in psychotropic medication)?

Risk Factors

Clinical inquiry and observation

Motto (1989) noted that the most straightforward way to determine the probability of suicide is to ask the patient directly. This approach emphasizes matter-of-factness, clarity, and freedom from implied criticism. A typical sequence might be to ask John the following questions:

1. Do you have periods of feeling low or despondent about how your life is going?

2. How long do such periods last? How frequent are they? How bad do they get? Does the despondency produce crying, interfere with daily activities, sleep, concentration, or appetite?

3. Do you have present feelings of hopelessness, discouragement, or self-criticism? Are these feelings so intense that life does not seem worthwhile?

4. Do thoughts of suicide come to mind? How persistent are such thoughts? How strong have they been? Did it require much effort to resist them? Have you had any impulses to carry them out? Have you made any plans? How detailed are such plans? Have you taken any initial action (such as hoarding medications, buying a gun or rope). Did the psychologist directly ascertain whether John had lethal means available to him (e.g., firearms, pills, etc.)?

5. Can you manage these feelings if they recur? If you cannot, is there a support system for you to turn to in helping to manage these feelings?

Motto (1989) pointed out that the brief inquiry above, when carried out in an empathic and understanding way, will provide the psychologist with a preliminary estimate of risk. This brief inquiry is most appropriate in settings where rapid decisions must be made (e.g., the emergency room, or consult service of a general hospital) or when a brief screening device is needed. The approach rests on the premise that "going directly to the heart of the issue is a practical and effective clinical tool, and patients and collaterals will usually provide valid information if an attitude of caring concern is communicated to them" (p. 247).

Extended assessment of suicide risk

When there is more time available than in an emergency setting, it behooves clinicians to use data from the specific risk factors for suicide, knowledge of the general formulation of clinical judgment, and their own clinical experience and training, combined with common sense, to make an estimate of risk. For example, if the patient has exhibited any previous suicidal behavior (e.g., John's previous attempt at age 17), this demonstrates a breach of resistance to pain, and the suicide attempt must be considered an indication of increased vulnerability (Motto, 1989). In addition, Clark et al. (1989) suggested that, when considering patients with moderate to severe affective disorders, the clinician "should not interpret the absence of any recent suicide attempts to mean that the patient is at relatively low risk for attempting suicide in the future . . . . suicide attempts made many years ago may have equal value to recent attempts when estimating an individual's predisposition to non-lethal attempts in the future" (p. 42). Also, as previously noted, Shneidman (1987, 1989) stressed the evaluation of perturbation, lethality, and environmental "press" as critical factors in the estimation of risk—all of which are evident in John's case.

John's psychologist did not immediately and directly explore the extent of the level of hopelessness and despair. She could have administered, either by paper and pencil or as interview questions, the Beck Hopelessness Scale, Scale for Suicide Ideation, and Depression Inventory. She might also have evaluated whether John met any of the criteria on Motto's risk estimator for suicide or on the Los Angeles Suicide Prevention Center's more demographic instrument. From the case material, it is not clear whether she explored with John (in any extended way) the specificity of thoughts, impulses, or actual plans to harm himself (Litman, 1974). The signs of termination behavior, actions that appear to negate the future, should also have been explored. Nor was John questioned about the availability or presence of lethal means in his home (e.g., a gun), even though as a military veteran he had at least basic training in the use of firearms. Furthermore, he had a family member (his grandfather) who killed himself using a firearm.

What is also unknown about this case is what John's *DSM-III-R* diagnostic category was. Did the psychologist make a formal diagnosis and ascertain how that diagnosis might affect the estimate of suicide risk? Many of the facts in the case material seem to point to signs of an affective disorder, alcohol abuse, or both. The association of depressive states with suicidal behavior is well-known (Motto, 1989). The risk of alcoholics eventually committing suicide was found to be over five times greater than that of nonalcoholics (Beck & Steer, 1989).

Bongar et al. (1989), Motto (1989), and Simon (1988) have suggested that clinicians should use a systematic decision-chart approach to the assessment and evaluation of the patient's potential for suicide or self-harm. Such a systematic

Figure 3.3   Clinical Assessment/Risk-Management Approach to
Detected Risk Factors

Risk Factors	Risk-Estimate
Subject: John Smith	
1. History of previous attempts	High
2. Lethality potential of previous attempts	Low
3. Positive psychiatric history	High
4. Depression or alcohol problem	High
5. Male, Caucasian, in late 40's	Moderate
6. Divorced and living alone	High
7. At risk of losing a job	High
8. Signs of acute perturbation	High
9. Available lethal means	High
10. Knowledge of firearms	High
11. Increase in self-hate or self-loathing	High
12. Strong feelings of depression/hopelessness	High
13. Feels he or she is a source of shame	High
14. Narcissistic injury or recent loss	High
15. Previous lack of therapeutic alliance	High
16. Increased medical utilization	High
17. Indirect signs of termination behavior	Moderate
18. Family history of suicide	Moderate
19. Physical signs of depression	High
20. Beck Depression Inventory Score	Not used
21. Beck Hopelessness Scale Score	Not used
22. Beck Scale for Suicide Ideation	Not used
22. Risk-Rescue or LSARS of previous attempt	Low
23. Risk Estimator for Suicide	Not used
24. Los Angeles SPC Score	Not used
25. Specific evaluation of pain threshold	High
26. Reasons for Living Inventory	Not used
27. Information from psychological testing	Not done
28. Requested information from collaterals	High
29. Requested information from physician/lawyer	Moderate
29. Requested previous treatment records	High
30. Contact with previous therapist	Moderate
31. Medication evaluation considered	High
32. Direct questioning about suicide	High
33. Consultation considered	High
34. Formal assessment of risk	High
35. Risk-benefit estimate used in treatment plan	High

High Risk Factors	**23** detected
Moderate Risk Factors	**5** detected
Unknown	**7** Factors not assessed or no information

Clinician's Estimate of Elevated Risk: "Moderate to High"*

Note. The risk detection profile for "John Smith" represents only one method for the assessment of suicide risk. The purpose of this decision-chart is to encourage psychologists systematically to assess and enumerate detected risks, and to incorporate them into their treatment/risk management planning. However, the clinician's own professional judgment, based on training, education, and experience always should be the central element in making the final decision with regard to estimated risk. Each clinician may well assign different weights to risk factors that are presented; therefore this listing system should be seen only as one possible model for assessment and intervention.

approach to the assessment of risk, using a checklist such as that outlined in Figure 3.3, is one way that the clinician can preempt the very problematic issue of prediction (Simon, 1988). The psychologist can then concentrate on *risk detection* and on incorporating these "detected" risks into the plan for treatment and disposition. (For an additional perspective on a concise systematic approach to the assessment of elevated risk, see Appendix D.)

It is essential to reemphasize that clinicians have not been held

> legally liable for inaccurate predictions of suicide per se. Only when they have failed to properly collect necessary data and logically assess it in making a prediction of suicide have lawsuits prevailed . . . When a risk benefit analysis is noticeably absent, the court is less able to evaluate the appropriateness of the decision-making process in assessing the risk of suicide. All suicide assessments should be recorded in the patient's chart at the time of the evaluation. For the suicidal outpatient, assessment should be made at each outpatient visit. The hospitalized patient should also have frequent assessments, particularly when a change in status is considered, such as room or ward change, pass, or discharge. (Simon, 1988, p. 86–87)

Simon (1988) also demonstrated how the use of a decision chart for assessment and risk estimation can easily be integrated into treatment planning; for example, defining risk categories such as high risk—immediate hospitalization; medium risk—hospitalization or frequent outpatient visits, reevaluate the treatment plan frequently, remain available to the patient; and low risk—continue with current treatment plan. Finally, the psychologist must understand that the final decision as to suicide risk is an intuitive judgment—"we are obliged to accept that no matter how much information is gathered, sooner or later all the data must be weighed together and an intuitive estimate of risk recorded. That it is only an educated guess does not diminish its importance or its value as a consideration in management and treatment planning" (Motto, 1989, p. 138).

Outpatient Management and Treatment of the Suicidal Patient

The primary function of competent clinical management is to provide optimal conditions for effective treatment. According to Motto (1979a), although "in some situations management decisions can have even greater therapeutic impact than formal treatment" (p. 3), the tendency is to exaggerate the importance of management in the case of the suicidal patient. Because "all other efforts are contingent on the patient's survival management decisions may well have a certain priority in the treatment plan because they are geared to assure survival" (p. 3). Because this is "sometimes at the expense of optimal treatment" (p. 3), Motto (1979a) stressed the need to understand that all interactions with patients have treatment implications.

The majority of material written in this area has focused on

> management (rather than treatment) of the suicidal client; that is, preventing the person in crisis from committing suicide until the crisis has passed. Once the client has been stabilized and equilibrium restored, it is generally assumed that therapy will be resumed as with any other client, whether the diagnosis is depression, borderline personality, or some other disorder. (Fremouw et al., 1990, p. 98)

This approach presents a number of problems, as described by Fremouw et al. (1990):

1. It is lacking in provisions to lower the probability of future suicidal crises (i.e., nothing has been done to assure that the next stressor will not precipitate another suicidal episode). This particular problem is most apparent when therapy focuses on one problem after another (the patient's marriage, job, money problems, etc.) without a close examination of the basic issues that precipitated the patient's considering suicide as an option.

2. A "therapy as usual" approach fails to understand that being suicidal is not an entirely transient phenomenon; it has both state and traitlike characteristics. (p. 99)

Many opportunities for intervention with patients in the suicidal state occur in the professional practice activities of clinicians whose experience with this particular problem is limited (Motto, 1979a). The purpose of this chapter is to help such psychologists by providing a practical response to the following question: What should I do when I have to make critical decisions and why? Which patients can be managed and treated in outpatient settings (including general principles in the outpatient management of the suicidal patient, fundamental emergency psychotherapy and crisis intervention skills), and a selection of authorities' recommendations for psychotherapy with seriously suicidal patients will be discussed.

Principles of Outpatient Management

It has been said that suicide is the most feared outcome in psychotherapy and can signal a calamitous, irrevocable failure in treatment (Gill, 1982). Kahn (1982b) noted that nowhere in the range of professional activities of the clinician is he or she under more intense and significant stress than when treating the potentially suicidal patient. The stress and anxiety that this clinical situation provokes in the therapist is a two-edged sword. It can mobilize the psychologist to greater clinical alertness and therapeutic vigilance. However, if the clinician becomes preoccupied with the issue and threat of a patient's suicide, it can divert the clinician from the primary task of attending to more disposition-based treatment—therapeutics that are solidly grounded in an understanding of the power of a sound therapeutic alliance and on a well-formulated treatment plan based on the detection of known elevated-risk factors (Bongar et al., 1989; Gill, 1982; Simon, 1988).

Typically, the outpatient management of suicide will involve patients in the low to medium (moderate) risk category (Bongar et al., 1989; Peterson & Bongar, 1989, in press; Simon, 1987, 1988). Although outpatient therapy is possible for persons at high suicidal risk, hospitalization is more usual in such cases, because the opportunities to control and anticipate suicide are greater in an inpatient setting. The first management decision in treating a suicidal patient is to determine treatment setting, which includes consideration of characteristics of both the patient and therapist, and a careful evaluation (including a clear definition of the risks and the rationale for the decisions that one is making). According to Motto (1979a), the central reason for not using outpatient management is the psychologist's firm judgment that "the patient is not likely to survive as an outpatient" (p. 3). However, the psychologist must never forget that each management decision is the result of the unique characteristics of the patient (including his or her social matrix) and the therapist's equally unique capabilities and tolerances for stress and uncertainty. As noted by Motto (1979a),

> At times, high-risk persons with near-psychotic levels of disorganization have been treated as outpatients because in work settings they seemed able to use their defenses—especially obsessive patterns—effectively; suicidal impulses were diminished remarkably as long as they were at work. Others can manage at home when home is experienced as a protective environment. When no readily available setting affords relief, a hospital becomes the preferred setting. (p. 3)

One of the first tasks in determining appropriate patient populations for outpatient management is to distinguish between acute clinical states related to *DSM-III-R* Axis I clinical syndromes and chronic suicidal behavior that is part of an Axis II personality disorder (Goldsmith, Fyer, & Frances, 1990; Simon, 1988). Simon (1988) pointed out that the clinician who treats a suicidal outpatient and who makes a gross error in deciding not to seek commitment for the patient meeting these legal criteria may be held liable. Important considerations that should be taken into account when contemplating hospitalization are (Simon, 1987, 1988):

1. Acutely suicidal patients often suffer from *DSM-III-R* Axis I disorders, typically major affective or schizophrenic disorders that require immediate hospitalization and inpatient treatment. The suicidal risk usually passes with the remission in the acute or recurrent episode of the illness. Psychologists must act promptly and affirmatively to hospitalize and to supervise such patients.

2. Chronically suicidal patients can more typically be treated as outpatients, and, usually, these patients meet the Axis II criteria for a personality disorder. However, inpatient management may be necessary when their suicidal impulses become acute and exacerbated because of a life crisis or if they also develop an Axis I clinical syndrome, typically an affective disorder. Chronically suicidal patients' behavior may be a way to deal with their inner sense of rage, secondary to a sense of low self-esteem; or they may use the suicidal crisis as a means of escape from their life turmoil and attempt to regain control. When such crises occur, a real risk of suicide does exist, and hospitalization may become necessary.

3. If these chronically suicidal patients are not hospitalized, they should be continuously reevaluated for suicide risk during each psychotherapeutic contact. The clinician must make sure that the

patient sees them as readily available, their medications must be closely monitored, and the patient's interpersonal support systems must be mobilized to help them deal with the intense stresses of these chronic suicidal crises.

4. The psychologist who works on an outpatient basis with a chronically suicidal patient must learn to be able to tolerate a certain level of chronic suicidal ideation in these patients in order to continue psychotherapy effectively. For psychologists who elect this management course, the well-documented risk–benefit analysis is *sine qua non* in the ongoing outpatient management plan.

Here, it is important to note Litman's cautionary dictum that most chronically suicidal patients have a history of contacts with mental health professionals; 20% of the suicides in Litman's study group were in treatment at the time of their death, and 50% were in treatment with psychiatrists (Litman, 1988). Litman pointed out that the actual on-going treatment of these difficult patients calls for flexibility and the use of a variety of therapeutic modalities. The major complication to treatment is "therapist burn-out."

Once the environment for treatment has been chosen, the psychologist must then determine the imminence of the risk (Fremouw et al., 1990). If he or she determines that there is a moderate to high risk of suicide, on the basis of the evaluation of a combination of demographic factors, the clinical interview, and any other sources of information (e.g., self-report measures, information from significant others, consultations, etc.) the first decision point is to determine whether outpatient management continues to be a viable option. That is, can the psychologist and other caretakers reasonably ensure the protection of the patient? If the probability of the suicidal behavior is judged to be "low enough to warrant continued outpatient treatment, then treatment could continue on an intensified basis . . . if, for a variety of reasons, outpatient treatment is not appropriate, then hospitalization is warranted" (Fremouw et al., 1990, p. 93).

The authors of this book noted that the determination of the level of danger in this decision is based on five considerations:

1. the imminence of the behavior (e.g., the immediacy of the risk; whether the patient is a clear and imminent danger to self at the present time);

2. the target of the danger (e.g., whether the suicidal behaviors occur in the context of angry dyadic exchanges, as is often the case, whether there is a possibility of concurrent homicidal and suicidal thoughts and impulses);

3. the clarity of the danger (e.g., whether and to what degree the patient is specific in what he or she plans to do; the intensity of

the impulses, whether the patient has selected the method, time, or place);

4. the intent of the behavior (whether there is a clear determination of both the patient's intention and of his or her motive to die); and

5. the lethality or probability of death (this must be assessed on separate dimensions, e.g., LSARS, Risk–Rescue).

In determining imminence and dangerousness, it is helpful to conceptualize the patient's "danger-to-self" thoughts, feelings, and behaviors along a thought–impulse–action continuum. Shneidman (1989), we recall, found that a communication of intent is present in 80% of completed suicides. Although placing this communication of intent by patients at the 50% to 70% level, Fawcett (1988) found that high-risk suicidal patients tend to communicate their intent to their significant other only, whereas those in the moderate- to mild-risk group more frequently threaten suicide to doctors, other family members, and so forth. It is clear that, except where contraindicated by toxic interpersonal matrices, comprehensive information gathering and collaboration with the family and significant others is a vital element in any successful management plan. (We will discuss this point in greater detail in chapter 6.)

We have found Shneidman's (1981c, 1989) basic model for psychotherapy with patients in the suicidal state to be the keystone to understanding the essentials of this clinical situation. Here, the concepts of perturbation and lethality will guide our understanding. Shneidman (1981c) defined these concepts in the following way:

- Perturbation refers to how upset (disturbed, agitated, sane–insane, discomposed) the individual is—rated on a 1 to 9 scale.
- Lethality refers to how lethal the individual is, that is, how likely it is that he or she will take his or her own life—also rated on a 1 to 9 scale. (p. 341)

We can arbitrarily divide the seriousness of the risk (i.e., lethality or suicidality) of all the patient's suicidal actions, deeds, and episodes (whether a verbal threat or behaviors that we ordinarily think of as attempts) into "three rough commonsense groupings: low, medium, and high" (Shneidman, 1981c, p. 342). *High lethality* is where the danger of "self-inflicted death is realistically large and imminent; what one might ordinarily call high suicide risks" (p. 342). Shneidman strongly believes that working intensively with a highly suicidal patient (i.e., someone who might be assessed as a 7, 8, or 9 on a 1-to-9 scale of lethality) is a special task—one that demands a different kind of therapeutic involvement, has different rules, and has a different theoretical rationale. Here, the fundamental principle for treating the acutely suicidal patient so as to decrease lethality is "by dramatically decreasing the felt perturbation" (Shneidman,

1981c, p. 342). (We will present the details of Shneidman's model for intensive psychotherapy later in this chapter.)[1]

Therapy represents the opportunity to translate our knowledge (albeit incomplete) of risk factors for suicide into a plan of action (Brent et al., 1988). Treatment of patients who are at high risk for suicide should ameliorate those risk factors that are most likely to result in suicide. Simon (1987) stressed that, although there is a loose fit between diagnosis and suicide, suicide rarely occurs in the absence of psychiatric illness. In adult suicides, more than 90% of suicide victims were mentally ill before their deaths. Recognizing that "the most basic management principle is to understand that most suicide victims kill themselves in the midst of a psychiatric episode (Barraclough et al., 1974; Dorpat & Ripley, 1960; Robins et al., 1959; Shaffer, 1974; Shaffer et al., 1985; Shaffi, 1986)" (Brent et al., 1988, p. 365), it is clear that proper diagnosis and treatment of acute psychiatric illness can lower the risk for suicide. Brent and his colleagues stressed the need to involve the family for support and improved compliance. They cautioned that clinicians take particular care in the treatment of any co-morbid medical and psychiatric condition, providing hope (particularly to new-onset patients), restricting the availability of lethal agents, and remaining alert to indications for psychiatric hospitalization.

Gill (1982) pointed out that suicidal impulses and behaviors occur in patients whose diagnoses range across the entire diagnostic spectrum and that a truly comprehensive discussion of the treatment of suicidal patients would have to address the treatment of each specific diagnostic group and situation—a task that is clearly beyond the scope of the present book. We shall limit our discussion, instead, to comments on the outpatient management of suicidal adult patients in general. We suggest that if a patient demonstrates even a low to moderate level of suicide risk and the psychologist decides to pursue outpatient management, he or she would be well advised to seek an immediate and formal consultation with an experienced colleague in order to discuss the risks and benefits of this course of action. The use of consultation provides a timely biopsy of the management plan (Gutheil, 1990) and demonstrates the psychologist's commitment to maintaining the highest levels of professional practice activities. In addition, the use of family or significant other involvement can dramatically increase the

---

[1]For more information on the treatment of specific diagnostic categories and special clinical populations and situations, the reader is directed to: Berman (1986b); Brent et al. (1988); Buie and Maltsberger (1989); Dubovsky (1988); Gutheil and Appelbaum (1982); Fremouw et al. (1990); Jacobs (1989a, 1989b); Kreitman (1986); Lesse (1989b); Litman (1989); Maltsberger (1986, 1988); Mann and Stanley (1988a, 1988b); Maris (1981, 1986, 1988, 1989a, 1989b); Motto (1986, 1989); Murphy (1986, 1988a, 1988b); Perr (1985a, 1985b, 1988); Peterson and Bongar (1989); Pfeffer (1988); Pokorny (1983); Pope (1989); Rachlin (1984); Rangell (1988); Richman and Eyman (in press); Robertson (1988); Robins (1985, 1986); Shneidman (1981a, 1981b, 1981c, 1984, 1985, 1986a, 1987, 1989); Simon (1987, 1988); Smith (1988); Swartz (1988); Swenson (1986); VandeCreek and Knapp (1983, 1989); Waltzer (1980); and Weishaar and Beck (1990).

protective net and allow "all the cards to be face-up on the table" vis-à-vis the proposed risk management plan.

In this regard, an important issue is the patient's competency and willingness to participate in management and treatment decisions (Gutheil, 1984). Simon cited Gutheil's (1984) recommendation to the patient: "If you don't level with me, I can't help you" (Simon, 1987, p. 263). Gutheil also noted that, for effective treatment to occur, it is essential to assess certain kinds of competencies and capacities, in particular, the patient's competence to participate in therapeutic alliance with the clinician.

The "Duty to Warn"

Previously, we have discussed the details of *Bellah v. Greenson*, but it may be helpful to cite briefly the words of the court in this particular case with regard to the formulation of decisions about duty to warn and suicidality. It is important to note (as we did in chapter 2) that some states have statutory avenues that allow such breaches of confidentiality. (We will be discussing the ethical and legal principles with regard to confidentiality in detail in chapter 6.)

In *Bellah v. Greenson* (1978), the parents of Tammy Bellah alleged that her psychiatrist, Dr. Greenson, had knowledge of Tammy's heavy drug use and suicidal tendencies prior to her self-destruction. Tammy's parents asserted that the proximate cause of her death was the psychiatrist's failure to take affirmative actions to prevent Tammy's overdose. They also alleged that Dr. Greenson should have informed them of their daughter's suicidal condition.

The court rejected the plaintiffs' contention that there was a duty on the part of the defendant to breach the confidence of a doctor–patient relationship by revealing disclosures made by their daughter about conditions that might cause her to commit suicide. The court held that a therapist is only required to disclose the contents of a confidential communication when the risk to be prevented thereby is the danger of violent assault and not when the risk of harm is self-inflicted harm or mere property damage. The court also rejected the plaintiffs' contention that the action was based on an oral contract and, therefore, subject to the 2 year statute of limitations. In short, although the *Bellah* court did decide that Dr. Greenson's standard of outpatient care could be decided by expert testimony (see the discussion of this case in chapter 2), the court refused to extend the *Tarasoff* "duty to warn" to cases of "danger to self."

Working With the Difficult Suicidal Patient

Our discussion of general management principles would be incomplete without explicitly addressing the issue of the reactions that a suicidal (and for that matter any difficult) patient invokes in his or her psychologist. In discussing what it is that makes some therapeutic encounters more difficult than others, some researchers focus on specific patient behaviors, such as suicidal gestures, violence, and the abuse of alcohol and drugs (Bachrach, 1983; Deutsch, 1984; Smith & Steindler, 1983; Wong, 1983). Others believe that it is not the patient alone, but rather a severely pathological family system that makes the treatment difficult (Wong, 1983). Still other researchers and clinicians argue that the major source of difficulty is the structure of the treatment system (Neill, 1979; Robbins, Beck, Mueller, & Miezener, 1988).

Another major camp maintains that there is no such thing as a difficult patient; that there are only difficulties arising in the unique intersection of subjectivities that constitute the psychotherapeutic situation. From this viewpoint, it is not the patient per se but, rather, the negative interaction between the patient and the therapist that renders treatment difficult (Steiger, 1967; Stolorow, Brandchaft, & Atwood, 1983). Fine (1984) stated that many psychotherapists' definition of a difficult patient, and their reluctance to treat such patients, is based on often unacknowledged or unrealized countertransference.

It may be useful to note that Lane's (1984) literature review of Freud's views on *negative therapeutic reaction* (NTR) demonstrated that there is no single definition of NTR and that NTR overlaps with other classifications such as the *difficult patient* and *resistance*. Lane argued that NTR is a type of resistance that interrupts treatment and makes the patient difficult and that the key to handling NTR and patient difficulty is to understand the protective function of the patient's defenses.

Basically, then, the argument from this countertransference position on the difficult patient is that the therapist plays a role in the patient's state of being difficult: "few patients, in other words, are difficult per se, and 'difficultness' may be largely a function of impaired interaction between two individuals" (Smith & Steindler, 1983, p. 107). Steiger and Hirsh (1965) elaborated, stating: "it is more correct . . . to speak of the difficult doctor–patient relationship rather than the difficult patient" (p. 1449). However, data from a preliminary investigation (Bongar, Forcier, & Peterson, in press) on the definitional aspects of difficult patients and the stresses that they engender in their therapists, indicate that every psychiatrist in the pilot study ($N = 25$) reported, in an in-depth interview format, that there truly are difficult patients—that certain kinds of patients are intrinsically more difficult to treat than others, thereby suggesting that patient difficulty is not solely an artifact of countertransference.

The stresses on psychotherapists who are involved in treating difficult patients have also been extensively discussed in the literature. Results of a study by Deutsch (1984) revealed that expression of anger toward the therapist, severely depressed patients, apparent patient apathy and lack of motivation, and premature termination were frequently cited as stressful behaviors, with patients' suicidal statements cited as the most stressful patient behaviors of all.

Therefore, it is of critical importance to note the intensity of the clinician's own personal reaction to the patient's suicidal communications, for it has been shown that countertransference feelings of anger, anxiety, and lack of control are common when interviewing suicidal patients. If these feelings on the part of the clinician are not carefully monitored, they can cloud accurate clinical judgment and even impede the correct formulation of the treatment plan (Smith, 1986).

Suicidal behavior, in particular, often elicits negative reactions on the part of the clinician. The reasons for this vary and range from a concern over the stigma of losing a patient to fear of the emotional trauma of such a loss to a fear of litigation (Fremouw et al., 1990). However, it is critically important, as Shneidman (1981c) recognized, that suicidal patients be treated without any iatrogenic elements: "Thus, in the treatment of the suicidal person there is almost never any place for the therapist's hostility, anger, sardonic attitudes, daring the patient, or pseudo-democratic indifference" (p. 342).

Maltsberger (1989) wrote that difficult and suicidal patients commonly evoke on the part of the therapist a strong countertransference wish to "do something active, powerful, healing, so we will not have to endure the empathic pain of acknowledging the patient's hopelessness. We want them to get better fast to help ourselves" (p. 416). The psychotherapist must be vigilant and ensure that negative reactions to a patient, whether countertransference or the understandable reaction to a difficult patient, do not lead to the psychotherapist colluding in behaviors that expose the patient to increased risk.

Both Motto (1979a) and Holmes and Rich (1990) pointed out that special obstacles may be introduced when the patient is another professional person (e.g., another psychologist or health care professional). We must take care to resist the impulse to rationalize higher risks away because of the patient's professional standing or role in the community. Motto further cautioned against lowering one's guard when the patient does not seem at high risk for suicide but threatens or implies that suicide will be resorted to "if you don't put me in the hospital," "if the doctor does not give me something to get rid of the pain," "if my wife doesn't come back," or "if they reduce my disability payments" (p. 6). He noted that there are enumerable variants of these statements, the common theme being that "someone else's action, or lack of it, is identified as responsible for the patient's suicidal impulse" (p. 6).

Motto (1979a) recommended that clinicians carefully consider and assess the patient's goals and the reasonableness of his or her request. Often the patient wants something that is justifiable, but, because this request is put in the form of an abrasive or threatening demand, it is experienced by the clinician (or by significant others) as manipulative, and an

> unreasoning resistance is generated, and the refusal is rationalized as "not playing into the patient's dependent needs." This can easily lead to a

power struggle in which the patient has the ultimate power, and a suicidal act may occur. This power struggle can be critical; often by the time that the patient is seen in a psychiatric setting, the family has exhausted its energies. (p. 6)

According to Motto, if the patient's demands have merit, they should be acknowledged and the clinician should do what he or she can to help the patient have these demands met—regardless of the irritation that the patient may have caused. Furthermore, the treatment plan should include a discussion of how much more readily others would respond to the patient's requests if they were phrased in a different manner. If the demands do not have merit, the needs that generated them should be identified if at all possible and an alternative means formulated to meet them.

Whenever a clinician is challenged as to whether she or he can thwart a patient's suicidal intent, it is generally "appropriate to acknowledge that the patient ultimately has control of that decision" (Motto, 1979a, p. 6). Making such an acknowledgment is a recognition and acceptance of reality and not a matter of manipulation. The psychologist must be comfortable with his or her own limitations in order to deal with this reality in an effective manner and to avoid feelings of frustration, anger, and resentment that can handicap her or his judgment and clinical effectiveness (Motto, 1979a).

Therefore, we recommend that psychologists routinely consider a consultation on any difficult and suicidal patient. At the conclusion of this chapter and in chapter 6 we will discuss this recommendation more extensively.

Standards of Outpatient Care

Honest errors of judgment are inevitable in clinical practice, and the courts have recognized that "the accurate prediction of dangerous behavior, and particularly suicide and homicide, are almost never possible. Thus, an error of prediction, or even of judgment does not necessarily establish negligence" (Stromberg, 1989, p. 468).

In the case of an outpatient suicide, the courts typically struggle with two central issues, foreseeability and causation (Simon, 1988). Specifically, their examination turns on whether the outpatient psychotherapist should have predicted the suicide and, if there was sufficient evidence for an identifiable risk of harm, whether the psychotherapist did enough to protect the patient (VandeCreek et al., 1987).

If a psychotherapist elects outpatient care for a suicidal patient, a number of strict management rules should be followed. However, the courts have tended to be less stringent in evaluating outpatient suicide in the absence of clear signs of foreseeability, because of the obvious increased difficulty in controlling the patient's behavior (Simon, 1988). The case law seems to put forth a basic rule that the psychotherapist should correctly recognize the risk of suicide and appropriately balance this risk with the benefits of greater control through hospitalization (Simon, 1987, 1988).

Psychologists in outpatient settings should be prepared to increase their treatment options for suicidal patients; for example, providing 24-hour coverage and adequate evening, weekend, and vacation backup arrangements (Harris, 1988; VandeCreek et al., 1987). The frequency of therapy appointments may also have to be increased (Farberow, 1957; Mintz, 1968), with the diagnosing clinician meeting much more frequently with the patient for increasingly greater amounts of time (Wekstein, 1979). In general, the clinician should maintain contact with ''life forces'' by talking to the part of the patient that wants to keep living and enlisting the cooperation of family members and friends (Farberow, 1957). By increasing the number of visits and contacts, psychologists diminish their reliance on long-term estimates of the eventual likelihood of suicide (Bongar et al., 1989; Schutz, 1982; Simon, 1988).

The telephone can be an invaluable instrument in the outpatient management of the suicidal patient. Through the judicious use of telephone ''check-in'' (Schutz, 1982) by the patient and the use of information from significant others in the patient's life (with appropriate acknowledgment of confidentiality considerations), the psychologist can sharpen the ongoing clinical risk assessment and allow for greater fine-tuning of the outpatient treatment plan (Bongar et al., 1989).

Psychologists who treat suicidal patients on an outpatient basis need to consider seriously routine consultation with a professional who has expertise in dealing with suicidal patients (Peterson & Bongar, 1990; VandeCreek et al., 1987). Patients may also be referred for appropriate consultation for medications that need to be monitored very carefully. For example, patients should never be given more than a week's supply of antidepressant medication and no more than a month's supply of sedative hypnotic, anxiolytic, or antipsychotic medications (Peterson & Bongar, in press; Slaby et al., 1986). The implementation of specific outpatient risk/benefit guidelines and documentation, the evaluation of personal competency to assess and treat suicidal patients, requests for case consultation, medication, and supervision, as well as addressing problems in establishing a standard of care will be discussed in chapter 6.

The Risks and Benefits of ''No Suicide'' Contracts

Patient–therapist contracts and agreements are a common therapeutic management strategy. Wekstein (1979) encouraged the psychotherapist to establish a contract describing the terms of therapy for all patients. Schutz (1982) suggested for suicidal patients that the clinician obtain a promise that the patient will control suicide impulses or will call the psychotherapist before attempting suicide. Psychologists, at times, may attempt to cement and formalize the therapeutic alliance through such verbal or written contracts with the patient (Peterson & Bongar, 1989; Simon, 1988). However, when negotiating a contract, the psychologist must weigh carefully the unique dynamics of each therapeutic relationship. For example, some patients may interpret such a contract to mean that they are permitted to call the psychotherapist only when they are highly dysfunctional, perturbed, and contemplating a lethal act (Bongar et al., 1989; Peterson & Bongar, 1989).

There are other limitations as well. Motto (1979a) pointed out that to the "extent that a relationship of mutual trust and respect is formed, a patient's agreement to continue in treatment, arrive at appointments, or not kill himself can be negotiated" (p. 4). He cautioned, however, that such agreements require an established therapeutic relationship, if they are to be at all relied upon. He also noted that, with adolescents, it is not reasonable to depend on such implicit contracts even when a good relationship exists. He further cautioned that contracts may become the means of articulating a power struggle with patients and that this must be avoided if at all possible. In addition, patients who have a compulsive need to be reasonable, rational, grateful, and cooperative may agree to therapeutic arrangements they cannot fulfill, precipitating an unbearable crisis.

Simon cited the case of *Stepakoff v. Kantar* (1985) in point of this standard. In this particular case, the plaintiff alleged that Dr. Kantar, the patient's psychiatrist, knew that the plaintiff's husband was suicidal and should have notified the patient's wife (the plaintiff) of that fact or made appropriate arrangements for hospitalization. In this case, the clinician thought that the patient, a manic depressive, had made a solid pact (i.e., a therapeutic contract) to contact the clinician if the patient felt suicidal. The clinician felt, in light of this apparently reliable agreement and the patient's defense mechanisms, that the patient was unlikely to commit suicide. The patient committed suicide anyway. Simon (1987) wrote:

> The state high court held that the psychiatrist did not owe the patient a specific legal duty to safeguard him from serious danger to himself. The psychiatrist's legal obligation to the patient was to treat him according to the standard of care and skill of the average psychiatrist. Beyond that standard, the psychiatrist did not have a duty to take reasonable preventive measures after diagnosing the patient as suicidal. The court stated that the duty owed by the psychiatrist to a suicidal outpatient was no different from that imposed on other physicians to other patients. (p. 263)

In short, although such contracts may be used to strengthen the therapeutic alliance, there are a number of specific limitations inherent in such contracts.

Simon (1988) arrived at the following conclusions: (a) Although some patients may accept such a contract, many patients state that, if self-destructive impulses arise, they cannot or will not want to contact their psychotherapist; (b) these contracts have no legal force; (c) the contract may falsely relieve the psychotherapist's concern and lower vigilance, without having any appreciable effect on the patient's suicide intent; and (d) such contracts may reflect the psychotherapist's attempt to control the inevitable stress and anxiety that are commonplace when treating the suicidal patient.

However, when such an instrument is used properly (i.e., as a clinical as opposed to a legal intervention), it can be an effective tool in evaluating both the patient's level of intent and sense of control. The agreement should be established to continue for a specific time frame and updated as it expires. (For an example of a sample contract, see Appendix C.)

Lethality, Method, and Responsibility

The psychologist should ensure that any weapons in the patient's possession are placed in the hands of a third party (Mintz, 1961; Schutz, 1982; Slaby et al., 1986). Because the availability of firearms and, especially, handguns plays such a prominent role as the "method of choice" for many completed suicides, the psychologist should assiduously assess the presence, access to, and knowledge of the patient with respect to this highly lethal means. This also necessitates a careful thinking-through of the patient's entire life–environment and of the way in which the patient spends each day, so as to determine proactively the presence of any potentially lethal means (e.g., hoarding of pills, access to poisons, whether the patient has a means in mind, such as hanging, jumping from a particular building, driving the car off the road, etc.).

Furthermore, it is worth mentioning again that the psychologist must not hesitate to contact others in the life of the patient and enlist their support in the treatment plan (Slaby et al., 1986). Litman (1982) recommended that, if a psychotherapist treats a high-risk outpatient who thinks he or she can function as an outpatient, it is the psychotherapist's responsibility to ensure that the risk is made known to all concerned parties (i.e., the family and significant others). We concur with Shneidman (1981c) and suggest that the number of high-risk suicidal patients that a psychologist treats at any given time should not exceed one or two (Mintz, 1961; Shneidman, 1981c) and certainly no more than two or three moderate- to high-risk patients at any one time (Peterson & Bongar, 1990; Wekstein, 1979).

It is necessary for the psychologist to realize that therapeutic concern cannot extend to an assumption of total responsibility for the patient's life. In short, the psychotherapist must avoid the trap of the omnipotent rescuer and, instead, convey to the patient a sense of enlightened caring and concern (Bongar et al., 1989; Gill, 1982; Peterson & Bongar, in press).

Shneidman (1981c) wisely counseled that, in general, any suicidal state is characterized by its transient quality, pervasive ambivalence, and dyadic nature. Psychologists and other mental health professionals are

> well advised to minimize, if not totally to disregard, those probably well-intentioned but shrill writings in this field which naively speak of an individual's "right to commit suicide"—a right which, in actuality, cannot be denied—as though the suicidal person were a chronic univalently self-destructive hermit. (p. 347)

Fremouw et al. (1990) added that a common misconception about suicide among mental health professionals is that suicide is to be expected in cases of severe hardship, especially in persons with terminal illnesses: "Often statements such as this are an indication of the speaker's belief that he or she could not bear to experience similar hardship. In reality, experience shows that human beings are capable of enduring tremendous adversity and still maintain a fierce determination to live" (p. 18). They cited a study (Brown, Henteleff, Barakat, & Rowe, 1986) that showed that, even in cases of incurable cancer, the large majority of patients wished to live as long as possible. The few who had contemplated suicide were found to suffer from clinical depression (i.e., a treatable condition).

However, Jacobs (1989b) pointed out that a key element in successful therapy is empathy: Patients must be allowed the freedom to feel their pain and to share it with their family, friends, or their psychotherapist. The clinician must call upon his or her empathic resources to feel the despair with the patient, in order to be able to sustain this empathic relationship and to face the specter of death. In Jacob's opinion, being able to sustain empathy is the most difficult aspect of psychotherapeutic work with suicidal patients. "It is so difficult that even people very close to suicidal persons often cannot maintain an empathic connection with them" (p. 332).

Medication Issues

Psychologists must be highly knowledgeable and up-to-date on common medications (psychotropic and otherwise) available for their patients. They must know both the generic and brand names, effects and side-effects, ranges for a therapeutic dosage, and contraindications for certain types of polypharmacy. Developing, maintaining, and using this knowledge requires a close and actively collaborative relationship with a medical colleague who is expert in prescribing for high-risk populations (see Appendix B.4).

For example, Peterson and Bongar (1989), in their chapter on suicide in outpatient psychiatry, recommended that psychiatrists routinely attend to the issue of risk in their manner of prescribing—that is, they should never give more than a week's supply or less of antidepressant medication and no more than a month's supply of a sedative hypnotic, anxiolytic, or antipsychotic. Psychiatrists should also keep track of the frequency of refills and, if necessary, contact the local pharmacist to determine if the patient has been obtaining lethal medications from multiple physicians.

The skills and techniques of therapy are varied; the relevance of biology and diagnosis must be thoroughly integrated (Jacobs, 1989b). Because many suicidal patients have a diagnosable affect or thought disorder, the utility of a patient's being given appropriate medication, whether it be antidepressant or antipsychotic, must always be considered. Such consideration is an essential part of the armamentarium of successful therapeutics. Therefore, in all cases where the patient presents with suicide as a clinical issue (and, for that matter, for all patients seen in a general clinical practice), the psychologist should routinely consider obtaining a consultation on the advisability of medication for the patient as part of the management plan.

Because there are divergent views on the definition or description of the pathological state underlying the suicidal impulse, it follows "that the use of psychotropic drugs with any given suicidal patient can be controversial" (Motto, 1979a, p. 5). For example, Motto cited the case of a patient whom he treated where "the therapist saw the problem as a characterological one for which no specific medication exists" (p. 5).

Motto advised that the prescribing physician should be concerned about the toxicological properties of psychotropic and other medications. For example, he urged that tricyclic antidepressants be used with great caution with high-risk depressed patients, noting that it is often difficult to prescribe a therapeutic dose without providing a potentially lethal supply. The answer that he suggested is to give frequent small prescriptions, rather than asking a family member to dispense the medication (the latter method expressing clear doubts about the patient's ability to resist suicidal impulses).

Even if the therapist does not consider the underlying pathology to be primarily depressive in nature, a trial of antidepressants may be considered in light of "the current practice and sentiment in the psychiatric community regarding the nature of suicidal states and their relationship to depression" (Motto, 1979a, p. 5). Recent empirical and epidemiological findings with regard to the Axis I diagnoses of suicide completers necessitate routine consideration of other medications. For example, recent findings indicate mood cycling and panic and anxiety disorders as high-risk diagnoses, in addition to the historically well-known relationships between suicide and depression, schizophrenia, and alcohol and substance abuse (Fawcett et al., 1987; Keller, 1988; Weissman et al., 1989).

Anecdotal information indicates that claims have been brought against both the prescribing psychiatrist and the patient's psychotherapist or psychologist when a patient kills himself or herself with a lethal overdose of prescription medication (M. Bogie, personal communication, April 1989). Harris (personal communication, May 1990) commented that, even when the psychologist is blameless with regard to the negligent prescribing,

> such claims can arise when the prescribing physician chooses to "go naked" (i.e., carry no malpractice insurance, often divesting himself or herself of assets)—the psychologist's professional liability policy may be seen by the plaintiffs and their attorney as the only "deep pocket" that offers any remedy and economic relief for the damages sustained by the plaintiffs.

Involving Family and Significant Others

Frances (1985) pointed out that in suicide treatment there are impressive advantages to involving couples and families in at least the evaluation phase of therapy. Whenever the presenting problem involves dysfunctional interactions in the couple or family, extending treatment efforts to include these significant others is also indicated. (The specific issues of confidentiality and the involvement of significant others will be discussed in chapter 6.)

Fawcett (1988) argued explicitly that there should be an increased awareness of the social matrix in suicide. One of the important implications from Fawcett and his colleagues' research is that coping behaviors can be viewed in interpersonal as well as intrapsychic terms and that there may be value in conjoint therapy with the patient who is depressed and his or her significant others (centered around the patient's and the significant other's needs for mutual interdependence) (Fawcett, 1988; Fawcett et al., 1987). This position has important implications for the consideration of family therapy and relationship network involvement as a routine element in outpatient care.

During the time of a suicidal crisis, Richman (1986) believes that there are a number of family characteristics that can increase the possibility of a patient's suicide; for example, the family's inability to accept necessary change, role and interpersonal conflicts, disturbed family structure, intolerance for crises, unbalanced or one-sided intrafamilial relationships, and affective difficulties (See Table 4.1). Although a complete discussion of the complexities of family and group therapy is beyond the scope of this book, the reader is directed to the work of Richman (1986) and Richman and Eyman (in press).

The point here is that the psychologist who works with suicidal patients must carefully guard against becoming the patient's only source of support (Fremouw et al., 1990). Besides reducing stressors in the patient's life, one of the goals of treatment is to help to develop multiple sources of support (e.g., family, group, etc.).

Clarkin (1985) stated that family therapy is a treatment format in which

Table 4.1

Characteristics of Families with Suicidal Potential

---

1. An inability to accept necessary change
   a. An intolerance for separation
   b. A symbiosis without empathy
   c. A clinging to early attachments at the expense of later ones
   d. An inability to mourn
2. Role and interpersonal conflicts, failures, and fixations
3. A disturbed family structure
   a. A closed family system
   b. A prohibition against intimacy outside the family
   c. An isolation of the potentially suicidal person within the family
   d. A quality of family fragility
4. Unbalanced or one-sided intrafamilial relationships
   a. A specific kind of scapegoating
   b. Double-binding relationships
   c. Sadomasochistic relationships
   d. Ambivalent relationships
5. Affective difficulties
   a. A one-sided pattern of aggression
   b. A family depression
6. Transactional difficulties
   a. Communication disturbances
   b. An excessive secretiveness
7. An intolerance for crises

Note. From *Family Therapy for Suicidal People* (p. 58) by J. Richman, 1986, Springer Publishing Company, Inc., New York 10012. Copyright 1986 by Springer Publishing Company, Inc. Used by permission.

psychodynamic, cognitive behavioral, experiential, and, especially, systems-strategic techniques are used. Whether the family format versus an individual and group format is indicated in any particular case requires answers to the following basic questions:

1. Is the patient's presenting problem intimately related to the family's current interaction patterns?

2. Does the presenting problem play a significant role in the stabilization and maintenance of current family homeostasis?

3. Is an individual psychotherapy format a real possibility for the identified patient, or are there powerful forces for group cohesion and homeostasis that preclude the differentiation that is vital for a successful individual treatment?

4. In formulating a management plan, has the psychologist correctly conceptualized the sequencing and staging that will be necessary

for the alleviation of any current crisis states and for producing symptom reduction?

5. Even if the family appears to be making a significant contribution to the presenting problem of the identified patient, what level of motivation does the family have to facilitate intervention in a family format?

Fremouw and colleagues (1990) cautioned that the involvement of family members necessitates a good deal of discretion on the part of the psychologist (e.g., examining any resistance on the part of the patient to the involvement of family and significant others, and the possibility that the patient may feel ashamed to let family know his or her "secret," thus lowering self-esteem).

Above all, the psychologist must take care to make an evaluation of the toxicity of the family and significant other matrix (e.g., where family and significant other involvement may do more harm than good). Parents with a history of severe emotional distress or psychopathology have been associated with suicidal behavior in their children (Fremouw et al., 1990), and a history of suicidal behavior on the part of a parent or family member predisposes a child to risk (Pfeffer, 1986). Where the significant other or family is seen as toxic, the option remains of involving other sources of support (e.g., group treatment, members of the clergy, friends, coworkers).

The correlation of social isolation and increased risk for suicide was substantiated by Maris's (1989b) own data and Lester's (1972) comments. A study conducted by Fawcett, Leff, and Bunney (1969), found that those individuals who were seen as being at a higher risk for suicide had demonstrated a lifelong inability to maintain warm and mutual interdependent personal relationships.

Where the suicidal patient's support system is weak or nonexistent, the psychologist should take advantage of established mental health resources such as day treatment or residential programs (Motto, 1979a). The psychologist should also consider group therapy, particularly psychotherapy groups that have been formed specifically to treat depressed and suicidal patients. Motto cautioned that, for the impulsive and labile patient who may not be able to reach the therapist at any given time, the patient should be given the numbers of suicide prevention and crisis centers. A high-risk patient who has no social supports may require hospitalization simply because of the lack of any sustaining social network.

Another consideration in assessing the benefits of family and group approaches for suicidal patients is explored by Richman (Richman, 1986; Richman & Eyman, in press), who pointed to the importance of assessing patient–group fit in considering nonindividual formats. Although the specifics of heterogeneous versus homogeneous group formats for suicidal patients are beyond the scope of this discussion (see Richman & Eyman, in press), Richman cited the success of a long-term homogeneous group of chronically suicidal patients that he had led for a number of years. Specifically, the group members help to support and to provide extended insights into each patient's chronic suicidal state.

Shneidman (1981c) observed that suicide is often a highly charged dyadic crisis. It follows that the psychologist, who usually deals with the patient in individual therapy (and who may even fend off the inquiries of spouse, other family members, friends, and coworkers in other circumstances) should consider the possibility of working with significant others. For example, if the patient is married, Shneidman advised meeting the spouse. The psychologist must assess whether

> the spouse is suicidogenic; whether they ought to be separated; whether there are misunderstandings which the therapist can help to resolve; or whether the spouse is insightful and concerned and can be used by the therapist as an ally and cotherapist. The same is true for homosexual lovers, for patient and parent, etc. (p. 348)

It is not always necessary that the significant other(s) be seen as often as the patient. The guiding principle is that "other real people in the patient's life be directly involved and, at the minimum, their role as hinderer or helper be assessed" (Shneidman, 1981c, p. 348).

Emergency Treatment and Crisis Intervention

It is critical for the psychologist who assesses or treats suicidal outpatients to know the resources that are available for emergencies and outpatient crises. In addition, the Board of Professional Affairs' Committee on Professional Standards of the American Psychological Association (Board of Professional Affairs, 1987a, 1987b) has stated that psychologists must be well-prepared to handle psychological emergencies and that it behooves all psychologists to

> make certain that they are prepared to develop intervention strategies that are appropriate to the demands of a psychological emergency. Thus, if adequate training was not obtained at the graduate level, then the educational and experience requirements will have to be obtained through postdoctoral or continuing education work. (p. 708)

Whether the psychologist works in a college counseling center, a community mental health agency, inpatient setting, or outpatient private practice, he or she is likely to see patients who present with an elevated risk for suicide. The psychologist must have the crisis intervention and emergency management tools necessary to deal with the problem of patient suicidality readily at hand. There is a consensus that crisis management principally entails therapeutic activism, the delaying of the patient's suicidal impulses, the restoring of hope, environmental intervention, and consideration of hospitalization (Fremouw et al., 1990). Regarding this last point, it is imperative that the clinician not become interested in a readiness to confront outpatient suicidality, to the extent of regarding hospitalization as a permanent interruption to ongoing therapy. Here, the danger is that, in an attempt to avoid this interruption, some psychotherapists may inadvertently expose their patients to even greater danger by avoiding hospitalization (Farberow, 1957).

Wekstein (1979) concurred with many of the psychotherapists previously cited. He stated that the diagnosing psychotherapist must be willing to see the patient for increasingly greater amounts of time, to keep in contact with the life forces by talking to the part of the patient that wants to be alive, and to ensure 24-hour availability by enlisting the cooperation of family members and friends. Moreover, as far as the psychotherapist's position is concerned, he or she should not work with more than one or two high-risk patients at a time. Wekstein also encouraged the psychotherapist to establish a contract describing the terms of therapy. Interestingly, Wekstein broke with the previously mentioned psychotherapists in his view of outpatient therapy, believing that hospitalization should be avoided if at all possible. However, he conceded that when one was working with suicidal patients who were alcoholic, suffering from psychoses, or have a psychopathic personality, hospitalization should be considered.

Slaby et al. (1986) felt that once high suicide risk has been determined, a social support system should be formed that enlists the help of family and friends. Moreover, pharmacotherapy, psychotherapy, or sociotherapy should be initiated, and the patient required to pay a return visit to the psychotherapist's office to ensure there is no need for hospitalization.

Pope (1986) discussed the practical implications of such recommendations. Specifically, the psychologist must know community crisis intervention resources and which hospital he or she might use for voluntary or involuntary hospitalization of suicidal patients, as well as have a thorough understanding of the procedures for each setting. Pope set forth a number of salient points with regard to emergency and crises intervention resources and skills with the suicidal patient. These include asking oneself the following questions and establishing the following guidelines.

- Do you have appropriate staff privileges and a working relationship with the hospital administration or staff?
- To what extent will you be involved with the treatment planning and implementation while the client is hospitalized?
- What are the boundaries of your authority? In all instances, but especially when services are provided within the context of an outpatient clinic or involve referrals, ensure that clear and ap-

propriate lines of responsibility are explicit and understood by everyone. Clients are apt to "fall between the cracks" when being referred or transferred from one clinician to another.

- Has your availability to the patient been clarified? To what extent are you available for phone contact between regularly scheduled sessions? Can you be reached late at night, on weekends, or during holidays? What are your clients to do if there are unforeseen crises and you are unavailable?
- Have you discussed (and from time to time reviewed) procedures with your clients? The more active your clients are in creating these plans the better. Are you and your clients satisfied that these plans are adequate? Think them through on a "worst-possible-case" basis and include sufficient backup options.
- How are your absences—both planned (e.g., vacations) and un-planned (e.g., illness)—to be handled? If a colleague will be pro-viding coverage for your clients, be sure that (a) your clients understand the arrangements, (b) you obtain appropriate informed consent from your clients to share important information, and (c) you adequately brief your colleague on the condition, situation, and needs of any suicidal clients. (Pope, 1986, pp. 19–20)

The issues of changes of therapist and therapist absences are worthy of a further cautionary note, because, as Motto (1979a) commented, the period of time surrounding a loss or change of a therapist is an especially vulnerable time for the suicidal patient. He cited an example in which, at one institution, an examination of four recent suicides revealed that three had occurred in the context of vacation interruptions. This problem is common in training institutions, be-cause trainees, interns, and residents often move in and out of clinical assignments and often leave the area after completion of training. In short, psychologists who see suicidal patients in outpatient settings must be certain that they can provide adequate service to their suicidal patients, such as 24-hour emergency coverage, crisis intervention, and adequate backup arrangements (Bongar, et al., 1989; Doyle, 1990; Harris, 1988; VandeCreek et al., 1987).

Stromberg (1989) stated that psychologist–practitioners should have a clear idea of what steps they can and should take once they believe that an attempted suicide is likely: "use of crisis intervention techniques, referral to an emergency service, referral to a psychiatrist for medication, and/or civil commitment" (p. 469). Stromberg concluded that

psychologists and other mental health professionals who do not have hospital admitting privileges should be cautious in accepting potentially suicidal patients, and should consider referring such patients to profes-

sionals who do have these privileges, and who are skilled in the management of dangerous patients. (p. 469)

Psychotherapy With Seriously Suicidal Patients

It would be presumptuous in this section to attempt inclusively to describe the
varieties and theoretical rationales for effective psychotherapy with seriously
suicidal patients (that task alone would entail a separate book). Instead, we shall
present the reader with a brief sampling of the positions of a few well-known
suicidologists and their general thoughts on this difficult and complex clinical
endeavor.

Shneidman's model of psychotherapy

Shneidman (1981c) developed the position that psychotherapy with an intensely
suicidal patient is a task that "demands a different kind of involvement. The
goal is different—not that of increasing comfort, which is the goal of most
ordinary psychotherapy, but the more primitive goal of simply keeping the person
alive" (p. 342). He further noted that there "may be as important a conceptual
difference between ordinary psychotherapy (with individuals where living or
dying is not the issue) and psychotherapy with acutely suicidal persons as there
is between ordinary psychotherapy and ordinary talk" (p. 344).

The main point in working with a lethally oriented patient (in the ordinary
give and take of talk, advice, listening, and interpretations) is the psychologist's
need to increase the patient's psychological sense of possible choices and the
patient's sense of being emotionally supported (Shneidman, 1981c). After a
careful assessment of the interpersonal matrix to ensure that the significant others
are on the life-side of the patient's ambivalence, the psychologist should judi-
ciously consider involving relatives, friends, and coworkers in the total treatment
process. The psychologist should also routinely involve consultants, ancillary
therapists, and all possible interpersonal community resources.

Keeping in mind the four components of the highly suicidal state (heightened
inimicality, elevated perturbation, conspicuous constriction of intellectual focus,
and the idea of cessation as a solution), Shneidman concluded that treatment
must decrease lethality; putting "a hook on perturbation and, doing what needs
to be done, pulls the level of perturbation down—and with that action brings
down the active level of lethality" (p. 345). Once the patient is no longer highly
suicidal, the psychologist can use the usual methods of psychotherapy.

Cognitive therapy of suicide

The critical importance of the cognitive revolution in our understanding of a
psychotherapeutic approach to suicide and the seminal contributions of Beck et
al. (1979), Ellis and Dryden (1987), Meichenbaum (1977), and Peterson and
Seligman (1984) have been cited by Fremouw et al. (1990). Fremouw and

colleagues pointed out that several common threads tie the cognitive theories together and that there are unique cognitive characteristics of suicidal individuals— these are, cognitive rigidity, dichotomous thinking, impaired problem-solving ability, hopelessness, irrational beliefs, and dysfunctional attitudes.

In chapter 3, we detailed the highly significant contributions of Beck and his colleagues and presented examples of the current practices at the University of Pennsylvania's Center for Cognitive Therapy. We believe that the Center's integrated approach to the assessment and management of suicidal ideation, impulses, and behavior is an excellent example of a comprehensive template that might be adopted by the clinician seeking a working model of high-level out- patient cognitive psychotherapeutic care. (For additional information, the reader is directed to a recent review on cognitive approaches to understanding and treating suicidal behavior by Weishaar & Beck, 1990.)

It is important for the cognitive therapist to include behavioral and affective work along with efforts to change cognitions (Fremouw et al., 1990). Effective psychotherapy with the suicidal patient includes identification of the following therapy change targets: affect, behavior, cognition, organic conditions, and situa- tional factors. This is very similar to earlier recommendations by Lazarus to examine the patient's *b*ehavior, *a*ffect, *s*ensations, *i*magery, *c*ognitions, *i*nterper- sonal life, and *d*rug–physiological/pharmacological status (B.A.S.I.C. I.D., Lazarus, 1981).

Specifically, Fremouw et al. (1990) posit that each of these components manifests itself differently and may require different interventions, depending on the "type" of suicide under consideration. For example, they believe that suicidal depressed patients, more often than other groups, will show a tendency toward dichotomous thinking, rigidity, belief in the necessity of love and achievement, and other cognitive vulnerabilities. For the communication/control attempter or threatener (psychiatric diagnoses often include a personality disorder), Fremouw and colleagues recommended dealing explicitly with suicide as an interpersonal problem-solving strategy, where the goal of therapy is to help the patient "give up the suicide option by developing alternative, more advantageous, strategies" (p. 128). (For more information, the reader is directed to Fremouw et al., 1990 and Linehan 1987.)

Psychodynamic approaches and the empathic method

According to the dynamic integration approach of Maltsberger, to understand the vulnerability to suicide is to understand the psychology of despair. The patient's subjective experience has two parts (a) the patient finding herself or himself in an intolerable affective state, flooded with emotional pain so intense and so unrelenting that it can no longer be endured, and (b) the patient recognizing her or his condition and giving up on herself or himself. Maltsberger believes that such a recognition is not merely a cognitive surrender, even though most hopeless patients probably have thought about their circumstances and reach a conscious cognitive decision to give up. What he described is a more important unconscious precognitive operation in which the self is abandoned as being unworthy of further concern (Maltsberger, 1986).

Buie and Maltsberger (1989) stated that effective psychotherapy of the suicidal patient recognizes that such persons have often not developed their own internal resources for self-soothing. These vulnerable patients must look to resources external to themselves for a sense of comfort, and, without these external resources, they experience aloneness (defined as a vacant, cold feeling of isolative and hopeless discomfort). These authors elaborated on Kohut's position (Kohut, 1971) that people need to feel valuable. Immature, narcissistic individuals often use idealized or mirrored external others (self-objects) to feel a sense of value, and, when these self-objects are lost, vulnerable patients "fall prey to dangerous affects of worthlessness or aloneness (sometimes to both at once). Their survival is then in danger" (Buie & Maltsberger, 1989, p. 61).

The psychotherapy of the suicidal patient, according to Buie and Maltsberger's dynamic formulation of risk, requires that the psychologist help patients to work through and understand their sense of murderous rage with a self-object that has disappointed them. The psychologist must provide help to the patient in resisting primitive conscience or self-contempt. Maltsberger (1989) pointed out that throughout history this kind of interior enemy has been given a variety of names (demon, dybuk, superego, hostile introject) and that an important aim of psychotherapy is to "exorcise, as best we can, interior enemies of this sort" (p. 358). The therapist must also be on guard against the false lure to the patient of a fantasized sense of peace through death.

Clark et al. (1989) stressed the importance of repeated assessments over time on a broad array of clinical features throughout the course of psychotherapy. They cited Smith (1985) in asserting "that serial assessments which pay attention to the vicissitudes of clinical symptoms, changing life stress, and long-standing character structure in concert would provide a better method of estimating suicide risk" (Clark et al., 1987, p. 926) throughout the course of treatment.

With regard to chronicity and suicidality, Roth (1989) commented that chronic suicidal ideation and a chronic sense of depression "leads us to ponder the state of chronicity and the therapeutic task deriving from it" (p. 355). He cited the dictum of Semrad: "Chronicity follows when the precipitating factor in the original regression has not been worked through and resolved" (Roth, 1989, p. 355).

Recently, Jacobs (1989b) proposed a synthesis of dynamic, existential, and self-psychological approaches to the psychotherapy of the suicidal patient, which he calls the "the empathic method." Specifically, Jacobs believes that psychotherapy must recognize the important distinction between depression and despair. Moreover, psychotherapists must be willing to accept the patient's despair–the therapist must use more of himself or herself in the course of therapy (Havens,

1974, 1989), employing both the psychodynamic and existential perspective in the treatment.

The image of "going below," is described by Havens (1989) as a process whereby the psychotherapist attempts to engage the patient by a deepening awareness of the painful experience. Jacobs (1989b) noted:

> once you have imagined and felt the despair. . . For now, you must sit with that feeling and demonstrate to the patient that you can tolerate their pain (Semrad, 1984). Again, this counters our usual responses to painful situations, where we look for mechanisms to immediately alleviate pain. (p. 334)

Jacobs contended that empathy is a technique that all clinicians who work psychotherapeutically with suicidal patients "can and must learn in order to bring patients back from the brink of disaster" (p. 335). He cited the findings of Havens (1974, 1989) and of Havens and Palmer (1984) as demonstrations of how empathy can turn despair around. A powerful element in psychotherapy of suicidal patients is conveying to them that their lives truly matter to the therapist.

Maltsberger (1989), in commenting on a clinical interview conducted by Havens (1989) with a chronically suicidal patient, pointed out that it is clear from the interview that Havens, if necessary, would be prepared to continue listening to the patient's despair for hours and hours—rather than giving up hope or waiting for some spontaneous movement. The central concern here is that the psychotherapist fashion herself or himself into a self-sustaining object in order to counteract the highly corrosive affects of worthlessness and despair. Maltsberger (1989) quoted Elvin Semrad, speaking about Freida Fromm-Reichman,

> that little old lady kept coming back and coming back and coming back and coming back until the patient could not stand it any longer. Something had to give. Semrad used to say if you will stay with a patient long enough without surrender one day the patient will say to himself, "If this doctor can care so much and be so interested in me, maybe I've got it wrong, maybe I've got something worthwhile that I can't see but he can." But one must wait. You cannot be in a hurry. (p. 359)

Jacobs (1989b) concluded that using the empathic method in therapy with a suicidal patient challenges the psychologist to be where the patient is—a place where "under ordinary circumstances, we would not choose to go. . . We must be able to see death in its darkest moments to make it possible to see the light" (p. 341).

Psychotherapeutic Activism and the Therapeutic Alliance

Finally, we would like to state clearly our feelings on the issue of psychotherapeutic activism and availability to the suicidal patient, and on the crucial importance of the therapeutic alliance. We feel, as do a number of senior suicidologist colleagues (e.g., Motto, 1979a; Shneidman, 1981c, 1984), that suicidal patients must be told that they can reach their psychologist at any time (day or night, including weekends and holidays). This entails providing patients with home telephone numbers and telling them when the psychologist will be out of town and how to reach him or her during this time. Motto (1979a) pointed out that this ready availability of the therapist is rarely abused; the suicidal patient's need is not so much to have the therapist immediately available as to know that the psychologist's concern extends beyond the ordinary conditions of psychotherapy. The same principle applies to a psychologist making special scheduling arrangements. Motto (1979a) labeled this effort *active relatedness.*

The forms that active relatedness can take were discussed by two prominent suicidologists, Bruce Danto and Norman Farberow:

Danto: There has to be a time when you shift gears and become an activist. Support may involve getting a patient a job, attending a graduation or play, visiting the hospital, even making house calls.

Farberow: There are instances where the therapist provided very frequent and long sessions (some lasting all day) as examples of the extraordinary measures which are sometimes required to enable someone to live. Providing this degree of availability to the client gives the client evidence of caring when that caring is absolutely necessary to convince that client life is both livable and worth living. . . In such circumstances, all other considerations—dependence, transference, countertransference, and so on—become secondary. These secondary issues can be "put on hold" during the crisis—can be directly and effectively addressed once the client is in less danger. (Pope, 1986, p. 17)

Peterson and Bongar (1989) suggested that the importance of continuity of care is critical and that having a single clinician or team working with the patient both in outpatient and inpatient management is essential. Shneidman (1981c, 1984) pointed out that, to decrease the immediate level of perturbation, a psychotherapist may even need to cater to the infantile idiosyncratic behavior and excessive dependence needs of the patient in the short run.

Eyman agreed that, during crisis intervention, with the short-term goal of overcoming a suicidal crisis, the psychotherapist indeed might foster whatever expectations the patient has, "including infantile ones, in order to engage the patient during the crisis" (Richman & Eyman, in press, p. 9). However, Eyman believes that it could be disadvantageous, and even dangerous in more long-term psychotherapeutic endeavors, for the therapist to continually gratify a patient's childlike wishes and that therapists must carefully avoid the trap of attempting to be the all-powerful "good parent" by supplying the "patient with immediate gratification and nurturance, while avoiding analyzing and understanding the reasons for the patient's 'suicidal urges' " (Richman & Eyman, in press, p. 9). Clearly, both Shneidman and Eyman agree that this particular element in clinical management is an area where psychologists will accrue the greatest benefits to their management efforts by attending to the issues of careful diagnosis, clear understanding of patient dynamics (including the psychologist's own reaction to the patient's suicidality), and distinguishing between acute suicidal conditions related to *DSM-III-R* Axis I syndromes and chronic suicidality related to *DSM-III-R* Axis II syndromes (Bongar et al., 1989; Goldsmith et al., 1990; Simon, 1987, 1988).

In acknowledgment of the importance and difficulties inherent in these management and treatment considerations, we would advocate having at least one "face-to-face" joint session with the patient and each of the therapists who will be serving as backups. This practice is common in certain medical specialities (e.g., obstetrics) where the familiarity of the patient with the other doctors who may be called upon to provide immediate care is seen as a usual, caring, and customary element in good general practice.

Psychotherapy Integration and the Therapeutic Alliance

Bongar et al., (1989), in their article on integrative approaches to the assessment and management of the suicidal patient, pointed out that one of the most significant factors in assessing suicide risk and determining the prognosis for the success of subsequent treatment is the quality of the therapeutic alliance (see also Jacobs, 1989b; Peterson & Bongar, 1989; Simon, 1987, 1988; Smith, 1988). The therapeutic alliance has been put forward by Simon (1988) as the bedrock indicator of the patient's willingness to seek help and sustenance through personal relationships during serious emotional crises. Maltsberger (1986) specifically addressed the issue of the absence of sustaining interpersonal relationships as a key factor in the clinical formulation of suicide risk. In short, the presence or absence of a good therapeutic alliance can be used as an ongoing and robust measure of the treatment's effect on the patient's vulnerability to suicide. These therapeutic alliance skills are so important that London (1986) commented that it is wise to consider training novice psychologists in the fundamental skill of establishing good interpersonal relationships as a prerequisite to the later development of specialized and advanced therapeutic proficiencies.

Our recommendations regarding standards for the management of the suicidal outpatient are consistent with a basic maxim for working with suicidal patients and borrows heavily from the philosophy of crisis intervention. That is, involvement with the suicidal patient should not be seen as an attempt to ameliorate the patient's entire personality or to cure all emotional illness (Shneidman, 1985), but rather as an attempt to meet the immediate need to keep the person alive.

Summary

Psychologists who evaluate and treat patients in outpatient settings must be certain they can provide adequate care for their suicidal patients, examining both personal and professional competencies as well as making adequate backup arrangements with a local hospital when patients require hospitalization. Backup and coverage must always be available during evenings, weekends, holidays, and vacations.

It also is important to realize that from a legal standpoint, the courts have a tendency to be less strict in evaluating outpatient suicide in the absence of clear signs that the suicide was foreseeable (because of the obvious increased difficulty in controlling the patient's behavior). Here, the courts' guiding principle has been that the psychologist correctly recognized the risk of suicide and appropriately balanced this risk with the benefits that might be obtained through the greater control available through hospitalization.

Psychologists who treat suicidal patients on an outpatient basis must seriously consider routine consultations with a senior clinician who has considerable expertise in dealing with this patient population. Even the experienced psychologist should understand that, in such emergent and high-risk situations, two perspectives are better than one.

When suicidal ideations emerge during the course of treatment, an important treatment option is to increase the frequency of visits to daily or even more frequent visits, for these visits by an outpatient at risk for suicide diminish the reliance of the clinician on long-term probabilistic determinations of risk. The judicious use of telephone check-in by the patient and the use of information and support from significant others in the patient's life (with appropriate acknowledgment of interpersonal matrix specifics and confidentiality considerations) can sharpen the ongoing clinical risk assessment and allow for greater fine-tuning of the outpatient treatment plan. Patients also may be referred for psychotropic medications, which need to be monitored very carefully.

Traditionally, if a psychologist elects outpatient care for the management of a suicidal patient, there are a number of rules that should be followed. For example, the psychologist should consider obtaining a promise that the patient will control his or her suicide impulses or will call the psychologist before attempting suicide. Here it is important to understand the drawbacks and limitations of this technique. The psychologist should ensure that any weapons or lethal means in a patient's possession are placed in the hands of a third party. There should be an increase in therapy sessions. The psychotherapist must contact others in the life of the patient (with a consent) and ask them to assist in support, if appropriate. Family, couples and group interventions should be thoroughly evaluated.

It is also essential that the psychologist understand the important differences between crisis management and intensive psychotherapy with suicidal patients and remain constantly aware of the particular strains inherent in working with this high-risk population. We recommend that the psychologist see no more than two high-risk patients in their practice activities at any given time.

Unfortunately, it is essential to note that managing an outpatient who is a high suicidal risk always exposes the psychologist to liability if the patient does commit suicide—regardless of how assiduously the clinician has followed recommended procedures. By following these procedures—that is, the judicious use of consultation, staying within one's areas of competency, and meticulous documentation—it is much more likely that the psychologist will prevail should any legal action be brought (or that the action will be dismissed or settled quickly). Most important, following these guidelines will improve the quality of overall clinical care and thus save lives.

However, such life-saving prevention efforts involve more than merely following the standards of one's profession. The psychologist who works with suicidal people must understand that a sensitive and deeply caring therapeutic relationship (in active collaboration, whenever possible, with the protective net of the patient's family and significant others) is still the best form of suicide prevention—and that the very nature of such a relationship will help to safeguard against a malpractice action.

Inpatient Management and Treatment of the Suicidal Patient

In previous chapters, we have detailed the difficulties and essential elements necessary to assess elevated risk, as well as the precautions and clinical management considerations needed to intervene in outpatient settings. This has included both a discussion of what patients are suitable for outpatient care, and where continued outpatient care is contraindicated. In the present chapter, we will examine the options available for the inpatient management of suicide.

Here, it is important to restate clearly that, although many of the following guidelines and court decisions have been applied more usually to psychiatrists (who historically have been the mental health professionals with the greatest responsibility for inpatient management), as psychologists in many states obtain hospital privileges and staff memberships that give them the independent authority to admit, discharge, and treat inpatients, the profession will be exposed to the same clinical and legal risks as psychiatrists. Furthermore, even psychologists who do not seek these privileges must understand the specifics, benefits, and limitations of this form of management and have ready access via a collaborative relationship to psychologists or psychiatrists who do have these privileges. Psychologists in a general practice setting are likely to confront, on a routine basis, issues concerning the decision to hospitalize, continuity of care, and discharge planning and aftercare of patients following their inpatient stay.

It is important to repeat that the most common legal action involving psychiatric care is the failure to reasonably protect patients from harming themselves. The courts have tended to impose much stricter standards on inpatient than on outpatient care, and most malpractice actions currently involve clinical activities related to inpatient care (negligent admission, treatment, supervision, discharge, etc.).

Initial Intake Evaluation Goals

A review of case law suggests that an acceptable standard of care requires an initial and periodic evaluation of suicide potential for *all* patients seen in clinical practice. Furthermore, the case law shows that reasonable care requires that a patient who is "either suspected or confirmed to be suicidal" must be the subject of certain affirmative precautions (Simon, 1988, p. 85). The psychologist who either fails to reasonably assess a patient's suicidality or fails to implement an appropriate management plan that is based on the detection of elevated risk is likely to be exposed to liability if the patient is harmed by a suicide attempt. Simon also noted that "the law tends to assume that suicide is preventable, in most circumstances, if it is foreseeable" (p. 85).

A survey of suicides in the Los Angeles area (Litman, 1982) found that 1% of patients being treated in general medical–surgical and/or psychiatric hospitals committed suicide during their hospital treatment; approximately one third of these suicides resulted in lawsuits against the hospitals. Psychiatric units were the targets of about half of these suits. Suicidal phenomena are ubiquitous in the hospital setting, and dangerousness to self is the most common reason for admission to a psychiatric unit (Friedman, 1989). Friedman pointed out that the frequency of completed suicide in patients with a history of psychiatric hospitalization is many times that of patients in the general population.

In addition to assessing and hospitalizing patients who present as a high risk of suicide at the initial inpatient admission evaluation, the clinician and staff will have to assess suicide risk in deciding issues of specific treatments, privileges, discharge, and so forth. The inpatient staff will also have to deal (sometimes continuously) with the presence of suicidal thoughts, gestures, and impulses within the context of the therapeutic milieu. (Although a complete review of hospital treatment of the suicidal patient is beyond the scope of this chapter, the reader is directed to the recent extended discussion and review of this topic by Friedman, 1989.)

Litman (1957) recommended that, in cases in which the psychotherapist believes that an outpatient is a high suicide risk even though he or she can function as an outpatient, it is the psychotherapist's responsibility to ensure that the risk is made known to all concerned parties (i.e., the family and significant others). The clinician must dispassionately provide the family and significant others with an informed consent as to the risks and benefits of both inpatient and outpatient treatment (Sadoff, 1990). As we have counseled before, psychologists may wish to consider routinely involving a senior colleague for a second opinion on this particular decision.

When reviewing the psychotherapists' positions on outpatient care of high-suicidal-risk patients, there is a general consensus (with one exception) that the outpatient environment exposes the patient to much greater danger, because the patient is not under 24-hour restrictive care. Thus, courts have typically seen a psychiatric decision to hospitalize as the more usual and customary one for a patient who is a high and imminent risk. Hospitals are usually deemed the environment where maximum protection can best be provided.

Klerman (1986) cautioned that clinicians should carefully examine their own policies and procedures for hospitalizing patients to ensure that their decisions are actual risk–benefit decisions that are focused on the optimal care and safety of the patient and not merely defensive reactions that are based on fear of litigation. (Such automatic hospitalizations of a patient at any level of risk can be a significant iatrogenic effect of treatment and can significantly impair the outpatient therapy.) Klerman further warned that, because of this threat of litigation, the psychotherapist may become so concerned about the question of hospitalization that important details in therapy are missed. Moreover, the inability of the psychotherapist to deal effectively with the anxiety of the situation may influence the course of the treatment and not necessarily in ways that are beneficial to the patient.

Therefore, any standard of care must take into account the ability of psychotherapists to make decisions effectively on the basis of their personal and professional tolerances and competencies and of their ability to render a decision that is based on the therapeutic relationship and the best interests of the patient. However, in identifying this decision point, it is critical to acknowledge that managing the suicidal outpatient is often stressful and threatening in any psychotherapeutic practice. Competent professionals must be able to deal constructively and proactively with their own appropriate apprehension and anxiety through affirmative policies and precautions that are of benefit to the patient (Simon, 1988). For despite the outpatient psychotherapist's best efforts, the patient may still require voluntary or involuntary hospitalization (Simon, 1988).

The Decision to Seek Inpatient Care

It is important to recognize that the clinician's decision to hospitalize the patient should not end at the point of admission (Schutz, 1982); rather, the referring psychologist should be aware of the type of facility that he or she is sending a patient to and should be certain of its capability to provide the minimum level of restraint necessary to ensure the safety of the patient. In addition to referring the patient to an appropriate hospital, Schutz noted that the therapist must provide adequate information to the institution to allow the professionals there to make a competent assessment of suicide risk for the patient. Moreover, if the psychologist is the primary inpatient attending clinician, the psychologist should provide his or her own supervision orders clearly to the staff of the hospital at the time of the request for admission. According to Schutz, if the therapist withholds key facts, provides inappropriate supervision orders, or, most important, fails to ensure that her or his orders were correctly carried out, the therapist may be liable.

A common legal "no win" situation for the attending psychotherapist is the choice of a low-security or a high-security ward. Schutz claimed that, if a patient feels threatened by high security, he or she may be put in a lower restriction ward. However, if the therapist feels that increased security would in no way inhibit therapeutic gains, then a high-security ward should be used. Unfortunately, the "no win" enters into the equation because both too little and too much inhibition can be grounds for liability. Too little security can expose the psychotherapist and hospital to a malpractice action, whereas too much inhibition may be considered an infringement of the patient's civil rights. In previous chapters, we have discussed the movement toward an open door as compared with a custodial model of inpatient care. We have also detailed in chapter 4 the criteria for triage (i.e., outpatient care vs. hospitalization, assessing dangerousness and imminence, etc.). The general standards of inpatient care, admissions procedures, the decision to choose voluntary or involuntary units, and general inpatient treatment interventions, as well as pass and discharge follow-up planning will now be discussed.

Principles of Inpatient Management

It will be helpful now to review the general principles of management.[1] Simon (1988, p. 84) stated that intervention in inpatient settings usually requires (a) screening evaluations, (b) case review by the clinical staff, (c) development of an appropriate inpatient and postdischarge treatment plan, and (d) implementation of that plan. He further noted that careful documentation of all assessments and management decisions (with careful and timely amendments that are responsive to any changes in the patient's clinical circumstances) are usually considered the foundation for clinically and legally sufficient inpatient care. It is important to remember that, although the courts have moved in recent years toward a more open-door policy, there is still a split in court decisions over the use of this technique. The psychologist should carefully assess both local and state standards in his or her area. (One's state psychological association, state department of mental health, and so forth are usually good resources for obtaining this information.)

---

[1]An in-depth discussion of specific inpatient management strategies and procedures is beyond the scope of the present chapter; however, the reader is directed to the works of Benensohn and Resnik (1973), Friedman (1989), Furrow (1980), Litman (1982), Schutz (1982), and Simon (1987, 1988) for specific risk management policies, standards of care, and safety precautions.

Because hospitals, inpatient attending staff, and other staff have been "put on notice" by the reason for the hospitalization (e.g., a suicide attempt, serious threats, impulses, etc.), affirmative precautions (e.g., constant one-on-one supervision or inpatient observation) must be extended to the suicidal patient. However, as Simon (1988) stated: There is "no such thing as a suicide-proof unit" (p. 95). The illusion of this possibility can be dangerous to patients and to staff. Litman (1982) also cautioned that hospitals should develop formal policies and standards for the inpatient management of suicide, that staff should be trained in these policies, and, most important, that quality assurance mechanisms should be in place to ensure that these policies are actually being applied.

It is critical to understand that the elements that make working with suicidal patients difficult are connected to reasons that many people enter the health care professions—to save lives, to cure people, and to master death (Jacobs, 1989b). As Jacobs pointed out, however, although death is an accepted occurrence in most medical specialities, it is a relatively uncommon event in mental health care. The fact that the possibility of death is ever present in the treatment of suicide can create a very difficult and discouraging situation in which to work. However, clinicians must not avoid situations in which patients seem beyond help or beyond hope. Jacobs (1989b) recalled that when he was a psychiatric resident at the Massachusetts Mental Health Center, the superintendent used to say "hospitals that don't have suicides are turning away sick people" (p. 331). As another psychiatric colleague put it, "the doctor who works with sick patients in an inpatient setting must realize and accept the very real possibility of patient suicide and subsequent litigation—no matter how good the care. This risk is part of the territory." In Simon's (1988) words: "Only a consistently heightened awareness that patients can and do commit suicide as inpatients is adaptive to reality" (p. 95).

In deciding which management strategies to use to assess dangerousness in inpatient care, Shneidman's (1981c, 1984, 1985, 1986a) model of psychotherapeutic assessment and intervention is of particular value in clarifying immediate treatment and management issues. That is, careful consideration must be given to levels of perturbation and levels of lethality as separate and equally important factors in the ongoing evaluation of suicidal risk. Shneidman noted that the level of perturbation, be it psychotic or situational, is easily measured in a patient with impaired coping skills and that lethality is assessed by the level of planning, intent, and availability of means. In addition, inpatient clinicians should carefully monitor levels of cognitive constriction, hopelessness, despair, and heightened inimicality. Recently, Shneidman proposed a model that adds Murray's concept of *press* to this equation. (For details, see Shneidman, 1986, 1989, as well as the section in chapter 3 of the present volume on the general formulation of clinical judgment—specifically, Figure 3.2—and Shneidman's perspective on psychological approaches to understanding suicide in chapter 1.)

The prevention of suicide in inpatient settings has both secondary and tertiary components. Tertiary prevention involves the reduction of morbidity and mortality in those patients who are actively suicidal. The decision to use inpatient care is often the first step in prevention. That is, the removal of the patient from toxic, stressful, and less-safe environments may be adequate measures to ensure the patient's safety. However, there are times when the hospital must use more restrictive measures such as seclusion rooms, physical restraint procedures, chemical restraints, and electroconvulsive therapy (ECT). Less restrictive measures include one-on-one nursing care, the confinement of the patient to common areas where each patient can be carefully observed, and the requirement that the patient wear bedclothes as a discouragement to leaving an open unit (Friedman, 1989).

Secondary prevention seeks to avoid the development of suicidal behavior in patients at high risk; that is, in the case of suicide, the entire inpatient ward constitutes a population at high risk for suicide. The milieu can play a key role in the prevention of suicidal thoughts and behaviors, and well-run inpatient units share certain factors, such as clarity in role definition, unambiguous lines of authority, and openness in communication. The acknowledgment of negative staff reactions to patients and actual countertransference phenomena is crucial to both the prevention and the treatment of the suicidal patient. These should be acknowledged in oneself and, to the extent appropriate, in one's colleagues (Friedman, 1989).

Ward and individual case consultation should routinely be considered with any difficult or high-risk management decision. The ward consultant's role is to make both specific recommendations and to facilitate the process of defining and sharing responsibility (Friedman, 1989). Often, openly negative reactions to the patient, countertransference phenomena, and so forth can be more easily identified with the consultant's support. Moreover, there is less of a tendency to act inappropriately on the basis of such feelings.

Standards of Inpatient Management

By now, the reader should clearly understand the extent to which the law demands that patients receive reasonable care in foreseeable situations (Litman, 1982). However, Litman remarked that the current standards for reasonable psychiatric care with regard to suicide prevention "are unclearly stated and inconsistently applied" (p. 213). He pointed out that courts have tended to hold institutions to standards of care that are equivalent to standards prevailing in the community. (In chapter 2, we detailed the legal perspective and the specific liabilities that are often alleged against the clinician, [e.g., failure to properly diagnose, failure to take adequate protective measures, early release of a patient, and failure to commit].)

The duty of a mental hospital can best be defined as follows: "the generally accepted standard of using reasonable care in the treatment of the patient. If, however, a hospital is on notice that a patient has suicidal tendencies, the hospital also assumes the duty of safeguarding the patient from self-inflicted injury or death" (Robertson, 1988, p. 193). The psychiatric hospital's duty of care is measured by the standards typically in use by such hospitals (or by general hospitals with psychiatric units) under similar circumstances. At the same time, as a rule, a general hospital is usually held to a lower standard of care than a psychiatric hospital. However, a general hospital that provides psychiatric care and has a psychiatric floor must adhere to the standards of psychiatric hospitals (Robertson, 1988).

This duty is proportionate to a patient's needs; the facility must provide the care that the patient's history and mental condition dictate as adequate. However, the hospital is not required to guard against or "take measures to avert what a reasonable person under the circumstances would not anticipate as likely to happen" (Robertson, 1988, p. 193). Just as in the liability of the individual clinician, the hospital's and staff's liability are based on foreseeability. Still, even when there is a private attending clinician in charge of the patient's care, the hospital and its staff must perform proper observations, make thorough evaluations, and take affirmative precautions if needed.

When litigation ensues, the two issues of foreseeability and causation are typically determined on the basis of the testimony of expert witnesses as to the performance of the attending clinician(s) and of the hospital and inpatient staff (Litman, 1982). Typically, the exercise of sound judgment provides a good defense for the hospital (Robertson, 1988). Hospitals usually are not found liable when a doctor has determined (in his or her opinion) that surveillance was adequate (see *Lichtenstein v. Montefiore Hospital and Medical Center*, 1977; *Sklarsh v. United States*, 1961).

As we have already stated, hospitals should formulate written administrative and professional policies concerning the care of suicidal patients. Moreover, these policies need to agree with the guidelines of the American Psychiatric Association and of the Joint Commission on Accreditation of Hospitals and be conventionalized for all hospitals (Litman, 1982).

Litman (1982) cited a number of cases in which the following problems were the cause of litigation:

- the patient was diagnosed as high risk, but an order for active suicide precautions was not followed correctly (verdict for the plaintiff of $125,000);
- the suicide attempt was not taken seriously and the physician did not take time to make a complete diagnostic evaluation (verdict for the plaintiff of $150,000);

- a small remote community hospital had a very small psychiatric unit and only a part-time psychiatrist available (the jury voted 9 to 3 not to impose liability, feeling that this unit should not be held to the high standards of an urban hospital); and
- the clinician had a daily working inpatient therapeutic relationship with the patient, pass and discharge risks were calculated and the treatment plan followed, but the doctor's risk–benefit decision turned out to be in error (i.e., while on a pass, the patient jumped to his death).

In this last case, Litman believed it was not negligent to have taken a calculated risk.

Robertson (1988, pp. 198–199) states that there are eight common allegations for a complaint for malpractice following a patient's suicide:

1. failure to predict;
2. failure to control, supervise, or restrain;
3. failure to take proper tests and evaluations of the patient to establish suicide intent;
4. failure to medicate properly;
5. failure to observe the patient continuously (24 hours) or on a frequent enough basis (e.g., every 15 minutes);
6. failure to take an adequate history;
7. inadequate supervision and failure to remove belt or other dangerous objects; and
8. failure to place patient in a secure room.

In summary, (as we have noted before but wish to emphasize here), for *both* inpatient and outpatient care of the suicidal patient, the courts frequently assess whether suicide risk was recognized and whether the clinician adequately balanced the risks of suicide against the benefits of greater control and supervision (Simon, 1988).

Voluntary and Involuntary Hospitalization

Even if it is apparent to the psychologist that a suicidal patient needs referral to an inpatient facility, constraints unique to a specific environment can make such placements quite difficult. For example, in Massachusetts, recent rulings by the Department of Mental Health require completion of extensive documentation every 3 hours when a patient is in seclusion or restraint. As a consequence, few private hospitals accept involuntary patients or patients who may require these precautions. In order to admit a patient into a state hospital in Massachusetts, the clinician must obtain approval of a screening team from the patient's mental health regional service area. Some local mental health teams will not give approval without first assessing the patient. The problem is that, although these requirements must be met, alternative placement is not guaranteed (Peterson & Bongar, 1990).

The following special considerations may need to be factored into any decision regarding voluntary hospitalization (Fremouw et al., 1990):

1. Are there voluntary units available that will accept a high-risk patient?

2. Does the psychologist feel that the voluntary setting will offer sufficient and appropriate forms of supervision? Does the voluntary unit also have access to a closed-door facility and 24-hour suicide watch precautions?

3. Does the patient have adequate finances (e.g., insurance) to afford this option?

4. Is the patient adequately motivated to seek a voluntary admission?

With regard to this last point, Fremouw and colleagues warned that patients may appear to acquiesce and to participate in a voluntary admission in order to avoid another course of action (e.g., to avoid being involuntarily hospitalized), only to leave against medical advice and fulfill their suicidal plans. In considering this possibility, Gutheil (1990) stressed the need to document and carefully assess both the patient's cooperation and competence to participate in such key management decisions. As we have previously noted, it is crucial in most cases to involve the family and significant others actively in an open and candid discussion of the risks and benefits of a voluntary as opposed to an involuntary milieu, in order to increase the levels of cooperation and to inform concerned parties about the actual abilities of both types of facilities to protect the patient from self-harm.

Initiating an involuntary hospitalization under a state's civil commitment guidelines may be one of the final options for the suicidal patient who meets the legislated criteria for mental illness and dangerousness (often interpreted as an imminent danger to the self). If a clinician is seeing a suicidal outpatient and makes a gross error in deciding not to seek commitment for the patient who meets these legal criteria, he or she may well be held liable (Simon, 1988).

There are a number of other considerations that need to be accounted for when contemplating hospitalization (Simon, 1987, 1988). For example, clinicians may need to consider the involvement of law enforcement agencies with a paranoid patient who has become overwhelmed by paranoid thoughts. These patients are not only at risk for suicide, but also for suicide–murder. If they feel that family members or other people in their immediate environment are part of conspiracies against them, paranoid patients may see suicide as the alternative (Allen, 1983).

Psychologists who see suicidal patients should be completely familiar with the mental health laws of their state and have immediate access to the resources for both voluntary and involuntary inpatient care. It is beyond the scope of this chapter to detail the commitment and hospitalization statutes and procedures for each state, the reader is advised to consult his or her state psychological association, state department of mental health, and psychology licensing boards. In addition, psychologists should contact the local screening teams of the department of mental health, the emergency rooms of local hospitals, and other similar crisis resources. Moreover, if it is possible, psychologists should establish proactive face-to-face collaborative relationships through visiting such facilities, emergency rooms, and screening teams and other pertinent care providers.

Civil commitment procedures vary from state to state. There are, however, general guidelines that

> have emerged from the Supreme Court rulings in *Addington v. Texas* (1979) and *O'Connor v. Donaldson* (1975). These cases established dangerousness as one criterion for civil commitment. Furthermore the Supreme Court in *Addington v. Texas* ruled that civil commitment requires a burden of proof as clear and convincing evidence (approximately 75% certainty) before a person can be committed to a psychiatric facility against his or her wishes. (Fremouw et al., 1990, pp. 94–95)

In the case of suicide, there are two general determinations that must be made in civil commitment. The first is whether the person suffers from a disorder or defect that is a diagnosable mental disorder. The definition of *mental disorder* or *mental defect* does not always mean *DSM-III-R* criteria and such definitions vary from state to state (Fremouw et al., 1990). The second determination is whether the person may present a "danger to self." In some jurisdictions, this requires "the identification of a recent overt act and not just an inferred state of dangerousness based on test data or speculation" (Fremouw et al., 1990, p. 95). For the specific local criteria for the determination of dangerousness, psychologists should carefully read their state's mental health and commitment laws.

It is important, however, to reiterate that criteria do vary from state to state. For example, in Texas, the clinician is required to obtain an evaluation by a second clinician and the signature of a justice of the peace to hold a patient against her or his will for 24 hours. Then, even if the patient is sent to a psychiatric screening facility for evaluation for possible hospitalization in the state hospital system, she or he may be released onto the street within 3 days. It is not uncommon to see such patients shortly return after a second suicide attempt (Peterson & Bongar, 1990). Such difficulties obviously create major problems for mental health professionals. Whether clinicians choose to admit it or not, the bureaucratic obstacles to inpatient hospitalization may color judgment about the possible risk of suicide (Peterson & Bongar, 1990).

Furthermore, the concept of the *least restrictive environment* has evolved in the case law, which in theory translates as the idea that "patients should be treated in a facility with the fewest restrictions of liberty possible" (*Wyatt v. Stickney*, 1971, cited in Fremouw et al., 1990, p. 95). Recently state courts have recognized the right of "involuntarily committed patients to refuse some types of psychiatric care if they are not in an emergency situation (*Rennie v. Klein* 1979 and *Rogers v. Okin 1979*)" (Fremouw et al., 1990, p. 95).

Other difficulties in hospitalization include the comorbidity of an alcohol or substance abuse diagnosis. Many substance abuse or alcohol treatment units will not accept suicidal patients, and few psychiatric units will accept patients with substance or alcohol abuse problems. These policies are sometimes supported by state laws or regulations (Peterson & Bongar, 1990). For example, a recent decision by the Massachusetts Department of Mental Health forbids admission of any patient with a primary substance abuse diagnosis to a state mental hospital. In addition to the issues surrounding involuntary admission, state hospital care, and dual diagnosis, the psychologist frequently finds that medical social services are unwilling or unable to help in finding appropriate after-care placement for these cases or to help in investigating the patient's financial status. Thus, the psychologist must not only deal with medical and psychiatric admission criteria for the units contacted, but must also review adequacy of funding for the patient.

The psychologist must understand the general differences in regular and emergency admissions (procedures that, again, vary from state to state). Usually, states require that the patient be represented by counsel in any regular civil commitment hearing and that the patient's due process rights be carefully respected (Fremouw et al., 1990). However, each state has its own procedures and criteria for the determination of an emergent involuntary admission for a limited time period (e.g., 72 hours, 5 days, etc.). The length of the involuntary stay is usually regulated by the imminence of the risk (based on a determination of dangerousness and the patient's mental disorder). (See Table 5.1.) Finally, it is crucial that all assessment and management decisions, case conferences, telephone contacts with screening teams, hospitals, the patient, and family be meticulously and contemporaneously documented.

Hospital Admission Issues

Friedman (1989) recommended that at an inpatient intake, the clinician carefully assess the following basic general factors and areas:

Table 5.1
*Typical Substantive Criteria for Civil Commitment**

Typical substantive criteria for civil commitment
• mentally ill
• dangerous to self or others
• unable to provide for basic needs

Miscellaneous criteria (in conjunction with one or more criteria above)
• gravely disabled (unable to care for self to the point of likely self-harm)
• refusing hospitalization
• patient is in need of hospitalization
• danger to property
• lacks capacity to make rational treatment decisions
• hospitalization represents least restrictive alternative

---

*Statutorily determined, varying from state to state
Note. From *Concise Guide to Clinical Psychiatry and the Law* (p. 79) by R. I. Simon, 1988, Washington, DC: American Psychiatric Press. Compiled and research by Steven B. Bisbing, Psy.D., J.D.–reprinted with permission.

1. demographic–historical data for elevated risk;
2. history of the present illness;
3. medical history;
4. psychiatric history;
5. family and personal history;
6. physical and laboratory examinations; and
7. mental status examination.

Once this assessment is completed, the clinician should proceed to clarify any diagnostic issues that are still in doubt and attempt to formulate a systematic psychological explanation for the behavior. For example, the clinician should specifically examine the role of psychiatric diagnosis, the interpersonal diagnosis, the role of aggression, the interpersonal matrix, impaired impulse control, loss and separation, and the meaning of death and suicide (Friedman, 1989). Additional criteria require assessment of imminence and dangerousness (as mentioned in previous sections). Here, the psychologist may wish to review the assessment recommendations and summary in chapter 3 and to note that several tools are available to help in the evaluation of ideation, intent, hopelessness, depression, and similar emotions and feelings, (for example, LSARS, Risk-Rescue, BDI, BHS, SIS, and SSI).

Suicide Attempt Versus Nonsuicidal Deliberate Self-Harm

After conducting the comprehensive assessment(s) of elevated risk and dangerousness already discussed, an important threshold issue is whether all patients with overdoses, self-inflicted wounds, and the like act out of suicidal intent. Although this uncertainty should not affect the routine components of the psychiatric evaluation, the intake and management issues raised by the non-suicidal self-harming patient may be quite distinctive. An additional question is whether the patient is to be admitted because of suicidal self-harm or another medical problem (only later expressing suicidal ideation or exhibiting suicidal behavior). These two situations call for very different interventions. The former will be the focus of this section. (For more information on the latter group [e.g., a reaction to illness or medical treatment], the reader is directed to Peterson et al., 1985.)

We have already noted that the most common method of suicide attempt is self-poisoning by pill ingestion (Jacobs, 1989a; Murphy, 1987). Most self-poisonings are impulsive acts in which patients ingest what is available—often more than one substance or drug at a time. There should be concern about the additive effects of barbiturates and benzodiazepines when they are ingested simultaneously (Jacobs, 1989a). Even more serious effects can occur when barbiturates are combined with alcohol: "In fact almost all cases of reported death from chloridazepoxide or diazepam occur because of the simultaneous ingestion of barbiturates, hypnotics and alcohol" (Jacobs, 1989a, p. 370). (For an extended discussion of suicide in emergency settings, see Bongar et al., 1990; Jacobs, 1989a.)

The precipitant for the pill-ingester is often interpersonal turmoil, and the attempt is frequently motivated at the reestablishment of a significant relationship (Jacobs, 1989a). If the patient does not require medical hospitalization, a crisis intervention approach should be taken to evaluate (a) levels of anger, (b) the other member(s) of the threatened relationship, and (c) any psychotherapeutic relationship (to see if the patient is experiencing dissatisfaction or problems in that area). Jacobs commented that the outpatient therapist should be contacted (and, if needed, the hospital intake clinician in the emergency room can offer to consult with the outpatient therapist regarding any reported difficulties). Finally, a careful investigation must be made of the relationship between intent and the patient's understanding of lethality. (Here the extent of the patient's knowledge of medication is very helpful.) "Even though the threat of life may have been relatively minimal, the patient may need hospitalization because of high intent. An important goal here is to engage the patient in treatment . . . this may, in fact be the major purpose for hospitalization" (Jacobs, 1989a, p. 370).

The second most common method for a suicide attempt is wrist cutting. Murphy (1987) estimated that this method figures in 10% of attempts (with 60% of attempters being females and 40% being males). As is the case for pill ingesters, it is crucial to investigate the relationship between intent and lethality in wrist cutters. Attempters with a more serious psychiatric illness (e.g., patients with psychoses, some borderline patients, intoxicated patients, etc.) should be hospitalized (Jacobs, 1989a). It must be kept in mind that all attempters have an increased risk for completed suicide and that every effort should be made to involve them in treatment.

However, some patients appear to engage in low-lethality self-mutilation or self-harming acts to ward off feelings of numbness or unreality. These are usually either dissociative states or represent an underlying psychotic process. Such acts have been classified recently either as deliberate self-harm (Pattison & Kahan, 1983) or as simple self-mutilation (Dingman & McGlashan, 1988). Superficial wrist cutting, other self-inflicted wounds, and some minimal overdoses known by the patient to have no likelihood of lethality fall into this category. Often, such patients deny suicidal intent and, on the basis of available data from reliable sources such as family and friends, do not have any of the behaviors that typify higher risk individuals. Even among patients with histories of suicidal behavior, the presence of this lesser degree of injury may decrease suicidal risk (Dingman & McGlashan, 1988). Management of these patients is quite different from that of suicidal patients in the high- and moderate-risk categories (Bongar et al., 1990; Peterson & Bongar, 1990).

To demonstrate the common occurrence of this issue in emergency room settings, it is useful to cite the details of a recent study on chronic visitors to the psychiatric emergency room who present with such deliberate self-harming behaviors. A retrospective chart review examined the records of all patients ($N = 1,580$) seen in the emergency mental health service at a major teaching hospital during a 1-year period. Twenty-four chronically "suicidal" patients were identified (the criteria for selection being that the patient had four or more visits to the psychiatric emergency room in the index year for the primary presenting problem of suicide). The diagnostic and demographic characteristics of these patients were compared with a matched "nonsuicidal" control group of chronic emergency room visitors. Nineteen out of the 24 chronically suicidal patients had a history of deliberate self-harm, whereas there was no mention of self-mutilation or suicidal behavior in the charts of the control group. These 24 suicidal patients (19 of them deliberate self-harmers), who made up a little over 1% of the patients seen that year in the psychiatric emergency service, accounted for over 12% of all psychiatric emergency room visits in the index year. Diagnostically, although both groups of patients had considerable *DSM-III-R* Axis I pathology, the chronically suicidal patients more often carried an Axis II diagnosis of borderline personality disorder. At the 36-month follow-up, none of the 24 chronically suicidal patients (or the 21 controls) had committed suicide or died by another cause (Bongar et al., 1990).

Accurate differential diagnosis of specific personality pathology is essential in the treatment of the chronically suicidal patient. In their extensive review of personality disorders and suicide, Goldsmith et al., (1990) found that it was critically important to differentiate between borderline personality disorders and antisocial personality disorders, because suicidality in these two diagnostic populations presents both a challenge to effective clinical care and, more important, involves differential assessment and treatment approaches to patient suicidality.

Patients admitted for self-harm can be further subdivided into three types on the basis of acknowledged intent: (a) patients who clearly state that their intent was suicidal, (b) patients who are noncommittal, and (c) patients who frankly deny any suicidal intent. An essential point here is the frequent incongruence between the stated intent of some patients after an attempt and their potential for future lethality (Peterson & Bongar, 1990).

Among patients denying any suicidal intent, there are times that certain fears prevent an honest discussion. First, there is the concern that acknowledgment of suicidal intent will void the patient's insurance coverage. Although the psychologist cannot guarantee that this will not occur, a discussion with medical or surgical consultants on the importance (in certain circumstances) of not commenting on intent in the medical discharge summary may help the patient. Second, the patient may be afraid that if he or she acknowledges suicidal intent, he or she will be "put away" by the psychologist. It is useful to explain to patients that the absence, rather than the presence, of clear information on this point may obligate the psychologist to recommend inpatient treatment. Third, more accurate information may allow the patient and psychologist to consider less restrictive alternatives. This approach may help to defuse patient resistance. Furthermore, there is always the case of the patient who refuses to speak to the psychologist. (Often, where there is evidence of suicidality and the patient is mute, the psychologist may have no alternative but an involuntary admission.) Again, communicating the consequences of an information gap may facilitate verbalization by more resistant patients (Peterson & Bongar, 1990).

In closing this section, it is useful to repeat Motto's (1979a) dictum that the clearest indication for admission is the clinician's judgment that the patient is not likely to survive as an outpatient. Although the option of day treatment exists, Motto remarked that he had not found this option satisfactory for patients at risk. He also added that such admission decisions (i.e., regarding chances of survival as an outpatient), even when aided by specific criteria, are still largely judgments based on intuition.

Where there is any indication of a wish to die—no matter how small—we agree with Murphy (1987), who cited the policy of the Royal Edinburgh Hospital and recommended that there be a hospital admission for every suicide attempter, however slight the medical seriousness of the act. This hospitalization gives the clinician and hospital time for a more extended evaluation to ensure stability, to offer maximum opportunity for continued evaluation of intent and impulses, and, finally, to allow the clinician and hospital a period of time to assess, coordinate, and plan treatment in collaboration with the interpersonal support matrix. Murphy cautioned that manipulative and chronically suicidal patients should not be encouraged to experience the admission as positively reinforcing (e.g., by limiting privileges, telephone calls, television, etc.). He also recommended a family conference as soon as possible and suggested family treatment and conflict resolution. He noted that, in the final analysis, suicide attempters do have a higher risk for completed suicide.

Inpatient Treatment and Milieu Considerations

Inpatient treatment requires an intense multidisciplinary and multimodal approach (Friedman, 1989), involving somatic, cognitive-behavioral, psychodynamic, group and family therapies, and so forth, in addition to formal involvement of the interpersonal matrix and an ongoing assessment of the level of psychosocial supports. All of these are part of a well-integrated and unified treatment plan (Friedman, 1989; Peterson & Bongar, 1989).[2]

Treatment for both inpatients and outpatients in an acute overwhelming suicidal state usually takes the form of massive support on the patient's own terms. Psychological interpretation at such vulnerable moments can too easily generate a feeling of lethal distance (Motto, 1979a). Motto, however, cautioned that this should not preclude "the use of dynamic understandings, but that such interpretation should be at a level and form that reflects acceptance, caring, and concern rather than intellectual explanation" (p. 5). He also stated that the therapist should be in close contact with the patient's psychosocial support system—family, close friends, priest–minister–rabbi, employer, and other important psychosocial resources—and should be available to provide support to the interpersonal matrix and advise them in acute situations. The permission to respond to inquiries from friends and relatives, and the dynamics involved, should be clarified as early in treatment as possible. Shneidman (1981c) cautions on the need for an early assessment of the position of the support system vis-à-vis being supportive or unsupportive of life-forces and the patient's survival.

Hospitalization on a closed psychiatric unit, coupled with vigorous somatic and psychotherapeutic treatment, remains the wisest counsel when the clinician is dealing with an acutely suicidal patient (Murphy, 1988). Litman (1988) warned that for chronically suicidal patients, the goal of treatment is often the postponement of death rather than a cure.

---

[2]For additional information on principles of specific treatments and standards of care, the reader is directed to the following sources: Bachrach (1983); Barraclough et al. (1974); Beck (1967, 1986); Beck, Rush, Shaw, and Emery (1975); Beck and Steer (1989); Beck et al. (1985); Farberow (1981); Fawcett et al. (1987); Friedman (1989); Gutheil and Appelbaum (1982); Klerman (1990); Litman (1982, 1988, 1989); Mann and Stanley (1988b); Maris (1986); Motto (1975, 1989); Murphy (1987, 1988b); Perlin and Schmidt (1976); Perr (1960, 1965, 1985a, 1985b, 1988); Peterson and Bongar (1989, 1990); Robertson (1988); Robins (1985); Roy (1986); Shaffer (1974); Shneidman (1981c, 1984, 1989); Simon (1987, 1988); Slaby et al. (1986); Smith (1986); Stanley and Mann (1988); Stone (1990); and Weishaar and Beck (1990).

Using as our foundation the extensive review by Friedman (1989) on inpatient care, the various specific modalities available for inpatient care and the effects of the milieu will be discussed. It should be stressed that for medicolegal purposes, all treatment decisions, changes, and impasses must be meticulously documented. (We will discuss the issue of documentation further in chapter 6.)

Somatic Treatments

Biological treatment is usually directed toward any underlying *DSM-III-R* diagnosis (e.g., depression, anxiety, psychosis). The most common underlying diagnoses for which biological inpatient treatments are routinely used are unipolar and bipolar affective disorder, schizophrenia, and organic brain disorder (including dependencies, intoxications, medical illnesses, and any other organic condition that may reduce the patient's abilities to control his or her impulses; Friedman, 1989). For severely depressed patients, antidepressant pharmacotherapy (with psychotherapy) and electroconvulsive therapy are two main treatment options (Murphy, 1988). Murphy also pointed out that, if substance or alcohol abuse is present, a detoxification program is indicated. Moreover, for the depressed schizophrenic patient, antidepressant medication may be added to the antipsychotic regimen. (For additional information on principles of somatic management and treatment, and specific recommendations for somatic interventions with the adult suicidal patient, the reader is directed to the work of Goldblatt & Schatzberg; 1990.)

Electroconvulsive Therapy (ECT)

Other factors favoring hospitalization are the necessity of intense diagnostic evaluation, careful interventions with medication and psychotherapy under controlled conditions, special treatments such as electroconvulsive therapy (ECT), or some combination of these. It has been estimated that suicide prevention efforts would be well served by a judicious increase in the use of ECT in the severest depressions (Murphy, 1988) and by a concerted effort to rule out any underlying physical disorders in persons with treatment-resistant emotional disorders with a suicidal component (Motto, 1986).

However, there must be a clear diagnostic picture—for example, atypicality of the depressive diagnostic picture may reduce the response rate (Murphy, 1988). Here, it is important to note that the use of ECT has been both clinically and politically controversial. (For a measured view of this method of therapy and suicide, the reader is directed to the work of Tanney, 1986.)

Inpatient Psychotherapy

In the previous chapter, we described several examples of psychotherapeutic techniques for working with highly suicidal patients on an outpatient basis.

149

Friedman (1989) noted that inpatient psychotherapy, as in the case of outpatient treatment, is based on the special characteristics of both patients and therapists. However, there are some general differences in the models of inpatient psychotherapy. (For more details, the reader is directed to Friedman, 1989.) For example, Friedman's general model for inpatient psychotherapy involves four concepts: focal therapy, the deficit model, the conflict model, and transference/countertransference.

Focal therapy

Inpatient therapy is carried out under several restraints. For example, it is time-limited for the most part. Not uncommonly, the patient will not be able to carry on with the inpatient therapist after discharge. Because of this limitation, it is of crucial importance that therapists and administrators be clear in every case about the goals and limitations of treatment. The initial sessions should be used to develop a sense of rapport and to develop a detailed formulation on the basis of history and diagnosis. These goals need to be clarified with the patient and family or significant others at the onset. A family conference at the start of treatment is often extremely helpful in this regard.

The usual focal points (Friedman, 1989) in the inpatient psychotherapy of the suicidal patient include:

- any suicide attempt (and the surrounding circumstances and fantasies);
- an evaluation of past and present loss experiences that may be central elements in any depressed–depairing–hopeless affect and suicidal ideation or impulses; and
- an examination of any negative therapeutic reactions, countertransference, and transference, as well as specifics of impasses in the outpatient treatment.

Friedman found that the establishment of a discharge date at the start of treatment can serve as a powerful tool to help accelerate the therapeutic movement (although it should be noted that the effect of this time limit should be discussed carefully and thoroughly with patient and family).

The deficit model

There are two essential components in the conceptualization of inpatient psychotherapy: the experiential and the psychodynamic (Friedman, 1989). These categories, of course, could be expanded almost infinitely to include many varieties of treatment. Some examples of salient intervention theorists include Beck, Rush, Shaw, and Emery, 1979, 1985; Farberow, 1981; Fawcett et al., 1987; Klerman et al., 1984; Litman, 1982, 1989; Maltsberger, 1986; Motto, 1979a, 1989; Shneidman, 1981c, 1984, 1986a, 1986b, 1989; and Smith, 1986.

Friedman's deficit conceptualization implies that the experiential aspect of therapy addresses structural and developmental deficits (e.g., ego weaknesses, failures of empathy and pathological object relations; see especially, the work of Buie & Maltsberger, 1989). Here, the approach is to create therapeutic circumstances that are more conducive to "adaptive internalization and structuralization" (Friedman, 1989, p. 397). Specific techniques include nonjudgmental, empathic listening; encouragement; tolerance of the expression of painful affects; a flexible response to the patient's needs; and consistent limit-setting.

Conflict model

Friedman (1989) noted that the analytic aspect of therapy focuses on the identification of conflicts and on fostering insight. For suicidal patients, such a model requires listening for fantasies associated with suicidal behavior (e.g., fantasies of revenge, rescue, wishes for dependency—and their accompanying fears of loss of self, abandonment, etc.). Specific techniques include the use of confrontation, clarification, and interpretation.

Transference and countertransference

In a dynamic and experiential approach, many of the patient's fantasies, wishes, fears, and so on appear in the transference and elicit countertransference responses by attending clinicians and ward staff (Friedman, 1989). Such countertransference feelings can include anger, guilt, or helplessness and may mirror the patient's own experiences (cf. Jacobs, 1989b). The recognition of these feelings provides important treatment information and "prevents defensive reactions on the therapist's part such as denial or indifference" (Friedman, 1989, p. 398). Others who specifically deal with this issue include Buie and Maltsberger (1989), Maltsberger (1986), and Smith (1986).

Group and family treatment, and social services

In 1989, Friedman wrote that an important risk factor is the absence of the interpersonal matrix and of other vocational and financial resources. He also noted that social services must be involved at the beginning of treatment, through the discharge planning stage, and in securing aftercare. Group treatment can be of particular benefit to patients with limited interpersonal support matrices (Motto, 1979a). In addition, family therapy can be a crucial component both in enlisting the family's support and in working through and understanding complex and toxic family structures, systems, and dynamics. (For details on the complexities of family and group approaches, see Richman & Eyman, in press; Richman, 1986.)

Friedman stated that a psychoeducational emphasis is one possible approach that can help to make the family an ally rather than a scapegoat (e.g., by presenting the patient's illness as something to be worked on collaboratively by patient, family, and staff). Information on family supports (or lack thereof) is a key element throughout inpatient treatment and in discharge planning. The involvement of the family and significant others is also an essential element in overall risk management (as we discuss in detail in chapter 6).

The Ward Milieu

In reviewing the records of patients who have successfully committed suicide, one invariably finds ample evidence and frequent notations by the inpatient staff of seclusive behavior, lack of involvement in the activities of the ward, and the avoidance of meaningful or genuine interpersonal relationships with staff and other patients (Simon, 1988). Assessing this milieu in evaluating and treating suicidal patients is essential. Suicidal behavior can occur in rashes or epidemics on inpatient units. Specifically, three circumstances increase the risk of suicidal behavior, namely, change, conflict, and collusion:

1. All inpatient units experience periods of *change*: staff turnover, trainees leaving, patients leaving and arriving, and so forth.

2. Circumstances generate staff *conflict*; that is, conflict arises superficially with a clinical disagreement over management decisions such as privileges, medications, transfer, and discharge. Often reflecting and underlying these specific disagreements are consciously philosophical differences between staff members, as well as deep power struggles and personality conflicts.

3. Occasionally, inpatient units experience circumstances of *collusion*, on both a conscious and unconscious level (e.g., indirect communication during staff meetings). Conscious collusion could include patients' forming a "suicide pact" and the conspiracy of silence that often ensues among other patients.

In conclusion, an evaluation and monitoring of the milieu for suicidal thoughts and behavior is vital for high-level treatment to occur (Friedman, 1989).

Unit Precautions and Privileges

Unit Precautions

Benensohn and Resnik (1973) presented guidelines for preventing suicides from occurring in a hospital ward. These psychotherapists took the most frequent methods of inpatient suicide (hanging, jumping, cutting, and lethal injection) and developed the following recommendations:

1. Count silverware and all other sharp objects before and after use by the patients.

2. Do not allow patients to spend much time alone in their rooms and abolish private rooms altogether.

3. Jump and hang-proof the bathrooms by installing breakaway shower rods and recessed shower nozzles and by removing exposed pipes and locating ventilation ducts at floor level.

4. Keep electrical cords to a minimum length.

5. Install windows of unbreakable glass with either tamper-proof screens or partitions too small to pass through. Keep all windows locked.

6. Keep all storage and utility rooms and adjacent stairwells, offices, and kitchens in sight. Security precautions need to be impressed on all nonclinical staff, including housekeepers and maintenance personnel.

7. Have visitors clear all gifts with staff, and search patients (for drugs, sharp objects, cords, and other such items) after their return from passes. Being able to receive a pass may signify that the patient is getting better and now has enough energy to carry out a suicide plan that the inertia of depression had previously made impossible.

Although these suggestions will not totally eradicate hospital suicide, they can reduce hospital liability, because "reasonable" care will have been provided by the hospital. (For additional information on ward administrative policy regarding suicide, see Doyle, 1990.)

Privileges, Passes, and Discharges

A crucial area for monitoring is the area of privileges. These should be assigned and monitored carefully and on a routine basis (Friedman, 1989). One third to one half of all hospital suicides occur on pass (Friedman, 1989). Rules and privileges should be seen as avenues of communication for both patient and staff. Friedman noted that one cannot prevent all suicides and that calculated risks must be made, but, by seeing privileges and passes as communications, a better effort at assessment and treatment is assured. Often the extension of privileges should proceed in a stepwise fashion (e.g., moving from limited freedoms to extended freedoms). For an excellent discussion and specific guidelines for pass and discharge considerations, the reader should consult Simon (1987, 1988) and see Table 5.2.

Typically, making the decision to allow a patient out on pass or to be discharged home is even more difficult than making the decision to hospitalize a suicidal patient. (For a detailed discussion of the specifics of pass procedures

Table 5.2
Suicidal Patients: Pass and Discharge Considerations

Benefits of release versus risk: analysis
• determined by direct evaluation
• consultation with all appropriate staff
• review of patient's current and past course of hospitalization

Evidence of posthospitalization self-care ability
• Can patient function without significant affective and cognitive impairment?

Capable and accessible to obtaining assistance
• Is patient physically and emotionally able to employ others for support?

Remission of illness
• What remains unchanged and can be dealt with as an outpatient?

Control by medication
• Can side effects be tolerated/managed outside hospital and will patient comply with treatment?

Support system
• Does family or significant others exist and are they stabilizing or destabilizing?

Timing of proposed release
• Does staff adequately know the patient?
• Has the patient adequately been acclimated to the therapeutic milieu, with sufficient time to develop meaningful relationships?
• Has sufficient time elapsed to evaluate the effectiveness of treatment (e.g., medication)?

Therapeutic alliance
• Will the patient continue to work with the psychiatrist?

Note. From *Concise Guide to Clinical Psychiatry and the Law* (p. 88) by R. I. Simon, 1988, Washington, DC: American Psychiatric Press. Copyright 1988 by American Psychiatric Press. Reprinted by permission.

and discharge considerations, see Simon, 1987.) Because a large percentage of patient suicides occur within 3 months of hospital discharge, posthospitalization follow-up by the clinician is a critical necessity (Simon, 1988). There are two circumstances that call for a conservative management attitude (Friedman, 1989). First, there is the situation of the initial evaluation of admission or an acute clinical change in the course of inpatient admission. Friedman recommended that, until a patient is thoroughly assessed, the clinician and institution exercise extreme vigilance and "err on the side of caution" (p. 393). The second set of circumstances that require a conservative attitude involves situations in which the patient is at high risk for suicide and in which there is a treatment that can be provided (e.g., medication, special psychotherapeutic interventions, ECT) that might alter the risk in a significant manner. (Here there must be clear and acute circumstances that provide both legal and clinical justification for such treatments.) A number of authorities (Friedman, 1989; Gutheil & Appelbaum, 1982;

Shneidman, 1981c; Simon, 1987, 1988) have recommended automatic consultation in both of these situations. (Furthermore, legal, regulatory, or hospital treatment guidelines may automatically require second or third opinions or the convening of a panel of clinicians to make certain extremely difficult management, treatment, and discharge decisions; Friedman, 1989.)

In all of the discharging activities, there should be a clear discussion of confidentiality, including the specific guidelines for each case and general guidelines for the unit. (We will discuss this issue in detail in chapter 6.) This kind of discussion offers an excellent opportunity for the psychologist to review with the patient the ethical considerations in life-threatening situations, as well as for clinicians to see that such legal and ethical concerns must always be considered on a case-by-case basis (Bongar et al., 1989). Simon (1988) has noted that generally the competent patient's request for confidentiality must be honored unless the patient is a clear danger to self or others. Shneidman (1984, 1986) argued strongly that the main goal of assessment and treatment is to defuse the potentially lethal situation and that confidentiality with suicidal patients is secondary to ensuring their safety. Therefore, in the case of suicide, the life-threatening nature of the situation overrides the patient's right to confidentiality, until the crisis is past.

Follow-Up Care

Follow-up care after successful inpatient treatment of an acute episode is critical, because the period immediately following discharge is a time of greatly elevated risk for the suicidal patient (Friedman, 1989). In one diagnostically heterogeneous sample of 94 patients, 65% of the suicides occurred within 3 months of discharge (Roy, 1986). Simon (1988) recommended that:

1. Clinicians carefully assess the patient's ability to participate competently in discharge planning and the need to involve the interpersonal support system in the follow-up plan at the earliest possible time.

2. Inpatient and outpatient clinicians monitor the implementation of the follow-up plan and structure the follow-up so as to encourage compliance (e.g., scheduling initial appointments while the patient is still in the hospital, using reminder letters or telephone calls, recruiting specific family or friends to ensure that the patient comes to the follow-up appointments and takes medications).

3. Inpatient clinicians should clearly communicate to the patient, family, and significant others the general limitations on the powers of inpatient clinicians and the limits of their power once discharge is effected.

Malpractice Actions Involving
Inpatient Management

The following court decisions on inpatient management illustrate repeatedly the twin criteria of foreseeability and causation. Psychotherapists and hospitals should diligently assess the suicidal potential of their patients and carefully implement affirmative treatments. The risk of suicide should be noted regularly in the management plan and be reevaluated at each significant juncture in treatment and whenever important management decisions are to be made (Vande-Creek & Knapp, 1983). In addition, a new evaluation should be made whenever family, staff, and significant others provide new information (see Farberow, 1981, for additional information on this point).

Failure to Use Good Judgment and to Evaluate

In *Kardas v. State* (1965), the wife of a patient who committed suicide filed a suit against the hospital and the patient's physician alleging failure to use good judgment. The physician had determined that the patient's condition did not present a risk of suicide. The instructions of the institute's physicians were that the patient be placed under "close observation." The patient was not permitted to leave the ward except on "accompanied walks," because he was excited at some times and depressed at others. Liability was not found and the court stated that the state, having through its physicians made a diagnosis of no suicidal tendency, was under no duty to guard against suicide, and, having been under no duty, could not be held liable in negligence for the patient's death. The state, that is, cannot be held liable for what, in retrospect, proved to be an error in judgment by the physician.

Failure to Evaluate and Failure to Observe

In *Smith v. United States* (1977), the widow and children of the patient brought suit against the Veterans Administration psychiatric hospital and its physicians after the patient was allowed to leave a locked ward without being evaluated and then threw himself in front of a train. The complaint alleged that there was both failure to evaluate and a failure to observe. The court found liability and stated that prior to releasing the patient from the locked ward, the accepted standard of care required that the patient be evaluated by a psychiatrist to determine whether he was sufficiently free from impulsive inclinations. It was also recognized that a proper evaluation by a psychiatrist of the patient on the day he was transferred, the day on which he committed suicide, would have detected the impulsive inclinations that caused the patient to commit suicide. He would not then have been granted the privileges that allowed him to kill himself. The family also alleged that physicians were negligent in failing to note that the patient did not return to the hospital at 4:30 p.m., when sign-out privileges ended. If he had been missed at that time and a search had been initiated, he might have been found and returned to the locked ward before his death at 5 p.m.

Negligent Supervision and Failure to Adequately Observe

In *Torres v. State* (1975), the administrator of the patient's estate brought suit against a state hospital and alleged negligent supervision when the patient jumped off a bridge. The court ruled that the suicide was not caused by negligent supervision received at the hospital. The patient was placed in an open ward and granted an honor card that allowed him to leave the ward during daylight hours; nothing in the record indicated that the treatment he received was other than medically sound and proper. The patient never exhibited violent or suicidal tendencies, and the possibility of his committing suicide as a result of his increased freedom was not a foreseeable risk for which the state could be held liable.

Failure to Take Adequate Precautions

In *Dimitrijevic v. Chicago Wesley Memorial Hospital* (1968), the administrator of the patient's estate brought suit against a private hospital after a patient jumped from an 11th floor window. The complainant alleged that the hospital was negligent in having the patient next to an unguarded window and not transferring him to a section of the hospital with locked doors and windows in accordance with a supervising physician's order. The court did not find liability and stated that, unless the attending physician recommended special precautions against the suicide, the hospital was under no duty to take such precautions. The court noted that the evidence was conclusive that the supervising physician, as well as a psychiatric resident, neither felt such instructions to be necessary nor gave them. The resident prescribed that the patient remain ambulatory, and the supervising physician was consulted by the hospital's administrator over the need for security precautions. Furthermore, the hospital contacted the supervising physician, who stated that the transfer was not an emergency and could be delayed until there was regular space available. The court concluded that the hospital had a right to rely on the instructions of the doctors.

In *Herold v. State* (1962), the husband of a woman who killed herself brought suit against a state hospital and the attendants when the patient was given a cloth and told to do some dusting. Approximately 10 minutes later, she was found hanging by the dust cloth in the nurses' bathroom. The court found liability and reversed a judgment in favor of the state dismissing a claim for a patient's wrongful death. The court entered judgment in favor of the patient's husband for her wrongful death by suicide. Following the patient's transfer, on the morning of the suicide, there were at least 31 patients in the open ward, with only two attendants present.

In *Zilka v. State* (1967), the administrator of the patient's estate brought suit after the patient died by a self-administered dose of rat poison. The plaintiff alleged that there was a failure to observe and no record of any medical determination that the patient was fit for less restricted freedom than she had in the security ward. The court did not find liability and concluded that a medical determination that the patient was fit for the more unrestricted freedom was made when she was allowed to go home for a week approximately 2 months prior to her death. It also stated that there was no evidence of any suicidal inclinations from that time to the day she died. At any time during the 9-year period when the patient was in and out of the hospital, the opportunity for her to take her life was always present. The court added that the fact that she did so while in the custody of the state hospital was one of those risks that society must be willing to accept if it is to hold out any hope for the mentally ill.

Negligent Assignment of Privileges

In *Schwartz v. United States* (1964), the administrator of the patient's estate brought suit against a government mental hospital after the patient hanged herself from a tree. The course of treatment for the patient included instituting a program of intensive individual psychotherapy that accorded the patient freedom of the grounds and allowed her personal articles of clothing while she was unaccompanied on the grounds of the hospital. The court concluded that the plaintiff had been unable to show that these medical judgments, all of which were rendered by qualified staff psychiatrists in the performance of their duties at the hospital, were not rendered with the degree of skill and learning ordinarily possessed and exercised by psychiatrists in the locality at that time. It was noted that the patient never manifested a suicidal attempt or gesture while at the hospital. In addition, the plaintiff's witness stated that, in his opinion, granting the patient ''grounds'' privileges constituted good medical practice.

Failure to Provide Adequate Supervision

In *Wilson v. State* (1961), the husband of a patient sued a state hospital when the patient, who had attempted suicide in the past, jumped to her death using an unlocked laundry chute. The husband alleged that the failure to lock a laundry chute door (which was a violation of the rules of the hospital), resulted in the patient's jumping through the chute and killing herself and was the proximate cause of her death. The court found liability and noted that on the day of the occurrence, the attendant had unlocked the door to permit another patient to throw some bags of laundry down the chute. Some difficulty between other patients in the room distracted the attention of the attendant, and she closed the door without locking it and went to quiet the disturbance. The attendant did not recall leaving the chute unlocked until some 2.5 hours later when she was informed that the patient was found at the bottom of the chute.

As all of these cases show, institutions can benefit from self-knowledge. Hospitals should ask the following question and come to the following conclusion: "Do we treat persons at special risk for suicide? If yes, then there must be a security area and policies for special management of suicidal persons" (Litman, 1982, p. 220). Such policies are best determined by a hospital suicide prevention committee that represents the staff and administration (Litman, 1982). Such a committee can establish written guidelines after a survey of the hospital security areas and after talking with staff and patients. It is critical that these policies be incorporated routinely into the training and supervision of all staff and attendings. Litman also stated that a reasonable performance requires that the "patient be evaluated for suicide risk, that a treatment plan be formulated, and that the staff follow the treatment plan according to the hospital's policies" (p. 220).

Summary

As psychologists in many states obtain hospital privileges and staff memberships that allow them the independent authority to admit, to discharge, and to treat inpatients, psychologists will be exposed to the same clinical and legal risks as their colleagues in psychiatry. Furthermore, even practicing psychologists who do not seek these privileges must understand the specifics, benefits, and limitations of inpatient management and have ready access via a collaborative relationship with a psychologist or psychiatrist colleague who does have these privileges. Routinely, psychologists in general practice settings confront the issues of decision to hospitalize, continuity of care, and the discharge planning and aftercare following a patient's inpatient stay.

One survey of suicides in the Los Angeles area found that 1% of patients who were being treated in general medical–surgical or psychiatric hospitals committed suicide while in the hospital (Litman, 1982). (Approximately one third of these suicides resulted in lawsuits against the hospitals.) A review of case law suggests that an acceptable standard of care requires an initial and periodic evaluation of suicide potential for *all* patients seen in clinical practice. Furthermore, well-known authorities and the case law tell us that demonstrating that reasonable care was taken requires that patients suspected or confirmed to be suicidal be the subject of certain affirmative precautions. The courts will often assume that suicide is preventable in most reasonable circumstances if it is foreseeable.

However, according to Litman (1982) and Perr (1988), the standards for reasonable psychiatric care (with regard to suicide prevention) are often perceived by clinicians and hospitals as unclearly stated and inconsistently applied. Generally, the courts have tended to hold institutions to standards of care that are equivalent to standards prevailing in the community. The psychiatric hospital's duty of care is measured by the standards used by psychiatric hospitals (or general hospitals with psychiatric units).

This duty is proportionate to a patient's needs (which means providing the adequate care that the patient's history and mental condition dictate). When litigation ensues, the two issues of foreseeability and causation are typically determined on the basis of the testimony of expert witnesses' opinions as to the performance of the attending clinician(s), hospital, and inpatient staff. The exercise of sound judgment provides a good defense for the hospital, and hospitals are usually not found liable when a clinician in charge of the patient's care has determined (in his or her opinion) that surveillance was adequate.

Psychologists need to know the special clinical and legal requirements when considering a voluntary or involuntary hospitalization (e.g., their state laws) and the appropriate questions to ask when making such a recommendation. Psychologists specifically need to understand the local criteria for a commitment and the difference between regular and emergency admissions (e.g., a mental disorder and dangerousness to self). In addition, the patient's cooperation and competence to participate in key management decisions must be documented and assessed. The clearest indication for admission is the clinician's judgment that the patient is not likely to survive as an outpatient.

It is also crucial in most cases to involve the family and significant others actively in an open and candid discussion of the risks and benefits of a voluntary versus involuntary milieu, the specifics of treatment, and discharge and follow-up planning. This is important both to increase the levels of cooperation and to depict realistically the actual abilities of inpatient facilities to treat the patient and to protect the patient from self-harm.

High-quality inpatient care necessitates an intense multidisciplinary and multimodal approach. The inpatient treatment of the suicidal patient may include somatic, cognitive-behavioral, psychodynamic, group, and family therapies, and so on, as well as formal involvement of the interpersonal matrix and an ongoing assessment of the level of psychosocial supports. All of which are a part of a well-integrated and unified treatment and management plan.

It is crucial that all assessment, treatment and management decisions, case conferences, telephone contacts with screening teams, hospitals, the patient, and family, and all other activities and interactions be meticulously and contemporaneously documented. A risk–benefit note should be written whenever any calculated risk is part of the management plan. Eight common allegations for a complaint for malpractice following a patient's suicide include: failure to predict; failure to control, supervise or restrain; failure to take proper tests and evaluations of the patient to establish suicide intent; failure to medicate properly; failure to observe the patient continuously (24 hours) or on a frequent enough basis (e.g., every 15 minutes); failure to take an adequate history; failure to supervise adequately and to remove dangerous objects; and failure to place the patient in a secure room.

In summary, both the legal system and an optimal clinical standard require that clinicians and hospitals make appropriate and reasonable efforts to foresee elevated suicide risk. Once an elevated risk is determined, clinicians and institutions must take affirmative precautions. Such precautions often entail balancing and carefully assessing both the risks and benefits of any subsequent management decision. For example, it is often necessary to balance the risk of therapeutically extending the patient's responsibilities, privileges, and freedoms against the benefit of greater control and supervision (e.g., a hospital admission, reassessing the level of privileges, transfer of patient to a more secure environment, and adequate care in discharge and follow-up planning).

In the next and final chapter we will examine specific risk management procedures in both suicide prevention and postvention and present guidelines and suggestions for high-quality risk management. As the reader has already determined from reading this and the preceding chapters, we believe that optimal risk management systems for suicidal patients must be based on an understanding of the importance of the therapeutic alliance, a thorough understanding of the clinical and legal knowledge base, an assessment of personal and professional competencies and limitations, routine consultation, involvement of the patient's significant others and family whenever possible, and a meticulous and timely documentation of the standard of care.

CHAPTER 6

Risk Management: Prevention and Postvention

Ignorance of the law can make the legal profession and the courts seem menacing to the average practitioner. However, a clinically useful understanding of the law may actually enhance clinicians' enjoyment of their practice activities by, in Simon's words, "making the law a working partner" (1988, p. xv). For, although psychologists are not required to be lawyers, they are required to practice within the law and should attempt to "incorporate legal issues into their management of patients—turning the law to clinical account for the benefit of the patients" (Simon, 1988, xv). Furthermore, mental health professionals have an ethical and moral duty to provide care for patients, a duty that often transcends any minimal standard that may be imposed by the law or regulatory agencies, a duty to strive for an optimal standard of care in their own practices.

In the current climate of increased malpractice actions against mental health professionals, it would be naive for the practicing psychologist not to consider appropriate clinical and legal management issues when treating certain high-risk populations (e.g., patients who are dangerous to self or others). Indeed, Simon (1988) argued that it would be not merely naive but foolhardy to ignore risk management procedures in the course of treating such patients. Here, the key is to know when to apply risk management practices and to make certain that patients are helped and not harmed by such practices (Simon, 1988).

Throughout this book, we have argued that the best overall risk management strategy remains a sensitive and caring therapeutic alliance within the context of the best possible clinical care. We discuss this alliance specifically at the end of this chapter. We turn now to what Harris (1990) has determined are the elementary techniques of successful risk management, techniques that, if understood and used effectively, significantly minimize the risk of being found negligent in a malpractice action and that are of substantial benefit and use in defending oneself against complaints filed with professional ethics committees, licensing boards, and other bodies by which one is held responsible.

Harris (1990) noted that psychologists who wish to incorporate high-quality risk management activities as part of their professional practice activities first and foremost, must understand the American Psychological Association's ethical standards and standards for the providers of psychological services (American Psychological Association, 1981a, 1981b, 1981c, 1981d, 1981e, 1987) and combine this understanding with specific laws and regulations that govern psychological practice in their state. Effective risk management includes the additional requirement of obtaining essential clinical assessment and management information on specific at-risk populations, understanding the relationship between the law and mental health practitioners, knowing the rules and limitations regarding confidentiality and informed consent, understanding how courts determine malpractice, and learning how professional liability insurance policies work (see Bennett, Bryant, VandenBos, & Greenwood, 1990 for a more extended discussion of these general issues and their relationship to professional liability). Also, Harris (1990) has emphasized the critical relationship between effective risk management and the important elements of documentation and consultation.

We noted earlier Guthiel's (1990) claim that these last two elements are "the twin pillars" of liability prevention (p. 338). He went on to state that good documentation provides a durable, contemporaneous record, not only of what happened, but of the exercise of the mental health professional's judgment, the risk–benefit analysis, and the patient's ability to participate in planning his or her own treatment. The use of consultation, then, provides a biopsy of the standard care, capturing in a practical way the reasoning of the " 'average and reasonable practitioner,' that mythical being who represents the reference standard for the determination of the standard of care and alleged deviations therefrom" (p. 338).

Before beginning our discussion of risk management, we feel that it is crucial to reiterate a statement made in the preface: The information contained in this book is no substitute for a timely and formal consultation with a knowledgeable attorney and with one's professional colleagues. In particular, psychologists with specific questions or those who are threatened with a suit should follow the suggestion of Wright (1981) and of VandeCreek and Knapp (1983) that the first step (when one has specific legal concerns or has reason to believe that a malpractice suit is imminent) is quite straightforward: Consult an attorney who is expert in matters of mental health and the law.

In the *Psychologist's Legal Handbook*, Stromberg and colleagues (1988) pointed out that practitioners are most likely to be found liable in the case of suicidal inpatients. The underlying assumption in such cases is that hospital-based practitioners have greater observational capabilities and control over their patients. In matters of outpatient suicide, a malpractice suit is often based on the family members' contention that the outpatient psychotherapist provided inadequate diagnosis and treatment. Specifically, the psychologist is likely to be held liable if "similarly situated practitioners would have provide more care or would have controlled the patient better" (p. 467).

A crucial premise here is that clinicians have a duty to take steps to prevent suicide if they can reasonably anticipate the danger. Thus, the central issues in determining liability are "whether the psychotherapist should have predicted that the patient was likely to attempt suicidal behavior, and (assuming there was an identifiable risk) whether the therapist did enough to protect the patient" (Stromberg, 1989, p. 467).

In this regard, Pope (1986) stressed the importance of staying within one's area of competence and of knowing one's personal limits, observing that work with the suicidal patient can be "demanding, draining, crisis filled activity. It is literally life or death work" (p. 19). In addition to obtaining adequate training and knowledge of the literature on suicide, psychologists must become familiar with the legal standards involving rights to treatment and to refuse treatment, as well as the rules regarding confidentiality, involuntary hospitalization, and so forth. He wrote that a standard of care must involve a screening for suicide risk during the initial contact and ongoing alertness to this issue throughout the course of treatment. There should also be frequent consultation and ready access to facilities (e.g., emergency teams, hospitals, crisis intervention centers, day treatment, etc.) needed to implement appropriate affirmative precautions. (See Appendix E for an example of an action guideline approach to legal issues in emergency psychiatry.)

The courts have been sympathetic to the difficulties that clinicians have in predicting suicides and, as a result, have rarely imposed liability in the absence of prior observable acts or verbal threats by the patient. For example, in the case of *Bogust v. Iverson*, a college guidance counselor was held not liable when a student committed suicide 6 weeks after sessions with the counselor had ended. The student had not talked about suicide and had not exhibited behavior that would have prompted the counselor to initiate procedures for a civil commitment of the student (Stromberg et al., 1988).

The general legal standard for patient care clearly includes a thorough understanding of the complexities of procedures for assessing elevated risk and specific clinical management techniques for the suicidal patient (Bongar et al., 1989). Mental health professionals have been held liable when they have not taken adequate precautions to manage patients. The courts will not necessarily defer to a psychologist's decisional process when they find that "due to a totally unreasonable professional judgment, he or she underestimated the need for special care, or failed to take the usual precautions" (Stromberg et al., 1988, p. 468).

Psychologists' assessment and treatment efforts represent an opportunity to translate knowledge (albeit incomplete) of elevated-risk factors into a plan of action. The management plan for patients who are at an elevated risk for suicide should ameliorate those risk factors that are most likely to result in suicide or self-harm (Brent et al., 1988). Here, there are several general principles that should guide the treatment of patients at elevated risk for suicide and that apply across broad diagnostic categories. The most basic principle is that, because most suicide victims take their own lives or harm themselves in the midst of a psychiatric episode (Barraclough et al., 1974; Dorpat & Ripley, 1960; Murphy, 1988; Robins et al., 1959; Shaffer, 1974; Shaffer, Gould, & Trautman, 1985; Shaffi, 1986), it is critical to understand that a proper diagnosis and a careful management and treatment plan of the acute psychiatric disorder could dramatically alter the risk for suicide (Brent et al., 1988). Although there is a loose fit between diagnosis and suicide, Simon (1988) noted that suicide rarely occurs in the absence of psychiatric illness; the data on adult suicides indicate that more than 90% of these suicide victims were mentally ill before their deaths.

In addition to these requirements for acute management, Gutheil (1990), Litman (1988), and Simon (1987, 1988) discussed the special precautions that clinicians must take when assessing and treating patients who present with chronic suicidal ideation and behavior (e.g., where the clinician takes repeated calculated risks in not hospitalizing). Gutheil (1990) noted that here the mental health clinician will feel the tension between short-term solutions (e.g., a protected environment) and long-term solutions (e.g., actual treatment of the chronicity).

Other general principles include family involvement for support and improved compliance; diagnosis and treatment of any comorbid medical and psychiatric condition; the provision of hope, particularly to new-onset patients; the restriction of the availability of lethal agents; and indications for psychiatric hospitalization (Brent et al., 1988). To this list, a risk management perspective would add the critical necessity of assessing personal and professional competencies in order to treat at-risk patients, as well as meticulous documentation and the routine involvement of a second opinion through consultation (Bongar et al., 1989).

All of our assessment and management activities should also include a specific evaluation of the patient's competency to participate in management and treatment decisions, especially the patient's ability to form a therapeutic alliance (Gutheil, 1984, 1990; Kahn, 1990; Luborsky, 1990). An essential element in strengthening this alliance is the use of informed consent; that is, patients have the right to actively participate in making decisions about their psychological care. Psychologists need to directly and continuously assess the quality of this special relationship to understand that the quality of this collaborative alliance is inextricably part of any successful treatment and management plan (Bongar et al., 1989; Gutheil, 1984, 1988, 1990; Kahn, 1990; Luborsky, 1990; Motto, 1979a; Shneidman, 1981c, 1984, Simon, 1987, 1988).

Suicide results from the complex interplay of a number of diagnostic (psychiatric and medical), constitutional, environmental, occupational, sociocultural, existential, and chance casual elements (Simon, 1988). It is not simply the result of misdiagnosis or inadequate treatment. Courts sometimes have trouble understanding that psychotherapists are ''ordinary mortals struggling with [this conundrum]'' (Simon, 1987, p. 264) and that neither psychologists nor any other mental health professionals are able to guarantee control over the behavior of their patients, particularly patients in outpatient treatment. Therefore, as the first step in presenting risk management guidelines for the assessment and treatment of the suicidal individual, we will discuss the issue of the psychologist's technical and personal competence to work with such high-risk patients.

Assessment of Technical and Personal Competence

Although the law does not record a case to date of negligent psychotherapy where the basis is a failure to cure or to relieve a psychiatric symptom, verbal psychotherapies are not without their own risks (Simon, 1987). Demonstrably, patients who are improperly diagnosed or given an inappropriate type of psychotherapy may indeed regress and present with suicidal ideation or behavior (Simon, 1987; Stone, 1989a, 1989b). Extreme therapies, as well as innovative or regressive therapies, in addition to sexual seduction by therapists and malignant countertransferences can be taken as evidence of treatment gone awry. The presence of such factors may increase the risk of suicide significantly (Simon, 1987). Stone (1989b) cautioned about the risks of forcing a patient to see that his or her reality situation is empty of possible gratification, as well as being cautious when the context of this malignant insight is such that the patient feels even more hopeless and helpless. Too often, therapy is less than adequate because of ideological, theoretical, or technical prejudices: ''Not all psychiatrists and other psychotherapists are equipped emotionally or technically to manage suicidal patients'' (Lesse, 1989b, p. 215).

The treatment of depression in an outpatient setting gives an excellent example of the kind of specific technical proficiency that needs to be brought to bear in a suicidal crisis. Ideally, those clinicians who undertake the treatment of severely depressed patients should have broad spectrum training, including an understanding of the limitations and benefits of the various psychosocial and organic therapies. In addition, any clinician who undertakes the management of severely depressed suicidal outpatients must have ready access to appropriate inpatient facilities in case a voluntary or involuntary hospitalization is indicated. The implicit requirement is that psychologists know the specific clinical and research literature on all recommended psychosocial interventions for depression, as well as the appropriateness of routinely requesting a consultation for psychotropic medication for the treatment of patients with affective disorders (Lesse, 1989b).

Technical proficiency also means that the psychologist who sees a suicidal patient in an outpatient setting must learn to distinguish carefully between acute suicidal states related to *DSM-III-R* Axis I clinical syndromes and to chronic suicidal behavior as part of an Axis II personality disorder; the care and management of these patients may differ dramatically. (Of course, patients with Axis II personality disorders could also develop an Axis I condition at any time.) An additional and obvious consideration in treating the suicidal patient is whether the assessment and treatment take place in an inpatient or outpatient setting (Simon, 1987, 1988).

Psychologists who treat depressed suicidal patients must be knowledgeable about current clinical and research developments. For example, a prudent psychologist might review the initial recommendations of the American Psychological Association's Women and Depression Task Force for the treatment of depression in female patients (Landers, 1989). Likewise, the psychologist might include an examination of recent changes in our empirical understanding of acute and chronic predictor variables (Beck & Steer, 1989; Fawcett et al., 1987), new models for examining attempter behavior (Clark et al., 1989), recent findings on high-risk populations (Weissman et al., 1989), and current comprehensive reviews on depression (Keller, 1988) and suicide (Mann & Stanley, 1988b). However much or little one opts to incorporate such new developments into one's own treatment planning (e.g., to adopt recent directive and prescriptive treatment recommendations for certain psychopathological conditions), one effect of exploring this information is to gain better understanding of one's own current applied and theoretical approach to intervention and to reassess one's competencies within the context of the changing theoretical and empirical knowledge base.

This is a matter of vital importance. For example, in the treatment of patients with severe depression, Lesse (1989b) found that not all mental health professionals

> are equipped by personality or training to manage severely depressed patients, let alone those who have suicidal preoccupations or drives. This pertains to senior personnel and residents alike. Senior personnel should not place residents in charge of suicidal patients. It is imperative that they should be extremely closely supervised by a highly trained and motivated senior staff. (p. 195)

Lesse contended that therapists with their own depressive propensities, those who are threatened by aggressive patients, and those who are unable to handle crisis or emergency situations should not treat depressed patients. He also recommended that severely depressed patients not be cared for by clinicians who do not have the capacity for intensive psychopathologic investigation.

In coming to terms with their own limitations, one must remember, as Welch

(1989) pointed out, that all mental health providers (psychiatrists, psychologists, social workers, psychiatric nurses, etc.) are limited to varying degrees as to their specific professional competencies. Welch continues: "One might further argue that the greatest threat to 'quality of care' comes not from those with limited training but from those with a limited recognition of the limitations of their own training" (p. 28).

Therefore, one of the initial tasks of the psychologist who is called on to treat the suicidal patient is the need to have evaluated a priori the strengths and limitations of his or her own training, education, and experience in the treatment of specific patient populations in specific clinical settings (e.g., they must possess an understanding of their own technical proficiencies and of their emotional tolerance levels for the intense demands required in treating suicidal patients). Specifically, psychologists must make the difficult and highly personal decision to conduct their own self-study of personal and professional competence to treat suicidal patients before the fact, and not wait to assess this competence when suicidal thoughts or behaviors emerge in patients whom they are seeing in treatment. Pope (1986) wrote that the American Psychological Association's (1981b) "Specialty Guidelines for the Delivery of Psychological Services by Clinical Psychologists" dictate that clinical psychologists limit their practice to demonstrated areas of professional competence, for example, "to ensure that you meet the legal, ethical and professional standards of competence in working with suicidal clients" (p. 19). Setting such limits requires self-knowledge. (Psychologists may also wish, as part of such a self-study process, to consult an up-to-date volume on general ethical principles, standards, and guidelines in professional practice; see Bennett et al., 1990.)

Documentation and Risk Management

Paranoia and Progress Notes

We now turn to the second key element in risk management activities: the need for meticulous and timely documentation. In a well-known article, Gutheil (1980) commented that the prudent mental health practitioner can use paranoia as a motivating force to make psychiatric records effective for forensic purposes, utilization review, and treatment planning. Gutheil's key principles are "If it isn't written down, it didn't happen" and "What you see is what you've got." As a general rule, he continued, clinicians should write their notes as if a lawyer were sitting on their shoulders, reviewing every word. Gutheil pointed out that using paranoia as a guiding reality principle in these litigious times is a sound basis for effective record-keeping, because

> We mental health professionals should face, with dispassionate resolute-
> ness, the cold fact that certain people are out to get us. These people are

called "lawyers," and the reason they are out to get us is simple: they are paid to do so. The plot is variously termed "malpractice litigation," "contemporary narcissistic entitlement" or the "American disease." The practice of suing thy neighbor for almost anything has become a serious contender for the title of the country's second most favorite sport. . . . These facts are familiar to anyone able to read a newspaper and need not be belabored, but it is this reality-based paranoia that may serve as our stimulus in attempting to achieve records unassailable from the viewpoints of utilization review, forensic considerations, and treatment. (pp. 479–480)

As Gutheil (1980) also pointed out, in theory, honest error is separable from negligence, but, in practice, juries often confound the distinction. There is no infallible protection against this fact of forensic life.

It is our opinion that, although it is indeed essential to understand the purposes and context of defensive record-keeping, the psychologist should never lose sight of the most important purpose of clinical records and the rationale that properly underlies the keeping of such meticulous, high-quality records: that such documentation is an organizing framework that can focus the psychologist's attention on making sound clinical judgments. This ethos of meticulousness is of particular importance in clinical situations that are suffused with uncertainty (Gutheil, 1990). Such circumstances (suicidal situations among them) have in common the taking of clinically based calculated risks and trial and error empiricism. They specifically require that the clinician "think out loud for the record." Gutheil cited the typical example of deciding not to hospitalize a suicidal patient:

> Not hospitalizing the patient is often clinically wise but, after a given patient commits suicide, even the soundest decision may appear dubious in hindsight. And, we must recall, it is with hindsight that the evidence at the trial is presented. It is unfortunate that juries often have difficulty seeing that for a treatment to be 80 percent effective, two people out of ten must succumb to dismal failure—and one of the two (or their next of kin) may be the plaintiff—without any aspersion being cast on the treatment itself. . . . There is no absolute defense against this problem, but "thinking out loud for the record" stacks the deck heavily in favor of error in judgment rather than negligence. (p. 482)

For example, in the case of not hospitalizing a suicidal outpatient, such informed record-keeping would often include "thinking out loud for the record" as to the dangers that the patient might be exposed to and the "careful articulation of the pros and cons, including known risks and disadvantages and the reasons for overriding them . . . specific dates, and names are included, showing that the treating professional did not operate alone and unchecked in making this difficult but commonly encountered decision'' (Gutheil, 1980, p. 482). The treatment planning builds explicitly on past observed and recorded data and consultations. Gutheil noted that ''as a general rule, the more uncertainty there is, the more one should think out loud in the record'' (p. 482).

Inadequate Documentation

The need for accurate documentation is a *sine qua non* of demonstrating professional competence (VandeCreek & Knapp, 1989). Detailed records showing accurate documentation of assessment, treatment, and consultative procedures are the soundest way for psychologists to prove that they provided adequate care:

> The lack of documentation can fatally cripple the defendant's case, even if the therapist had acted in a conscientious and professionally sound manner. Numerous case consultations have supported this conclusion, including a case where the consultant believed there was no negligence on the part of the treating staff, but ''the almost complete lack of records left a legitimate issue as to the fact and so the settlement against the hospital and psychiatrist was made'' (Perr, 1985, p. 217). The settlement in that case was for $500,000. (VandeCreek & Knapp, 1989, p. 30)

Fremouw et al. (1990) cited the case of *Abille v. United States* (1980), in which the court implied that, if good notes had been kept (documenting the rationale for the change of an inpatient's status from suicidal to a lower level of precaution), the psychiatrist may not have been found liable—''that in the absence of notes, a breach of duty and failure to follow professional standards had occurred'' (p. 8).

The Power of Documentation

The power of documentation in retrospectively evaluating the quality of assessment and treatment is underscored by the observation that ''clinicians who make bad decisions but whose reasoning has been articulated clearly and whose justification for the intervention is well documented often come out better than clinicians who have made reasonable decisions but whose poor documentation leaves them vulnerable'' (Gutheil, 1984, p. 3). A good clinical record should be explicit about treatment decisions such as whether to hospitalize or not to hospitalize the patient, as well as those concerning therapeutic impasses; passes, discharges, and other privileges; any uncertainty about diagnosis; and evaluation of psychosocial supports. In addition, VandeCreek and Knapp (1989) noted that the clinician should carefully document any decisions to reduce the frequency of observations of suicidal patients. Each significant decision point should also include a risk–benefit analysis that indicates all actions that one considered, the reasons that led one to take an action, and the reasons that led one to reject an action. The record must indicate specifically why consultation and supervision were or were not employed and include a written record of the consultant's recommendations. Furthermore, Gutheil (1980) pointed out that "malpractice suits, it must be obvious, have been won or lost on matters of timing. . . . For this reason alone, as well as for the clinical need to reconstruct events with accuracy, the use of time notations (as well as dates) is a useful habit to develop" (p. 482).

For example, in a situation where the psychologist has a duty to protect the patient, the optimal clinical record would show that the psychologist considered hospitalizing the patient and that the clinical decision-making process based on this particular patient's history and his or her current clinical situation led the psychologist to take certain actions and reject others. The record would also indicate explicitly the use of informed consent and the participation of the competent patient (and, when appropriate, their significant others) in formulating the current management and treatment plan. If the patient (or family) is operating or acting in a manner that goes against the psychologist's professional judgment, there must be a detailed accounting of what actions were taken.

In addition to taking care to indicate timing in their charts, clinicians must document assessment, treatment, and consultation decisions in a timely manner. In patient suicides that lead to litigation, attention is often focused on the last evaluation performed by the clinician and or staff before the patient's suicide (Gutheil, 1984). Gutheil found that the questions raised after a patient's suicide center on whether the clinician adequately evaluated and documented his or her decision on the risk–benefits of various affirmative precautions, particularly once an elevated risk has been detected.

It should be noted that clinicians who attempt to alter the clinical record "after the fact" are making a fatal mistake. Gutheil (1980) pointed out the temptation (especially for novices) to

> plug into previous notes the significant but forgotten details. This is occasionally referred to as "fudging" and is as self-defeating as it is useless. Clearly, the best approach is to note the details the first time around, but, even for the best of clinicians, omissions may occur. The soundest approach then is candor. Noting the present date, one states something like: "Reviewing the notes of August–September, I find no mention of . . ." Such brief updates, made when the omission is noted and—one hopes—before the subpoena arrives, can fill in the gaps while preserving integrity and forensic validity. (p. 481)

As must be clear by now, therefore, one of the central, if not the most central, risk management activities that psychologists can engage in is to incorporate the routine practice of keeping meticulous and timely chart notes into all of their assessment and treatment activities. Such record keeping is often the best possible defense against the retrospective evaluation of the standard of care that occurs in malpractice actions. As a rule in malpractice litigation, if you failed to record an action in your records, there is a good chance the jury will assume that you failed to carry out the assessment or treatment effectively or completely, regardless of how convincing you are as a witness. In any forensically charged or uncertain situation, the practitioner's records should include a complete and highly detailed report of what actually happened and the reasons why he or she acted as he or she did.

In summary, the chart should reflect which sources of information were consulted, what factors went into the clinical decisions, and how the factors were balanced by the use of a risk–benefit assessment. Such risk–benefit notes are the decisional road marks in a psychotherapist's clinical formulation of the management and treatment plan (Simon, 1988).

Obtaining Previous Medical and Psychotherapy Records

It is a grave error to ignore the written records from a patient's previous treatment (Simon, 1987, 1988). For patients with a history of suicidal behavior, if possible, the psychologist should obtain permission to telephone previous psychotherapists for the full history of suicidal behavior. With the patient's permission, the psychologist may also wish to contact family members who can help to determine the gravity of past suicide attempts (Simon, 1987, 1988).

All of this information needs to be recorded and incorporated into the ongoing treatment plan. The absence of efforts to obtain previous medical and psychotherapy records is one of the signs of inadequate clinical care.

A Psychologist's Risk–Benefit Note

A model risk–benefit progress note includes

1. a completed assessment of risk;
2. the information that alerted the clinician to that risk;
3. which high-risk factors were present in that situation and in the patient's background;
4. what low risk factors (e.g., reasons to live, care of minor child, etc.) were present;
5. what questions were asked and what answers were given; and
6. how this information (the patient's history, and one's own clinical and evaluative judgments) led to the actions taken and rejected.

The analyses documented in the progress note should include the specific pros and cons of each action from a clinical and a legal perspective. One should state with whom one formally consulted, what was communicated to them, the nature of their response, and the actions they recommended. Additionally, one should indicate whether the recommendations were clear-cut. If there were alternative recommendations from the consultant, they should be described in detail, together with the rationale for not exercising those alternatives. If the opinions of consultants differed from one's own or from each other, note the sources of difference.

Whenever possible, the risk–benefit note should detail the psychologist's understanding of the role of informed consent and the right of the competent patient to participate collaboratively in the decision-making process. Specifically, the chart should describe the psychologist's efforts to involve the competent patient (and, where indicated, their significant others) in an open discussion of the risks and benefits of a particular course of action. If there is any disagreement in this process, it is wise to advise the patient and family immediately that they have the right to obtain a second opinion and to facilitate such a consultation. (We will discuss the importance of informed consent in detail in a later section of this chapter.)

Overall then, in the written record, the psychologist must present a chronologically specific recitation of all actions taken, their results, and the impact of the results on future actions, as well as patient behaviors in response to these actions. All calls to hospitals and to significant others should be recorded contemporaneously. The record should be as timely as possible, but this should not prevent one from including details at a later date that one neglected in the heat of the moment. However, altering or rewriting the record after one discovers that there may be questions about one's decisions (e.g., a law suit) can destroy the possibility of any adequate defense. As Hoge and Appelbaum (1989) noted "no single act so destroys the clinician's credibility in court" (p. 620).

Obviously, no practitioner will be able to obtain all of the information recommended for every forensically significant situation. The more information that is contained in the record, however, the more the record will demonstrate that, even though the result may have been extremely unfortunate, the practitioner behaved in a reasonable professional manner, given the information that she or he had at the time. The extra time and effort that will be required to draft comprehensive records pays high dividends should the tragedy of a patient suicide occur. Harris (1990) commented that it is better to spend the time imagining a lawyer on your shoulder now than to face a phalanx of plaintiff attorneys in the future without the protection of adequate documentation.

Even with good records, it will be difficult to demonstrate that the unfortunate result was not caused by the psychologist's negligence and to persuade the jury to resist the temptation to decide with their emotions and compensate the plaintiff victim for his or her terrible loss. Psychologists who have good records will have a much easier time convincing juries and lawyers that they are competent, caring professionals who, when confronted by a difficult clinical situation, behaved in a professional manner. Excellent records may even discourage the plaintiff's attorneys from pursuing legal action in the first place, or at least encourage them to avoid costly litigation and to propose settlement for a reasonable amount (Harris, 1990).

Involving the Patient and Family in Management and Treatment

Research indicates that it may be advisable to warn the patient's support system and significant others of the patient's potential for suicide and to increase their involvement in management and treatment (VandeCreek & Knapp, 1989). Such involvement can be a strong factor in promoting the patient's recovery. Observing that suicide is often a highly charged dyadic process, Shneidman (1981c) urged support group involvement in suicide prevention efforts. He also stated that, at the very least, the psychologist must carefully assess the interpersonal matrix for the role of significant others as either helpers or hinderers in the treatment process. If the patient actually does commit suicide, the therapist has established the communication channels and, ideally, good relations with the family that may facilitate a healthy resolution of ensuing sorrow and grief.

Legally speaking, it also is the case that the family is less likely to initiate litigation against the psychologist if such good relations have been achieved. Simon (1988) modified Sadoff's ''dereliction of duty directly causing damages'' (Sadoff, 1975) to the ''4Ds'' of a *Duty* of care—*Deviation* from the standard of care—*Damage* to the patient—*Directly* the result of the deviation from the standard of care (see Table 6.1).

It is Gutheil's (1990) contention that, in the real world, the determination of malpractice rests less on the 4Ds than on the malignant synergy of ''a bad outcome from whatever cause, in concert with 'bad feelings' in the plaintiffs,

Table 6.1
The 4Ds of Malpractice Assessment

- A doctor–patient relationship creating a **DUTY** of care must be present.
- A **DEVIATION** from the standard of care must have occurred.
- **DAMAGE** to the patient must have occurred.
- The damage must have occurred **DIRECTLY** as a result of deviation from the standard of care.

Note. From *Concise Guide to Clinical Psychiatry and the Law* (p. 6) by R. I. Simon, 1988, Washington, DC: American Psychiatric Press. Copyright 1988 by American Psychiatric Press. Reprinted by permission.

including guilt, rage, grief, surprise, betrayal, and a sense of being left alone with the bad outcome (psychological abandonment)'' (p. 335). The suicide of a loved one is a catastrophic outcome to treatment, and one which Gutheil believes is destined to leave in its wake a host of bad feelings toward the clinician. Litigation over suicide may provide a mechanism for the displacement of the family's guilt onto the clinician, serving the grieving family as an ''antidepressant'' mechanism for grief avoidance. (We will address the particular importance of sensitive postventive work with survivors later in this chapter.)

Legal Considerations of Informed Consent and Confidentiality

When psychologists formulate a treatment plan, they face the important task of involving the patient in the treatment process. However, the law of informed consent is often confusing to mental health professionals, who tend to see this task as an intrusion by the legal system into the treatment process, and who reduce it ''to a meaningless, mechanistic ritual of form signing'' (Hoge & Appelbaum, 1989, p. 613). If the psychologist, instead, sees the process of informed consent as an opportunity to increase communication and collaboration between the psychotherapist and patient, this particular task ''can have a powerful therapeutic influence of its own'' (Hoge & Appelbaum, 1989, p. 613).

The legal and ethical rationale for informed consent is based on the principle that patients should have the right to participate actively in making decisions about their psychological care. Not only are patients likely to cooperate more in a treatment they have had an active role in selecting, but the likelihood is greater that the chosen treatment will specifically address the patient's real concerns (Hoge & Appelbaum, 1989). However, it is important to be aware of the exceptions to the requirement for informed consent (Simon, 1988):

1. emergencies (where immediate treatment is needed to prevent imminent harm);

2. a waiver (where the patient knowingly and voluntarily waives his or her right to be informed);

3. therapeutic privilege (where the psychologist determines that a complete disclosure might have deleterious effects on the patient's well-being); and

4. incompetence on the part of the patient to give consent.

(For a detailed discussion of informed consent and competency see Simon, 1988, pp. 26–42.)

Hoge and Appelbaum (1989) noted that legal definitions have tended to be vague in screening for incompetence. They recommended that clinicians conceptually use the following hierarchy (in order of increasing stringency). The clinician must ask whether the patient can:

1. show evidence of a choice concerning treatment;

2. achieve a factual understanding of the issues at hand;

3. rationally manipulate the information provided to him or her; and

4. appreciate the nature of the situation and the consequences of the decision.

Failure in any of these standards may warrant a judicial determination of competence (Hoge & Appelbaum, 1989). However, there are situations—for example, emergencies when any delay of treatment could result in harm to the patient—in which the requirements of informed consent are suspended. "The law is willing to presume that a reasonable person would consent in such circumstances" (Hoge & Appelbaum, 1989, p. 614). (For a complete and in-depth discussion of the complexities of specific theories of informed consent, see Appelbaum, Lidz, & Meisel, 1987.)

Patients and Their Families as Collaborative Risk Management Partners

In order to integrate informed consent into treatment, the psychologist must approach it as a highly individual process. However, many mental health professionals see informed consent as a static one-time event, rather than a dynamic element in ongoing treatment. Although the use of forms as evidence for informed consent can play an excellent subordinate role in clarifying specific issues (such as the limitations of therapy, the role of psychologist and patient, limitations in confidentiality, etc.), the psychologist must see such forms as only the first step in an ongoing process of information-giving and collaboration (Hoge & Appelbaum, 1989; for examples of such comprehensive forms, see Harris, 1988).

Providing pertinent information to both patient and family over the course of treatment allows not only active collaboration, but also fosters close monitoring of the patient's and family's concerns. Indeed, under the rules of informed consent, the patient (and often the family) has the right to be told about the risks and benefits of the suggested course of action and of any reasonable alternative treatments (Bennett et al., 1990). This information should be given in a "neutral dispassionate manner, utilizing to the extent possible a scientific approach to the pros and cons of alternative forms of treatment" (Sadoff, 1990, p. 332).

We agree in spirit with Sadoff that, in the forensically charged area of elevated risk assessment and precautionary action, both competent patients and their families should be provided with as much information as possible to allow them—except when it is clinically contraindicated by a toxic interpersonal matrix—to collaborate and participate as active partners in each facet of the risk–benefit plan. Specifically, this involves the psychologist in detailing all available options, including a discussion of the nature and purpose of the proposed treatment, its risks and benefits, and the availability of alternative treatments and their risks and benefits (see Table 6.2).

Not only can such an open discussion of the risks and benefits facilitate cooperation, widen the protective net, and increase available sources of vital information, but such an open sharing of the risks with patients and family can lessen the experience of shock and surprise should the tragedy of a patient's suicide occur. Yet the delicate problem remains of how to involve the support group without violating patient confidentiality. This last point leads us to the issue of the suicidal patient and confidentiality.

The Issue of Confidentiality

Confidentiality is often referred to as the patient's right not to have communications that are given in confidence disclosed to outside parties without the patient's implied or expressed authorization (Simon, 1988). Once a doctor–patient relationship is established, the mental health professional assumes an "automatic duty to safeguard patients' disclosures" (Simon, 1988, p. 57). Yet the duty to maintain confidentiality is not absolute, and there are clearly situations where breaching confidentiality is both ethically and legally valid.

Simon (1988) pointed out that the competent patient's request for the maintenance of confidentiality must be honored unless the patient is a clear danger to himself or herself or to others. However, the legal duty to warn or inform third parties exists in some jurisdictions only if the danger of physical harm is threatened toward others (Simon, 1988).

Table 6.2
Informed Consent: Reasonable Information to be Disclosed

While there exists no consistently accepted set of information to be disclosed for any given medical or psychiatric situation, as a rule of thumb, five areas of information are generally provided:
1. Diagnosis–description of the condition or problem
2. Treatment–nature and purpose of proposed treatment
3. Consequences–risks and consequences of the proposed treatment
4. Alternatives–viable alternatives to the proposed treatment
5. Prognosis–projected outcome if treatment is not accepted

Note. From *Concise Guide to Clinical Psychiatry and the Law* (p. 29) by R. I. Simon, 1988, Washington, DC: American Psychiatric Press. Copyright 1988 by American Psychiatric Press. Reprinted by permission.

Psychologists must understand laws and regulations related to breaching confidentiality when patients are a "danger to self." For example, in 1988, the Commonwealth of Massachusetts enacted a new psychology licensing law, imposing a limited statutory "duty to commit" on psychologists who see patients as imminently dangerous to themselves (*Massachusetts General Law*, 1988). This statute allows a limited breach of confidentiality by the psychologist to help safeguard the patient and to help with treatment where the patient is an imminent danger to himself or herself, and where the patient refuses or is unable to follow the recommendations for outpatient treatment or voluntary hospitalization. Of course, a hospitalization under such circumstances often involves the family and significant others (Harris, 1990).

Pope, Tabachnick, and Keith-Spiegel (1988) have commented that

> Apparently the argument made by the defense in many of the early "duty to protect" cases (e.g., *Tarasoff v. Regents of the University of California*, 1976), that absolute confidentiality is necessary for psychotherapy, is not persuasive for many psychotherapists: Breaking confidentiality is seen by a large number of practitioners as uniformly good practice in cases of homicidal risk, suicidal risk, and child abuse. (p. 550)

Shneidman (1981c) went even further and stated that confidentiality, when a patient has exhibited suicidal behavior, should not be an important issue between psychologists and their patients. He argued forcibly that the main goal of suicidal therapy is to defuse the potentially lethal situation. Thus, to hold to the principle of confidentiality is contradictory to a basic tenet of an ethical psychotherapeutic relationship.

The official policy of the American Psychological Association states that psychologists have a primary obligation to respect the confidentiality of information obtained from persons in the course of their work and that they may reveal such information to others only with the consent of the person or her or his legal representative, except in those unusual circumstances when not doing so would result in clear danger to the person or to others (Keith-Speigel & Koocher, 1985). Where appropriate, psychologists should inform their patients of the legal limits of confidentiality (see Bennett et al., 1990).

As Simon (1988) pointed out, the *Principles of Medical Ethics* state that a "physician may not reveal the confidences entrusted to him in the course of medical attendance . . . unless he is required to do so by law or unless it becomes necessary in order to protect the welfare of the individual or community" (p. 96).

Gutheil (1984) noted that, with patients for whom suicidal issues are predominant, it is important to assess their ability to participate in therapeutic alliance with the clinician:

> The patient who is collaborative, who sees the issue as a joint problem for both patient and clinician, is in a completely different position from the patient who sees himself as being acted upon. . . . The distinction between the patient who can cooperate but does not and the patient who is too sick to cooperate may mean the difference between success and failure in the litigation area. (Gutheil, 1984, p. 3)

Therefore, at the most basic level, we believe that clinicians have a professional duty to take appropriate affirmative measures to prevent their patients from harming themselves. At times, this may necessitate communicating with family members about the specifics of a patient's case, attempting to ameliorate toxic family interactions with the patient, or mobilizing support from the family and significant others. In the Commonwealth of Massachusetts, for example, the new psychology licensing law specifically allows psychologists to do so, should they determine that their patient meets the Commonwealth's criteria for hospitalization.

Breaching Confidentiality

In general, ethical considerations require that clinicians provide their patients with complete information about the limits to confidentiality. In addition, they should give careful thought to how they would handle various types of requests to release information or breach confidences before the specific situations occur. They should consider the lengths to which they would go to protect their patients' confidentiality; for example, whether they would retain an attorney to fight a request on demand for information or fully discuss the implications of a privilege waiver with their patients upon receiving a subpoena. Finally, when an actual situation arises, a consultation with a senior colleague, an attorney or both may help to sort out the various options available and the clinical implications and management strategies associated with each strategy.

Here, the essential advice is to develop a good understanding of the issues involved in breaching confidentiality with suicidal patients before the fact. Psychologists should develop a well-thought out policy on breaching confidentiality before being required to implement it and seek consultation in any situation of uncertainty.

As with all other individual rights recognized by our society, the courts have held that the right to privacy must be balanced against the rights of other individuals and against the public interest (i.e., the legitimate regulatory functions of government) to determine which should prevail. As a result of this balancing process, the courts have created many exceptions to the general rule of therapeutic confidentiality. Indeed, some would say that there are so many exceptions that the term *therapeutic confidentiality* is now an oxymoron (Harris, 1988). The critical point is that the psychologist should inform patients of the exceptions that exist to confidentiality before the patient enters treatment.

Simon (1988) wrote that common sense and good judgment can lead to a decision to breach patient confidentiality, specifically where "a patient will probably commit suicide and the act can be stopped only by the psychiatrist's intervention. . . . However, any limitations on the maintenance of confidentiality should be explained to patients from the beginning of any evaluation or treatment" (pp. 60–61). Furthermore, Stromberg et al. (1988) noted that:

> Ethically, the therapist may be bound to disclose information concerning a patient in an emergency, when disclosure would obviously be best for the patient. Courts have increasingly defined "emergency" narrowly so that it does not cover all breaches of confidentiality which a particular therapist views as appropriate but only those made because the patient's health is seriously and imminently at stake. (p. 14)

Stromberg et al. continued that the scope of the disclosure should be limited to what is necessary for providing appropriate care and that, for example, disclosures made in good faith in seeking a civil commitment of the patient would be largely protected.

We believe that, if a breach of confidentiality is necessary to save the patient's life, the psychologist is bound to take this step. We agree with Shneidman (1981c) that, if such a breach of confidentiality is necessary to defuse a lethal situation, the psychologist must do so and "not ally herself/himself with death" (p. 348). (For an extended discussion of the complex ethical and legal dilemmas that often emerge when working with suicidal patients, [e.g., the issues of rational suicide and euthanasia] see Amchin, Wettstein, & Roth, 1990.)

Consultation With Other Professionals

Mental health professionals have historically been reluctant to obtain second opinions, mostly because of the issue of confidentiality. The basic argument has been that a psychotherapist could not disclose information to a second therapist because it would negatively affect the patient. As an unfortunate example of this attitude, one recent study found that only 27% of clinicians (psychologists, psychiatrists, and social workers) routinely seek consultation to assist in their assessment of suicide (Jobes et al., 1990). However, a very different pattern emerges in medical specialities other than psychiatry, where it is routine and customary to obtain consultation or a second opinion when conflicts or uncertainties arise.

There is almost no instance in the therapist's professional life when consultation with a colleague is more important than when dealing with a highly suicidal patient (Shneidman, 1981c). The additional perspective is essential if

181

the clinician is to "keep in mind the total picture of the patient and not be blinded by his or her theoretical constructs" (Sadoff, 1990, p. 335).

Pope (1986), who collected the comments of experienced psychologists on avoidable pitfalls and direct guidance in treating suicidal patients, cited the comments of Peck and of Strupp:

> **Peck:** Many therapists fail to consult. . . . Review the situation and get an outside opinion.
>
> **Strupp:** There is too often a failure to have in place a network of services appropriate for suicidal clients in crisis. Whether it is an individual private practitioner, a training program run by a university department of psychology, a small psychology clinic, or psychologists associated in group practice—there needs to be close and effective collaboration with other mental health professionals such as psychiatrists and physicians and with facilities equipped to handle suicidal emergencies. . . . I'm not talking about pro forma arrangements but a genuine and effective working relationship. In all cases involving suicide risk, there should be frequent consultation and ready access to appropriate hospitals. (p. 22)

We would argue that any time a psychologist writes a risk–benefit progress note in a situation of uncertainty in assessment or management (even when only a low level of elevated risk is detected), she or he should also weigh the value of obtaining a formal consultation. Here, a careful risk–benefit analysis that examines both sides of the risk equation (the hidden benefits and risks as well as overt ones) will do much to refute an allegation of negligence.

However, even the best risk–benefit analysis "may prove wrong in hindsight" (Gutheil, 1990, p. 37). The aftermath of a patient's suicide tends to trigger in involved observers what some decision analysts have called the "hindsight bias": "the observer's perception that what happened was inevitable (and hence predictable or foreseeable) because, in fact, it happened" (Gutheil, 1990, p. 336). Gutheil observed that hindsight bias is often accompanied by "magical thinking": a form of reasoning characterized by extremes of categorical thinking (e.g., hospitalize or not hospitalize, medicate differently, should not have granted privileges, etc.), coupled with the perception that the clinician is the only active agent and that the patient is an inert or helpless being completely under the clinician's control (Gutheil, 1990).

However, a good risk management analysis does not preclude a bad outcome. Although a risk–benefit analysis (prior to any decision to take a calculated risk in the management plan) demonstrates that the clinician has weighed both sides of the equation, a simultaneous consultation for any high-risk decision or in any clinical situation of uncertainty provides a useful biopsy of the standard of care (Gutheil, 1990). Such consultation, in conjunction with documentation of this decision-making process, can serve as durable proof that the clinician has not been negligent in confronting the decision in question. In particular, the consultation captures, in a practical manner, the reasoning of the hypothetical "reasonable and average practitioner" and, more important, "frees the clinician from the accusation of ideologic insularity; the 'second opinion' may thus provide invaluable input, especially in moments of crisis" (Gutheil, 1990, p. 338).

Furthermore, the use of consultation may aid in providing a shift in treatment, help in dealing with a therapeutic impasse, and help to assuage the fears and subsequent guilt of the family and significant others if the treatment should happen to fail (Sadoff, 1990).

Consultation Questions

Although the following list of discussion points is not exhaustive, it does suggest the sort of specific questions that should be discussed with a consultant when treating the suicidal patient. These include reviewing

1. the overall management of the case, specific treatment issues, uncertainties in the assessment of elevated risk or in diagnosis. This can include a review of the mental status examination, history, information from significant others, the results of any psychological tests and data from risk estimators, suicide lethality scales, and so on. The psychologist's formulation of the patient's *DSM-III-R* diagnosis, together with any other specific psychotherapeutic formulations, clinical assessments, and evaluation of any special treatment and management issues (e.g., comorbidity of alcohol/ substance abuse, physical illness, etc.) should also be reviewed.

2. issues of managing the patient with chronically suicidal behavior, patient dependency, patient hostility and manipulation, toxic interpersonal matrices, lack of psychosocial supports; and the patient's competency to participate in treatment decisions. An assessment of the quality of the therapeutic alliance and the patient's particular response to the psychologist and to the course of treatment (e.g., intense negative or positive transference, etc.) should also be discussed.

3. the psychologist's own feelings about the progress of treatment and feelings toward the patient (e.g., the psychologist's own feelings of fear, incompetency, anxiety, helplessness, or even anger) and any negative therapeutic reactions such as countertransference, and therapist burnout.

4. the advisability of using medication, the need for additional medical evaluation (e.g., any uncertainties as to organicity or neurologi-

cal complications) or both. Reevaluation of any current medications that the patient is taking (e.g., effectiveness, compliance in taking medication, side-effects, polypharmacy) should be included in this review of medication options.

5. the indications and contraindications for hospitalization. Some considerations should be what community crisis intervention resources are available for the patient with few psychosocial supports, day treatment options, emergency and backup arrangements and resources, and planning for the psychologist's absences.

6. indications and contraindications for family and group treatment. This discussion should include the possible use of other types of psychotherapy and somatic interventions, and questions on the status of and progress in the integration of multiple therapeutic techniques.

7. the psychologist's assessment criteria for evaluating dangerousness and imminence (i.e., does the consultant agree with the clinician's assessment of the level of perturbation and lethality?). The specifics of the patient's feelings of despair, depression, hopelessness, cognitive constriction, and impulses toward cessation should also be discussed.

8. the issues of informed consent and confidentiality, and the adequacy of all current documentation on the case (e.g., intake notes, progress notes, utilization reviews, family meetings, supervisor notes, telephone contacts, etc.).

9. whether the consultant agrees with the psychologist's current risk–benefit analysis and management plan. Does the consultant agree that the dual issues of foreseeability and the need to take affirmative precautions have been adequately addressed?

The art of calling in a consultant and formally documenting the answers to these sample questions and others that may be pertinent in particular cases will provide powerful evidence that the psychologist did not act "mindlessly, impetuously or arrogantly . . . and suggests that the clinician was concerned with discovering the standard of care before proceeding" (Hoge & Appelbaum, 1989, pp. 619–620). Again, the opinion of a sensible colleague can be the best immediate "cross-validity check" on the standard of care.

Identifying Appropriate Consultants

In high-risk situations, one should routinely seek professional consultations from colleagues, preferably ones who are senior, have forensic expertise, or both. These consultants should be retained professionally and given sufficient information to provide reasonable advice, and their advice should be carefully recorded in the psychologist's records. It is important to remember that in a malpractice case, the standard of care will be retrospectively determined through expert testimony. Where one's own judgment is buttressed by the judgments of one or two senior colleagues, it is far easier to demonstrate that one behaved appropriately, even when the result was unfortunate. In situations of calculated risk and uncertainty and where time and clinical circumstances permit, it is desirable to arrange for the patient to actually be evaluated by another psychologist or psychiatrist.

Some authorities have stated that consultation need not be formal, that is, a short telephone consultation or corridor consultation can often serve as a "quick biopsy of the community standard, enabling the clinician to demonstrate that the plan seemed reasonable to another member of the same professional group in the same community, thus undercutting the idea that the clinician's care deviated from that standard" (Gutheil, 1984, p. 3). However, as a risk management tool, we believe that seeking a consultation must be a more formal process. In order for the consultation to be more forensically effective it must be a formal one, one where the psychologist and the consultant provide notes for the written record and where both consultant and psychologist of record formally acknowledge that a consultant relationship is in effect. There must be a durable written recording of the consultation, because, as Gutheil (1984) noted, the courts suffer from a "particular kind of concrete thinking; that is, if you did not write it, it did not happen. Such thinking reflects the incredible power of documentation in the assessment and intervention process" (p. 3).

Harris (1990) stated that one of the simplest ways to indicate the formality of such consultative activities is for the psychologist to pay the consultant for consultation time and for the consultant to provide a written risk management note for the chart. Additional avenues of formalizing such relationships could be written policy guidelines indicating who will serve as the consultant for particular clinical dilemmas in a clinic, hospital, group practice, and health maintenance organization. In summary, we agree with Shneidman's dictum that "suicide prevention is not best done as a solo practice" (1981c, p. 344) and that routine consultation is the wisest possible course of action in the assessment and management of the suicidal patient.

Furthermore, although legal standards of care are "fixed at a minimum level by necessity" (Simon, 1988, p. xv), we believe that psychologists have an ethical and personal duty to strive toward a professional standard of care at the maximum level of proficiency (i.e., a more optimal standard). Such a maximal standard of care is solidly grounded on an understanding of when to seek appropriate consultation, together with a thorough knowledge of the clinical and legal knowledge base, a solid proficiency in specific clinical assessment and management procedures, a careful assessment of personal and professional competencies, the involvement of patient and family as informed and collaborative risk management partners, and the understanding of the power of careful, durable documentation. These risk management efforts in the care of the suicidal patient are a reflection of the best traditions of psychology—activities that seek always to constitute in practice a high standard of care on behalf of patients.

Training and Supervision

A recent study that investigated the incidence, impact, and methods of coping with patient suicide during the training years of psychology graduate students found that 1 in 6 students had experienced a patient's suicide at some time during their training. Trainees with patient suicides reported levels of stress that were equivalent to that found in ''patient samples with bereavement and higher than that found with professional clinicians who had patient suicides'' (Kleespies et al., 1990, p. 257). This study also found that trainees who had lost a patient to suicide responded (in order of frequency) with feelings of shock, guilt or shame, denial or disbelief, feelings of incompetence, anger, depression, and a sense of being blamed. After the suicide, trainees frequently turned to their supervisors, both for emotional support and for help in understanding the suicide.

Many psychologists serve as supervisors of trainees, interns, employees, and other colleagues. (One estimate places 64% of psychologists spending at least part of their professional time in supervision; VandeCreek & Harrar 1988.) Although to date very few court cases in the mental health field are based solely on supervisor negligence, ''Slovenko (1980) has warned that supervisor liability may be the 'lawsuit of the future' . . . the principles under which supervisor liability can be claimed have been established in other fields such as medicine and could be applied to professional psychology'' (VandeCreek & Harrar, 1988, p. 13).

According to VandeCreek and Harrar (1988), supervisor negligence can be found if the following three criteria are met:

1. A professional relationship of any duration exists between supervisor and supervisee.

2. The behavior of the supervisor or supervisee fell below an accepted standard of care for the profession.

3. A patient was injured; and the substandard care of the supervisee or supervisor was the proximate cause of the patient's injury.

Simon (1987, 1988) and VandeCreek and Harrar (1988) observed that under the doctrine of *respondeat superior* (let the master respond), psychiatrists, psychologists, and other mental health professionals may be held monetarily responsible for the negligent acts of others working under their supervision, control, or direction. Under a doctrine of vicarious liability, the one who controls the conduct of the treatment may be required to pay damages to the plaintiff. Simon (1987), however, cautioned that there is very little case law on the specific subject of clinical supervision in the field of mental health and negligence.

Psychologists should be on guard particularly when assigning what might be construed as high-risk activities to trainees or interns, for the supervisor is expected to exercise very close supervision and control. They should carefully note the training and competencies of supervisees and make certain that they do not assign to a trainee a patient whose problems may be beyond the trainee's level of training, education, and experience. Because there is very little formal graduate training currently offered in the study of suicide (Bongar & Harmatz, 1989), we would recommend that all supervisors and training programs require that new trainees, interns, and staff receive formal didactic and supervised experience in the management of both acute and chronic suicidal states. Such training should be part of the trainee orientation for training sites, psychological service centers, hospitals, and elsewhere. (This training would also include close and early case supervision on this specific high-risk task for trainees, interns, and staff.)[1]

Additional factors come into play when the alleged substandard treatment was not directly provided by the supervising psychologist. VandeCreek and Harrar (1988) stressed that supervisors will typically be held responsible for the actions of their trainees under the doctrine of *respondeat superior* and that patients (and their families) have the right to an informed consent as to the trainee status of the psychotherapist. There is an ethical and legal obligation to tell patients of the therapist's trainee status and level of experience. The failure to provide patients with this information may expose both trainee and supervisor to "possible lawsuits alleging fraud, deceit, misrepresentation, invasion of privacy, breach of confidentiality, and lack of informed consent" (VandeCreek & Harrar, 1988, p. 14).

In particular, the doctrine of informed consent mandates that supervisors share enough information with the patient regarding the trainee's level of education and experience and regarding the expected level of care so that a prudent patient can make an informed decision about his or her own care. As VandeCreek and Harrar (1988) pointed out: "While some psychologists have worried that sharing this information might scare off most clients, an equally persuasive argument can be made to the client that teaching facilities, with close supervision by experts, can provide exceptionally good care" (p. 14).

These statements to patients about the expert quality of the supervision

---

[1]For additional guidelines and recommendations for the supervision of clinical practice, the reader is directed to the work of Alonso (1985), Beutler (1988), Kaslow (1984), Langs (1979), Norcross (1984), Peterson (1985), Stoltenberg and Delworth (1987), and to a recent comprehensive bibliography on supervision in clinical and counseling psychology (Robiner & Schofield, 1990).

mandates that the supervisors themselves be well trained and knowledgeable in working with suicidal patients. It is essential to note that, even when a patient gives informed consent to care by a trainee, the patient has not thereby consented to receive substandard care. Some courts have concluded that trainees should follow the "same standards of care as professionals who provide the same service" (e.g., *Emory University v. Porubiansky*, 1981). It should be noted that when a patient is harmed, the student, supervisor, employing hospital, agency, or clinic—and, possibly, the sponsoring educational institution—may all be made defendants, and liability may be alleged as either direct or vicarious.

These statements are illustrated by the case of *Peck v. The Counseling Service of Addison County* (1985). A patient, Mr. Peck, told his counselor that he might burn down his father's barn as an act of angry revenge. After discussing this threat with the patient, the counselor decided that the patient would not carry out his threat. The patient burned down his father's barn the next day. The counseling center had no written policy guidelines for the assessment of dangerousness, and the counselor did not discuss this case with her supervisor. The court concluded that the counselor was negligent for her failure to notify the family of the threat. This ruling was based on her failure to obtain previous treatment records, to obtain a complete history of the patient's condition, and to consult with her supervisor (VandeCreek & Harrar, 1988; VandeCreek & Knapp, 1989). The counseling service was found negligent for not having provided clear written guidelines for the management of dangerous patients:

> The lack of a policy is an example of failure to exercise the right of control. Had the Service had such a policy, the supervisor and the agency might have been absolved of liability if the counselor had failed to follow them. (VandeCreek & Harrar, 1988, p. 15)

In assessing and treating suicidal patients, we support the recommendation that policy guidelines for the management of dangerous patients be required in all institutions that offer supervised clinical experience. Furthermore, although not explicitly required, we also recommend that any time a patient presents with even a mild-to-moderate level of elevated suicide risk, the supervisor meet with the patient (along with the trainee) to ensure that all foreseeable elements of the elevated-risk profile have been ascertained and that the management plan demonstrates affirmative precautions for safeguarding the patient. We believe that this procedure not only protects the patient, but can serve as a valuable modeling experience for trainees observing their supervisor at work in this high-risk endeavor.

Finally, as in the case of all nonsupervised clinical care, all assessments and management precautions should be meticulously documented. If the training site does not require that the supervisor actually sign every individual progress note after reviewing the trainee's work, we would urge that, at the very minimum, the supervisor sign off on (and, if indicated, amend) any risk–benefit analysis in the chart (e.g., where the assessment and management precautions for dangerousness are documented).

Postvention

The Emotional Aftermath

The tragedy of patient suicide requires work with the bereaved parties, including the psychologist, in a process called *postvention*, those "appropriate and helpful acts that come after the dire event itself" (Shneidman, 1981b, p. 349). Postvention consists of those activities that can help to reduce the aftereffects of a traumatic event in the lives of the survivors. "Its purpose is to help survivors live longer, more productively, and less stressfully than they are likely to do otherwise" (Shneidman, 1981b, p. 350).

At this point, it is worth repeating that empirical findings show that the average professional psychologist involved in direct patient care has better than a 1 in 5 chance of losing a patient to suicide at some time during his or her professional career, with the odds climbing to better than 50/50 for psychiatrists (Chemtob, Hamada, Bauer, Torigoe, & Kinney, 1988; Chemtob, Hamada, Bauer, Kinney, & Torigoe, 1988). Even a psychologist in training, has between a 1 in 6 and a 1 in 7 chance of losing a patient to suicide (Brown, 1987; Kleespies et al., 1990). It is clear that, despite the psychologist's best efforts, the tragedy of a patient's suicide can still occur. When it does occur, family, friends, and the psychologist all experience a flood of intense and negative feelings.

Shneidman (1981b) wrote that the reactions of the "survivor victims" following the sudden death of a loved one by suicide are likely to include feelings of shame, guilt, hatred, and perplexity and that family members can become obsessed with thoughts of death for sometime afterward, seeking reasons, casting blame, and often punishing themselves. Ness and Pfeffer (1990), in a review of sequelae of bereavement resulting from suicide, found that there may be a difference between bereavement because of suicide and bereavement because of other types of death (however, these data are far from conclusive). Ness and Pfeffer also observed that "[s]uicide of a family member may also be a risk factor for suicide of the bereaved individual. . . . there is a highly consistent set of findings that social attitudes are more blaming toward individuals who have been bereaved because of suicide" (p. 284).

The reaction of the patient's psychologist is often no less severe. As mentioned earlier, psychologists who lose a patient to suicide often respond to the loss in a manner similar to persons who have experienced the sudden death of a family member (Chemtob et al, 1988).

Drawing on information communicated by more than 200 psychotherapists interviewed shortly after a patient's suicide, Litman (1965) found two broad types of reactions. Therapists reacted with emotions of grief, guilt, depression, personal inadequacy, and sometimes anger. Some of the psychotherapists noted partial identification with dead patients in their own dreams or symptomatic actions (e.g., the death of a patient was often followed by accident proneness). Denial was the most common defense mechanism. (This was also the most common mechanism used by family, friends, and others close to suicides.) Although a number of therapists reported that they would try not to work again with suicidal patients, many others expressed the view that patient suicide was an inevitable occupational hazard and resolved to learn from the tragedy and use the experience to improve their work with all present and future patients. Therapists also reported that it was helpful to work through the pain in their own personal treatment and to formally review the case with colleagues.

Fremouw et al. (1990) pointed out that, if a suicide occurs in an inpatient setting, hospital policies and procedures often require that there be a review of the case (in some instances even a formal psychological autopsy). Such a procedure attempts to identify errors of omission or commission and, of equal importance, can help the attending clinicians and staff discuss their feelings of loss, anger, and responsibility. (For a detailed discussion of such procedures, see Cotton, 1989.)

Clearly a complete discussion of the voluminous clinical literature on postvention is beyond the scope of this book. As a starting point, readers interested in the extensive clinical material available on suicide survivorship and in practical information on postvention, should see the work of Cotton (1989), Dunne, McIntosh, and Dunne-Maxim (1987), Friedman (1989), Litman (1965), and Shneidman (1981b). However, before proceeding with our discussion of the legal aftermath, it may be helpful to cite briefly Shneidman's general recommendations for postventive work with survivors, which set the course of our own suggestions.

Shneidman found that the efforts of postvention are grounded in earlier work on grief, crisis therapy, and bereavement (e.g., Caplan, 1964; Lindeman, 1944; Parkes, 1972). These findings seem to indicate that grief is itself a "dire process, almost akin to a disease, and that there are subtle factors at work that can take a heavy toll unless they are treated and controlled" (Shneidman, 1981b, p. 350). Postventive efforts are not limited to the initial stage of shock, but are more often "directed to the longer haul, the day-to-day living with grief over a year or more following the first shock of loss" (Shneidman, 1981b, p. 351). Usually postvention extends over the months following the tragedy and shares many of the characteristics of psychotherapy. The following are some general principles for postvention:

1. It is best to begin postventive therapy as soon as possible after the suicide (e.g., within the first 72 hours).

2. Talk with the survivors, they often offer remarkably little resistance and are generally eager to have an opportunity to talk to a professional.

3. Negative emotions (e.g., anger, envy, guilt, shame, etc.) about the decedent or about death itself should be explored, but not at the very beginning of the postventive treatment.

4. The psychologist conducting postvention activities should play the important role of reality tester—acting not as an echo of conscience but as the quiet voice of reason.

5. The psychologist should be alert to any signs of declining health and mental well-being; medical evaluation of all survivors is crucial.

6. Pollyannish optimism or banal platitudes should be avoided.

7. It is important to acknowledge that grief work takes time. It can extend from several months to a lifetime.

Recently, Ness and Pfeffer (1990) provided the following guidelines for persons who work with individuals bereaved as a result of suicide:

1. Survivors never resolve their feelings entirely, and therefore any overly ambitious therapeutic goals in this direction may frustrate rather than help the bereaved individual.

2. Some of these bereaved individuals may respond positively to peer group experiences.

3. A family history of suicide should be asked about in interviewing any patient, since some patients may be reluctant to reveal this information.

4. If a patient commits suicide while in therapy, the clinician should make an active effort to talk with the family. Such support at such a crucial moment may have long-lasting benefit for the family members, not to mention the clinician. (p. 284)

Survivor groups have been formed to help suicide survivors with their loss. The American Association of Suicidology has listings of over 120 support groups for survivors and these groups share the goals of education, helping survivors ventilate their feelings, activating social support, and referring survivors for additional professional help when needed (Fremouw et al., 1990).

Gutheil (1988, 1990) noted that outreach to the survivors is both ethically necessary and clinically crucial. Furthermore, because malpractice actions often result from a combination of bad outcome and bad feelings, the psychologist who initiates postvention immediately (and who does not leave the surviving family members with a feeling of being abandoned) is also practicing sound risk management (Ruben, 1990). Berman and Cohen-Sandler (1983) wrote that by increasing the survivors' understanding and gradual acceptance of the loss through postventive work, the psychologist may also "prevent the hasty, emotionally driven initiation of malpractice lawsuits" (p. 17). In short, in making a serious commitment to helping the other survivors deal with their feelings of guilt, grief, rage, and other emotions, the psychologist reflexively helps herself or himself. At the heart of postvention activities is the need to let the other survivors know that the psychologist cares about their welfare and is willing to make himself or herself available to the survivors. (Of course, the deceased patient's confidentiality must be carefully maintained throughout all such activities.)

With regard to confidentiality, it is important to note that, even though the patient has committed suicide, "a factor that may be known publicly, the confidentiality of the physician–patient or psychotherapist–patient relationship (which is protected by state law) still pertains to all information that the therapist possesses about the patient" (Ruben, 1990, pp. 629–630). Psychologists need to understand that the right to devulge such information now "belongs to the legal representative of the deceased. Therefore, if the therapist receives requests from the police who are investigating the patient's death . . . the clinician must obtain a release of information from the patient's administrator or estate executor in order to comply" (p. 630).

In summary, we would like to underscore our position that the wisest and most important step that a clinician can take after a patient's suicide is to consult with a knowledgeable senior colleague about postvention steps. From their different perspectives, the clinician and the consultant can better formulate plans for immediate postvention efforts with the patient's family, as well as reach out to other friends and members of the interpersonal matrix. (This may include postvention with other clinical staff involved in the patient's care; see Cotton, 1989; Friedman, 1989.)

Stromberg et al. (1988) pointed out that, in serious circumstances such as suicides, a psychologist should be aware that every statement she or he makes can be subjected to later judicial scrutiny: "A routine expression of sympathy ('I'm really sorry this happened; I feel so bad') may be characterized later as an admission of legal liability. Therefore, the psychologist should be careful about what is said" (p. 496).

Thus, we must caution the reader: Any discussion with a colleague, or even with one's own family or friends, of the deceased patient's care is usually considered nonprivileged information that is open to the legal discovery process. That is, the plaintiff attorneys will subpoena colleagues and ask what was told to them about your concerns regarding the patient's suicide. Discussions of feelings and concerns regarding possible errors in management or treatment should always be confined to the context of a psychotherapeutic or legal consultation (Ruben, 1990). In particular, clinicians should refrain from making statements to others concerning "their role or responsibility for the patient's death" (Ruben, 1990, p. 623).

Discussing the details of the case in which there is no psychotherapist–patient privilege (i.e., as with the psychologist's own therapist), no attorney–client privilege, and no institutional safeguards against the uncontrolled use of confidential information (e.g., a hospital's peer review/quality assurance meetings) may be a grave error from a legal perspective. The lawyers for the defendant psychologist in the first meeting with their client will invariably ask the question: "Doctor, have you discussed this case with anyone since the patient's suicide?" Defendant attorneys know that any statements made to friends and colleagues about the patient's death may be discoverable by the plaintiff attorneys.

A personal psychotherapeutic consultation for the psychologist-survivor (where all information is privileged) allows the clinician to begin immediately to process the terrible acute emotional aftermath, *before* meeting with other survivors. A personal psychotherapist and a postvention consultant can serve as firm anchors in reality to help in discussion of the management of the psychologist's other patients in this period of intense emotional turmoil. The psychologist and postvention consultant may wish to discuss the advisability of jointly meeting with the family. Here, the postventive consultant can serve as a valuable postvener for both the patient's family and the clinician.

Regrettably, given the current legal climate, only the most naive mental health professional would not consider consulting an attorney immediately following a patient's suicide. Therefore, in addition to consulting with a senior and experienced clinical colleague, we strongly urge psychologists to consult immediately with an attorney who is expert in matters of mental health and the law, allowing the attorney, for example, to help examine professional liability coverage and to assist in notification of the insurance carrier (an often mandatory duty). Furthermore, retaining personal legal counsel will ensure that the clinician's interests are specifically being looked out for. (Please note that the attorney appointed by the insurance carrier has the insurance company and its settlement aims foremost in mind and will ethically advise the psychologist of this fact.)

The legal mechanisms and details that are brought into play should a malpractice action be brought (e.g., what the plaintiff's lawyers will allege, the role of expert witnesses in determining the standard of care, etc.) are discussed in the following sections. Again, we caution that reading the following sections is no substitute for a consultation with a competent attorney.

The Legal Aftermath

In addition to the emotional havoc that the suicide wreaks on survivors (including the patient's psychologist), clinicians are likely to experience fears and realistic apprehensions over the possibility of subsequent malpractice litigation. For, as discussed earlier, currently, the most common legal action involving psychiatric care is the suicide of a patient.

Gutheil (1988) found that in the first 1,200 cases reviewed by the American Psychiatric Association's Insurance Trust, suicide led the list of all possible causes for a suit by a factor of 2. Gutheil also commented that these figures do not do justice to the problem, because the data do not include missed diagnosis (of suicidality) or attempted suicide.

In actual legal practice, there are three types of suicides that can lead to litigation (Gutheil, 1988, 1990):

- outpatient suicides (leading to such questions as whether the clinician should have hospitalized the patient);
- inpatient suicides (prompting attempts to prove failure to observe closely enough, inappropriate transfer, incorrect allocation of privileges, etc.); and
- suicide following discharge or when a patient escapes from an institution (implying that better follow-up and aftercare should have been provided or better precautions taken to prevent escape).

There are also three typical legal conceptualizations of the deceased patient in malpractice actions following a patient suicide (Gutheil, 1988, 1990):

- the patient is a child and the clinician, a negligent and incompetent parent.
- the patient is a product—a defective one, manufactured by the clinician, the institution, or both.
- the bereaved spouse, parents, and children are victims, and the clinician's insurance policy is a ready source of funds for the bereaved.

As we have previously discussed in the section on informed consent, there is one emerging conceptualization that may be effective in refuting attempts by the plaintiff's attorney to portray the patient in a suicide case as an inert being—a helpless child in the hands of her or his negligent caretakers (Gutheil, 1990): the patient's competence (or capacity) to weigh the risks and benefits of "giving or withholding information" (Gutheil, 1990, p. 338) from the hospital staff about his or her suicidal intentions. If the patient's ability to weigh these factors is carefully assessed and that assessment is documented, the patient may realistically be viewed as "an active agent who has some control over the choice of reporting to staff his or her clinical state" (p. 338). However, it is crucial to distinguish this situation from situations in which the patient is too "depressed, psychotic, intoxicated, or otherwise impaired to participate" (p. 338). Gutheil concluded that lay juries appear to be able to comprehend the "distinction between a patient

who can't report on his or her own potential for suicide and one who 'won't' ''
(Gutheil, 1990, p. 338).

The value of any such determination relies on a solid grounding in good
clinical care and an understanding of risk–benefit analysis (e.g., the accuracy of
the clinician's assessments to determine foreseeability and subsequent affirmative
actions). As noted earlier, the courts recognize that the prediction of the course
of a mental disorder is a professional judgment of high responsibility and, in
some cases, a judgment that involves a measure of calculated risk (Robertson,
1988).

The crucial importance of outreach and compassion toward the bereaved
survivors cannot be overemphasized. It is unethical, heartless, and the poorest
possible defensive risk management practice to ''abandon'' the family and friends
after a patient's suicide out of a fear of litigation. Ruben (1990) states that not
talking or meeting with the family after the patient's suicide is a most foolhardy
course of action: ''it has the greatest potential for inciting family members to
initiate legal actions against the therapist'' (p. 625).

Underscoring the enormity of this particular mistake, Litman (1982) details
the circumstances of the following case: A 22-year-old first year student at a
prestigious Eastern law school became discouraged and depressed during the
first year. He was seen in the student health clinic complaining of an inability
to study and of the classic signs of depression, including suicidal ideation. After
he spent two nights sleeping in the college infirmary and being watched by an
off-duty policeman, his parents flew in from the West Coast with the intention
of taking the patient home, but were told by a psychiatric social worker at the
infirmary and by the psychiatrist in charge that they were being overly protective
and that better treatment could be provided in a local teaching hospital. The
patient was admitted on a weekend and was seen for a brief period by the on-duty
admitting physician and for a brief time by the staff psychiatrist. In neither
instance was there an evaluation of the patient's suicide potential, nor was there
a definite treatment plan or case disposition. On Sunday morning, the patient
appears to have

> telephoned an ex-girl friend in New York. He then ingested a lethal
> amount of caustic poison which he found in an unlocked utility room
> where it was used for urine testing, and then jumped from a window to
> a lawn below. He survived the fall but died subsequently of the poison.
> (Litman, 1982, p. 214)

Litman (1982) further reported that in this case the hospital staff made no
effort to talk with the bereaved parents, and it was extremely difficult for the
parents to obtain any information at all about what had happened to their son.
''Finally they consulted an attorney in order to find a way to obtain information

about what had happened'' (p. 214). Eventually this legal consultation led to a malpractice lawsuit for negligence. The crucial point is that, according to Litman (who had agreed to serve as an expert witness for the family), even 2 years after the death the hospital could have settled this case ''by giving the parents a full explanation, publicly admitting guilt, and paying the legal expenses already accumulated'' (p. 214). In fact, Litman had actually attempted to arrange this. Five years after the patient's death, the case went to trial. One week into the trial, when it had become obvious to the hospital, clinical staff, and their counsel that there was no defense, ''the hospital and staff settled for $185,000 in damages and a full public admission of negligence'' (Litman, 1982, p. 214). Litman commented that this particular hospital was staffed by ''renowned doctors from the world's best medical schools. Nevertheless, there were numerous gross violations of minimal standards of care and prudent judgment (both before and after the death)'' (Litman, 1982, p. 214).

The role of the attorneys

Once the plaintiffs consult an attorney and decide to bring a malpractice action, the attorneys for both plaintiff and defendant will request copies of all documentation pertinent to the case (e.g., all outpatient and hospital charts, files from police and medical examiners's offices). The plaintiff's attorney may have already done this prior to bringing a suit to evaluate the strength of the case. The attorneys will also obtain sworn statements and depositions from a variety of sources (e.g., the attending clinicians, hospital staff, friends, relatives, associates of the patient). These witnesses will be asked, under oath, to give information about the deceased patient and the circumstances of the patient's death (Litman, 1982).

Before proceeding to the specific theories of negligence and what the attorneys for plaintiff and defendant will allege in an actual trial situation, it may be helpful to make a few comments on the realities of malpractice actions. Perhaps the most important factor in understanding the special dynamics of malpractice suits is that these cases do not try well before a jury. Insurance carriers, being realists, will always bear in mind the substantial cost of courtroom litigation, which, when combined with the uncertainty of outcome, makes settlement an appealing expedient. A settlement will fix the amount of the loss ''at a dollar figure which is invariably much less than the dollar value of the damage claim and avoids the risk of prolonged litigation ending in a substantial jury award'' (Slawson et al., 1974, p. 62).

From experience, the insurance carrier knows that in the courtroom drama of a malpractice action, there can be no certainty as to the verdict. Even when evidence in support of the defendant seems overwhelming, an emotional verdict for the plaintiff is always possible because of the spontaneous tendency on the part of members of a jury to identify with the bereaved and suffering plaintiffs.

Regardless of the strength or technical elegance of the legal defense, it may at times carry less weight with jurors than their understandable and natural wish to offset the plaintiffs' suffering and loss. For the jury has two essential tasks: They must decide if there "has been a wrong and if so, how much money will right it" (Slawson et al., 1974, p. 62).

Robertson (1988), however, contended that jurors can, at times, be seen as cynical—that juries can be reluctant to reward the suicide plaintiff. He reasoned that such jurors may believe that suicide is ultimately a person's own responsibility and, if one is serious about committing suicide, no effort on the part of a clinician could have prevented the tragedy. For some jurors, suicide may be seen as a sin, whereas others will privately express surprise that plaintiffs can bring a suit following the suicide of a loved one. It is the role of the plaintiff's attorney to defuse and to discuss these attitudes during jury selection.

The plaintiff's attorney will seek to educate the jurors, to bring them to accept the notion that mental health professionals are charged routinely with evaluating suicide potential and that it is the usual and customary role of the mental health professional to take affirmative precautions to protect patients from themselves. The most commonly used conceptualization in reaching the hearts of the jurors is to equate the patient with a helpless child who desperately needs and relies on the parental figure of the psychotherapist for protection—that is, the patient has a diminished capacity or competence to care for himself or herself and is therefore not responsible for his or her actions. The plaintiff's attorney may make the emotional argument that "after all, suicide is really the act of dying of sadness" (Robertson, 1988, p. 199).

The plaintiff's attorney will use a similar theme for proving that the patient was not guilty of comparative negligence because he or she was not rational or had impaired judgment. Robertson (1988) noted that it is often necessary (as a specific strategy) to demonstrate that the patient was not negligent when he or she refused voluntary hospitalization.

Common legal defenses

For psychologists used to the more empathic and sensitive realm of psychotherapy, some defense strategies may seem to exhibit a callousness of the worst possible sort. Yet such defensive practices are the reality of a malpractice trial. The following are examples of common defense strategies (Robertson, 1988):

1. ***Best judgment defense***
   The defense will portray the defendant as an honest practitioner who used her or his best judgment after careful testing, evaluation, and consultation. Robertson commented that this particular defense is often more "effective on appeal than at the jury level" (p. 199). However, if the defendant did not review the patient's records or

conduct an adequate examination for elevated risk, there is no basis for this defense.

2. *Impossible to predict*

This particular defense is usually based on the statistical impossibility of predicting suicide and is often documented by the lack of suicide ideation, impulses, gestures, or attempts. The defendant psychologist must demonstrate that the patient, the patient's family, or both parties denied any suicidal threats, gestures, impulses, or ideas and that there was no foreseeable clinical reason to have expected the patient's suicide.

3. *Blaming the family*

This particular defense, although appearing heartless, callous, and reprehensible to many clinicians, is considered by lawyers to be an effective challenge—a way of attempting to shift the focus of responsibility to the family. For example, the defense will attempt to show that a spouse or other family member sometimes refused to tell clinicians about a prior suicide history. Robertson commented that defense lawyers will allege a failure on the part of the family to monitor medications, to properly observe the patient at home, and to report a change in the patient's condition (as the family had agreed to do in the management plan). Lawyers for the defense at times will also attempt to show that the surviving spouse or family "drove" the patient to suicide. (Robertson commented that, if a marriage is rocky and there is evidence of the surviving spouse's infidelity, a marital separation, or intense family strife, the jury is more likely to punish the surviving spouse or family than to "reward" the survivors.)

4. *Family or widow/widower guilt complex*

This is a similar, and in the eyes of those in the helping professions, callous and superficial view of the tragedy. Yet, lawyers will commonly allege that the family or surviving spouse "feels guilty over the suicide and is seeking to assuage that guilt" (Robertson, 1988, p. 200). Defense lawyers will allege that this survivor guilt is projected onto the luckless defendant, "whose only crime was to care enough to be there at the end and console the family after the death" (p. 200). Robertson further noted that this is a "touchy" argument and should not be used to "bury" the surviving spouse or family but, instead, to excuse them and the defendant from any culpability.

5. *Intervening or supervening causes*

This defense typically rests on the premise that some suicides occur after the patient is discharged or is no longer in active treatment.

A change in circumstances or intense aggravation caused by someone else might have precipitated the suicide (unbeknownst to the defendant).

6. *Contributory or comparative negligence*
The defense will try to prove, using expert testimony, that the patient was not irrationally incompetent and that the patient was responsible for her or his actions as much as any other plaintiff. For example, the defense will try to use the concealment of a history of previous suicide attempts or the patient's refusal to be hospitalized. Robertson noted that a jury could then reduce any award by the percentage of comparative negligence.

7. *The missing defendant*
Here, defense attorneys will state that the "real" culprit is actually a prior or subsequent treating health care professional (e.g., former or subsequent therapist). If the suicide occurs months after the defendant treated the patient, "the subsequent treating doctor should be impleaded" if there is evidence that "she or he failed to diagnose the patient's condition" (Robertson, 1988, p. 201). However, it is often a better defense strategy to enlist the cooperation of prior or subsequent treating clinicians, rather than alienating them. (The records of prior treatment can help to establish that there was no history of suicide, and the former therapist can help to substantiate that there was no prior evidence of suicidal ideation, impulse, or behavior.)

8. *The least restrictive alternative*
Effective mental health treatment recognizes that, at times, the least restrictive environment alternative, rather than hospitalization (with constant observation), is the best course of treatment. The clinician may consider the least restrictive alternative or the use of appropriate alternative treatments. (This is sometimes referred to as the "respectable minority" defense.)[2]

In the case of a patient's suicide and the determination of the psychologist's liability—despite contrary instructions from the bench—the jurors may feel that the fact of suicide shows negligence and choose to indemnify the plaintiffs on that basis. For as health care becomes more impersonal, "the professional liability

---

[2]For a recent debate on this particular defense, the reader is directed to published discussion between Gutheil (1990) and Sadoff (1990) and to the recent debate between Klerman (1989) and Stone (1989a). For specific examples of defense malpractice panel briefs, trial opening statements, and cross-examinations of expert witnesses, see Robertson (1988), Appendix D, and chapters 8 and 9.

carrier has been cast in the role of a legitimate resource in case of untoward result'' (Slawson et al., 1974, p. 62).

The role of expert witnesses

It is the role of the expert witness to provide testimony to help guide the court relative to accepted standards of professional practice and any departures therefrom. However, it is important to understand that courts have been known to elevate standards and do have the authority to determine what is adequate (see especially, Berman & Cohen-Sandler's, 1983, analysis of *Hellig v. Carey*, 1974). In an occasional situation, the breach of duty may be considered so reckless or egregious as to be within the common knowledge of a prudent layman, and no expert testimony would be required. Usually, the facts about adequacy and propriety of treatment are in dispute, and so expert opinion is presented by both the plaintiff and the defendant. In the end, the credibility of the expert testimony may be the determining factor (Rachlin, 1984).

Berman and Cohen-Sandler (1983), in their discussion of expert testimony and the standard of care, stated that in malpractice actions following a suicide, the issue is what constitutes ''reasonable'' professional judgment. They wrote that, unlike the medical sciences, there is ''little in mental health treatment that is unequivocally considered standard'' (p. 6). In fact, ''a variety of activities, some viewed as deviant or even radical may not be unacceptable or unreasonable'' treatments (p. 6). They concluded that, if a clinician deviates from a prevailing standard, negligence would be found ''only if, on the basis of expert testimony, such treatments were deemed unreasonable'' (p. 6).

Therefore, when litigation ensues, the two issues of foreseeability and causation are typically determined on the basis of the testimony of expert witnesses' opinions as to the performance of the attending clinician(s), hospital, and inpatient staff (Litman, 1982). For example, in *Meier v. Ross General Hospital* (1968), where a patient was admitted because he was suicidal (and had previously attempted to kill himself), the patient was left in a second-floor room with a window that was not secured (i.e., unbarred and easily opened wide). The patient jumped from the window and killed himself. The court, after hearing expert testimony, held that since the hospital knew there was a likelihood of suicide, it was obliged to use reasonable care in protecting the patient. However, Robertson (1988) noted that in *Vistica v. Presbyterian Hospital and Medical Center* (1967), the court decided that no expert witnesses were needed: The patient was hospitalized as suicidal, the hospital knew this, and clearly did not take needed affirmative precautions.

Berman and Cohen-Sandler (1983) pointed out that, although reasonableness has been measured by customary professional standards, this standard is neither objective nor fixed. For example, they found that ''the more extensive the involvement one has in suicidology, the greater the perception of a gap between observed and accepted levels of care'' (p. 18).

To qualify as an expert witness, a professional ''must demonstrate that he or she has acquired special knowledge of the subject matter about which testimony is to be given'' (Berman & Cohen-Sandler, 1983, p. 7). The specific competency of the expert is usually attested to by the statement that she or he is duly licensed to practice her or his profession. However, it has been noted by Berman and Cohen-Sandler (1983) that, in cases of suicide, the possession of a particular degree or license may not by itself be sufficient. They found that ''no clear guidelines are provided by the legal system'' (p. 7) for the qualifications of the expert witness in the cases of suicide. For example, is expertise defined by the label of *suicidologist* (an expert in treatment and research in the study of suicide) or by a certain level of experience in working with suicidal patients? This question is still open to debate, and no professional discipline appears to have exclusive rights to serve as an expert in providing testimony to the court regarding the standard of care of another mental health colleague. Psychologists, sociologists, nurses, and social workers have all served as expert witnesses in cases of malpractice against professionals in other disciplines (e.g., psychiatrists). It is crucial, however, that the expert witness stay within his or her statutory and professionally defined areas of practice competencies when offering expert testimony (Robertson, 1988).

Expert witnesses, like the attorneys, will examine all clinical material (e.g., charts, intake sheets, emergency room notes) and all sworn statements and depositions obtained by the attorneys. They will also examine police and medical examiner's files and records and, while serving as expert, meet repeatedly with their clients to go over any specific ambiguities and uncertainties. Ultimately, they will provide their opinion to those who retained them and, if called upon to do so in court, on very specific issues such as foreseeability and failure to take affirmative precautions in the provision of a standard of care (Litman, 1982).

Finally, it may be useful to restate that there are always areas of indecision, gray areas where clinicians will disagree, resulting in differences of opinion among both treating clinicians and expert witnesses (Sadoff, 1985). Not uncommonly, highly respected and nationally renowned clinicians and clinical researchers in their roles as expert witnesses for each side completely disagree in their retrospective evaluation of the standard of care.[3]

A key contributor to any confusion or disagreement over rules within the context of the legal system has been ''attributing to professional people the capacity to predict and control the behavior of the mentally ill'' (Perr, 1988,

---

[3]For examples of such published differences of opinion in both the legal and clinical realm, the reader is directed to discussions between Maltsberger (1989), Roth (1989), Gutheil (1990), and Sadoff (1990) and to the recent debate between Klerman (1989) and Stone (1989a).

p. 4). With regard to this latter point, we stress again the importance of expert witnesses remaining within their specific area of expertise (see Perr, 1985a, 1985b; 1988; Sadoff, 1985).

Berman and Cohen-Sandler (1983) stated that, regardless of discipline, suicidologists serve as "expert witnesses (as well they should) in malpractice actions involving nonsuicidologists" (pp. 15–16). One benefit to patients from the use of a suicidologist as an expert witness is that, through his or her testimony, he or she aims to raise the current standards that are often so "minimal that only the most blatantly foolish actions are determined to be negligent" (Berman & Cohen-Sandler, 1983, p. 15). We wish to emphasize that an important goal of this book is to establish sound guidelines for clinical practice based on a comprehensive and flexible understanding of both clinical and legal realities, rather than on arbitrarily dictated "cookbook" abstractions. Although raising the standard of care through such testimony may result in an increase in the court's expectation of higher standards of treatment (and, in the short run, result in an increase in successful malpractice actions against practitioners), a higher standard for treatment has the long-term potential benefit of clinicians routinely providing an improved level of care.

Summary

We believe that for *every* patient seen in professional psychological practice there are a few essential steps that can dramatically reduce one's exposure, should a malpractice action be brought. These steps provide a set of standards that will ensure the highest level of professional treatment for the patients under our care, suicidal patients in particular.

Practice and Risk Management Guidelines

For each patient seen as part of a psychologist's professional practice activities, there must be an initial evaluation and assessment, regular ongoing clinical evaluations and case reviews, consultation reports and supervision reports (where indicated), and a formal treatment plan. All of these activities need to demonstrate specifically a solid understanding of the significant factors used to assess elevated risk of suicide and how to manage such risk—with a documented understanding of the prognosis for the success (or possible paths to failure) of subsequent outpatient (or inpatient) treatment or case disposition.

Documentation

Psychologists must be aware of the vital importance of the written case record. In cases of malpractice, courts and juries often have been observed to operate on the simplistic principle that "if it isn't written down, it didn't happen" (no matter what the subsequent testimony or elaboration of the defendant maintains). Defensive clinical notes, written after the fact, may help somewhat in damage control, but there is no substitute for a timely, thoughtful, and complete chart record that demonstrates (through clear and well-written assessment, review, and treatment notes) a knowledge of the epidemiology, risk factors, and treatment literature for the suicidal patient. Such a case record should also include (where possible) a formal informed consent for treatment, formal assessment of competence, and a documentation of confidentiality considerations (e.g., that limits were explained at the start of any treatment).

Information on previous treatment

Psychologists must obtain, whenever possible, all previous treatment records. These records should include not only psychological records but also medical records.

Involvement of the family and significant others

When appropriate, psychologists should involve the family and significant others in the management or disposition plan. The family and significant others are good sources of information (both current and background) and can serve as an integral and effective part of the support system.

Consultation on present clinical circumstances

Psychologists should routinely obtain consultation and/or supervision (or make referrals) on all cases where suicide risk is determined to be even moderate, and after a patient suicide or serious suicide attempt. They should also obtain consultation on and/or supervision on (or refer) cases that are outside their documented training, education, or experience, as well as when they are unsure of the best avenue for initiating or continuing treatment. The principle that two perspectives are better than one should always guide the clinician in moments of clinical uncertainty.

Sensitivity to medical issues

Clinicians should be knowledgeable about the effects of psychotropic medication and make appropriate referrals for a medication evaluation. If the psychologist decides that medication is not indicated in the present instance, he or she should thoroughly document the reasoning for this decision in the written case record. Where appropriate, the patient (and, when it is indicated, the patient's family or significant others) should be included in this decision-making process. Psychologists need to know the possible organic etiologies for suicidality and seek immediate appropriate medical consultation for the patient when they detect any signs of an organic condition.

Knowledge of community resources

Psychologists who see suicidal patients should have access to the full armamen-tarium of resources for voluntary and involuntary hospital admissions, day treat-ment, 24-hour emergency backup, and crisis centers. This access can be direct or indirect (through an ongoing collaborative relationship with a psychologist or psychiatrist colleague).

Consideration of the effect on self and others

If a patient succeeds in committing suicide (or makes a serious suicide attempt), psychologists should be aware not only of their legal responsibilities (e.g., they must notify their insurance carrier in a timely fashion), but, more important, of the immediate clinical necessity of attending to both the needs of the bereaved survivors and to the psychologist's own emotional needs. (The psychologist must acknowledge that it is both normal and difficult to work through feelings about a patient's death or near-death and that he or she, having lost a patient to suicide, is also a suicide survivor.) The concern should be for the living. After consultation with a knowledgeable colleague and an attorney, immediate clinical outreach to the survivors is not only sensitive and concerned clinical care, but in helping the survivors to deal with the catastrophic aftermath via an effective clinical postven-tion effort, the psychologist is also practicing effective risk management.

Preventive preparation

Most important, psychologists must be cognizant of all of the standards above and take affirmative steps to ensure that they have the requisite knowledge, training, experience, and clinical resources prior to accepting high-risk patients into their professional care. This requires that all of these mechanisms be in place *before* the onset of any suicidal crisis.

Afterword

An Abiding Concern for Patient Welfare

Suits against mental health professionals are traumatic experiences, yet they remain a relatively rare occurrence (when compared to the large number of suits against the practitioner in nonpsychiatric medical specialities). The fear of being sued probably has more widespread and deleterious effect on clinicians than do actual lawsuits. Although there is no specific set of clinical practices that can absolutely guarantee a psychologist that she or he will be immune from either losing a patient to suicide or from being sued (and being held liable), there are some sources of reassurance as well as ways to reduce overall risk when assessing or treating a suicidal patient (Hoge & Appelbaum, 1989).

Pope (1986) stated that, in assessing and treating the suicidal patient, "perhaps most importantly communicate that you care" (p. 20). Although individual psychologists may differ in the ways that they demonstrate such caring, they can truly extend themselves in their management efforts to demonstrate their commitment to doing whatever needs to be done to keep the patient alive and that every effort will be made to help the patient to decrease his or her pain, perturbation, and lethality.

Psychologists must resist the temptation to use inappropriate defensive clinical practices that, while limiting their liability exposure, may not be to the patient's benefit. Such temptations—for example, ordering excessive precautions or treatments to prevent or limit liability or avoiding procedures or treatments out of fear of a suit, even though such treatments may be to the patient's benefit—are both "unconscionable and potentially legally catastrophic" (Simon, 1988, p. 7). The psychologist who practices such inappropriate behaviors is not automatically shielded from charges of negligence. On the contrary, psychologists pursuing such defensive practices that may harm their patients can be sued for falling below the accepted standard of care.

Instead, the guiding principle in all our efforts toward the care of the suicidal patient should always be to keep the benefit to the patient foremost in our mind. Hoge and Appelbaum (1989) observed that, when a clinician is uncertain of what to do in a particular situation, the best course is "that which is consonant with the patient's therapeutic interests" (p. 619). They further noted that even if this "leads to a poor result . . . acting in the patient's interests will almost always be taken as evidence of good faith on the therapist's part" (p. 619). They concluded that too many psychotherapists become needlessly paralyzed in the face of difficult decisions with potential legal ramifications "when a return to first clinical principles is really all that is necessary" (p. 619).

Optimizing Levels of Care

Throughout this book, we have detailed the clinical and legal knowledge base, and have recommended guidelines for assessment and management of the suicidal patient on the basis of an optimal rather than minimal standard of care. Such specific issues as consultation, durable documentation, assessment of personal and professional competency, and involvement of the family and interpersonal matrix are all key elements in high-quality clinical practice and risk management. However, our efforts toward the detection of elevated risk and the taking of affirmative precautions (on the basis of detected risk) must, ultimately, rest on a foundation of highly individualized, systematic, and integrative care within the context of a sound therapeutic alliance (Bongar et al., 1989).

The Therapeutic Alliance

When seeing patients in ongoing treatment, one of the most significant factors used to assess suicide risk and to determine the prognosis for the success of subsequent treatment is the quality of the therapeutic alliance (Bongar et al., 1989; Gutheil, 1990; Hoge & Appelbaum, 1989; Peterson & Bongar, 1989; Simon, 1988; Smith, 1988). This relationship has been put forward by Simon (1988) as the bedrock indicator of the patient's willingness to seek help and sustenance through personal relationships during serious emotional crises. In addition, Maltsberger (1986) specifically addressed the issue of the absence of sustaining interpersonal relationships as a key factor in the clinical formulation of suicide risk. Clinicians, in seeking to understand clinical and legal requirements, should "emphasize principles that can be generalized to new situations, rather than blind rules" (Hope & Appelbaum, 1989, p. 620). Above all, legal regulation must be seen in the context of the clinician–patient relationship (Hoge & Appelbaum, 1989; Simon, 1988). The presence or absence of a good working therapeutic alliance can be used as an ongoing and robust measure of the treatment's effect on the patient's vulnerability to suicide (Bongar et al., 1989).

One of the reasons that mental health professionals are sued less often than professionals in other health care specialities is the emphasis that mental health clinicians have traditionally placed on developing and maintaining a good psychotherapist–patient relationship. "It is an axiom among malpractice attorneys that clinicians who maintain good relationships with their patients do not get sued, even in the face of unfortunate outcomes" (Hoge & Appelbaum, 1989, p. 619). Psychologists and other health care providers are neither omniscient nor omnipotent, and the law does not require that we be so. When our best efforts fail, we share with other survivors a "despair born of death too soon" (Slawson et al., 1974, p. 63).

In conclusion, as psychologists, we might do well to focus our clinical efforts on Shneidman's basic maxim for working with suicidal patients (Shneidman, 1985). This rule borrows heavily from the philosophy of crisis intervention "to see our involvement with the suicidal patient not as an attempt to ameliorate the patient's entire personality or to cure all emotional illness, but rather as an attempt to meet the immediate need to keep the person alive" (Bongar et al., 1989, pp. 64–65).

References

Abille v. United States, 482 F.Supp. 703 (N.D. Cal. 1980).

Abram, H. S., Moore, G. I., & Westervelt, F. B. (1971). Suicidal behavior in chronic dialysis patients. *American Journal of Psychiatry, 127*, 1199.

Achte, K. (1988). Suicidal tendencies in the elderly. *Suicide and Life-Threatening Behavior, 18*(1), 55–64.

Alcohol, Drug Abuse, and Mental Health Administration. (1989). *Report of the Secretary's Task Force on Youth Suicide: Vols. I–IV*. (DHSS Publication Nos. ADM 89-1621–1624). Washington, DC: U.S. Government Printing Office.

Allen, N. H. (1983). Homicide followed by suicide: Los Angeles, 1970–1979. *Suicide and Life-Threatening Behavior, 13*(3), 155–165.

Alonso, A. (1985). *The quiet profession: Supervisors of psychotherapy*. New York: Macmillan.

Alvarez, A. (1971). *The savage god*. New York: Random House.

Alvarez, A. (1976). Literature in the nineteenth and twentieth centuries. In S. Perlin (Ed.), *A handbook for the study of suicide* (pp. 31–60). New York: Oxford University Press.

Amchin, J., Wettstein, R. M., & Roth, L. H. (1990). Suicide, ethics, and the law. In S. J. Blumenthal & D. J. Kupfer (Eds.), *Suicide over the life cycle: Risk factors, assessment, and treatment of suicidal patients* (pp. 637–664). Washington, DC: American Psychiatric Press.

American Jurisprudence. (1981). *2d Volume 61 Review* New York: The Lawyer's Cooperative Publishing Co.

American Psychiatric Association. (1987). *Diagnostic and statistical manual of mental disorders* (rev. 3rd ed.). Washington, DC: Author.

American Psychological Association. (1981a). Ethical principles of psychologists. *The American Psychologist, 36*(6), 633–638.

American Psychological Association. (1981b). Specialty guidelines for the delivery of psychological services by clinical psychologists. *The American Psychologist, 36*(6), 640–651.

American Psychological Association. (1981c). Specialty guidelines for the delivery of services by counseling psychologists. *The American Psychologist, 36*(6), 652–663.

American Psychological Association (1981d). Specialty guidelines for the delivery of services by industrial/organizational psychologists. *The American Psychologist, 36*(6), 664–669.

American Psychological Association (1981e). Specialty guidelines for the delivery of services by school psychologists. *The American Psychologist, 36*(6), 670–681.

American Psychological Association (1987). General guidelines for providers of psychological services. *The American Psychologist, 42*(1), 712–723.

Appelbaum, P. S., Lidz, C. W., & Meisel, A. (1987). *Informed consent: Legal theory and clinical practice.* New York: Oxford University Press.

Arana, G. W., & Hyman, S. (1989). Biological contributions to suicide. In D. G. Jacobs & H. N. Brown (Eds.), *Suicide: Understanding and responding: Harvard Medical School perspectives on suicide* (pp. 73–86). Madison, CT: International Universities Press.

Asarnow, J. R., Carlson, G. A., & Guthrie, D. (1987). Coping strategies, self-perceptions, hopelessness, and perceived family environments in depressed and suicidal children. *Journal of Consulting and Clinical Psychology, 55*, 361–366.

Asberg, M., Bertillson, L., & Martensson, B. (1984). CSF monoamine metabolites, depression, and suicide. *Advances in Biochemical Psychopharmacology, 39*, 87–97.

Asberg, M., Traskman, L., & Thoren, P. (1976). 5-HIAA in the cerebrospinal fluid: A biochemical suicide predictor? *Archives of General Psychiatry, 33*, 1193–1197.

Bachrach, L. L. (1983). Planning services for chronically mentally ill patients. *Bulletin of the Menninger Clinic, 47*, 163–188.

Barraclough, B., Bunch, J., Nelson, B., & Sainsbury, P. (1974). A hundred cases of suicide: Clinical aspects. *British Journal of Psychiatry, 125*, 355–373.

Bassuk, E. L. (1982). General principles of assessment. In E. L. Bassuk, S. C. Schoonover, & A. D. Gill (Eds.), *Lifelines: Clinical perspectives on suicide* (pp. 17–46). New York: Plenum.

Battin, M. P. (1982). *Ethical issues in suicide.* Englewood Cliffs, NJ: Prentice Hall.

Battin, M. P. (1983). Suicide and ethical theory. *Suicide and Life-Threatening Behavior, 13*(4), 231–239.

Battin, M. P., & Mayo, D. J. (Eds.). (1980). *Suicide: Philosophical issues.* New York: St. Martin's Press.

Beck, A. T. (1967). *Depression: Clinical, experimental, and theoretical aspects.* New York: Harper & Row.

Beck, A. T. (1986). Hopelessness as a predictor of eventual suicide. In J. J. Mann & M. Stanley (Eds.), *Psychobiology* (pp. 90–96). New York: Academy of Sciences.

Beck, A. T., Brown, G., Berchick, R. J., Stewart, B. L., & Steer, R. A. (1990). Relation of hopelessness to ultimate suicide: A replication with psychiatric outpatients. *American Journal of Psychiatry, 147*(2), 190–195.

Beck, A. T., Kovacs, M., & Weissman, A. (1975). Hopelessness and suicidal behavior. *Journal of the American Medical Association, 234*, 1146–1149.

Beck, A. T., Kovacs, M., & Weissman, A. (1979). Assessment of suicidal intention: The scale for suicide ideation. *Journal of Consulting and Clinical Psychology, 47*, 343–352.

Beck, A. T., Resnik, H. L. P., & Lettieri, D. J. (Eds.). (1986). *The prediction of suicide*. Philadelphia, PA: The Charles Press Publishers.

Beck, A. T., Rush, A. J., Shaw, B. F., & Emery, G. (1979). *Cognitive therapy of depression: A treatment manual*. New York: Guilford Press.

Beck, A. T., Schuyler, D., & Herman, I. (1974). Development of suicidal intent scales. In A. T. Beck, H. L. P. Resnik, & D. J. Lettieri (Eds.), *The prediction of suicide* (pp. 45–56). Bowie, MD: The Charles Press Publishers.

Beck, A. T., & Steer, R. A. (1987). *Beck Depression Inventory: Manual*. San Antonio, TX: The Psychological Corporation.

Beck, A. T., & Steer, R. A. (1988). *Beck Hopelessness Scale: Manual*. San Antonio, TX: The Psychological Corporation.

Beck, A. T., & Steer, R. A. (1989). Clinical predictors of eventual suicide: A 5- to 10-year prospective study of suicide attempters. *Journal of Affective Disorders, 17*, 203–209.

Beck, A. T., Steer, R. A., Kovacs, M., & Garrison, B. (1985). Hopelessness and eventual suicide: A 10-year prospective study of patients hospitalized with suicidal ideation. *American Journal of Psychiatry, 142*, 559–563.

Beck, A. T., Steer, R. A., & Ranieri, W. F. (1988). Scale for suicide ideation: Psychometric properties of a self-report version. *Journal of Clinical Psychology, 44*(4), 500–505.

Beck, A. T., Weissman, A., Lester, D., & Trexler, L. (1974). The measurement of pessimism: The Hopelessness Scale. *Journal of Consulting and Clinical Psychology, 42*(1), 861–865.

Bell v. New York City Health & Hospitals Corporation, 90 A.D. 2d 270, 456 N.Y.S.2d 787 (1982).

Bellah v. Greenson, 146 Cal. Rptr. 535 (1978).

Benesohn, H., & Resnik, H. L. P. (1973). Guidelines for "suicide proofing" a psychiatric unit. *American Journal of Psychotherapy, 26*, 204–211.

Bennett, B. E., Bryant, B. K., VandenBos, G. R., & Greenwood, A. (1990). *Professional liability and risk management*. Washington, DC: American Psychological Association.

Berman, A. (1983). *Training committee report*. Unpublished manuscript. (Available from the American Association of Suicidology, 2459 South Ash, Denver, CO 80222)

Berman, A. (1986a). A critical look at our adolescence: Notes on turning 18 (and 75). *Suicide and Life-Threatening Behavior, 16*(1), 1–12.

Berman, A. (1986b). Adolescent suicides: Issues and challenges. In S. M. Bronheim, P. R. Magrab, & R. B. Shearin (Eds.), *Seminars in adolescent medicine: Adolescent depression and suicide* (pp. 269–277). New York: Thieme Medical Publishers.

Berman, A. L., & Cohen-Sandler, R. (1982). Suicide and the standard of care: Optimal versus acceptable. *Suicide and Life-Threatening Behavior, 12*(2), 114–122.

Berman, A. L., & Cohen-Sandler, R. (1983). Suicide and malpractice: Expert testimony and the standard of care. *Professional Psychology: Research and Practice, 14*(1), 6–19.

Berman, A. L., & Jobes, D. (in press). *Adolescent suicide: Assessment and intervention.* Washington, DC: American Psychological Association.

Beutler, L. E. (1988). Introduction to the special series: Training to competency in psychotherapy. *Journal of Consulting and Clinical Psychology, 56,* 651–652.

Beutler, L. E. (1989). Differential treatment selection: The role of diagnosis in psychotherapy. *Psychotherapy, 26*(3), 271–281.

Beyer, H. A. (1982). Suicide: A legal perspective. In E. L. Bassuk, S. C. Schoonover, & A. Gill (Eds.), *Lifelines: Clinical perspectives on suicide* (pp. 225–228). New York: Plenum.

Black, D. W., & Winokur, G. (1990). Suicide and psychiatric diagnosis. In S. J. Blumenthal & D. J. Kupfer (Eds.), *Suicide over the life cycle: Risk factors, assessment, and treatment of suicidal patients* (pp. 135–154). Washington, DC: American Psychiatric Press.

Blaker, K. P. (1972). Systems theory and self-destructive behavior. *Perspectives in Psychiatric Care, 10,* 168–172.

Blumenthal, S. J. (1990). An overview and synopsis of risk factors, assessment, and treatment of suicidal patients over the life cycle. In S. J. Blumenthal & D. J. Kupfer (Eds.), *Suicide over the life cycle: Risk factors, assessment, and treatment of suicidal patients* (pp. 685–734). Washington, DC: American Psychiatric Press.

Board of Professional Affairs, Committee on Professional Standards. (1987a). Casebook for providers of psychological services. *The American Psychologist, 42*(7), 704–711.

Board of Professional Affairs, Committee on Professional Standards. (1987b). General guidelines for providers of psychological services. *The American Psychologist, 42*(7), 712–723.

Bogust v. Iverson (1960). 10 Wis. 2d 129, 102 N.W. 2d 228.

Bohanan, P. (1943). *African homicide and suicide.* Princeton, NJ: Princeton University Press.

Bongar, B., Forcier, L. A., & Peterson, L. G. (in press). Views on difficult and dreaded patients: A preliminary investigation. *Medical Psychotherapy.*

Bongar, B. & Harmatz, M. (1989). Graduate training in clinical psychology and the study of suicide. *Professional Psychology: Research and Practice, 20*(4), 209–213.

Bongar, B. & Harmatz, M. (1990, August). Clinical psychology graduate education in the study of suicide: Availability, resources, and importance in NCSPP versus CUDCP programs. In B. Bongar & E. A. Harris (Chairs), *Contemporary developments in the assessment and management of the suicidal patient.* Symposium conducted at the meeting of the American Psychological Association, Boston, MA.

Bongar, B., Peterson, L. G., Golann, S., & Hardiman, J. J. (1990). Self-mutilation and the chronically "suicidal" emergency room patient. *Annals of Clinical Psychiatry, 2*(3), 217–222.

Bongar, B., Peterson, L. G., Harris, E. A., & Aissis, J. (1989). Clinical and legal considerations in the management of suicidal patients: An integrative overview. *Journal of Integrative and Eclectic Psychotherapy, 8*(1), 53–67.

Boyd, J. (1983). The increasing rate of suicide by firearms. *New England Journal of Medicine, 308,* 872–898.

Brent, D. A., & Kolko, D. J. (1990). The assessment and treatment of children and adolescents at risk for suicide. In S. J. Blumenthal & D. J. Kupfer (Eds.), *Suicide over the life cycle: Risk factors, assessment, and treatment of suicidal patients* (pp. 253–302). Washington, DC: American Psychiatric Press.

Brent, D. A., Kupfer, D. J., Bromet, E. J., & Dew, M. A. (1988). The assessment and treatment of patients at risk for suicide. In A. J. Frances & R. E. Hales (Eds.), *American Psychiatric Press Review of Psychiatry: Vol. 7* (pp. 353–385). Washington, DC: American Psychiatric Press.

Brown, H. N. (1987). The impact of suicides on therapists in training. *Comprehensive Psychiatry, 28*(2), 101–112.

Brown, H. N. (1989). Patient suicide and therapists in training. In D. G. Jacobs & H. N. Brown (Eds.), *Suicide: Understanding and responding: Harvard Medical School perspectives on suicide* (pp. 415–434). Madison, CT: International Universities Press.

Brown, J., Henteleff, P., Barakat, S., & Rowe, C. J. (1986). Is it normal for terminally ill patients to desire death? *American Journal of Psychiatry, 143,* 208–211.

Brown, L., Ebert, M. H., Goyer, P. F., Jimerson, D., Klein, W. J., Bunney, W. E., & Goodwin, F. K. (1982). Aggression, suicide, and serotonin: Relationship to CSF amine metabolites. *American Journal of Psychiatry, 139*(6), 741–746.

Buda, M., & Tsuang, M. T. (1990). The epidemiology of suicide: Implications for clinical practice. In S. J. Blumenthal & D. J. Kupfer (Eds.), *Suicide over the life cycle: Risk factors, assessment, and treatment of suicidal patients* (pp. 17–38). Washington, DC: American Psychiatric Press.

Buglass, D., & Horton, J. (1974). A scale for predicting subsequent suicidal behavior. *British Journal of Psychiatry, 124,* 573–578.

Buie, D. H., & Maltsberger, J. T. (1989). The psychological vulnerability to suicide. In D. G. Jacobs & H. N. Brown (Eds.), *Suicide: Understanding and responding: Harvard Medical School perspectives on suicide* (pp. 59–71). Madison, CT: International Universities Press.

Bursztajn, H., Gutheil, T. G., Hamm, R. M., & Brodsky A. (1983). Subjective data and suicide assessment in light of recent legal developments: Part II. Clinical uses of legal standards in the interpretation of subjective data. *International Journal of Law and Psychiatry, 6*, 331–350.

Butcher, J. N. (1989). *The Minnesota Report: Adult Clinical System MMPI-2*. Minneapolis, MN: University of Minnesota Press.

Butcher, J. N., Dahlstrom, W. G., Graham, J. R., Tellegen A., & Kaemmer, B. (1989). *MMPI-2: Manual for administration and scoring*. Minneapolis, MN: University of Minnesota Press.

Camus, A. (1959). *The myth of Sisyphus and other essays*. New York: Knopf.

Caplan, G. (1964). *Principles of preventive psychiatry*. New York: Basic Books.

Carlino v. State, 294 N.Y.S.2d 30 (1968).

Center for Cognitive Therapy Policy Manual. (1989). (Available from the Center for Cognitive Therapy, Department of Psychiatry, University of Pennsylvania, 133 South 36th Street, Philadelphia, PA 19104.)

Charles, S. C., Wilbert, J. R., & Franke, K. J. (1985). Sued and nonsued physicians' self-reported reactions to malpractice litigation. *American Journal of Psychiatry, 142*(4), 437–440.

Chemtob, C. M., Bauer, G. B., Hamada, R. S., Pelowski, S. R., & Muraoka, M. Y. (1989). Patient suicide: Occupational hazard for psychologists and psychiatrists. *Professional Psychology: Research and Practice, 20*(5), 294–300.

Chemtob, C. M., Hamada, R. S., Bauer, G. B., Kinney, B., & Torigoe, R. Y. (1988). Patient suicide: Frequency and impact on psychiatrists. *American Journal of Psychiatry, 145*, 224–228.

Chemtob, C. M., Hamada, R. S., Bauer, G. B., Torigoe, R. Y., & Kinney, B. (1988). Patient suicide: Frequency and impact on psychologists. *Professional Psychology: Research and Practice, 19*(4), 421–425.

Clark, D. C. (1988). Depression and suicide: Editor's commentary. *Suicide Research Digest, II*(1), 2.

Clark, D. C. (1990). Panic disorder: Summary and editor's commentary. *Suicide Research Digest, IV*(1), 3–4.

Clark, D. C., Gibbons, R. D., Fawcett, J., & Scheftner, W. A. (1989). What is the mechanism by which suicide attempts predispose to later suicide attempts? A mathematical model. *Journal of Abnormal Psychology, 98*(1), 42–49.

Clark, D. C., Young, M. A., Scheftner, W. A., Fawcett, J., & Fogg, L. (1987). A field test of Motto's Risk Estimator for Suicide. *American Journal of Psychiatry, 144*(7), 923–926.

Clarkin, J. F. (1985). Considering family versus other therapies after a teenager's suicide attempt. *Hospital and Community Psychiatry, 36*(10), 1041–1046.

Clopton, J. R. (1974). Suicidal risk via the Minnesota Multiphasic Personality Inventory (MMPI). In C. Neuringer (Ed.), *Psychological assessment of suicide risk* (pp. 118–133). Springfield, IL: Charles C. Thomas.

Cohen E., Motto, J., & Seiden, R. (1966). An instrument for evaluating suicide potential. *American Journal of Psychiatry, 122*, 886–891.

Cole, J. K., & Magnussen, M. (1966). Where the action is. *Journal of Consulting and Clinical Psychology, 30*(1), 539–545.

Cotton, P. G., Drake, R. E., Whitaker, A., & Potter, J. (1989). Guidelines for dealing with suicide on a psychiatric inpatient unit. In D. G. Jacobs & H. N. Brown (Eds.), *Suicide: Understanding and responding: Harvard Medical School perspectives on suicide* (pp. 405–413). Madison, CT: International Universities Press.

Cummings, N. A., & VandenBos, G. R. (1979). The general practice of psychology. *Professional Psychology: Research and Practice, 10*(1), 430–440.

Cross, C. K., & Hirschfeld, R. M. A. (1985). Epidemiology of disorders in adulthood: Suicide. In J. O. Cavenar & R. Michels (Eds.), *Psychiatry: Vol. 6* (pp. xx–xx). Philadelphia, PA: J. B. Lippincott.

Cull, J. G., & Gill, W. S. (1982). *Suicide Probability Scale (SPS) Manual.* Los Angeles: Western Psychological Services.

Dahlstrom, W. G., Welsh, G. S., & Dahlstrom, L. E. (1972) *An MMPI handbook: Vol. I.* Minneapolis, MN: University of Minnesota Press.

Dalton v. State, 308 N.Y.S.2d 441 (Suppl. Ct. N.Y. App. 1970).

Davidson, H. A. (1969). Suicide in the hospital. *Hospitals, J. A. H. A., 43*, 55–59.

Deutsch, C. J. (1984). Self-report sources of stress among psychotherapists. *Professional Psychology: Research and Practice, 15*, 833–845.

Diekstra, R. F. W. (1990). An international perspective on the epidemiology and prevention of suicide. In S. J. Blumenthal & D. J. Kupfer (Eds.), *Suicide over the life cycle: Risk factors, assessment, and treatment of suicidal patients* (pp. 533–570). Washington, DC: American Psychiatric Press.

Dillman v. Hellman, 283 So. 2d 388 (Fla. Dist. Ct. App. 1973).

Dimitrijevic v. Chicago Wesley Memorial Hospital, 92 Ill. App. 2d 251, 236 N.E.2d 309 (1968).

Dingman, C. W. & McGlashan, T. H. (1988). Characteristics of patients with serious suicidal intentions who ultimately commit suicide. *Hospital and Community Psychiatry, 39*, 295–299.

Dinnerstein v. State, 486 F.2d 34 (Conn. 1973).

Dorpat, T. L., Anderson, W. F., & Ripley, H. S. (1968). The relationship of physical illness to suicide. In H. L. P. Resnik (Ed.), *Suicidal behaviors* (pp. 209–219). Boston: Little, Brown & Co.

Dorpat, T. L., & Ripley, H. S. (1960). A study of suicide in the Seattle area. *Comprehensive Psychiatry, 1*, 349–359.

Dorwart, R. A., & Chartock, L. (1989). Suicide: A public health perspective. In D. G. Jacobs & H. N. Brown (Eds.), *Suicide: Understanding and responding: Harvard Medical School perspectives on suicide* (pp. 31–55). Madison, CT: International Universities Press.

Douglas, J. D. (1967). *The social meaning of suicide.* Princeton: Princeton University Press.

Doyle, B. B. (1990). Crisis management of the suicidal patient. In S. J. Blumenthal & D. J. Kupfer (Eds.), *Suicide over the life cycle: Risk factors, assessment, and treatment of suicidal patients* (pp. 469–498). Washington, DC: American Psychiatric Press.

Dubovsky, S. L. (1988). *Concise guide to clinical psychiatry.* Washington, DC: American Psychiatric Press.

Dunne, E. J., McIntosh, J. L., & Dunne-Maxim, K. (1987). *Suicide and its aftermath: Understanding and counseling the survivors.* New York: W. W. Norton.

Durkheim, E. (1951). *Suicide.* (J. A. Spaulding & G. Simpson, Trans.). Glencoe IL: The Free Press. (Original published in 1897 as *Le Suicide*).

Earls, F., Escobar, J. I., & Manson, S. M. (1990). Suicide in minority groups: Epidemiologic and cultural perspectives. In S. J. Blumenthal & D. J. Kupfer (Eds.), *Suicide over the life cycle: Risk factors, assessment, and treatment of suicidal patients* (pp. 571–598). Washington, DC: American Psychiatric Press.

Egeland, J. A., & Sussex, J. N. (1985). Suicide and family loading for affective disorders. *Journal of the American Medical Association, 254*(7), 915–918.

Eisenthal, S. (1974). Assessment of suicide risk using selected tests. In C. Neuringer (Ed.), *Psychological assessment of suicide risk* (pp. 134–149). Springfield, IL: Charles C. Thomas.

Ellis, A., & Dryden, W. (1987). *The practice of rational-emotive therapy.* New York: Springer.

Ellis, T. E. (1986). Toward a cognitive therapy for suicidal individuals. *Professional Psychology: Research and Practice, 17*(2), 125–130.

Emory University v. Porubiansky, 282 S.E.2d 903 (1981).

Engel, G. L. (1977). The need for a new medical model: A challenge for biomedicine. *Science, 196,* 129–136.

Evans, G., & Farberow, N. L. (1988). *The encyclopedia of suicide.* New York: Facts on File.

Exner, J. (1978). *The Rorschach: A comprehensive system: Vol. 2. Current research and advanced interpretation.* New York: Wiley.

Exner, J. (1986). *The Rorschach: A comprehensive system: Vol. 1* (2nd ed.). New York: Wiley.

Eyman, J. R. (1987). *Unsuccessful psychotherapy with seriously suicidal borderline patients.* Paper presented at the joint meeting of the American Association of Suicidology and the International Association of Suicidology, San Francisco, CA.

Eyman, J. R., & Eyman, S. K. (in press). *Assessment of suicide risks using psychological tests.*

Farberow, N. L. (1957). The suicidal crisis in psychotherapy. In E. S. Shneidman & N. L. Farberow (Eds.), *Clues to suicide* (pp. 119–130). New York: McGraw-Hill.

Farberow, N. L. (Ed.). (1980). *The many faces of suicide: Indirect self-destructive behavior.* New York: McGraw-Hill.

Farberow, N. L. (1981). Suicide prevention in the hospital. *Hospital and Community Psychiatry, 32*, 99–104.

Farberow, N. L., Helig, S., & Litman, R. (1968). *Techniques in crisis intervention: A training manual.* Los Angeles: Suicide Prevention Center.

Fatuck v. Hillside Hospital, 45 A.D.2d 708, 356 N.Y.S.2d 105 (N.Y. 1974).

Fawcett, J. (1988, May). Interventions against suicide. In D. G. Jacobs & J. Fawcett (Chairs), *Suicide and the psychiatrist: Clinical challenges.* Paper presented at a symposium of the Suicide Education Institute of Boston, in collaboration with The Center for Suicide Research and Prevention, at the annual meeting of the American Psychiatric Association, Montreal, Quebec, Canada.

Fawcett, J., Leff, M., & Bunney, W. E. (1969). Suicide: Clues from interpersonal communication. *Archives of General Psychiatry, 21*, 129–137.

Fawcett, J., Scheftner, W., Clark, D. C., Hedeker, D., Gibbons, R., & Coryell, W. (1987). Clinical predictors of suicide in patients with major affective disorders: A controlled prospective study. *American Journal of Psychiatry, 144*(1), 35–40.

Fine, R. (1984). Countertransference reactions to the difficult patient. *Current Issues in Psychoanalytic Practice, 1*, 7–22.

Fowler, R. C., Rich, C. L., & Young, D. (1986). San Diego Suicide Study II: Substance abuse in young cases. *Archives of General Psychiatry, 43*(10), 962–965.

Frances, A. J. (1985). Afterword. *Hospital and Community Psychiatry, 36*(10), 1046.

Frederick, C. J. (1978). Current trends in suicidal behavior. *American Journal of Psychotherapy, 32*(2), 172–200.

Frederick, C. J., & Resnik, H. L. P. (1989). How suicidal behaviors are learned. In S. Lesse (Ed.), *What we know about suicidal behavior and how to treat it* (pp. 21–46). New York: Jason Aronson.

Friedman, R. S. (1989). Hospital treatment of the suicidal patient. In D. G. Jacobs & H. N. Brown (Eds.), *Suicide: Understanding and responding: Harvard Medical School perspectives on suicide* (pp. 379–402). Madison, CT: International Universities Press.

Fremouw, W. J., de Perczel, M., & Ellis, T. E. (1990). *Suicide risk: Assessment and response guidelines.* New York: Pergamon Press.

Freud, S. (1917). Mourning and melancholia. *Standard Edition: Vol. 14* (pp. 237–258). London: Hogarth Press.

Furrow, B. R. (1980). *Malpractice in psychotherapy.* Lexington, KY: D. C. Heath and Co.

Garfinkel, B. D. (1989). School-based prevention programs. Alcohol, Drug Abuse, and Mental Health Administration *Report of the Secretary's Task Force on Youth Suicide: Vol. III. Prevention and intervention in youth suicide* (pp. 3-294–3-304) (DHSS Publication No. ADM 89-1623). Washington, DC: U.S. Government Printing Office.

Gibbs, J., & Martin, T. (1964). *Status integration and suicide.* Eugene, OR: University of Oregon Press.

Gibbs, J. T. (1988). Conceptual, methodological, and sociocultural issues in black youth suicide: Implications for assessment and early intervention. *Suicide and Life-Threatening Behavior, 18*(1), 73–89.

Gill, A. D. (1982). Outpatient therapies for suicidal patients. In E. L. Bassuk, S. C. Schoonover, & A. D. Gill (Eds.), *Lifelines: Clinical perspectives on suicide* (pp. 71–82). New York: Plenum.

Goldblatt, M. J., & Schatzberg, A. F. (1990). Somatic treatment of the adult suicidal patient: A brief survey. In S. J. Blumenthal & D. J. Kupfer (Eds.), *Suicide over the life cycle: Risk factors, assessment, and treatment of suicidal patients* (pp. 469–498). Washington, DC: American Psychiatric Press.

Goldfried, M. R., & Wachtel, P. L. (1987). Clinical and conceptual issues in psychotherapy integration: A dialogue. *International Journal of Eclectic Psychotherapy, 6*(2), 131–144.

Goldring, N., & Fieve, R. R. (1984). Attempted suicide in manic-depressive disorder. *American Journal of Psychotherapy, 38*(3), 373–383.

Goldsmith, S. J., Fyer, M., & Frances, A. (1990). Personality and suicide. In S. J. Blumenthal & D. J. Kupfer (Eds.), *Suicide over the life cycle: Risk factors, assessment, and treatment of suicidal patients* (pp. 155–176). Washington, DC: American Psychiatric Press.

Goldstein, L. S., & Buongiorno, P. A. (1984). Psychotherapists as suicide survivors. *American Journal of Psychotherapy XXXVIII*(3), 392–398.

Gould, M. S., Shaffer, D., & Kleinman, M. (1988). The impact of suicide in television movies: Replication and commentary. *Suicide and Life-Threatening Behavior, 18*(1), 90–99.

Gregory v. Rubenson, 338 S.W.2d 88 (Mo. 1966)

Gutheil, T. G. (1980). Paranoia and progress notes: A guide to forensically informed psychiatric record-keeping. *Hospital and Community Psychiatry, 31*(7), 479–482.

Gutheil, T. G. (1984). Malpractice liability in suicide. *Legal aspects of psychiatric practice, 1,* 1–4.

Gutheil, T. G. (1988). Suicide and suit: Liability and self-destruction. In D. G. Jacobs & J. Fawcett (Chairs), *Suicide and the psychiatrist: Clinical challenges.* Paper presented at a symposium of the Suicide Education Institute of Boston, in collaboration with The Center for Suicide Research and Prevention, at the annual meeting of the American Psychiatric Association, Montreal, Quebec, Canada.

Gutheil, T. G., & Appelbaum, P. S. (1982). *Clinical handbook of psychiatry and the law*. New York: McGraw-Hill.

Gutheil, T. G., Bursztajn, H., Hamm, R. M., & Brodsky, A. (1983). Subjective data and suicide assessment in light of recent legal developments: Part I. Malpractice prevention and the use of subjective data. *International Journal of Law and Psychiatry, 6*, 317–329.

Halgin, R. P. (1985). Teaching integration of psychotherapy models to beginning therapists. *Psychotherapy, 22*(3), 555–563.

Harrar, W. R., VandeCreek, L., & Knapp, S. (1990). Ethical and legal aspects of clinical supervision. *Professional Psychology, 21*(1), 37–41.

Harris, E. A. (1988, October). *Legal issues in professional practice*. Workshop materials for the Massachusetts Psychological Association, Northampton, MA.

Harris, E. A. (1990, April). Risk management. Workshop sponsored by the American Psychological Association Insurance Trust, San Francisco, CA.

Havens, L. (1974). The existential use of the self. *American Journal of Psychiatry, 131*, 1–10.

Havens, L. (1989). Clinical interview with a suicidal patient. In D. G. Jacobs & H. N. Brown (Eds.), *Suicide: Understanding and responding: Harvard Medical School perspectives on suicide* (pp. 343–353). Madison, CT: International Universities Press.

Havens, L. L., & Palmer, H. L. (1984). Forms, difficulties, and tests of empathy. *Hillside Journal of Clinical Psychiatry, 6*(2), 285–291.

Helling v. Carey, 83 Wash. 2d 514 P.2d 981 (1974).

Hendin, H. (1989). Student suicide. In S. Lesse (Ed.), *What we know about suicidal behavior and how to treat it* (pp. 439–452). Northvale, NJ: Jason Aronson.

Hendren, R. L. (1990). Assessment and interviewing strategies for suicidal patients over the life cycle. In S. J. Blumenthal & D. J. Kupfer (Eds.), *Suicide over the life cycle: Risk factors, assessment, and treatment of suicidal patients* (pp. 235–252). Washington, DC: American Psychiatric Press.

Henry, A. F., & Short, J. E. (1954). *Suicide and homicide*. Glencoe, IL: The Free Press.

Herold v. State 15 App. Div. 2d 835, 224 N.Y.S.2d 369 (3d Dep't 1962).

Hirsch v. State, 168 N.E.2d 372 (1960).

Hirschfeld, R., & Davidson, L. (1988). Risk factors for suicide. In A. J. Frances & R. E. Hales (Eds.), *American Psychiatric Press review of psychiatry: Vol. 7* (pp. 307–333). Washington, DC: American Psychiatric Press.

Hoge, S. K., & Appelbaum, P. S. (1989). Legal issues in outpatient psychiatry. In A. Lazare (Ed.), *Outpatient psychiatry* (pp. 605–621). Baltimore, MD: Williams and Wilkins.

Holinger, P. C., & Offer, D. (1982). Prediction of adolescent suicide: A population model. *American Journal of Psychiatry, 139*, 307–309.

Holinger, P. C., & Offer, D. (1989). Sociodemographic, epidemiological, and individual attributes. In Alcohol, Drug Abuse, and Mental Health Administration *Report of the Secretary's Task Force on Youth Suicide: Vol. II, Risk Factors for Youth Suicide* (DHSS Publication No. ADM 89-1622. Washington, DC: U.S. Government Printing Office.

Holmes, V. F., & Rich, C. L. (1990). Suicide among physicians. In S. J. Blumenthal & D. J. Kupfer (Eds.), *Suicide over the life cycle: Risk factors, assessment, and treatment of suicidal patients* (pp. 599–618). Washington, DC: American Psychiatric Press.

Inwald, R. E., Brobst, K. E., & Morrissey, R. F. (1987). *Hillson Adolescent Profile Manual.* Kew Gardens, NY: Hillson Research.

Jacobs, D. G. (1988, May). Introduction: Models for understanding and responding. In D. G. Jacobs & J. Fawcett (Chairs), *Suicide and the psychiatrist: Clinical challenges.* Paper presented at a symposium of the Suicide Education Institute of Boston, in collaboration with The Center for Suicide Research and Prevention, at the annual meeting of the American Psychiatric Association, Montreal, Quebec, Canada.

Jacobs, D. G. (1989a). Evaluation and care of suicidal behavior in emergency settings. In D. G. Jacobs & H. N. Brown (Eds.), *Suicide: Understanding and responding: Harvard Medical School perspectives on suicide* (pp. 363–377). Madison, CT: International Universities Press.

Jacobs, D. G. (1989b). Psychotherapy with suicidal patients: The empathic method. In D. G. Jacobs & H. N. Brown (Eds.), *Suicide: Understanding and responding: Harvard Medical School perspectives on suicide* (pp. 329–342). Madison, CT: International Universities Press.

Jobes, D. A., Eyman, J. R., & Yufit, R. I. (1990). Suicide risk assessment survey. Paper presented at the annual meeting of the American Association of Suicidology, New Orleans, LA.

Johnson v. United States, 409 Fed. Supp. 1283, Md. Fam. Law (1981).

Joint Commission on Accreditation of Hospitals (JCAH). (1991). *1991 Accreditation manual for hospitals, AMH Vol. I: The Standards.* (Available from the JCAH, 1 Renaissance Blvd., Oakbrook Terrace, Illinois 60181.)

Kahn, A. (1982a). The moment of truth: Psychotherapy with the suicidal patient. In E. L. Bassuk, S. C. Schoonover, & A. D. Gill (Eds.), *Lifelines: Clinical perspectives on suicide* (pp. 83–92). New York: Plenum.

Kahn, A. (1982b). The stress of therapy. In E. L. Bassuk, S. C. Schoonover, & A. D. Gill (Eds.), *Lifelines: Clinical perspectives on suicide* (pp. 93–100). New York: Plenum.

Kahn, A. (1990). Principles of psychotherapy with suicidal patients. In S. J. Blumenthal & D. J. Kupfer (Eds.), *Suicide over the life cycle: Risk factors, assessment, and treatment of suicidal patients* (pp. 441–468). Washington, DC: American Psychiatric Press.

Kapantais, G., & Powell-Griner, E. P. (1989). *Characteristics of persons dying from AIDS: Preliminary data from the 1986 National Mortality Followback Survey* (Advance data report Number 173) Washington, DC: National Center for Health Statistics.

Kaplan, A. G., & Klein, R. B. (1989). Women and suicide. In D. G. Jacobs & H. N. Brown (Eds.), *Suicide: Understanding and responding: Harvard Medical School perspectives on suicide* (pp. 257–282). Madison, CT: International Universities Press.

Kardas v. State 24 App. Div. 2d 789, 263 N.Y.S.2d 727, (3d Dep't 1965).

Kaslow, F. W. (Ed.). (1984). *Psychotherapy for psychotherapists*. New York: Haworth.

Keith-Spiegel, P., & Koocher, G. P. (1985). *Ethics in psychology*. New York: Random House.

Keller, M. B. (1988). Afterword to section II: Unipolar depression. In A. J. Frances & R. E. Hales (Eds.), *American Psychiatric Press review of psychiatry: Vol. 7* (pp. 284–287). Washington, DC: American Psychiatric Press.

Kermani, E. J. (1982). Court rulings on psychotherapists. *American Journal of Psychotherapy, 36*(2), 248–254.

Kety, S. S. (1990). Genetic factors in suicide: Family, twin, and adoption studies. In S. J. Blumenthal & D. J. Kupfer (Eds.), *Suicide over the life cycle: Risk factors, assessment, and treatment of suicidal patients* (pp. 127–134). Washington, DC: American Psychiatric Press.

Kleespies, P. M., Smith, M. R., & Becker, B. R. (1990). Psychology interns as patient suicide survivors: Incidence, impact, and recovery. *Professional Psychology: Research and Practice, 21*(4), 257–263.

Klein, J. I., & Glover, S. I. (1983). Psychiatric malpractice. *International Journal of Law and Psychiatry, 6,* 131–157.

Klerman, G. L. (Ed.). (1986). *Suicide and depression among adolescents and young adults*. Washington, DC: American Psychiatric Press.

Klerman, G. L. (1987). Clinical epidemiology of suicide. *Journal of Clinical Psychiatry, 48*(Suppl.), 33–38.

Klerman, G. L. (1989). Psychotherapy on trial? Osheroff versus Chestnut Lodge. *Harvard Medical School Mental Health Letter, 6*(1), 4.

Klerman, G. L. (1990). The psychiatric patient's right to effective treatment: Implications of Osheroff versus Chestnut Lodge. *American Journal of Psychiatry, 147*(4), 409–418.

Klerman, G. L., Weissman, M. M., Rounsaville, B. J., & Chevron, E. S. (1984). *The interpersonal psychotherapy of depression*. New York: Basic Books.

Kohut, H. (1971). *The analysis of the self*. New York: International Universities Press.

Krapvika v. Maimonides, 60 A.D.2d 871, 501 N.Y.S.2d 429 (1986).

Kreitman, N. (1986). The clinical assessment and management of the suicidal patient. In A. Roy (Ed.), *Suicide* (pp. 181–195). Baltimore, MD: Williams and Wilkins.

Landers, S. (1989). Modern day stresses give rise to depression. *American Psychological Association Monitor, 20*(10), 32.

Lane, R. C. (1984). The difficult patient, resistance, and the negative therapeutic reaction: A review of the literature. *Current Issues in Psychoanalytic Practice, 1*, 83–106.

Langs, R. (1979). *The supervisory experience.* New York: Jason Aronson.

Lann, I. S., & Moscicki, E. K. (1989). Introduction: Strategies for studying suicide and suicidal behavior. *Suicide and Life-Threatening Behavior, 19*(1), xi–xiii.

Lazare, A. (1987). Shame and humiliation in the medical encounter. *Archives of Internal Medicine, 147*, 1653–1658.

Lazarus, A. A. (1981). *The practice of multimodal therapy: Systematic, comprehensive and effective psychotherapy.* New York: McGraw-Hill.

Leenaars, A. A., & Balance, W. D. (1984). A predictive approach to suicide notes of young and old people from Freud's formulations with regard to suicide. *Journal of Clinical Psychology, 40*(6). 1362–1364.

Lesse, S. (1989a) Preface. In S. Lesse (Ed.), *What we know about suicidal behavior and how to treat it* (pp. ix–xiv). Northvale, NJ: Jason Aronson.

Lesse, S. (1989b). The range of therapies with severely depressed suicidal patients. In S. Lesse (Ed.), *What we know about suicidal behavior and how to treat it.* (pp. ix–xiv). Northvale, NJ: Jason Aronson.

Lester, D. (1972). *Why people kill themselves.* Springfield IL: Charles C. Thomas.

Lester, D. (1988). Suicide in women: An overview. In D. Lester (Ed.), *Why women kill themselves* (pp. 3–15). Springfield, IL: Charles C. Thomas.

Lewinsohn, P. M., Garrison, C. Z., Langhinrichsen, J., & Marsteller, F. (1989). *The assessment of suicidal behavior in adolescents: A review of scales suitable for epidemiological and clinical research* (Report prepared under NIMH contract numbers 316774 and 316776). Rockville, MD: Child and Adolescent Disorders Research Branch, National Institute of Mental Health.

Liberman, R. P., & Eckman, T. (1981). Behavior therapy versus insight-oriented therapy for repeated suicide attempters. *Archives of General Psychiatry, 38*(10), 1126–1130.

Lichtenstein v. Montefiore Hospital and Medical Center, 56 App. Div. 2d 281, 392 N.Y.S.2d 18, (1st Dep't 1977).

Lifton, R. J., Shuichi, K., & Reich, M. R. (1979). Mishima Yukio: The man who loved death. *In Six Lives/Six Deaths.* New Haven, CT: Yale University Press.

Lindeman, E. (1944). Symptomatology and the management of acute grief. *American Journal of Psychiatry, 101*, 141–148.

Linehan, M. M. (1981). A social-behavioral analysis of suicide and parasuicide: Implications for clinical assessment and treatment. In H. Glazer & J. Clarkin (Eds.), *Depression: Behavioral and directive intervention strategies* (pp. 229–294). New York: Garland.

Linehan, M. M. (1985). The reasons for living inventory. In P. Keller & L. Ritt (Eds.), *Innovations in clinical practice* (pp. 321–330). Sarasota, FL: Professional Resource Exchange.

Linehan, M. M. (1987). Dialectical behavior therapy: A cognitive behavioral approach to parasuicide. *Journal of Personality Assessment, 1*, 328–333.

Litman, R. E. (1957). Some aspects to the treatment of the potentially suicidal patient. In E. S. Shneidman & N. L. Farberow (Eds.), *Clues to suicide* (pp. 11–118). New York: McGraw-Hill.

Litman, R. E. (1965). When patients commit suicide. *American Journal of Psychotherapy, 19*, 570–576.

Litman, R. E. (1967). Sigmund Freud on suicide. In E. S. Shneidman (Ed.), *Essays in self-destruction* (pp. 324–344). New York: Science House.

Litman, R. E. (1968). Sigmund Freud on suicide. *Bulletin of Suicidology, July,* 11–23.

Litman, R. E. (1971). Suicide prevention: Evaluating effectiveness. *Life-Threatening Behavior, 1*(3), 155–162.

Litman, R. E. (1980). Psycholegal aspects of suicide. In E. A. Curran (Ed.), *Modern legal medicine, psychiatry, and forensic science* (pp. 841–853). Philadelphia, PA: F. A. Davis Company.

Litman, R. E. (1982). Hospital suicides: Lawsuits and standards. *Suicide and Life-Threatening Behavior, 12*(4), 212–220.

Litman, R. E. (1988, May). Treating high-risk chronically suicidal patients. In D. G. Jacobs & J. Fawcett (Chairs), *Suicide and the Psychiatrist: Clinical Challenges.* Paper presented at a symposium of the Suicide Education Institute of Boston, in collaboration with The Center for Suicide Research and Prevention, at the annual meeting of the American Psychiatric Association, Montreal, Quebec, Canada.

Litman, R. E. (1989). Suicides: What do they have in mind. In D. G. Jacobs & H. N. Brown (Eds.), *Suicide: Understanding and responding: Harvard Medical School perspectives on suicide* (pp. 143–154). Madison, CT: International Universities Press.

London, P. (1986). Major issues in psychotherapy integration. *International Journal of Eclectic Psychotherapy, 5*(3), 211–216.

Luborsky, L. (1990). Who is helped by psychotherapy? *Harvard Mental Health Letter, 7*(2), 4–5.

Mack, J. E. (1989). Adolescent suicide: An architectural model. In D. G. Jacobs & H. N. Brown (Eds.), *Suicide: Understanding and responding: Harvard Medical School perspectives on suicide* (pp. 221–238). Madison, CT: International Universities Press.

Mack, J. E., & Hickler, H. (1981). *Vivienne: The life and suicide of an adolescent girl.* Boston: Little Brown.

Mackenzie, T. B., & Popkin, M. K. (1990). Medical illness and suicide. In S. J. Blumenthal & D. J. Kupfer (Eds.), *Suicide over the life cycle: Risk factors, assessment, and treatment of suicidal patients* (pp. 205–234). Washington, DC: American Psychiatric Press.

Malinowski, B. (1926). *Crime and custom in savage society.* New York: Routledge.

Maltsberger, J. T. (1986). *Suicide risk: The formulation of clinical judgment.* New York: New York University Press.

Maltsberger, J. T. (1988). Suicide danger: Clinical estimation and decision. *Suicide and Life-Threatening Behavior, 18*(1), 47–54.

Maltsberger, J. T. (1989). Discussion of Leston Havens' interview. In D. G. Jacobs & H. N. Brown (Eds.), *Suicide: Understanding and responding: Harvard Medical School perspectives on suicide* (pp. 357–360). Madison, CT: International Universities Press.

Mann, J. J., & Stanley, M. (1988a). Foreword to section III: Suicide. In A. J. Frances & R. E. Hales (Eds.), *American Psychiatric Press review of psychiatry: Vol. 7* (pp. 287–288). Washington, DC: American Psychiatric Press.

Mann, J. J., & Stanley, M. (1988b). Afterword to section III: Suicide. In A. J. Frances & R. E. Hales (Eds.), *American Psychiatric Press review of psychiatry: Vol. 7* (pp. 422–426). Washington, DC: American Psychiatric Press.

Mann, J. J., Stanley, M., McBride, A., & McEwen, B. S. (1986). Increased serotonin and B-adrenergic receptor binding in the frontal cortices of suicide victims. *Archives General Psychiatry, 43*, 954–959.

Maris, R. W. (1976). Sociology of suicide. In S. Perlin (Ed.), *A Handbook for the study of suicide.* New York: Oxford University Press.

Maris, R. W. (1981). *Pathways to suicide: A survey of self-destructive behaviors.* Baltimore, MD: Johns Hopkins University Press.

Maris, R. W. (1983). Suicide: Rights and rationality. *Suicide and Life-Threatening Behavior, 13*(4), 223–230.

Maris, R. W. (1986). Preface to the special issue: Biology of suicide. *Suicide and Life-Threatening Behavior, 16*(2), v–viii.

Maris, R. W. (1988). Preface: Overview and discussion. In R. W. Maris (Ed.), *Understanding and preventing suicide: Plenary papers of the first combined meeting of the AAS and IASP (pp. vii–xxiii).* New York: Guilford.

Maris, R. W. (1989a). Preface: Strategies for studying suicide and suicidal behavior. *Suicide and Life-Threatening Behavior, 19*(1), ix–x.

Maris, R. W. (1989b). The social relations of suicide. In D. G. Jacobs & H. N. Brown (Eds.), *Suicide: Understanding and responding: Harvard Medical School perspectives on suicide* (pp. 87–125). Madison, CT: International Universities Press.

Maris, R. W. (1990). Forensic suicidology: Litigation of suicide cases and equivocal deaths. In B. Bongar (Chair), *Management of the suicidal patient: Ethical and legal considerations.* Symposium conducted at the meeting of the American Psychological Association, Boston, MA.

Massachusetts General Law, Chapter 112 Section 129A, April (1988).

McCann, J. T., & Suess, J. F. (1988). Clinical applications of the MCMI: The 1-2-3-8 codetype. *Journal of Clinical Psychology, 44*(2), 181–186.

McEvoy, T. L. (1974). Suicidal risk via the thematic apperception test. In C. Neuringer (Ed.), *Psychological assessment of suicide risk* (pp. 3–17). Springfield, IL: Charles C. Thomas.

McIntosh, J. (1988). Suicide: Training and education needs with an emphasis on the elderly. *Gerontology and Geriatric Education, 7*(3), 125–139.

McIntosh, J., Santos, J. F., Overholser, J. C., & Hubbard, R. W. (forthcoming). *Suicide in the elderly.* Washington, DC: American Psychological Association. Manuscript submitted for publication.

Meichenbaum, D. B. (1977). *Cognitive-behavior modification.* New York: Plenum Press.

Meier v. Ross General Hospital, 69 Cal. 2d 420, 71 Cal. Rptr. 903, 445 P.2d 519 (1968).

Menninger, K. (1938). *Man against himself.* New York: Harcourt Brace Jovanovich.

Menninger, K. (1989). Afterword: Reflections on suicide. In D. G. Jacobs & H. N. Brown (Eds.), *Suicide: Understanding and responding: Harvard Medical School perspectives on suicide* (pp. 483–484). Madison, CT: International Universities Press.

Menninger, W. W. (1989). The impact of litigation and court decisions on clinical practice. *Bulletin of the Menninger Clinic, 53*(3), 203–14.

Meyer, R. G. (1989). *The clinicians handbook: The psychopathology of adulthood and adolescence (2nd ed.).* Boston: Allyn and Bacon.

Meyer, R. G., Landis, E. R., & Hays, J. R. (1988). *Law for the psychotherapist.* New York: W. W. Norton.

Mintz, R. S. (1968). The psychotherapy of the suicidal patient. In H. L. P. Resnick (Ed.), *Suicidal behaviors: Diagnosis and management.* Boston: Little Brown.

Miskimins, R. W., DeCook, R., Wilson, L. T., & Maley, R. F. (1967). Prediction of suicide in a psychiatric hospital. *Journal of Clinical Psychology, 23*, 296–301.

Moore v. United States, 222 F.Supp. 87 (Mo. 1963).

Morgan, A. C. (1989). Special issues of assessment and treatment of suicide risk in the elderly. In D. G. Jacobs & H. N. Brown (Eds.), *Suicide: Understanding and responding: Harvard Medical School perspectives on suicide* (pp. 239–255). Madison, CT: International Universities Press.

Motto, J. A. (1975). The recognition and management of the suicidal patient. In F. Flash & S. Draghi (Eds.), *The nature and treatment of depression.* New York: Wiley.

Motto, J. A. (1977). The estimation of suicide risk by use of clinical models. *Suicide and Life-Threatening Behavior, 7*(4), 236–245.

Motto, J. A. (1979a). Guidelines for the management of the suicidal patient. *Weekly Psychiatry Update Series: Lesson 20, 3*, 3–7. (Available from Biomedia, Inc., 20 Nassau Street, Princeton, NJ 08540).

Motto, J. A. (1979b). The psychopathology of suicide: A clinical approach. *American Journal of Psychiatry, 136*(4–B), 516–520.

Motto, J. A. (1986). Clinical considerations of biological correlates of suicide. *Suicide and Life-Threatening Behavior, 16*(2), pp. 1–20.

Motto, J. A. (1989). Problems in suicide risk assessment. In D. G. Jacobs & H. N. Brown (Eds.), *Suicide: Understanding and responding: Harvard Medical School perspectives on suicide* (pp. 129–142). Madison, CT: International Universities Press.

Motto, J. A., Heilbron, D. C., & Juster, R. P. (1985). Development of a clinical instrument to estimate suicide risk. *American Journal of Psychiatry, 142*(6), 680–686.

Murphy, G. (1984). The prediction of suicide. *American Journal of Psychotherapy, XXXVIII*(3), 341–349.

Murphy, G. E. (1986). The physician's role in suicide prevention. In A. Roy (Ed.), *Suicide* (pp. 171–179). Baltimore, MD: Williams and Wilkins.

Murphy, G. E. (1987). Suicide and attempted suicide. In J. O. Cavenar (Ed.), *Psychiatry: Volume 1* (pp. 1–18). Philadelphia, PA: J. B. Lippincott.

Murphy, G. E. (1988a). The prediction of suicide. In S. Lesse (Ed.), *What we know about suicidal behavior and how to treat it* (pp. 47–58). Northvale, NJ: Jason Aronson.

Murphy, G. E. (1988b). Prevention of suicide. In A. J. Frances & R. E. Hales (Eds.), *American Psychiatric Press review of psychiatry: Vol. 7* (pp. 403–421). Washington, DC: American Psychiatric Press.

Murray, H. (1938). *Explorations in personality*. New York: Oxford University Press.

National Center for Health Statistics (1986). *Annual summary of births, marriages, divorces, and deaths: United States, 1985*. Washington, DC: author.

Neill, J. R. (1979). The difficult patient: Identification and response. *Journal of Clinical Psychiatry, 40*, 209–212.

Nemiah, J. C. (1982). Foreword. In E. L. Bassuk, S. C. Schoonover, & A. D. Gill (Eds.), *Lifelines: Clinical perspectives on suicide*. New York: Plenum.

Ness, D. E., & Pfeffer, C. R. (1990). Sequelae of bereavement resulting from suicide. *American Journal of Psychiatry, 147*(3), 279–285.

Norcross, J. C. (1984). The training of clinical psychologists: Some training predictions and recommendations. *The Clinical Psychologist, 37*(1), 23–24.

Neuringer, C. (1974a). Problems in assessing suicide risk. In C. Neuringer (Ed.), *Psychological assessment of suicide risk* (pp. 3–17). Springfield, IL: Charles C. Thomas.

Neuringer, C. (1974b). Rorschach inkblot test assessment of suicidal risk. In C. Neuringer (Ed.), *Psychological assessment of suicide risk* (pp. 74–94). Springfield, IL: Charles C. Thomas.

O'Connor v. Donaldson, 442 U.S. 563 (1975).

Osborne, D. (1985). The MMPI in psychiatric practice. *Psychiatric Annals, 15*(19), 542–545.

Osgood, N. J. (1985). *Suicide in the elderly: A practitioners guide to diagnosis and mental health intervention*. Rockville, MD: Aspen.

Osgood, N. J., & Thielman, S. (1990). Geriatric suicidal behavior: Assessment and treatment. In S. J. Blumenthal & D. J. Kupfer (Eds.), *Suicide over the life cycle: Risk factors, assessment, and treatment of suicidal patients* (pp. 341–380). Washington, DC: American Psychiatric Press.

Pallis, D. J., Barraclough, B., Levey, A., Jenkins, J., & Sainsbury, P. (1982). Estimating suicide risk among attempted suicides: The development of new clinical scales. *British Journal of Psychiatry, 141,* 37–44.

Pallis, D. J., Gibbons, J. S., & Pierce, D. W. (1984). Estimating suicide risk among attempted suicides: II. Efficiency of predictive scales after the attempt. *British Journal of Psychiatry, 144,* 139–148.

Paradies v. Benedictine Hospital, 431 N.Y.S.2d 175 (Appl. Div. 1980).

Parkes, C. (1972). *Bereavement.* New York: International Universities Press.

Pattison, E. M., & Kahan, J. (1983). The deliberate self-harm syndrome. *American Journal of Psychiatry, 140,* 867–872.

Peck v. The Counseling Service of Addison County, 499 A.2d 422 (1985).

Peck, M. L., Farberow, N. L., & Litman, R. E. (Eds.). (1985). *Youth suicide.* New York: Springer.

Perlin, S., & Schmidt, C. W. (1976). Psychiatry. In S. Perlin (Ed.), *A handbook for the study of suicide* (pp. 147–163). New York: Oxford University Press.

Perr, I. N. (1960). Suicide responsibility and the hospital psychiatrist. *Cleveland-Marshall Law Review, 9*(3), 427–440.

Perr, I. N. (1965). Liability of hospital and psychiatrist in suicide. *American Journal of Psychiatry, 122*(6), 631–638.

Perr, I. N. (1974). Suicide and civil litigation. *Journal of Forensic Sciences, 19*(2), 261–266.

Perr, I. N. (1979). Legal aspects of suicide. In L. D. Hankoff & B. Einsidler (Eds.), *Suicide: Theory and clinical aspects* (pp. 91–100). Littleton, MA: PSG Publishing.

Perr, I. N. (1985a). Psychiatric malpractice issues. In S. Rachlin (Ed.), *Legal encroachment on psychiatric practice.* San Francisco: Jossey-Bass.

Perr, I. N. (1985b). Suicide litigation and risk management: A review of 32 cases. *Bulletin of American Academy of Psychiatry and the Law, 13*(3), 209–219.

Perr, I. N. (1988). The practice of psychiatry and suicide litigation. *New Developments in Mental Health Law, 8*(1), 4–19.

Peterson, C. & Seligman, M. E. P. (1984). Causal explanations as a risk factor for depression: Theory and evidence. *Psychological Review, 91,* 347–374.

Peterson, D. R. (1985). Twenty years of practitioner training in psychology. *American Psychologist, 40,* 441–451.

Peterson, L. G., & Bongar, B. (1989). The suicidal patient. In A. Lazare (Ed.), *Outpatient psychiatry: Diagnosis and treatment* (2nd ed.) (pp. 569–584). Baltimore, MD: Williams and Wilkins.

Peterson, L. G., & Bongar, B. (1990). Training physicians in the clinical evaluation of the suicidal patient. In M. Hale (Ed.), *Teaching methods in consultation-liaison psychiatry* (pp. 89–108). Basel, Switzerland: Karger.

Peterson, L. G., Bongar, B., & Netoski, M. (1989). Regional use of violent suicidal methods: An analysis of suicide in Houston, Texas. *American Journal of Emergency Medicine, 7*(2), 21–27.

Pfeffer, C. R. (1986). *The suicidal child.* New York: Guilford.

Pfeffer, C. R. (1988). Suicidal behavior among children and adolescents: Risk identification and intervention. In A. J. Frances & R. E. Hales (Eds.), *American Psychiatric Press review of psychiatry: Vol. 7* (pp. 386–402). Washington, DC: American Psychiatric Press.

Phillips, D. P., & Carstensen, L. L. (1988). The effect of suicide stories on various demographic groups, 1968–1985. *Suicide and Life-Threatening Behavior, 18*(1), 100–114.

Piotrowski, C., Sherry, D., & Keller, J. W. (1985). Psychodiagnostic test usage: A survey of the Society for Personality Assessment. *Journal of Personality Assessment, 49*(1), 115–119.

Pisel v. Stamford Hospital, 180 Conn. 314, 430 A.2d 1 (1980).

Pokorny, A. D. (1964a). A follow-up study of 618 suicidal patients. *American Journal of Psychiatry, 122,* 1109–1116.

Pokorny, A. D. (1964b). Suicide rates in various psychiatric disorders. *Journal of Nervous and Mental Disease, 139*(6), 499–506.

Pokorny, A. D. (1983). Prediction of suicide in psychiatric patients. *Archives of General Psychiatry, 40,* 249–257.

Pope, K. (1986, January). Assessment and management of suicidal risks: Clinical and legal standards of care. *Independent Practitioner,* 17–23.

Pope, K. (1989, January). Malpractice suits, licensing disciplinary actions, and ethics cases. *Independent Practitioner,* 22–26.

Pope, K. S., Tabachnick, B. G., & Keith-Spiegel, P. (1988). Good and poor practices in psychotherapy: National survey of beliefs of psychotherapists. *Professional Psychology: Research and Practice, 19*(5), 547–552.

Rachlin, S. (1984). Double jeopardy: Suicide and malpractice. *General Hospital Psychiatry, 6,* 302–307.

Rachlin, S., & Schwartz, H. I. (1986). Unforeseeable liability for patients' violent acts. *Hospital and Community Psychiatry, 37*(7), 725–731.

Rainer, J. D. (1984). Genetic factors in depression and suicide. *American Journal of Psychotherapy, 38*(3), 329–340.

Rangell, L. (1988). The decision to terminate one's own life: Psychoanalytic thoughts on suicide. *Suicide and Life-Threatening Behavior, 18*(1), 28–46.

Rennie v. Klein, 462 Fed. Supp. 1131 (1979).

Rich, C. L., Fowler, R. C., Fogarty, L. A., & Young, D. (1988). San Diego Suicide Study III: Relationships between diagnoses and stressors. *Archives of General Psychiatry, 45*(6), 589–592.

Rich, C. L., Motooka, L., Mitchell, S., Fowler, R. C., & Young, D. (1988). Suicide by psychotics. *Biological Psychiatry, 24*(5), 595–601.

Richman, J. (1986). *Family therapy for suicidal people.* New York: Springer Publishing.

Richman, J., & Eyman, J. R. (in press). Psychotherapy of suicide: Individual, group, and family approaches. In D. Lester (Ed.), *Understanding suicide: The state of the art.* Philadelphia, PA: The Charles Press.

Rigler, D. (1982). Ericksonian hypnosis in a pediatric hospital. In J. Zeig (Ed.), *Ericksonian hypnosis and psychotherapy.* New York: Brunner/Mazel.

Robbins, J. M., Beck, P. R., Mueller, D. P., & Miezener, D. A. (1988). Therapists' perceptions of difficult psychiatric patients. *Journal of Nervous Disorders and Ment Diseases, 176*, 490–497.

Robertson, J. D. (1988). *Psychiatric malpractice: Liability of mental health professionals.* New York: John Wiley.

Robiner, W. N., & Schofield, W. (1990). References on supervision in clinical and counseling psychology. *Professional Psychology: Research and Practice, 21*(4), 297–312.

Robins, E. (1985). Suicide. In H. I. Kaplan & B. J. Sadock (Eds.), *Comprehensive Textbook of Psychiatry: Volume IV* (pp. 311–1315). Baltimore, MD: Williams & Wilkins.

Robins, E. (1986). Completed suicide. In A. Roy (Ed.), *Suicide* (pp. 123–133). Baltimore, MD: Williams and Wilkins.

Robins, E., Murphy, G. E., Wilkinson, R. M., Gassner, S., & Kays, J. (1959). Some clinical considerations in the prevention of suicide based on a study of 134 successful suicides. *American Journal of Public Health, 49*, 888–898.

Robins, L. N., & Helzer, J. E. (1986). Diagnosis and clinical assessment: The current state of psychiatric diagnosis. *Annual Review of Psychology, 37*, 409–432.

Robins, L. N., & Kulbok, P. A. (1988). Epidemiological studies in suicide. In A. J. Frances & R. E. Hales (Eds.), *American Psychiatric Press review of psychiatry: Vol. 7* (pp. 289–306). Washington, DC: American Psychiatric Press.

Rogers v. Okin, 478 Fed. Supp. 1342 (1979).

Rosen, G. (1976). History. In S. Perlin (Ed.), *A handbook for the study of suicide* (pp. 3–30). New York: Oxford University Press.

Roth, S. (1989). Discussion of Leston Havens' interview. In D. G. Jacobs & H. N. Brown (Eds.), *Suicide: Understanding and responding: Harvard Medical School perspectives on suicide* (pp. 354–357). Madison, CT: International Universities Press.

Roy, A. (1986). Preface. In A. Roy (Ed.), *Suicide* (p. vii). Baltimore, MD: Williams and Wilkins.

Roy, A. (1988, May). Risk factors in suicide. In D. G. Jacobs and J. Fawcett (Chairs), *Suicide and the psychiatrist: Clinical challenges.* Paper presented at a symposium of the Suicide Education Institute of Boston, in collaboration with the Center for Suicide Research and Prevention, at the annual meeting of the American Psychiatric Association, Montreal, Quebec, Canada.

Ruben, H. L. (1990). Surviving a suicide in your practice. In S. J. Blumenthal & D. J. Kupfer (Eds.), *Suicide over the life cycle: Risk factors, assessment, and treatment of suicidal patients* (pp. 619–636). Washington, DC: American Psychiatric Press.

Rubinstein, D. (1983). Epidemic suicide among Micronesian adolescents. *Social Science and Medicine, 17*(10), 657–665.

Runyon v. Reid, 510 P.2d. 943 (Okla. 1973).

Rush, A. J., & Beck, A. T. (1989). Cognitive therapy of depression and suicide. In S. Lesse (Ed.), *What we know about suicidal behavior and how to treat it* (pp. 283–306). Northvale, NJ: Jason Aronson.

Sadoff, R. L. (1975). *Forensic psychiatry: A practical guide for lawyers and psychiatrists.* Springfield, IL: Charles C. Thomas.

Sadoff, R. L. (1985). Malpractice in psychiatry: Standards of care and the expert witness. *Psychiatric Medicine, 2*(3), 235–243.

Sadoff, R. L., & Gutheil, T. G. (1990). Expert opinion: Death in hindsight. In R. I. Simon (Ed.), *American Psychiatric Press review of clinical psychiatry and the law:Vol 1* (pp. 329–339). Washington, DC: American Psychiatric Press.

Sainsbury, P. (1986). The epidemiology of suicide. In A. Roy (Ed.), *Suicide* (pp. 17–40). Baltimore, MD: Williams and Wilkins.

Schein, H. M. (1976). Obstacles in the education of psychiatric residents. *Omega, 7,* 75–82.

Schutz, B. M. (1982). *Legal liability in psychotherapy.* San Francisco, CA: Jossey-Bass.

Schwartz v. United states, 226 F. Supp. 84 (D.C. Dist. Col. 1964).

Schwartz, A. J., & Whitaker, L. C. (1990). Suicide among college students: Assessment, treatment, and intervention. In S. J. Blumenthal & D. J. Kupfer (Eds.), *Suicide over the life cycle: Risk factors, assessment, and treatment of suicidal patients* (pp. 303–340). Washington, DC: American Psychiatric Press.

Semrad, E. V. (1984). Psychotherapy of the psychoses. *Samiska, 8,* 1.

Shaffer, D. (1974). Suicide in childhood and early adolescence. *Journal of Child Psychology and Psychiatry, 15,* 275–291.

Shaffer, D., Gould, M., & Trautman, P. (1985, September). Suicidal behavior in children and young adults. Paper presented at the Psychobiology of Suicidal Behavior Conference, New York, NY.

Shaffi, M. (1986, October). Psychological autopsy study of suicide in adolescents. Paper presented at the Child Depression Consortium, St. Louis, MO.

Shneidman, E. S. (1981a). Postvention: The care of the bereaved. *Suicide and Life-Threatening Behavior, 11*(4), 349–359.

Shneidman, E. S. (1981b). Psychotherapy with suicidal patients. *Suicide and Life-Threatening Behavior, 11*(4), 341–348.

Shneidman, E. S. (1981c). *Suicidal thoughts and reflections 1960–1980.* New York: Human Sciences Press.

Shneidman, E. S. (1984). Aphorisms of suicide and some implications for psychotherapy. *American Journal of Psychotherapy, 38*(3), 319–328.

Shneidman, E. S. (1985). *Definition of suicide.* New York: John Wiley & Sons.

Shneidman, E. S. (1986a). Some essentials of suicide and some implications for response. In A. Roy (Ed.), *Suicide* (pp. 1–16). Baltimore, MD: Williams and Wilkins.

Shneidman, E. S. (1986b). Suicidal logic. In W. S. Sahakian, B. J. Sahakian, & P. L. Sahakian-Nunn (Eds.), *Psychopathology today: The current status of abnormal psychology* (3rd ed.) (pp. 267–281). Itasca, IL: Peacock Press.

Shneidman, E. S. (1987). A psychological approach to suicide. In G. R. Vanden-Bos & B. K. Bryant (Eds.), (pp. 147–183). *Cataclysms, crises, and catastrophes: Psychology in action.* Washington, DC: American Psychological Association.

Shneidman, E. S. (1988). Some reflections of a founder. *Suicide and Life-Threatening Behavior, 18*(1), 1–12.

Shneidman, E. S. (1989). Overview: A multidimensional approach to suicide. In D. G. Jacobs & H. N. Brown (Eds.), *Suicide: Understanding and responding: Harvard Medical School perspectives on suicide* (pp. 1–30). Madison, CT: International Universities Press.

Shneidman, E. S., Farberow, N. L., & Litman, R. E. (1970). *The psychology of suicide.* New York: Science House.

Simon, R. I. (1987). *Clinical psychiatry and the law.* Washington, DC: American Psychiatric Press.

Simon, R. I. (1988). *Concise guide to clinical psychiatry and the law.* Washington, DC: American Psychiatric Press.

Sklarsh v. United States, 194 F.Supp. (E.D.N.Y. 1961).

Slaby, A. E., Lieb, J., & Tancredi, L. R. (1986). *Handbook of psychiatric emergencies* (3rd ed.). New York: Medical Examination Publishing Co.

Slawson, P. F., Flinn, D. E., & Schwartz, D. A. (1974). Legal responsibility for suicide. *Psychiatric Quarterly, 42,* 50–64.

Slawson, P. F., & Guggenheim, F. G. (1984). Psychiatric malpractice: A review of the national loss experience. *American Journal of Psychiatry, 141*(8), 979–981.

Slovenko, R. (1985). Forensic psychiatry. In H. I. Kaplan & B. J. Sadock (Eds.), *Comprehensive textbook of psychiatry: Vol. IV* (pp. 1960–1990). Baltimore, MD: Williams & Wilkins.

Smith v. United States, 437 F.Supp. 1004 (ED Pa. 1977).

Smith, J. (1986). *Medical malpractice psychiatric care.* Colorado Springs, CO: Shepards/McGraw-Hill.

Smith, K. (1985). Suicide assessment: An ego vulnerabilities approach. *Bulletin of the Menninger Clinic, 48*(5), 489–499.

Smith, K. (1988). *The psychotherapy of suicidal patients.* Paper presented at the annual meeting of the American Association of Suicidology, Washington, DC.

Smith, K., Conroy, R. W., & Ehler, B. D. (1984). Lethality of suicide attempt rating scale. *Suicide and Life-Threatening Behavior, 14*(4), 215–242.

Smith, K. & Crawford, S. (1986). Suicidal behavior among "normal" high school students. *Suicide and Life-Threatening Behavior, 16*(3), 313–25.

Smith, K., & Eyman, J. R. (1988). Ego structure and object differentiation in suicidal patients. In H. D. Lerner & P. M. Lerner (Eds.), *Primitive mental states and the Rorschach* (pp. 175–202). Madison, CT: International Universities Press.

Smith, K., & Maris, R. (1986). Suggested recommendations for the study of suicide and other life-threatening behaviors. *Suicide and Life-Threatening Behavior, 16*(1), 67–69.

Smith, R. J., & Steindler, E. M. (1983). The impact of difficult patients upon treaters. *Bulletin of the Menninger Clinic, 47*, 107–116.

Smith, S. (1977). The golden fantasy: A regressive reaction to separation anxiety. *International Journal of Psychoanalysis, 58*, 311–324.

Speer v. United States, 512 F.Supp. 670 (1981).

Stanley, M., & Mann, J. J. (1988). Biological factors associated with suicide. In A. J. Frances & R. E. Hales (Eds.), *American Psychiatric Press review of psychiatry: Vol. 7* (pp. 334–352). Washington, DC: American Psychiatric Press.

Stanley, M., Stanley, B., Traskman-Bendz, L., Mann, J. J., & Meyendorff, E. (1986). Neurochemical findings in suicide completers and attempters. *Suicide and Life-Threatening Behavior, 16*(2), 204–218.

Steer, R. A., & Beck, A. T., (1988). Use of the Beck Depression Inventory, Hopelessness Scale, Scale for Suicide Ideation, and Suicidal Intent Scale with adolescents. *Advances in Adolescent Mental Health, 3*, 219–231.

Steiger, W. A. (1967). Managing difficult patients. *Psychosomatics, 8*, 305–308.

Steiger, W. A., & Hirsh, H. (1965). The difficult patient in everyday medical practice. *Medical Clinics of North America, 49*, 1449–1465.

Stengel, E. (1965). *Suicide and attempted suicide.* Bristol, United Kingdom: MacGibbon and Kee Limited.

Stepakoff v. Kantar, 393 Mass. 836, 473 N.E.2d 1131 (1985).

Stolorow, R. D., Brandchaft, B., & Atwood, G. E. (1983). Intersubjectivity in psychoanalytic treatment: With special reference to archaic states. *Bulletin of the Menninger Clinic, 47*, 117–128.

Stoltenberg, C. D., & Delworth, U. (1987). *Supervising counselors and therapists.* San Francisco, CA: Jossey-Bass.

Stone, A. A. (1989a). A response to Dr. Klerman. *Harvard Medical School Mental Health Letter, 6*,(1), 3–4.

Stone, A. A. (1989b). Suicide precipitated by psychotherapy. In S. Lesse (Ed.), *What we know about suicidal behavior and how to treat it* (pp. 307–319). Northvale, NJ: Jason Aronson.

Stone, A. A. (1990). Law, science, and psychiatric malpractice: A response to Klerman's indictment of psychoanalytic psychiatry. *American Journal of Psychiatry, 147*(4), 419–427.

Strickland, B. R. (1987). On the threshold of the second century of psychology. *The American Psychologist, 42*(12), 1055–1056.

Stromberg, C. D. (1989). Requests for patient's records. *Register Report, 15*(4), 14–15.

Stromberg, C. D., Haggarty, D. J., Leibenluft, R. F., McMillan, M. H., Mishkin, B., Rubin, B. L., & Trilling, H. R. (1988). *The psychologist's legal handbook.* Washington, DC: The Council for the National Register of Health Service Providers in Psychology.

Swartz, M. (1988). Malpractice liability for suicide: Clinical, legal, and rhetorical dimensions. *The Psychiatric Forum, 14*(1), 45–53.

Swenson, E. V. (1986). Legal liability for a patient's suicide. *The Journal of Psychiatry & Law, 14*(3), 409–434.

Szasz, T. (1986). The case against suicide prevention. *The American Psychologist, 41*(7), 806–812.

Tanney, B. L. (1986). Electroconvulsive therapy and suicide. *Suicide and Life-Threatening Behavior, 16*, 198–222.

Tarasoff v. Regents of the University of California, 551 P.2d 334, 131 Cal. Rptr. 14, Ca. Sup. Ct. (1976).

Texarkana Memorial Hospital, Inc. v. Firth, 746 S.W.2d 494 (1988).

Topel v. Long Island Jewish Medical Center, 431 N.E.2d 293 (1981).

Torres v. State, 49 App. Div. 2d 966, 373 N.Y.S.2d 696, (1975).

Traskman, L., Asberg, M., Bertilsson, L., & Sjostrand, L. (1981). Monoamine metabolites in CSF and suicidal behavior. *Archives of General Psychiatry, 38*, 631–636.

Tuckman, J., & Youngman, W. F. (1968). A scale for assessing suicide risk of attempted suicides. *Journal of Clinical Psychology, 24*, 17–19.

Vaillant, G. E., & Blumenthal, S. J. (1990). Introduction—Suicide over the life cycle: Risk factors and life-span development. In S. J. Blumenthal & D. J. Kupfer (Eds.), *Suicide over the life cycle: Risk factors, assessment, and treatment of suicidal patients* (pp. 1–16). Washington, DC: American Psychiatric Press.

Van Praag, H. M. (1986). Affective disorders and aggression disorders: Evidence for a common biological mechanism. *Suicide and Life-Threatening Behavior, 16*(2), 21–47.

VandeCreek, L., & Harrar, W. (1988). The legal liability of supervisors. *Psychotherapy Bulletin, 23*(3), 13–17.

VandeCreek, L., & Knapp, S. (1983). Malpractice risks with suicidal patients. *Psychotherapy: Theory, Research and Practice, 20*(3), 274–280.

VandeCreek, L., & Knapp, S. (1989). *Tarasoff and beyond: Legal and clinical considerations in the treatment of life-endangering patients.* Sarasota, FL: Professional Resource Exchange, Inc.

VandeCreek, L., Knapp, S., & Herzog, C. (1987). Malpractice risks in the treatment of dangerous patients. *Psychotherapy: Theory, Research, and Practice, 24*(2), 145–153.

Vistica v. Presbyterian Hospital, 67 Cal. 2d 465, 62 Cal. Rptr. 577, 432 P.2d 193 (1967).

Waltzer, H. (1980). Malpractice liability for a patient's suicide. *American Journal of Psychotherapy, 34*(1), 89–98.

Weishaar, M. E., & Beck, A. T. (1990). Cognitive approaches to understanding and treating suicidal behavior. In S. J. Blumenthal & D. J. Kupfer (Eds.), *Suicide over the life cycle: Risk factors, assessment, and treatment of suicidal patients* (pp. 469–498). Washington, DC: American Psychiatric Press.

Weisman, A. D., & Worden, J. W. (1972). Risk-rescue in suicide assessment. *Archives of General Psychiatry, 26*, 553–560.

Weisman, A. D., & Worden, J. W. (1974). Risk-rescue in suicide assessment. In A. T. Beck, H. L. Resnik, & D. L. Lettieri (Eds.), *The prediction of suicide.* Bowie, MD: The Charles Press Publishers.

Weissman, M. M., & Klerman, G. L. (1982). Depression in women: Epidemiology, explanations, and impact on the family. In M. Notman & C. Nadelson (Eds.), *The woman patient.* New York: Plenum.

Weissman, M. M., Klerman, G. L., Markowitz, J. S., & Ouelette, R. (1989). Suicidal ideation and suicide attempts in panic disorder and attacks. *New England Journal of Medicine, 321*, 1209–1214.

Wekstein, L. (1979). *Handbook of suicidology: Principles, problems, and practice.* New York: Brunner/Mazel.

Welch, B. (1989). A collaborative model proposed. *American Psychological Association Monitor, 20*(10), 28.

Wilson v. State (1961, 3d Dept.) 14 App. Div. 2d 976, 221 NYs2d 354.

Wilson, M. (1981). Suicidal behavior: Toward an explanation of differences in female and male rates. *Suicide and Life-Threatening Behavior, 11*(3), 131–140.

Winchel, R. M., Stanley, B., & Stanley, M. (1990). Biochemical aspects of suicide. In S. J. Blumenthal & D. J. Kupfer (Eds.), *Suicide over the life cycle: Risk factors, assessment, and treatment of suicidal patients* (pp. 97–126). Washington, DC: American Psychiatric Press.

Wise, M. G., & Rundell, J. R. (1988). *Concise guide to consultation psychiatry.* Washington, DC: American Psychiatric Press.

Wong, N. (1983). Perspectives on the difficult patient. *Bulletin of the Menninger Clinic, 47*, 99–106.

Wright, R. (1981). What to do until the malpractice lawyer comes. *The American Psychologist, 36*, 1535–1541.

Wyatt v. Stickney, 325 Fed. Supp. 781 (1971).

Youngstrom, N. (1990). Malpractice premiums jump 50 percent August 1. *American Psychological Association Monitor, 21*(8), 16.

Yufit, R. I. (1988). *Manual of procedures—assessing suicide potential: Suicide assessment team.* Unpublished manual (Available from Robert I. Yufit, Ph.D., Department of Psychiatry and Behavioral Sciences, Division of Clinical Psychology, Northwestern University Medical School, Chicago, IL).

Yufit, R. I. (1989). Developing a suicide screening instrument for adolescents and young adults. In Alcohol, Drug Abuse, and Mental Health Administration *Report of the Secretary's Task Force on Youth Suicide: Vol. IV* Strategies for the Prevention of Youth Suicide (pp. 4-129–4-144). (DHSS Publication No. ADM 89-1624). Washington, DC: U.S. Government Printing Office.

Yufit, R. I., & Benzies, B. (1979). *Preliminary manual Time Questionnaire: Assessing suicide potential.* Palo Alto, CA: Consulting Psychologists Press.

Zilboorg, G. (1937). Considerations on suicide with a particular reference to that of the young. *American Journal of Orthopsychiatry, 7,* 15–31.

Zilka v. State, 52 Misc. 2d 891, 277 N.Y.S.2d 312, (1967).

Zubin, J. (1974). Observations on nosological issues in the classification of suicidal behavior. In A. T. Beck, H. L. Resnik, & D. L. Lettieri (Eds.), *The prediction of suicide* (pp. 3–25). Bowie, MD: The Charles Press Publishers.

Zung, W. W. K. (1974). Index of potential suicide (IPS). In A. T. Beck, H. L. Resnik, & K. L. Lettieri (Eds.), *The prediction of suicide* (pp. 221–249). Bowie, MD: The Charles Press Publishers.

Appendix A
Rates of Completed Suicide in the United States

Rates of Completed Suicide by Sex and Age per 100,000 Resident Population

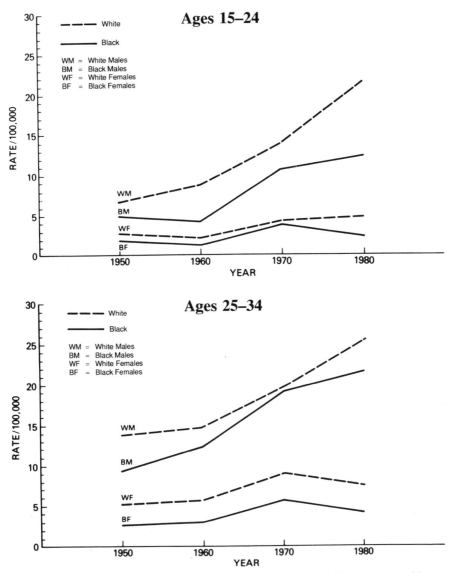

Note. From *Report of the Secretary's Task Force on Youth Suicide: Vol. III Prevention and Intervention in Youth Suicide* (pp. 3-192–3-195) by Alcohol, Drug Abuse, and Mental Health Administration, 1989, Washington, DC: U.S. Government Printing Office.

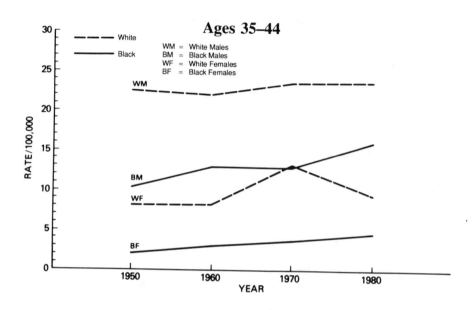

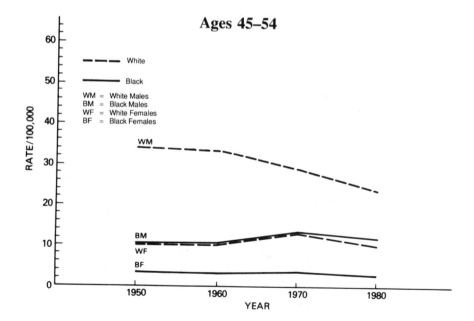

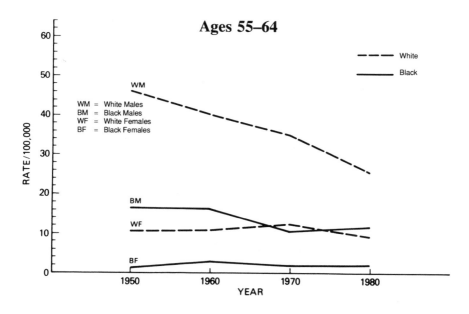

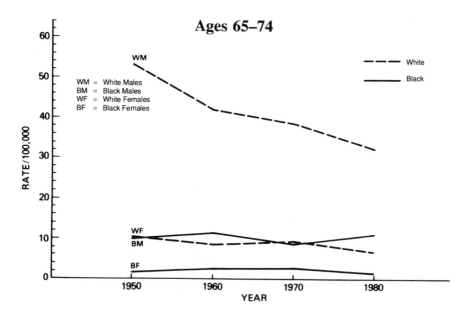

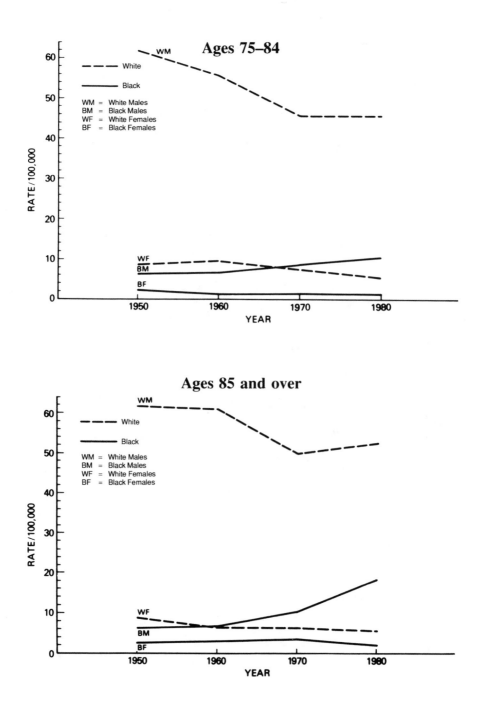

Appendix B
Suicide Risk Estimators
and Scales

Appendix B.1
The California Risk Estimator for Suicide

The Suicide Risk Assessment Scale

Instructions

1. The Suicide Risk Assessment Scale is designed to estimate the risk of suicide in adults aged 18-70, during a two-year period following the time of assessment.
2. The Scale is primarily applicable to persons known to be at some risk, such as those in a serious depressive state, having suicidal thoughts or impulses, or having made a recent suicide attempt.
3. The Scale is to be administered by a clinician, not self-administered. Responses to the items in the first column are best determined in the course of a clinical interview. The information need not be obtained in the listed order.
4. *The subjective judgement of the interviewer is to be used throughout in categorizing the response, as data provided in the clinical situation may be incomplete, ambiguous or conflicting.*
5. For the one most appropriate response category in the second column, the indicated "assigned score" in the third column should be entered into the last column as the "actual score." *If any data are missing or unobtainable, score that item zero.*
6. Total the fifteen actual scores and determine from the Table of Risk what category of risk is scored. This is expressed in three ways: (a) numerically, on a scale of one to ten, representing the decile of risk, (b) descriptively, from "Very Low" to "Very High," and (c) an estimated percentage of risk during the two years following assessment.

The Suicide Risk Assessment Scale is intended as a supplement to, not a substitute for, clinical judgement. A thorough evaluation is indicated in any serious emotional disturbance. Individual uniqueness suggests that when the Scale is not consistent with clinical judgement, clinical judgement should be given precedence.

Date: _____   Total Score: _____

Subject: _____   Risk category, Table of Risk: _____

Interviewer: _____   Risk category, Clinical Estimate: _____

Time needed to administer: _____   Comment: _____

Ease of administration: 1   2   3   4   5   _____

   (circle number)   Easy   Difficult

245

Item	Response Category	Assigned Score	Actual Score
1. Age at last birthday	Find age in table and enter corresponding score.	See table (page 248)	
2. Type of occupation	Executive Administrator Professional Owner of business Semiskilled worker Other	48 48 48 48 48 0	
3. Sexual orientation	Bisexual and sexually active Homosexual, not sexually active Other	65 65 0	
4. Financial resources	Negative (debts exceed resources) None 0 to $100 Over $100	0 0 35 70	
5. Threat of significant financial loss	Yes No	63 0	
6. Stress unique to subject's circumstances, *other than* loss of finances or relationship, threat of prosecution, illegitimate pregnancy, substance abuse or poor health.	Severe Other	63 0	
7. Hours of sleep per night (approximate nearest whole hour)	0–2 3–5 6 or more	0 37 74	
8. Change of weight during present episode of stress (approximate)	No change 10% or more weight loss Less than 10% loss Weight gain	0 0 60 60	
9. Ideas of persecution or reference	Moderate or severe Other	45 0	
10. Intensity of present suicidal impulses	Questionable, moderate or severe Other	100 0	

(continued)

Item	Response Category	Assigned Score	Actual Score
11. If current suicide attempt made, seriousness of intent to die.	Unequivocal Ambivalent, weighted toward suicide Other or not applicable	88 88 0	
12. Number of prior psychiatric hospitalizations	None 1 2 3 or more	0 21 43 64	
13. Result of prior efforts to obtain help	No prior efforts Some degree of help Poor, unsatisfactory, or variable outcome	0 0 55	
14. Emotional disorder in family history	Depression Alcoholism Other	45 45 0	
15. Interviewer's reaction to the person	Highly positive Moderately or slightly positive Neutral or negative	0 42 85	
		Total Score	

Table of Risk			
Total Score	Decile of Risk	Relative Risk	Approximate Suicide Rate
0–271	1	Very low	Less than 1%
272–311 312–344	2 3	Low	1–2.5%
345–377 378–407 408–435 436–465	4 5 6 7	Moderate	2.5–5%
466–502 503–553	8 9	High	5–10%
over 553	10	Very High	Over 10%

Age-Score Table					
Age	Score	Age	Score	Age	Score
18	0	36	45	54	80
19	3	37	47	55	81
20	6	38	49	56	83
21	9	39	51	57	85
22	12	40	53	58	86
23	14	41	55	59	88
24	17	42	57	60	90
25	20	43	59	61	91
26	22	44	61	62	93
27	25	45	63	63	95
28	27	46	65	64	96
29	29	47	67	65	98
30	32	48	69	66	99
31	34	49	71	67	101
32	36	50	72	68	102
33	39	51	74	69	104
34	41	52	76	70	106
35	43	53	78		

Note. From "Development of a Clinical Instrument to Estimate Suicide Risk" by J. A. Motto, D. C. Heilbron, and R. P. Juster, American Journal of Psychiatry, 142(6), pp. 680–686, 1985. Copyright 1982, the American Psychiatric Association. Reprinted by permission.

Appendix B.2
Los Angeles Suicide
Prevention Center Scale

	Rating for Category
Age and Sex (1–9)	
Male	
50 plus (7–9)	( )
35–49 (4–6)	( )
15–34 (1–3)	( )
Female	
50 plus (5–7)	( )
35–49 (3–5)	( )
15–34 (1–3)	( )
Symptoms (1–9)	
Severe depression: sleep disorder, anorexia, weight loss, withdrawal, despondency, loss of interest, apathy (7–9)	( )
Feelings of hopelessness, helplessness, exhaustion (7–9)	( )
Delusions, hallucinations, loss of contact, disorientation (6–8)	( )
Compulsive gambling (6–8)	( )
Disorganization, confusion, chaos (5–7)	( )
Alcoholism, drug addiction, homosexuality (4–7)	( )
Agitation, tension, anxiety (4–6)	( )
Guilt, shame, embarrassment (4–6)	( )
Feelings of rage, anger, hostility, revenge (4–6)	( )
Poor impulse control, poor judgment (4–6)	( )
Other (describe):	
Stress (1–9)	
Loss of loved person by death, divorce, or separation (5–9)	( )
Loss of job, money, prestige, status (4–8)	( )
Sickness, serious illness, surgery, accident–loss of limb (3–7)	( )
Threat of prosecution, criminal involvement, exposure (4–6)	( )
Change(s) in life, environment, setting (4–6)	( )
Success, promotion, increased responsibilities (2–5)	( )
No significant stress (1–3)	( )
Other (describe):	
Acute Versus Chronic (1–9)	
Sharp, noticeable and sudden onset of specific symptoms (1–9)	( )
Recurrent outbreak of similar symptoms (4–9)	( )
No specific recent change (1–4)	( )
Other (describe):	

(continued)

	Rating for Category
Suicidal Plan (1–9)	
Lethality of proposed method—gun, jumping, hanging, drowning, knife, pills, poison, aspirin (1–9)	( )
Specific detail and clarity in organization of plan (1–9)	( )
Specificity in time planned (1–9)	( )
Bizarre plan (1–9)	( )
Rating of previous suicide attempt(s) (1–9)	( )
No plans (1–3)	( )
Other (describe):	
Resources (1–9)	
No sources of support (family, friends, agencies, employment) (7–9)	( )
Family and friends available, unwilling to help (4–7)	( )
Financial problems (4–7)	( )
Available professional help, agency or therapist (2–4)	( )
Family and/or friends willing to help (1–3)	( )
Stable life history (1–3)	( )
Physician or clergy available (1–3)	( )
Employed (1–3)	( )
Finances no problem (1–3)	( )
Other (describe):	
Prior Suicidal Behavior (1–7)	
One or more prior attempts of high lethality (6–7)	( )
One or more prior attempts of low lethality (4–5)	( )
History of repeated threats and depression (3–5)	( )
No prior suicidal or depressed history (1–3)	( )
Other (describe):	
Medical Status (1–7)	
Chronic debilitating illness (5–7)	( )
Pattern of failure in previous therapy (4–6)	( )
Many repeated unsuccessful experiences with doctors (4–6)	( )
Psychosomatic illness, e.g., asthma, ulcer, hypochondria (1–3)	( )
No medical problems (1–2)	( )
Other (describe):	

(continued)

	Rating for Category
Communication Aspects (1–7)	
Communication broken with rejection of efforts to reestablish by both patient and others (5–7)	( )
Communications have internalized goal, e.g., declaration of guilt, feelings of worthlessness, blame, shame (4–7)	( )
Communications have interpersonalized goal, e.g., to cause guilt in others to force behavior, etc. (2–4)	( )
Communications directed toward world and people in general (3–5)	( )
Communications directed toward one or more specific persons (1–3)	( )
Other (describe):	
Reaction of Significant Others (1–7)	
Defensive, paranoid, rejected, punishing attitude (5–7)	( )
Denial of own or patient's need for help (5–7)	( )
No feelings of concern about the patient; does not understand the patient (4–6)	( )
Indecisiveness, feelings of helplessness (3–5)	( )
Alternation between feelings of anger and rejection and feelings of responsibility and desire to help (2–4)	( )
Sympathy and concern plus admission of need for help (1–3)	( )
Other (describe):	

The Los Angeles Suicide Prevention Center Suicide Potential Scale is designed to serve principally as a clinical aid in the evaluation of a client (e.g., an office patient or a caller to a telephone crisis service) who has identified himself or herself as suicidal. The pressing need at this point is to evaluate how seriously suicidal is the person. The answer to that question determines whether the process is continued in the office or the phone, whether emergency procedures are initiated to hospitalize, whether other resources such as family, relatives, neighbors, etc. are enlisted, or other resources and actions are considered.

The LASPC Scale is aimed at providing the assessor with a ready reference list of significant factors in estimating the current suicidal risk. Although numbers are used to arrive at a final score, the score does not imply a rigidly defined level of self-destructive status, but rather a general level which may guide appropriate and adequate response.

Scoring of the Suicide Potential Scale is clinically oriented. Ten categories are listed containing varied numbers of items in each. After each item, numbers are given suggesting the usual range of score for each item. The highest score for any item is nine, the lowest score is one. Some items suggest a range of 3 points (e.g., 4–6, 7–9, etc.); some may range over the entire scale (e.g., 1–9); some may have lesser ranges (e.g., 4–7, 1–5). The rater may apply any score within the suggested range, selecting the score on the basis of intensity, or prominence of that particular variable.

The score for each category is the highest score found for any of the variables checked within that category. The highest possible score within the first 6 categories is 9; the highest possible score in the last 4 categories is 7. Suicide potential is arrived at by:

1. Add all the category scores to find the total (the range is 82–10).   _____

2. Divide the total by 10   _____

3. Round the answer to the nearest whole number above   _____

4. Circle the number in the box below to indicate the degree of risk

Suicide Potential

1 2 3	4 5 6	7 8 9
low risk	medium risk	high risk

Scoring Aids for Each Category

Age and Sex

Age and sex offer a general framework for evaluating the suicidal situation. Both statistics and experience have indicated that the suicide rate for committed suicide in general rises with increasing age, and that men are more likely to kill themselves than women. A suicidal communication from an older male tends to be most dangerous; from a young female, least dangerous. Rates among young people have risen in the past two decades, suggesting greater risk. Each case requires further individual appraisal in which the criteria listed below have been found to be useful.

Symptoms

Each symptom is scored on the basis of the intensity with which it is expressed. Among the most common symptoms are depression, psychosis and anxiety. Depression may be expressed physically with vegetative symptoms (sleep and/or appetite disorders, lack of energy, exhaustion, apathy, etc.) as well as emotionally (despondency, despair, loss of interest, withdrawal from social contacts, loss of sexual drive, etc.). Problems with attention and concentration, feelings of loss of ability to think clearly, and poor judgment also indicate depressive states. Psychotic states are high risk because of unpredictability. They are characterized by delusions, hallucinations, loss of contact or disorientation, or highly unusual ideas and experiences. Anxiety appears in high levels of tension and agitation.

Feelings of guilt, shame, rage, hostility and revenge accompanying the anxiety increase the risk. The combination of agitation and depression in which the person is unable to tolerate her or his feelings and exhibits impaired judgment, poor impulse control, restlessness and fearfulness rate the highest level of risk.

Stress/Acute Versus Chronic Factors

Though listed separately, stress and acute versus chronic factors are always considered together. All of the variables listed under stress may be found as precipitating or as long-term stress. Most frequently the stress involves loss, or the threat of loss, of dependency and/or companionship sources such as loss of a loved one by separation, divorce or death; loss of social self-image, such as loss of job, money, prestige, or status; loss of physical self-image through serious illness, surgery, accident, etc.; and loss of reputation through criminal involvement, prosecution, exposure of sexual acting out, etc. Increased anxiety and tension may appear as a result of success through a promotion or increased responsibilities. Stress must always be evaluated from the client's point of view. Ratings of stress level may increase or lessen depending on the status of the client's coping and defensive resources. Some diagnostic categories indicate a poor history of personal, social and emotional functioning, such as borderline, psychotic states in remission, substance abuse, etc. A sudden, recent crisis with the appearance of unusual symptoms indicates an acute stage which may be more readily resolved.

Suicide Plan

Presence or absence of suicide plan will change the rating of risk level markedly. The second element is specificity versus vagueness. Three main elements are considered in appraising this category: (a) the lethality of the proposed method; (b) the availability of the means; and (c) the degree of planning of the details. A method involving a gun or jumping or hanging (with essentially immediate results) is of higher lethality than one which depends on the use of pills or wrist cutting (in which the feasibility of rescue or intervention is present). If the gun is at hand, the threat of its use is much more serious than when no gun is available. If the person indicates by many specific details that much time has been spent in making preparations, such as changing a will, writing notes, collecting pills, bought a rope, and set a date, the level of risk rises markedly. Evaluation of any plan that is obviously bizarre depends on the client's psychiatric diagnosis. A psychotic person with suicidal impulses is high risk and may make a bizarre attempt as a result of psychotic ideation. If prior suicidal behavior is known and suicide attempts have occurred, ratings of their seriousness help in assessing the current risk (see *Prior Suicidal Behavior*).

Resources

A suicidal client frequently feels alone and unloved. If factually true, the risk is very much increased. External resources may be found in family, relatives, friends, fellow employees, neighbors, and professional help (i.e., therapist, case worker, physician, attorney, probation officer, etc.). Clergy may also serve as a significant resource for some individuals. Often the client has either exhausted or angered significant resources, such as family or friends, so that they are available but rejecting, thus increasing the risk. Financial problems tend to exacerbate all the situations above as well as serving as its own source of anxiety and depression.

Prior Suicidal Behavior

Research and experience have indicated that a history of prior suicidal behavior markedly increases risk. If the prior suicidal behavior is one of attempts, detailed inquiry should be made to determine the lethality (see *Suicidal Plan*). Attempts of high lethality indicate higher risk than attempts of low lethality. A history of repeated threats along with depression indicate the possible development of suicidal behavior as a means of coping with distressing problems.

Medical Status

The presence of a chronic, debilitating illness needs to be explored especially when it has involved change in self-image and/or self-concept. "Loss of future" may have resulted in serious depression. For persons with chronic illness, the relationship with their physician, their family, or even the hospital becomes significant in terms of resources for support. Psychosomatic illnesses may indicate a process previously developed to excessive levels of anxiety which may not be functioning as effectively currently. A pattern of previous failure in therapy may contribute to feelings of hopelessness when in the midst of current depressive feelings that there is any help possible.

Communication Aspects

Suicidal behavior is often best understood as a communication. It is a form of demanding attention and a response and implies that previous efforts to communicate by more usual methods have not succeeded. The most serious situation occurs when both sender and intended receiver are rejecting efforts to reestablish communication. This may indicate a loss of hope, which heightens suicidal risk. Communications may be verbal, behavioral, or both, and may be direct, indirect, or both. The message may be directed at specific individuals or to the world at large. When directed to an individual it may contain accusations, hostility, blame, with demands for changes in behavior and feelings on the part of the other. Other communications may express feelings of guilt, inadequacy, worthlessness, anxiety and tension. When the communication is directed to specific persons, the reactions of these persons are important in the evaluation of the suicidal danger (see *Reactions of Significant Others*).

Reactions of Significant Others

Reactions of the significant others may vary from rejecting, punishing, and defensive; through denial of the possibility of suicide; through lack of understanding; through disinterest and withdrawal. Active, punishing rejection indicates the highest risk, especially if the significant other has been an important source of dependency gratification in the past.

Note. From *The Prediction of Suicide* (pp. 74–79) edited by A. T. Beck, H. L. P. Resnik, and D. J. Lettieri, 1986, Philadelphia, PA: The Charles Press Publishers. Copyright 1974 by Dr. Norman Farberow. Reprinted with permission from The Charles Press Publishers and Dr. Norman Farberow.

Appendix B.3
Risk-Rescue Rating

Patient _____ Age ____ Sex ____   Risk Score _____

Circumstances _____   Rescue Score _____

_____   Risk-Rescue
                                                Rating _____

RISK FACTORS	**RESCUE FACTORS**

1. Agent used:
   1. Ingestion, cutting, stabbing
   2. Drowning, asphyxiation, strangulation
   3. Jumping, shooting
	1. Location:
	   3. Familiar
	   2. Nonfamiliar, nonremote
	   1. Remote

2. Impaired consciousness:
   1. None in evidence
   2. Confusion, semicoma
   3. Coma, deep coma
	2. Person initiating rescue:*
	   3. Key person
	   2. Professional
	   1. Passerby

3. Lesions/Toxicity:
   1. Mild
   2. Moderate
   3. Severe
	3. Probability of discovery by a rescuer:
	   3. High, almost certain
	   2. Uncertain discovery
	   1. Accidental discovery

4. Reversibility:
   1. Good, complete recovery expected
   2. Fair, recovery expected with time
   3. Poor, residuals expected, if recovery
	4. Accessibility to rescue:
	   3. Asks for help
	   2. Drops clues
	   1. Does not ask for help

5. Treatment required:
   1. First aid, emergency ward care
   2. House admission, routine treatment
   3. Intensive care, special treatment
	5. Delay until discovery:
	   3. Immediate 1 hour
	   2. Less than 4 hours
	   1. Greater than 4 hours

Total Risk Points: _____	Total Rescue Points: _____

RISK SCORE		**RESCUE SCORE†**	
5. High risk	(13–15 risk points)	1. Least rescuable	(5–7 rescue points)
4. High moderate	(11–12 risk points)	2. Low moderate	(8–9 rescue points)
3. Moderate	(9–10 risk points)	3. Moderate	(10–11 rescue points)
2. Low moderate	(7–8 risk points)	4. High moderate	(12–13 rescue points)
1. Low risk	(5–6 risk points)	5. Most rescuable	(14–15 rescue points)

*Self-rescue automatically yields a rescue score of 5.
†If there is undue delay in obtaining treatment after discovery, reduce final rescue score by one point.

Note. From ''Risk-Rescue Rating in Suicide Assessment'' by A. Weisman and J. W. Worden, 1972, *Archives of General Psychiatry, 26*, pp. 553–560. Copyright 1972, American Medical Association. Reprinted by permission.

Appendix B.4
Lethality of Suicide
Attempt Rating Scale

K. Smith, PhD., R.W. Conroy, MD, and B.D. Ehler, RPh
The Menninger Foundation

ABSTRACT: An 11-point (0–10) scale for measuring the degree of lethality of suicide attempts is presented. The scale has nine example "anchors" and uses the relative lethality of an extensive table of drugs. The psychometric studies show the scale to be of at least equal-interval, possibly even ratio measurement level. The equal-interval quality allows suicidal behaviors to be specified in numeric relationship to each other relieving us of the burden of using unquantified labels such as "mild," "moderate," and "serious." Having a standardized, commonly used reference scale should greatly facilitate our research and clinical efforts to communicate our findings. The scale can be used reliably by nonmedical personnel with no prior training.

It could be effectively argued that in spite of years of suicide research, we have neglected to adequately define our principal subject: suicide behavior. We are referring to a very practical impediment to our abilities to perform scientific studies and to communicate about attempts of varying lethalities. We are not referring to the "prediction" of suicide, but to the inability to communicate in consensual terms about the seriousness of an act already performed. "High lethality," "low lethality," "mild," "moderate," and "serious" suicide potential are all descriptors without standard reference points. By using such unscaled adjectives in our scientific work we inflict upon ourselves a degree of imprecision similar to that of a physicist scientifically describing light intensity with the words "dim," "bright," and "blinding" instead of using units of "candle-power." In suicide research, a few instruments have been proposed for such a standard but none of them has more than reliability data to support its use. Reliability ratings are, of course, important but not enough, given the sophisticated questions being posed in the literature, such as whether there is a continuum of suicidal people or just two slightly overlapping groups: "attempters" and "completers"; or if a person has made a "mildly" lethal attempt, how probable is it that he/she will later make a more "serious" one. Those who are serious students of the suicide literature know how perplexing it is to try to compare the findings by different researchers who use different yardsticks to communicate their definitions of "mild" and "serious."

Figure B.4.1 graphically illustrates some of the problems that can result when scaling is ignored. The scale points of two fictitious "measures" of lethality are displayed on what is imagined to be the full spectrum of suicide lethality. Such distributions of actual scale points can be determined by procedures such as those applied in this paper. Observe the "gaps" in measurement between points 3 and 4 of scale S_1 and points 1 and 2 of scale S_2. There is no way the reader or even the researcher can know of such missing data without scaling procedures. Note also the relative ability of each scale to discriminate lethality. Scale S_1 is sensitive to attempts of low lethality but not to distinguishing among serious attempts. Scale S_2 is insensitive at both the lower and higher ranges of lethality. The insensitivity of the lower region is seen in the fact that there is only one scale point for the bottom half of the scale and no scale point anchoring the end of the range. It is insensitive in the higher range because it does not differentiate the range of high-risk attempts and secondly because points 3 and 4 may be so close together as to be only different numbers applied to clinically indistinguishable differences in lethality. Again, you would not have such information without "scaling" the instruments. With these scales, an S_2 rating of 1 (least lethality) appears close to the S_1 rating of 3 (moderately severe lethality). Such unseen scale biases can produce major confusion in attempts to understand the degrees of lethality reported in the literature.

In addition to the lack of scaling information, the existing instruments have other properties which encourage the development of a new scale. Setting aside most "suicide prediction" scales, because they seldom include methods of objectively measuring lethality, the most pertinent scales are those reported by Beck, Schuyler, and Herman (1974); Dorpat and Boswell (1963); Farberow and Shneidman (1961); Freeman, Wilson, Thigpen, and McGee (1974); Motto (1965); and Weisman and Worden (1974). In our search for a suitable scale, we could see some advantage to constructing an instrument that did not depend on obtaining the patient's judgments about his/her "intent," "premeditation," "understanding" of the dangerousness of the method chosen, and so forth. While this information may help to predict future risk, we were in accord with comments made by Pierce (1977) and echoed by Engelsmann and Ananth (1981) that such

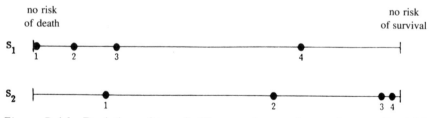
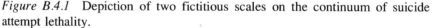

Figure B.4.1 Depiction of two fictitious scales on the continuum of suicide attempt lethality.

information may be distorted due to the patient's unwillingness to cooperate fully in revealing his/her state of mind just prior to an attempt, or by what was said by family or consultants to him/her about what he/she had done, or by such sequelae as a clouded consciousness resulting from the drugs or other agents used during the attempt. Our own work had impressed us with how often those patients, making the most mild attempts, would speak about their acts in vivid, overly dramatic detail, making a conscious effort to exaggerate the facts. Furthermore, we suspect that the more objective details of the actual attempt convey a more balanced picture of conscious and unconscious motivations (see Farberow & Shneidman, 1961, pp. 65–67) than occurs when selective weight is given to motivations of which the patient is aware. A final and very significant advantage of a scale which does not focus on a patient's admitted intent is that it can be applied to attempts recorded in medical records, coroner reports, and information obtained from the person's relatives and friends. We wanted a scale that would work equally well with or without a patient to interview. This goal excluded the use of Beck's "Circumstances Related to Suicide Attempt" section of his "Suicide Intent Scale" (SIS), Dorpat and Boswell's five-point (3 anchors) scale, and Pierce's (1977) modification of Beck's SIS.

Another problem is found in scales which emphasize the length of time between initiation of a method and death, a relationship variously termed "reversibility of method" (Freeman, Thigpen, & McGee, 1972), "rescue" (Weisman & Worden, 1972), and "point of no return" (Farberow & Shneidman, 1961, p. 64). The problem with this construct is that ingestions of very lethal drugs usually end up being given the same weight as ingestions of 10 aspirin and less weight than other less lethal acts. The justification for such a position is that it usually takes more time for the poisons to be effective and therefore the person has allowed more time for rescue. While this may be true, we also have reason to suspect that people tend to use the methods that are available, which in our increasingly drug-oriented society is increasingly likely to be drugs (e.g., Lester & Murrel, 1982). We wanted a scale that would allow more flexibility and realism in rating substance ingestions. This goal ruled out Farberow and Shneidman's hierarchy of methods which was actually not an empirical scale except in the hands of others, for example, Exner and Wyle (1977); Freeman, Thigpen, Wilson, and McGee's (1974) scales; and Weisman and Worden's (1974) scales.

Because research is often performed by nonmedical mental health professionals, we wanted a scale that was not too medically technical, yet allowed one to accurately appraise the seriousness of the act and approximate the lethality of ingested substances. Because of its reference to "necrotizing lesions," assessing damage to "large and small arteries" and the need to judge the "expected time of medical recovery," Weisman and Worden's (1974) scale was further faulted. Furthermore, while the Sterling-Smith Toxicology Index (1974) was a potential strength of the Weisman and Worden effort, the index tends to overrate the seriousness of ingestions and is too limited in the number of drugs it covers ($N = 30$).

Finally, we wanted a scale that could discriminate small increments of lethality so that sensitive empirical differences would not be obscured. We wanted a scale with at least seven points and because of that we did not use Motto's four "grades." Also, Motto (1965) did not supply inter-rater reliability information, nor a systematic guide for rating overdoses.

None of these instruments had any scaling information so it was not possible to know whether the scale items tended to bunch at one end or the other, where the gaps in measurement were, or whether adjacent points truly represented clinically and statistically separate judgments. To remedy such problems we wanted to develop a linear, interval level scale. We were also aware that most authors of scales had not made clear the discipline of the raters, an oversight that we suspected could significantly obscure the possibility that special training or knowledge might be required to use the scale reliably. We therefore wanted to test the ability of psychologists and social workers in addition to that of physicians and nurses to use the instrument.

As a starting point we selected the "Lethality of Intent" and "Lethality of Method" scales suggested by McEvoy (1974) largely because they were nine-point scales with some seemingly nice gradations of change in the degree of lethality. There were no scaling or reliability studies reported on the scales. Smith and Conroy combined aspects of these two scales into one, made refinements in wording and item definitions, and added anchors as they rated 718 attempts made by 200 suicidal patients. Their reliability on an earlier version of the scale was previously reported to be 0.91 (Smith, 1981). Continued refinement eventuated in Ehler and Smith's development of the part of the scale that deals with the lethality of various ingested substances. There are 170 substances listed along with their lethal ranges (based upon notion of the LD_{50}–see reference notes for Table B.4.3 for the 120- and 170-lb. person. This particular list represents all the substances that our patients have reported ingesting during attempts for which an LD_{50} could be located. For further details the reader is referred to the "Instructions for Approximating Ingestion Lethality," below. We now turn to a study of the psychometric properties of the scale.

Method

Twenty-four experienced psychiatric staff members volunteered to rate and scale the items.[1] The staff was drawn from four disciplines: psychiatry, psychology, social work, and nursing. These participants were first asked to perform the

---

[1]The authors are aware that 24 raters is not a large number and that their results would need to be substantiated by larger samples of more diverse observers.

scaling task on the nine anchor points. They were given nine cards, each containing one of the anchors, and asked to arrange the cards according to increasing degrees of lethality. The participants were then asked to separate the cards spatially so that the distance between adjacent cards reflected the participant's appraisal of the relative degree of change in lethality. The relative spacing between cards was then recorded on a 101-point scale anchored at one (0.0) end by "absolutely no realistic chance of dying" and at the other end (100.0) by "absolutely no realistic chance of surviving." The scale was marked in five-point increments. As a second task the participants were asked to use an intact version of the nine-point scale to rate 24 suicide attempt vignettes. This rating provided the reliability portion of the study. Finally, the participants were asked to indicate where on the scale they would make the distinction between "mild" and "serious" attempts.

Results

The scaling procedure resulted in the means and standard deviations seen in Table B.4.1. As can be observed (see Figure B.4.2), the scale points span the full range of lethality and possess relatively good differentiation. When adjacent scale point means were evaluated for the degree of overlap, all points were found to be significantly different from each other ($p < 0.01$). The Newman-Keuls procedure was used to help correct for spurious levels of significance due to multiple t tests. That the scale points do differ significantly from each other suggests that they do represent different perceived levels of lethality. The 101-point scale was reduced to an 11-point scale with the individual scale points rounded to the closest whole number. The one exception was scale point 33.8,

Table B.4.1

Mean Placements and Standard Deviations of the Nine Anchors Along with the Resulting Eleven-Point Scale

Item	Mean placement	SD	11–pt. scale conversion
A	0.0	0.0	0.0
B	8.6	5.5	1.0
C	18.8	9.6	2.0
D	33.8	13.6	3.5
E	50.8	7.0	5.0
F	69.1	9.1	7.0
G	82.0	5.4	8.0
H	91.9	3.8	9.0
I	99.4	2.2	10.0

no risk
of death

no risk
of survival

Figure B.4.2 Depiction of actual scale points of the Smith, Conroy, and Ehler Scale on the continuum of suicide attempt lethality.

which was rounded to 3.5. No scale point was compromised by more than 0.2 points. With the reduction of scale values accomplished, the ordinal nine-point scale with which we had started emerged as nine anchor points on an 11-point equal-interval scale. Eight of the anchors fall directly on the cardinal numbers of the scale. The fourth anchor, 3.5, is 1.5 units from its adjacent points (2.0 and 5.0) on this equal-interval scale. Proportionality and, thus, ratio properties are achieved by this range of 0 to 10. To examine further the equal-interval properties of the scale, an analysis suggested by Torgerson (1958) was employed. The scale placements of the 24 participants were randomly divided into two groups and plotted against each other. As Torgerson notes, an interval scale is suggested when the resulting coordinates produce, within the bounds of sampling error, a straight line.

Figure B.4.3 shows the essentially straight-line plot for these data. As Torgerson further advises, the ratio between the same scale points of both groups should not differ by more than sampling error. As tested by χ^2, all ratios are within the sampling error, further confirming the equal-interval quality.

The intraclass correlation of all raters irrespective of discipline affiliation is quite good at both the group level ($r_k = 0.99$) and for individual raters ($r_i = 0.85$). To be most conservative, the variance attributed to "disciplines" and "individual differences among raters" was included in the error terms where possible. There were no significant differences found in reliability among disciplines (see Table B.4.2). "Level" differences were found only in two disciplines, nursing ($F = 2.6564$, df 5/19, $p < 0.05$) and social work ($F = 5.1540$, df 5/19, $p < 0.001$). A study of individual variations showed the actual differences to be quite small. The range for nursing was from 4.71 to 5.12 (mean = 4.82). For social work the range was from 4.42 to 5.62 (mean = 4.86). A 0.30 to 0.76 of a point shift in scale values is likely to be of little clinical significance on an 11-point scale.

There was some discipline variation in judging the point after which an attempt was considered to be "serious." On the 101-point scale, psychologists and nurses made the demarcation at 50.0. Psychiatrists were somewhat lower at 43.3, with social workers lowest of all, at 35.0. The overall mean for all participants was 45.0. Transposing this to the 11-point scale, then, means that clinicians would label as "serious" all suicidal behavior above scale point 3.5.

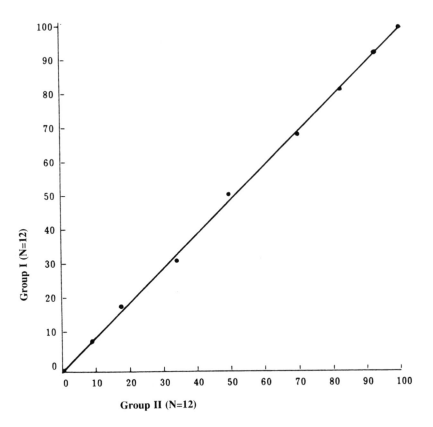

Figure B.4.3   Test of ratio properties using two randomly selected groups.

Discussion

The results confirm the development of an 11-point, equal-interval scale with nine anchors that can reliably be used to measure the lethality of suicide attempts. It has also been shown that the scale can be used reliably by nonmedical personnel as well as physicians and nursing staff. A principal advantage of the scale is that it can be applied to historical data, as it is not dependent on a patient's willingness to accurately discuss his/her "intent."

The clinicians in this study were not "taught" the scale but only given it along with the written instructions about its use. It appears likely that the reliability of the instrument would be even higher if the participants had discussed the instructions and practiced their application prior to the reliability study. The fact that the scale could be rated so well without careful study or experience is a valuable property.

Table B.4.2
Intraclass Reliability Coefficients by Disciplines

	r_i	r_k
Social Workers	.812602	.962987
Psychiatrists	.850175	.971467
Nurses	.867339	.975142
Psychologists	.884018	.978601

r_i is the reliability of an individual rater within a discipline.
r_k is the reliability of the group as a whole. r_k is the intraclass coefficient usually reported in the literature even though the estimate of an individual's ability to reliably rate is best conveyed by r_i.

The clinician's evaluation of seriousness helps to define the range of behaviors they wish most to be able to anticipate. Their rating of "serious" appears motivated most by considerations of the lethality of method, rather than the circumstances of the attempt. In our previous work (e.g., Smith, 1981) we have generally used a much more stringent definition of seriousness, one equivalent to scale point 8. Because of the decreased level of ambivalence seen in the scale points of 8 and above, we will probably continue to use 8 as our research benchmark of "seriousness." We have already shown that those with an 8 or higher have similar personality characteristics that tend to distinguish them from those 7 and below (Smith, 1982).

It appears quite likely that the scale possesses the even higher scale properties of a "ratio" level scale, as it does have an "absolute zero" point. If this could be further documented through additional scaling studies, clinicians and researchers would be in a position to qualify attempts relative to each other (e.g., "his last attempt was twice as serious as his first"). As it now stands, the attempts should probably still be qualified by a scale number that closely approximates such information.

While the research usefulness of the scale should be clear, it is also mentioned that the scale is being used clinically in our setting. All suicide attempts occurring within the hospital are rated on the scale. The advantage of such rating is in providing a more objective frame of reference to evaluate an attempt. Sometimes clinicians, out of the countertransference elicited by a suicide act, over- or underreact to the event. It is our assumption that by more accurately appraising the attempt, staff are in a better position to render treatment. It also appears that inquiring about and then rating the lethality of all attempts made *prior* to a hospitalization will help staff to be aware of an incoming patient's suicide potential.

References

Beck, A. T., Schuyler, D., & Herman I. (1974). Development of suicidal intent scales. In A. T. Beck, H. L. P. Resnik, & A. J. Lettieri (Eds.), *The prevention of suicide* (pp. 45–56). Bowie, MD: Charles Press Publishing, Inc.

Dorpat, T. L., & Boswell, J. W. (1963). An evolution of suicidal intent in suicide attempts. *Comprehensive Psychiatry, 4*, 117–125.

Englesmann, F., & Ananth, J. (1981). Suicide rating scales. *Psychiatric Journal of the University of Ottawa, 6*, 47–51.

Exner, J. E., & Wyle, J. (1977). Some Rorschach data concerning suicide. *Journal of Personality Assessment, 41*, 339–348.

Farberow, N. L., & Shneidman, E. D. (Eds.). (1961). *The cry for help.* New York: McGraw-Hill.

Freeman, D. V., Wilson, K., Thigpen, J., & McGee, R. (1974). Assessing intention to die in self-injury behavior. In C. Neuringer (Ed.), *Psychological assessment of suicidal risk*, (pp. 18–42). Springfield, IL: Charles C Thomas.

Lester, D., & Murrell, M. E. (1982). The preventive effect of strict gun control laws on suicide and homicide. *Suicide and Life-Threatening Behavior, 12*, 131–140.

McEvoy, T. L. (1974). Suicide risks via the Thematic Apperception Test. In C. Neuringer (Ed.), *Psychological assessment of suicidal risk*, (pp. 95–117). Springfield, IL: Charles C Thomas.

Motto, J. A. (1965). Suicide attempts: A longitudinal view. *Archives of General Psychiatry, 13*, 516–520.

Pierce, D. W. (1977). Suicidal intent in self-injury. *British Journal of Psychiatry, 130*, 377–385.

Smith, K. (1981). Using a battery of tests to predict suicide in a long-term hospital: A quantitative analysis. *Journal of Clinical Psychology, 37*, 555–563.

Smith, K. (1982–1983). Using a battery of tests to predict suicide in a long-term hospital: A clinical analysis. *Omega, 13*, 261–275.

Smith, K., Conroy, R. W., & Ehler, B. (1984). Lethality of suicide attempt rating scale. *Suicide and Life-Threatening Behavior, 14*(4), Winter, 215–242.

Sterling-Smith, R. S. (1974). A medical toxology index. In A. T. Beck, H. L. P. Resnick, & A. J. Lettieri (Eds.), *The prevention of suicide*, (pp. 214–220). Bowie, MD: Charles Press Publishing, Inc.

Torgerson, W. S. (1958). *Theory and methods of scaling.* New York: John Wiley & Sons, Inc.

Weisman, A. D., & Worden, J. W. (1974). Risk-rescue rating in suicidal assessment. In A. T. Beck, H. L. P. Resnick, & A. J. Lettieri, (Eds.), *The prevention of suicide* (pp. 193–213). Bowie, MD: Charles Press Publishing, Inc.

Appendix B.4.A
Scale Points[1]

Instructions

The range of this scale is from 0.0 to 10.0. While it has nine example "anchoring" points, a person may be rated in between anchoring points if that seems most appropriate. The suicide attempt lethality rating is a composite of two assessments: the actual lethality of the method used, and the circumstances surrounding the attempt. Lethality of method refers to the life-threatening impact of the specific act, such as where and how deeply the person was lacerated, or the type and dosage of medication consumed. Examples of various methods appropriate to a lethality level are provided at each scale point. Ingestions of chemicals and medication overdoses should be evaluated using Table B.4.3 and associated instructions. The severity of method is then modified by an assessment of the circumstances surrounding the attempt. Some pertinent circumstantial questions are: was the person alone; did he/she tell anyone before or after the attempt was made; could he/she have expected someone to "inadvertently" disrupt the attempt; did he/she take steps to hide the act or prevent help; how much medical intervention was required; and did the attempt result in a serious medical threat to life (e.g., unconsciousness). These kinds of circumstantial events are used to adjust the "method" rating so that the *lethality of the whole attempt* is reflected in the rating.

Three other guidelines are offered:

1. An attempt that involved a "communication" should not be rated higher than 7.0 unless the communication *follows* an unusually severe method (e.g., calling someone after shooting self)

2. An attempt in which a very deadly method was used should be rated no less than 3.5

3. The rating of 5.0 should be used only when there is insufficient information *and* when the method seemed potentially very lethal (e.g., "patient ingested an unknown number of barbiturates"). A "very lethal dose" of a drug would involve amounts nearer the higher end of the LD_{50}. When the amount of drugs ingested is "unknown," Table B.4.3 should be consulted to determine the potential lethality of the overdose.

---

[1]While the authors of the original paper worked to ensure that all information contained in their tables was accurate, as of the date of the publication of the original article, as medical research and clinical practice advance, standards of practice may change. For this reason, we recommend that psychologists consult with a knowledgable medical colleague with regard to the use of the material contained in Appendix B.4.

Table B.4.3

Drug	LD$_{50}$	How supplied	Lethal range for a 120 lb. person in caps, tabs or ounces	Lethal range for a 170 lb. person in caps, tabs or ounces
Acetaminophen				
(Tylenol–Reg. Strength)	200–1,000 mg Kg	325 mg tab	34–168	47–237
*(Tylenol–Extra Strength)	200–1,000 mg Kg	500 mg tab	22–109	31–155
*(Anacin–3)	200–1,000 mg Kg	500 mg tab	22–109	31–155
	140 mg/Kg causes		23 reg. strength	33 reg. strength
	liver damage		16 extra strength	22 extra strength
Allerest				
Composed of:				
2 mg Chlorpheniramine	25–250 mg/Kg	tab	78	110
18.7 mg Phenylpropanolamine	2,000 mg			
4 mg Chlorpheniramine	25–250 mg/Kg	cap	29	41
*50 mg Phenylpropanolamine	2,000 mg			
Alprazolam	approx. 8,000 mg	0.5 mg tab	12,457	17,669
(Xanax)		1 mg tab	6,229	8,834
Amitriptyline HCl	35–50 mg/Kg	10 mg tab	191–273	271–387
(Elavil)		25 mg tab	76–109	108–155
		50 mg tab	38–55	54–77
		75 mg tab	25–36	36–52
		100 mg tab	19–27	27–39
		150 mg tab	13–18	18–26
***Amphetamine**	100–200 mg	5 mg tab	20–40	20–40
(Dextroamphetamine)	(not prorated by	10 mg cap	10–20	10–20
(Dexedrine)	body weight)	15 mg cap	7–13	7–13
***Amytal**	1,500 mg	50 mg tab	23	33
	(not prorated by	100 mg tab	12	17
	body weight)			
***Amytal Sodium**	1,500 mg	65 mg tab	18	25
	(not prorated by	200 mg cap	6	8
	body weight)			
Arsenate of Lead	100–500 mg	—	78–389 mg	110–552 mg
Arsenic	200 mg	—	156 mg	221 mg
	(not prorated by body weight)			
Artane	100–1,000 mg	2 mg tab	39–390	55–550
(Trihexyphenidyl)	(not prorated by	5 mg cap	16–160	22–220
	body weight)			
Asendin	50–500 mg/Kg	50 mg tab	55–550	77–770
(Amoxapine)		100 mg tab	27–270	39–390
		150 mg tab	18–180	25–250

(continued)

Drug	LD$_{50}$	How supplied	Lethal range for a 120 lb. person in caps, tabs or ounces	Lethal range for a 170 lb. person in caps, tabs or ounces
Aspirin, ASA (Bufferin, Ascriptin) (Acetylsalicylic Acid)	30,000 mg 200–500 mg/Kg	325 mg tab	34–84	48–119
Atarax (Hydroxyzine HCl)	25–250 mg/Kg	10 mg tab 25 mg tab 50 mg tab	136–1,360 55–550 27–270	193–1,930 77–770 39–390
Ativan (Lorazepam)	50–500 mg/Kg	0.25 mg tab 0.5 mg tab 1 mg tab 2 mg tab	10,900–109,000 5,450–54,500 2,725–27,250 1,363–13,630	15,460–154,600 7,730–77,300 3,865–38,650 1,933–19,330
Aventyl see Nortriptyline HCl	—	—		
Benadryl (Diphenhydramine HCl)	20–40 mg/Kg	25 mg cap 50 mg cap	44–88 22–44	62–124 31–62
Bufferin see Aspirin	—	—		
Caffeine	183–250 mg/Kg	65 mg tab	153–209	218–297
***Carbamezine** (Tegretol)	100–500 mg/Kg	200 mg tab	27–136	39–193
Centrax see (Prazepam)				
***Chloral Hydrate** (Noctec)	2,000–10,000 mg	250 mg cap 500 mg cap	6–31 3–16	9–44 4–22
Chlordiazepoxide HCl (Librium)	50–500 mg/Kg	5 mg cap 10 mg cap 25 mg cap	545–5,450 273–2,730 109–1,090	773–7,730 387–3,870 155–1,550
Chlorpromazine HCl (Thorazine)	15–150 mg/Kg	10 mg tab 25 mg tab 50 mg tab 100 mg tab 200 mg tab	82–820 33–330 16–160 8–80 4–40	116–1,160 46–460 23–230 12–120 6–60
***Codeine**	500–800 mg	15 mg tab 30 mg tab 60 mg tab	26–41 13–21 7–11	36–58 18–29 9–15
Compazine (Prochlorperazine)	15–150 mg/Kg	5 mg tab 10 mg tab 15 mg tab	164–1,640 82–820 55–550	232–2,320 116–1,160 77–770
Compoz (Diphenhydramine)*	20–40 mg/Kg	25 mg tab	44–88	62–124

(continued)

Drug	LD_{50}	How supplied	Lethal range for a 120 lb. person in caps, tabs or ounces	Lethal range for a 170 lb. person in caps, tabs or ounces
*Contac Composed of: 4 mg Chlorpheniramine 50 mg Phenlpropanolamine	25–250 mg/Kg 2,000 mg	cap	29	41
Cope Composed of: 421 mg Aspirin 15 mg Methapyrilene	30,000 mg 50 mg/Kg	tab	53	75
Coricidin Composed of: 2 mg Chlorpheniramine 325 mg Aspirin	25–250 mg/Kg 30,000 mg	tab	70	99
Coricidin D Composed of: 2 mg Chlorpheniramine 12.5 mg Phenylpropanolamine 325 mg Aspirin	25–250 mg/Kg 2,000 mg 30,000 mg	tab	65	92
Coumadin	100 mg (not prorated by body weight)	2 mg tab 5 mg tab 10 mg tab	39 16 8	55 22 11
Cylert (Pemoline)	2,000 mg (not prorated by body weight)	37.5 mg tab	41	59
Dalmane (Flurazapam HCl)	50–500 mg/Kg	15 mg cap 30 mg cap	181–1,810 91–910	257–2,570 129–1,290
Darvocet-N (Propoxyphene napsylate)	35 mg/Kg	50 mg tab 100 mg tab	38 19	54 27
Darvon (Propoxyphene HCl)	35 mg/Kg	32 mg cap 65 mg tab	60 30	85 42
*Demerol (Meperidine HCl)	1,000 mg (not prorated by body weight)	50 mg tab	16	22
*Depakene (Valproic Acid)	50–500 mg/Kg	250 mg cap	11–110	15–150
Desipramine HCl (Norpramin) (Pertorfrane)	35–50 mg/Kg	25 mg tab 50 mg tab 75 mg tab 100 mg tab 150 mg tab	76–109 38–55 25–36 19–27 12–18	108–155 54–77 36–52 27–39 18–25
*Dexol bleach	5 ml to 30 ml 1/6 to 1 oz	liquid	1/6 to 1 oz	1/4 to 1 1/4 oz

(continued)

269

Drug	LD$_{50}$	How supplied	Lethal range for a 120 lb. person in caps, tabs or ounces	Lethal range for a 170 lb. person in caps, tabs or ounces
Diazepam HCl (Valium)	50–500 mg/Kg	2 mg tab 5mg tab 10 mg tab	1,360–13,630 545–5,450 273–2,730	1,933–19,330 773–7,730 387–3,870
Dilantin (Phenytoin)	100–500 mg/Kg	100 mg cap	55–273	77–770
Diphenhydramine HCl (Benadryl)	20–40 mg/Kg	25 mg cap 50 mg cap	44–88 22–44	62–124 31–62
***Doriden** (Glutethamide)	100–500 mg/Kg	250 mg tab 500 mg tab	22–109 11–55	31–155 16–77
Doxepin HCl (Sinequan, Adepin)	35–50 mg/Kg	10 mg cap 25 mg cap 50 mg cap 75 mg cap 100 mg cap 150 mg cap	191–273 76–109 38–55 25–36 19–28 13–18	271–387 108–155 54–77 36–52 27–39 18–26
***Dramamine** (Dimenhydrinate)	25–250 mg/Kg	50 mg tab	27–270	39–390
Drawing Ink	480–960 cc 16–32 oz	liquid	12–24	18–36
Dristan tablets Composed of: 2 mg Chlorpheniramine 5 mg Phenylephrine 325 mg Aspirin 16.2 mg Caffeine	25–250 mg/Kg 1,000 mg 200–500 mg/Kg 183–250 mg/Kg	tab	65	92
***Dristan capsules** Composed of: 4 mg Chlorpheniramine 50 mg Phenylephrine	25–250 mg/Kg 1,000 mg	cap	16	22
Elavil see Amitriptyline	—	—		
Empirin see Aspirin	—	—		
***Empirin #1, #2, #3, #4** Composed of: 325 mg Aspirin Codeine (8, 15, 30, 60mg)	200–500 mg/Kg 500–800 mg	#1 tab #2 tab #3 tab #4 tab	51–82 26–41 13–21 7–11	73–117 36–58 18–29 9–15
***Equagesic** Composed of: 250 mg Aspirin 25 mg Ethoheptazine 150 mg Meprobamate	200–500 mg/Kg 1,000 mg 100–500 mg/Kg	tab	19–23	28–33

(continued)

Drug	LD$_{50}$	How supplied	Lethal range for a 120 lb. person in caps, tabs or ounces	Lethal range for a 170 lb. person in caps, tabs or ounces
*Equanil	100–500 mg/Kg	200 mg tab	27–136	39–193
(Meprobamate)		400 mg tab	14–68	20–97
*Ethchlorvynol	100–500 mg/Kg	200 mg cap	27–136	39–193
(Placidyl)		500 mg cap	11–55	16–78
		750 mg cap	7–35	10–50
*Ethinamate	100–500 mg/Kg	500 mg cap	11–55	16–78
(Valmid)				
Etrafon Triavil		2–10 tab	191–226	271–320
(Amitriptyline)	35–50 mg/Kg	2–25 tab	76–100	108–142
(Trilafon)	15–150 mg/Kg	4–10 tab	191–195	271–276
		4–25 tab	76–93	108–133
		4–50 tab	38–51	54–72
*Excedrin				
Composed of:		tab	19–48	28–68
250 mg Aspirin	200–500 mg/Kg			
250 mg Acetaminophen	200–1,000 mg/Kg			
65 mg Caffeine	183–250 mg/Kg			
*Fiorinal				
Composed of:		tab	23–31	33–44
50 mg Butalbital	200–500 mg/Kg	cap		
200 mg Aspirin	200–500 mg/Kg			
40 mg Caffeine	183–250 mg/Kg			
Flurazepam HCl				
see Dalmane	—	—		
Furniture Polish	30–480 cc	liquid	1–12 oz	1–18 oz
(80% Kerosene)	1–16 oz			
*Glutethamide				
see Doriden	—	—		
Haldol	15–150 mg/Kg	0.5 mg tab	1,635–16,350	2,319–23,190
(Haloperidol)		1 mg tab	818–8,180	1,160–11,600
		2 mg tab	409–4,090	580–5,800
		5 mg tab	164–1,640	232–2,320
		10 mg tab	82–820	116–1,160
		20 mg tab	41–410	58–580
Hydroxyzine HCl				
see Atarax	—	—		
Imipramine HCl	35–50 mg/Kg	10 mg tab	191–273	271–387
(Tofranil)		25 mg tab	76–109	108–155
		50 mg tab	38–55	54–76
Iodine, Tincture	2,000 ml	liquid	3 oz	4 oz
	3.5 oz			
Librium				
see Chlordiazepoxide HCl	—	—		

(continued)

Drug	LD$_{50}$	How supplied	Lethal range for a 120 lb. person in caps, tabs or ounces	Lethal range for a 170 lb. person in caps, tabs or ounces
Lighter Fluid Composed of: petroleum distallates	30–250 cc 1–8 oz	liquid	1–6 oz	1–9 oz
Lithium Carbonate	serum level of 3–4 mEg/L	300 mg cap 300 mg tab	Serum level can be reached with as few as 15–20 caps	Serum level can be reached with as few as 15–20 caps
Lomotil Composed of: 2.5 mg Diphenoxylate HCl 0.025 mg Atropine Sulfate	200 mg	tab	62	88
Lorazepam see Ativan	—	—		
Loxapine (Loxitane)	50–500 mg/Kg	5 mg cap 10 mg cap 25 mg cap 50 mg cap	550–5,500 275–2,750 110–1,100 55–550	770–7,700 385–3,850 154–1,540 77–770
Ludiomil (Maprotiline HCl)	35–50 mg/Kg	25 mg tab 50 mg tab	76–109 38–55	108–155 54–78
Mellaril (Thioridazine HCl)	15–150 mg/Kg	10 mg tab 25 mg tab 50 mg tab 100 mg tab 150 mg tab 200 mg tab	82–820 33–330 16–160 8–80 6–60 4–40	116–1,160 46–460 23–230 12–120 9–90 6–60
*Meperidine HCl see Demerol	—	—		
Meprobamate (Miltown, Equanil, Meprospan)	100–500 mg/Kg	200 mg tab 400 mg tab	27–136 14–68	39–193 20–97
Mercury salts (liquid Mercury is *not* toxic to the body since it is not absorbed)	500–1,000 mg (not prorated by body weight)	found in insecticides	500–1,000 mg	500–1,000 mg
*Methadone (Dolophine HCl)	100 mg (not prorated by body weight)	5 mg tab 10 mg tab	16 8	22 11
Methanol	60–250 ml	liquid	2–6 oz	2–9 oz
Methapryilene HCl	50 mg/Kg	25 mg tab	109	155
Methaqualone (Quaalude)	100–500 mg/Kg	150 mg tab 300 mg tab	37–183 19–93	52–260 26–130

(continued)

Drug	LD$_{50}$	How supplied	Lethal range for a 120 lb. person in caps, tabs or ounces	Lethal range for a 170 lb. person in caps, tabs or ounces
*Methylphenidate HCl (Ritalin)	200 mg	5 mg tab 10 mg tab 20 mg tab	31 16 8	44 22 11
Methyprylon (Noludar)	100–500 mg/Kg	50 mg tab 200 mg tab 300 mg cap	109–545 27–136 18–91	155–773 39–194 26–129
Miltown see Meprobamate	—	—		
Mistletoe Composed of: Tryamine Betaphenethylamine	"considered dangerous"	berries	unknown	unknown
Moban (Molindone HCl)	15–150 mg/Kg	5 mg tab 10 mg tab 25 mg tab 50 mg tab 100 mg tab	164–1,640 82–820 33–330 16–160 8–80	232–2,320 116–1,160 46–460 23–230 12–120
Mysoline (Primidone)	100–500 mg/Kg	50 mg tab 250 mg tab	109–545 22–109	155–773 31–155
*Nail Polish (Toluene)	5–30 cc 1/6–1 oz	liquid	1/6 to 1 oz	1/4 to 1 1/4 oz
Nail Polish Remover (Acetone)	30–240 cc 1–8 oz	liquid	1–6 oz	1–8 oz
Nardil (Pheneizine SO$_4$)	25–100 mg/Kg	15 mg tab	91–364	129–517
Navane (Thiothixene HCl)	15–150 mg/Kg	1 mg cap 2 mg cap 5 mg cap 10 mg cap 20 mg cap	820–8,200 410–4,100 164–1,640 82–820 41–410	1,160–11,600 580–5,800 232–2,320 116–1,160 58–580
*Nembutal (Pentobarbital)	1,000 mg (not prorated by body weight)	50 mg cap 100 mg cap	16 8	22 11
*Noctec see Chloral Hydrate	—	—		
Nodoz Composed of: 100 mg Caffeine	183–250 mg/Kg	tab	100–136	141–193
Noludar see Methprylon	—	—		
Norpramin see Desipramine HCl	—	—		

(continued)

Drug	LD$_{50}$	How supplied	Lethal range for a 120 lb. person in caps, tabs or ounces	Lethal range for a 170 lb. person in caps, tabs or ounces
Nortriptyline HCl (Aventyl, Pamelor)	35–50 mg/Kg	10 mg cap 25 mg cap 75 mg cap	191–273 76–109 25–36	271–387 108–155 36–52
Nytol (Pyrilamine maleate)	40 mg/Kg	25 mg tab	87	124
Oleander leaves	3,000 mg (not prorated by body weight)	—	2,336 mg	3,313 mg
Oxazepam (Serax)	50–500 mg/Kg	10 mg cap 15 mg cap 30 mg cap	273–2,730 182–1,820 91–910	387–3,870 258–2,580 129–1,290
Paint thinner	"several ounces"	liquid	several ounces	several ounces
Pamelor see Nortriptyline HCl	—	—		
***Paraldehyde**	30–100 cc 1–3 oz	liquid	1–2 oz	1–3.3 oz
Parnate (Tranycypromine SO$_4$)	25–100 mg/Kg	10 mg tab	136–545	193–773
Pemoline see Cylert	—	—		
***Pentazocine** (Talwin)	300 mg (not prorated by body weight)	50 mg tab	5	7
***Pentobarbital** (Nembutal)	1,000 mg (not prorated by body weight)	50 mg cap 100 mg cap	16 8	22 11
Percodan (Oxycodone)	500 mg (not prorated by body weight)	4.5 mg tab 2.25 mg tab	78 156	110 220
Perfume Alcohol, methyl	60–250 cc 2–8 oz	liquid	2–6 oz	2–9 oz
Perphenazine HCl (Trilafon)	15–150 mg/Kg	2 mg tab 4 mg tab 8 mg tab 16 mg tab	409–4,090 205–2,050 102–1,020 51–510	580–5,800 290–2,900 145–1,450 73–730
Phenelzine SO$_4$ see Nardil	—	—		
Phenobarbital	1,500 mg	15 mg tab 30 mg tab 60 mg tab 100 mg tab	78 39 20 12	110 55 28 17

(continued)

Drug	LD_{50}	How supplied	Lethal range for a 120 lb. person in caps, tabs or ounces	Lethal range for a 170 lb. person in caps, tabs or ounces
Phenytoin see Dilantin	—	—		
Placidyl see Ethclorvynol	—	—		
Potassium Cyanate	840 mg/Kg	powder		
Prazepam (Centrax)	50–500 mg/Kg	5 mg tab 10 mg tab	273–2,730 137–1,370	387–3,870 194–1,940
Propa-pH (Benzoyl Peroxide)	250 mg/Kg	cream 30 gm tubes	6.5 tubes	9 tubes
***Propoxyphene napsylate** see Darvocet-N	—	—		
***Propoxyphene HCl** see Darvon	—	—		
Protriptyline HCl (Vivacti)	35–50 mg/Kg	5 mg tab 10 mg tab	382–546 191–273	542–774 271–387
Pyrilamine maleate	40 mg/Kg	25 mg tab	87	124
Quaalude see Methaqualone	—	—		
Quiet World Composed of: 227 mg Aspirin 162 mg Acetaminophen 25 mg Pyrilamine maleate	200–500 mg/Kg 200–1,000 mg/Kg 40 mg/Kg	tab	48–58	68–83
Rat Poison (Warfarin)	10–100 mg daily	(single dose not dangerous; it takes *repeated* ingestions)		
Ritalin see Methylphenidate	—	—		
***Robaxin** (Methocarbamol)	50–500 mg/Kg	500 mg tab 750 mg tab	5–50 4–40	8–80 6–60
Seconal (Secobarbital)	2,000 mg (not prorated by body weight)	50 mg cap 100 mg cap	31 16	44 22
Serax see Oxazepam	—	—		
Shaving Lotion Composed of: Alcohol, methyl	600–800 cc 20–27 oz	liquid	20–27 oz	20–27 oz
Silicone Shoe Waterproofer	30–480 cc 1–16 oz	liquid	1–12 oz	1–18 oz

(continued)

Drug	LD$_{50}$	How supplied	Lethal range for a 120 lb. person in caps, tabs or ounces	Lethal range for a 170 lb. person in caps, tabs or ounces
Sinequan see Doxepin HCl	—	—		
Sleepeze (Pyrilamine maleate)	40 mg/Kg	25 mg tab	87	124
Sodium Hydroxide	5,000 mg (not prorated by body weight)	—		
Sominex (Pyrilamine maleate)	40 mg/Kg	25 mg tab	87	124
Sominex-2 (Diphenhydramine HCl)	20–40 mg/Kg	25 mg tab	44–88	62–124
Stelazine see Trifluoperazine	—	—		
*Sudafed (Pseudoephedrine)	1,000 mg (not prorated by body weight)	30 mg tab 60 mg tab 120 mg tab	26 13 7	36 18 9
*Talwin see Pentazocine	—	—		
Tegretol see Carbamezine	—	—		
Ten-O-Six Lotion	32 oz	liquid	24 oz	36 oz
Thioridazine HCl see Mellaril	—	—		
Thiothixene HCl see Navane	—	—		
Thorazine see Chlorpromazine HCl	—	—		
Tofranil see Imipramine HCl	—	—		
Tranyl cypromine SO$_4$ (Parnate)	25–100 mg/Kg	10 mg tab	136–545	193–773
*Triclos	2,000–10,000 mg (not prorated by body weight)	750 mg tab	2–12	3–17
Trifluoperazine (Stelazine)	15–150 mg/Kg	1 mg tab 2 mg tab 5 mg tab 10 mg tab	818–8,180 409–4,090 164–1,640 82–820	1,160–11,600 580–5,800 232–2,320 116–1,160
Trilafon see Perphenazine	—	—		

(continued)

276

Drug	LD$_{50}$	How supplied	Lethal range for a 120 lb. person in caps, tabs or ounces	Lethal range for a 170 lb. person in caps, tabs or ounces
*Tuinal Composed of: 50 mg Amobarbital 50 mg Secobarbital	1,500 mg 1,500 mg (not prorated by body weight)	100 mg cap	12	17
Tylenol, Tylenol *Extra Strength see Acetaminophen	—	—		
Valium see Diazepam HCl	—	—		
*Valmid see Ethinamate	—	—		
*Valproic Acid (Depakene)	50–500 mg/Kg	250 mg cap	11–10	15–150
Vivarin Composed of: 200 mg Caffeine	183–250 mg/Kg	tab	50–69	71–97
Vivactil see Protriptyline HCl	—	—		
Xanax see Alprazolam	—	—		

Note. From "Lethality of Suicide Attempt Rating Scale" by K. Smith, R. W. Conroy, and B. D. Ehler, 1984, *Suicide and Life-Threatening Behavior, 14*(4), pp. 215–242. Copyright 1984 by Guilford Publications. Reprinted by permission.

Drugs and chemicals that have an asterisk (*) are lethal in relatively low doses. Unknown doses of drugs without the asterisk should probably be rated below 3.5, while those with an asterisk should be rated at 5.0 or perhaps higher, given proper consideration of other circumstances. Further instructions for rating overdoses are provided in Table B.4.3.

Appendix B.4.B
Definitions of Scale Points*

0.0   Death is an impossible result of the "suicidal" behavior

Cutting: Light scratches that do not break the skin; usually done with pop can "pull tabs," broken plastic, pins, paper clips; reopening old wounds also is included at this level. Wounds requiring sutures must be rated at a higher level.

---

*These scale points were suggested by T. L. McEvoy (1974) but have been revised and further defined with anchoring examples by the authors; revision completed 5/5/83.

Ingestion: This includes mild overdoses and the swallowing of objects such as money, paper clips, and disposable thermometers. Ten or fewer ASA, Tylenol®, "cold pills," laxatives, or other over-the-counter drugs; mild doses of tranquilizers or prescribed medications (usually fewer than 10 pills). Putting broken glass into one's mouth but not swallowing would be rated in this category.

Other: Clearly ineffective acts which are usually shown by the patient to staff or others (e.g., going outside in cold weather with only a nightgown on after telling parents she was going to commit suicide by "freezing myself to death").

1.0   Death is very highly improbable. If it occurs it would be a result of secondary complication, an accident, or highly unusual circumstances

Cutting: Shallow cuts without tendon, nerve, or vessel damage. These wounds may require some very minor suturing. Cutting is often done with something sharp such as a razor. Very little blood loss. Scratches (as opposed to cuts) to the neck are first rated here.

Ingestion: Relatively mild overdoses or swallowing of nonsharp glass or ceramics, events usually brought by the patient to staff attention. Twenty or fewer ASA, laxatives, and/or over-the-counter meds (e.g., Sominex, Nytol®, 15 or fewer Tylenol). Small doses of potentially lethal medications (e.g., six Tuinal, four Seconal) are also common; fewer than 20 (10 mg.) Thorazine tablets.

Other: Tying a thread, string, or yarn around neck and then showing to staff.

2.0   Death is improbable as an outcome of the act. If it occurs it is probably due to unforeseen secondary effects. Frequently the act is done in a public setting or is reported by the person or by others. While medical aid may be warranted, it is not required for survival.

Cutting: May receive but does not usually *require* medical intervention to survive.

> *Examples:* Relatively superficial cuts with a sharp instrument that may involve slight tendon damage. Cuts to the arms, legs, and wrists will require suturing. Cuts to the side of the neck are first rated in this category and should not require suturing.

Ingestion: May receive but does not usually *require* medical intervention to survive.

> *Examples:* Thirty or fewer ASA and/or other over-the-counter pills; fewer than 100 laxatives; twenty-five or fewer Regular Strength Tylenol; drinking of toxic liquids (12 ounces or less), shampoo or astringent (e.g., Ten-O-Six® Lotion), lighter fluid or other petroleum-based products (less than two ounces). Small doses of potentially lethal medications (e.g., 21 65-mg. Darvon, 12 tablets of Fiorinal, "overdosed on phenobarbital but only enough to make him very drowsy," 10–15 50-mg. Thorazine tab-

lets), greater quantities of aspirin might be taken when staff is notified within minutes by the patient. Fourteen or fewer lithium carbonate tablets. The patient may swallow small quantities of cleaning compounds or fluids such as Comet® cleanser (less than four tablespoons).

Other: Nonlethal, usually impulsive and ineffective methods.

> *Examples:* Inhaling deodorant without respiratory distress occurring, swallowing several pieces of sharp glass, evidence of failed attempt to choke self with a piece of pillowcase (e.g., rash-type abrasions.)

3.5   Death is improbable so long as first aid is administered by victim or other agent. Victim usually makes a communication or commits the act in a public way or takes no measures to hide self or injury.

Cutting: Deep cuts involving tendon damage (or severing) and possible nerve, vessel, and artery damage; cuts to the neck will require sutures but no major vessels were severed. Blood loss is generally less than 100 cc. Cuts to neck go beyond scratching but do not actually sever main veins or arteries.

Ingestion: This is a significant overdose and may correspond to the lower part of the LD_{50} range.

> *Examples:* Fewer than 60 ASA or other over-the-counter pills. Higher doses may be taken but patient insures intervention (e.g., 64 Sominex). Over 100 laxatives; 50 or fewer Tylenol. Potentially lethal overdoses (e.g., 60 Dilantin capsules plus half a fifth of rum) but done in such a way as to insure intervention (e.g., in front of nursing staff, telling someone within 1 hour). Signs of physiological distress may be present such as nausea, elevated blood pressure, respiratory changes, convulsions, and altered consciousness stopping short of coma. Lighter fluid (three or more ounces); 15–20 lithium carbonate tablets.

Other: Possibly serious actions that are quickly brought by the patient to staff's attention (e.g., tied a shoelace tightly around neck but came to staff immediately).

5.0   Death is a fifty-fifty probability directly or indirectly, or in the opinion of the average person, the chosen method has an equivocal outcome. Use this rating only when (a) details are vague; (b) a case cannot be made for rating either a 3.5 or 7.0.

Cutting: Severe cutting resulting in sizable blood loss (more than 100 cc) with some chance of death. Cutting may be accompanied by alcohol or drugs, which may cloud the issue.

Ingestion: Reports of vague but possibly significant quantities of lethal medications. Unknown quantities of drugs that are lethal in small dosages (those with an * in Table B.4.3) also belong here.

Examples: "Take a large number of chloral hydrate and Doriden"; "took 60 ASA and an undetermined amount of other medications."

Other: Potentially lethal acts.

Examples: Trying to put two bare wires into an electrical outlet with a nurse present in the room; jumping headfirst from a car driven by staff going 30 miles an hour; unscrewing a light bulb in the lounge and putting finger in socket with patients around.

7.0 Death is the probable outcome unless there is "immediate" and "vigorous" first aid or medical attention by victim or other agent. One or both of the following are also true: (a) makes communication (directly or indirectly); (b) performs act in public where he is likely to be helped or discovered.

Cutting: Cuts are severe.

Examples: Eloping and "slashing neck with razor" (including severing jugular) but returning to hospital on own and asking for help; while alone cut head with shard of glass and "almost bled to death"—called doctor after cutting. Eloping and very severely cutting self in a public restroom or motel–cuts led to hemorrhagic shock with vascular collapse–patient makes direct request for help after cutting.

Ingestion: Potentially lethal medications and quantities. This would involve a dose which, without medical intervention, would kill most people (usually at the upper end of the LD_{50} range or beyond).

Examples: Eloping and ingesting approximately two bottles of ASA and then returning to the hospital; 50 Extra-Strength Tylenol, eloping to motel and ingesting large quantities of Inderal, Dalmane, Mellaril, and three quarters of a fifth of bourbon, then making indirect communication of distress; took 23 100-mg. tablets of phenobarbital but told roommate immediately who told staff; 16–18 capsules of Nembutal–left note with a friend who missed the note resulting in the patient almost dying.

Other: Lethal actions performed in a way that maximizes chances of intervention.

Examples: Tied towel tightly around neck–airway cut off–tried to untie it but passed out on floor–found cyanotic and in respiratory arrest–had seen staff making rounds before attempt; string wrapped several times around neck and tied to bed–face flushed when found.

8.0 Death would ordinarily be considered the outcome to the suicidal act, unless saved by another agent in a "calculated" risk (e.g., nursing rounds or expecting a roommate or spouse at a certain time). One or both of the following are true: (a) makes no direct communication; (b) takes action in private.

Cutting: Severe gashes with major and quick blood loss. May be partially hidden from staff, spouse, or friends.

> *Examples:* Patient went into bathroom of his room, left the door open and severely cut one wrist resulting in major blood loss; death would have occurred had he not been found 30 minutes later by nursing staff on rounds.

Ingestion: Clearly lethal doses and no communication is made.

> *Examples:* Taking a lethal overdose of barbiturates but vomiting before going into a coma; overdosed on 900 mg Stelazine in apartment alone; overdosed on phenobarbital plus alcohol, found comatose in her bed. Took 20 Tuinal and became very sleepy while visiting friends–the friends became suspicious and took her to emergency room–in coma for 36 hours; took 15 Tuinal–found unconscious at home in tub of warm water.

Other: Most common here are hangings and suffocations which may or may not succeed but are performed so that a calculated chance of intervention could interrupt.

> *Examples:* Tying belt very tightly around neck and strangling self in shower; tied shoelace lightly around neck and going to bed–found at rounds to be cyanotic; blocked airways with plastic and had tied a stocking tightly around neck–found on top of her bed gurgling and pale but not cyanotic; elopes and attempts to drown self in nearby pond but in broad daylight; jumps in front of fast-moving car (over 30 mph); plastic bag over head–found deeply cyanotic; played Russian roulette and drew a "pass."

9.0   Death is a highly probable outcome: "Chance" intervention and/or unforeseen circumstances may save victim. Two of the following conditions also exist: (a) no communication is made; (b)effort is put forth to obscure act from helpers' attention; (c) precautions against being found are instituted (e.g., eloping).

Cutting: Severe, usually multiple cuts involving severe blood loss.

> *Examples:* Severely cutting arm with razor and bleeding into wastebasket then got into bed (it was bedtime so being in bed did not arouse suspicion)–found unconscious and in shock; savagely biting a 2-cm piece of skin out of wrist, losing four pints of blood and found in shock under

bed covers; cut neck in arts and crafts bathroom (when shop was closed) with three-inch blade, found unconscious; severely cut throat with a broken pop bottle in unit shower–this was done when most patients were away from the unit–difficulty breathing when found; cut neck and wrist in bathtub at home–died by drowning–had "hoped" husband would happen by to discover.

Ingestion: Clearly lethal doses.

> *Examples:* Drinking several ounces of nail polish remover–found covered in bed gagging, pale with large amount of foaming exudate coming from mouth–mildly comatose; took 30 500-mg Doriden tablets right before bedtime–in bed, appeared to be asleep but was actually unconscious in a deep coma.

Other: Highly lethal means employed.

> *Examples:* Plastic bag over head tied tightly with a scarf–found unconscious with head in toilet; drove head on into a gasoline truck but survived with minor scratches and bruises; stuffed plastic in both nostrils and oral pharynx, completely closing airways–she appeared to be sleeping in bed under covers; eloped to another city in car, tied plastic hose to exhaust and suffocated in parking lot; hanged self in closet with door closed–not breathing when cut down; jumped from 90-foot bridge into water–was unconscious when found. Gunshot to chest area (if shotgun used, rate 10.0); jumped headfirst from three-story building.

10.0   Death is almost a certainty regardless of the circumstances or interventions by an outside agent. Most of the people at this level die quickly after the attempt. A very few survive through no fault of their own.

Cutting: Just cuts as severe as in 9.0, except that the likelihood for intervention is even more remote. Blood loss is severe and quick.

> *Examples:* Eloping to an empty house and severely cutting wrists and neck with razor—when a policeman happened by the patient was sitting in a large pool of blood, warded off the policeman with the razor.

Ingestion: Because of the time usually involved before a toxin can take effect there are very few instances of overdosing that can be considered this serious.

> *Examples:* Some that have been serious are: ingesting furniture polish, paint thinner, and many prescription medications while alone in the house with no one expected by; overdose on large quantities of Dalmane and barbiturates with husband out of town and no children or other live-in

companions in the household; ingested 60 Nembutal, went into secluded, wooded area in mid-winter, covered self with leaves which caused him not to be found for several days.

Other: These are the most common types of attempts at this level.

Examples: Jumping off a tall building (four or more floors); jumping in front of cars on a freeway and being hit; eloping and hanging self in gym locker building at night; secretly eloping and drowning self in lake at a time when there was no activity in the lake area and when he would not be expected to be on the unit; gunshot to the head and any effort involving a shotgun.

Appendix B.4.C
Instructions for Approximating
Ingestion Lethality Using Table B.4.3

Several drugs and chemicals known to have been ingested during suicide attempts are listed in column 1 of the associated table. Some of the preparations are combinations of other drugs; if a drug in column 1 is a combination, its principal ingredients are listed directly below it under the heading "Composed of." When a drug in column 1 is known by more than one name, alternate product names are listed directly below it in parentheses. Column 2 provides the LD_{50} range for each of these drugs.[1] When the range is not known, a single number is provided which represents the best estimate of the midpoint of the missing range. The third column is entitled "How supplied." The last two columns show the lethal range or midpoint of each substance for a 120-lb person (column 4) and a 170-lb person (column 5).

To use the table, you need only know how much of a drug was consumed and the person's approximate weight. There are two "comparison weights": 120 lbs and 170 lbs. If the person actually weighs *less* than the comparison weight, the lethality of the dose should be considered proportionally *more* severe. Conversely, if the person weighs *more* than a comparison weight, the dose would *not* be as lethal. *If the weight is not known, then women should be judged against column 4 and men against column 5.*

If the amount of a substance ingested is near the upper limit of the LD_{50} range (given the person's weight), the appropriate lethality rating, not taking into

---

[1] The LD_{50} is the dosage or range of doses found to kill 50% of the subjects by whom it was ingested. The LD_{50} numbers are cast in terms of milligrams of drug/kg of body weight. Should you be interested in the amount of a drug needed to approximate the LD_{50} range for a particular person, multiply the LD_{50} of that drug by the patient's weight in kilograms (1 kg = 2.2 lb).

account other circumstances, is 7.0. When only a single LD_{50} number is provided, then it should be counted as the benchmark for a 7.0. An amount close to the lower end of the LD_{50} range is more coordinate with a rating of 3.5. Once the lethality rating based on the LD_{50} is established, other circumstances surrounding the attempt must be considered. The influence of other circumstances will probably result in a raising or lowering of the original rating. Therefore, the final rating will include LD_{50} data modified by circumstantial information and will best reflect the lethality of the *whole attempt.*

If alcohol is ingested with the other drugs, then the lethality of the drugs should be slightly increased. If, on the other hand, the person is an alcoholic or drug abuser, then the lethality of the drugs ingested is somewhat diminished as the liver is more conditioned to ridding itself of toxins. Where these issues become a factor is when a dose is of borderline lethality.

An *asterisk* before the name of a drug indicates that the drug is lethal in relatively small amounts.[2] "Unknown" doses of drugs with an asterisk should probably be rated at 5.0 or perhaps higher, given proper consideration of other circumstances. "Unknown" doses of drugs without the asterisk should probably be rated 3.5 or below.

---

[2]The criterion for this degree of lethality was established by finding the *median* number of the tablets or capsules taken in a study of 112 overdoses. It was found that 50% of the patients had consumed 30 or *more* tablets/capsules. In Table B.4.3, an asterisk indicates drugs which, in doses as small as 30 tablets/capsules, reach lethal range for a 120-lb person. These evaluations of drug lethality are based on the most common potencies in which the tablets/capsules are dispensed. If the most common potency of a certain tablet/capsule is unknown, the least potent available dose is used in the evaluation. The criterion, therefore, recognizes those drugs that would be potentially lethal in amounts consumed by 50% of the overdosing patients.

Note. From "Lethality of Suicide Attempt Rating Scale" by K. Smith, R. W. Conroy, and B. D. Ehler, 1984, *Suicide and Life-Threatening Behavior*, *14*(4), pp. 215–242. Copyright 1984 by the Guilford Press. Reprinted by permission.

Appendix B.5
A Suicide Screening Checklist (SSC)
for Adolescents and Young Adults

	Yes	No	Uncertain

Suicide history: (max. = 18)
1. Prior attempt
2. 2 or more prior attempts in past year (highly lethal = × 2)
3. Prior suicide threats, ideation
4. Suicidal attempts in family (× 2)
5. Completed attempts in family (× 3)
6. Current suicidal preoccupation, threats, attempt (× 2); detailed, highly lethal* plan (× 2); access to weapon, medication in home (× 4); all three 'yes' = 8
7. Preoccupation with death

Psychiatric History: (11)
8. Psychosis and hospitalization (× 3)
9. Diagnosis of schizophrenia or manic depressive illness (× 3)
10. Poor impulse control (current = × 3)
11. Explosive rage episodes (underline: chronic, single, recent, single past)
12. Accident-proneness (frequency, examples)

School (when relevant): −(9)
13. Grade failure
14. Rejection
15. Poor social relations
16. On probation or dropped out of school (× 2)
17. Disciplinary crisis (× 2)
18. Anticipation of severe punishment
19. Unwanted change of schools

Family: (27)
20. Recent major negative change, usually a loss (death, divorce, serious health problem); (irreversible loss = × 3; divorce = × 3; both 'yes' = × 6)
21. Loss of emotional support, estranged; early loss of parent (× 3)
22. Loss of employment (parent or self)
23. Major depression in parent, sibling (× 2)
24. Alcoholism in family member (× 2)
25. Psychiatric illness in family member (× 2); (23–25 Yes = 6 × 2)
26. History of sexual abuse

Societal: (3)
27. "Contagion" suicide episode
28. Economic down-shift in community
29. Loss of major support system (group, job, career problems)

(continued)

	Yes	No	Uncertain

Personality and Behavior; cognitive style: (60)
30. Anger, rage (intense = × 2; held in × 4; Both = 6)
31. Depression (intensely depressed = × 2; agitated depression = × 4; Both = 6)
32. Hopelessness (× 4) (30, 31, 32, all Yes = 6 + 6 + 4 = 16)
33. Mistrust (paranoid = × 2)
34. Disgust, despair
35. Withdrawn, isolate (2)
36. Low "future time" perspective (× 2)
37. High "past" orientation (× 2) (yes on 36, 37 = 4 × 2 = 8)
38. Rigidity or perfectionism (× 2) (Both = 4)
39. Lack of belonging (× 2)
40. Indifference, lack of motivation (boredom = × 2)
41. Worthlessness, no one cares
42. Shame or guilt (Both = × 2)
43. Helplessness
44. Inability to have fun (× 2)
45. Extreme mood or energy fluctuation (Both = × 2)
46. Giving away valuables

Physical: (14)
47. Male (× 3); Caucasian (× 2); (both 'yes' = 5)
48. Significantly delayed puberty
49. Recent physical injury resulting in deformity, impairment (permanent = × 2)
50. Marked obesity (+20%)**
51. Marked recent underweight or anorexia (−15%)** (more than 20% = × 3)**
52. Sleep disturbed (onset, middle, early awakening)
53. Ongoing physical pain

Interview behavior: (20)
54. Non-communicative, encapsulated (× 4)
55. Negative reaction of patient to interviewer (× 4)
56. Negative reaction of interviewer to patient
57. Increasing "distance" during interview (× 3)
58. Increasing hostility, non-cooperation (× 2)
59. Highly self-critical, self-pitying (Both = × 2)
60. Discusses death, suicide (× 4)

Total Score: _____ (Max. = 162)

Suicide Potential Range Risk Guidelines: *Severe* (110 to 162)
(*Tentative ranges*–to be evaluated by field-testing): *Moderate* (60 to 109)
  Low (below 60)

Confidence Level: _____ High _____ Low   Reasons for low confidence rating:

*"High lethality" defined as method with low degree of reversibility, low risk for rescue (46, 47), substantial medical injury (e.g., comatose).
**Use standard height-weight tables per appropriate age-range.

Manual For Use and Scoring the
Suicide Screening Checklist (SSC):
(Abbreviated Version)

The SSC is completed during and following an interview that includes major focus on areas to be evaluated. When necessary, available friends or relatives may be utilized to collect relevant data to supplement the primary source of patient interview data.

It is critical, initially, to develop as good a level of rapport as possible to ensure maximal amount of involvement and candidness. Inability to develop a high level of rapport is often important data in itself, as lack of cooperation or disruptively high anxiety may be symptomatic of the current level of coping and adaption, as well as ego function.

Care must also be taken to watch for manipulative behavior, in which the person may be desiring to create a negative image to elicit sympathy, attention, etc., or to create a positive image of good psychological health, either due to denial, or because the person is trying to hide their suicidal intent. The degree of manipulation may also be seen in a positive light, as a reflection of the person's maneuverability and skills at seeking control and mastery.

Scoring

Each item is to be scored as present (yes), absent (no), uncertain or unclear (unc).

Weighted items are scored according to the number (multiplier) in parenthesis. If the data fit the highest weighted score when there is more than one score listed, the higher multiplier should be used. For example, if #36 and #37 are both "yes," the total score for the two items is 8 (2 + 2 = 4 × 2 = 8). In #6, a "detailed, highly lethal plan" would be scored a "3," whereas "preoccupation" alone is scored a "2."

Total the scores of all 60 items.

Try to minimize the number of "uncertain" scores (Each "uncertain" score receives a zero score.) Use the cut-off score ranges as guidelines to clinical judgment. A high score should be considered ominous, even if not supported by your own clinical judgment.

On the other hand, a low SSC score that is not supported by clinical judgment needs careful exploration to ascertain if a "false negative" has been obtained. An examination of positive scores on key "item clusters," when a low overall score has been obtained, merits special close scrutiny of the total picture. Secondary (i.e., sequential) screening is usually indicated.

"Low level of confidence" must be evaluated, as this rating raises the question of the validity of the total score. Added sources of data are usually needed.

With successive SSC revisions, based on criterion validity, the total scores and cut-off score ranges should assume increasing levels of objectivity.

A SSC score above 120 or below 20 should be viewed with skepticism, and suggests that responses are being slanted to create a "sick" or "healthy" profile. Until a formal "lie scale" is developed, it is sometimes useful to repeat the same questions at a later point in the interview, to determine the reliability of the original response.

Be wary of the effects of licit or illicit drug usage on mood and level of involvement. Verify amounts consumed if possible and be aware of side effects.

Attempt to corroborate questionable response data by questioning accompanying family members or close friends. Usually a sufficient degree of trust can be established in the interview to minimize doubts about degree of manipulation. Establishing an adequate rapport is important, so that the pattern and total score of an adequate screening instrument can provide decisive data in the diagnostic process, which is a vital reason for its incorporation into decision-making.

Note. From *Report of the Secretary's Task Force on Youth Suicide: Vol. IV* (pp. 4-129–4-144) by Alcohol, Drug Abuse, and Mental Health Administration, 1980, Washington, DC: U.S. Government Printing Office. Copyright 1989 by Dr. Robert Yufit. Reprinted by permission. Suicide Screening Checklist is part of a paper commissioned by the Centers for Disease Control.

Appendix C
An Antisuicide Contract

An Antisuicide Contract

As part of my therapy program, I, _____ , agree to
the following terms: (name)

1. I agree that one of my major therapy goals is to live a long life with more
pleasure and less unhappiness than I now have.

2. I understand that becoming suicidal when depressed or upset stands in the
way of achieving this goal, and I therefore would like to overcome this tendency. I
agree to use my therapy to learn better ways to reduce my emotional distress.

3. Since I understand that this will take time, I agree in the meantime to refuse
to act on urges to injure or kill myself between this day and _____ .
                                                        (date)

4. If at any time I should feel unable to resist suicidal impulses, I agree to
call _____ at _____ or _____ . If this person
            (name)   (number)   (number)
is unavailable, I agree to call _____ at _____ or go
                                    (name)   (number)
directly to _____ at _____ .
              (hospital or agency)   (address)

5. My therapist, _____ , agrees to work with me in
scheduled sessions to help me learn constructive alternatives to self-harm and to be
available as much as is reasonable during times of crisis.

6. I agree to abide by this agreement either until it expires or until it is openly
renegotiated with my therapist. I understand that it is renewable at or near the
expiration date of _____ .
                      (date)

_____   _____
             Signature   Date

_____   _____
         Therapist's Signature   Date

Note. From *Suicide Risk: Assessment and Response Guidelines* (p. 102) by W. J. Fremouw, M. de
Perczel, and T. E. Ellis, 1990, New York: Pergamon Press. Copyright 1990 by Pergamon Press.
Reprinted by permission.

Appendix D
Other Suicide Risk Factor Checklists

Appendix D.1
Suicide Risk Factors Checklist

Psychiatric

Major depression–particularly endogenous
Alcohol dependence–rate 50 × the general population, 25% of all suicides
Drug addiction–10% die by suicide
Personality disorders–especially borderline and compulsive
Schizophrenia—frequently with command hallucinations
Organic psychoses
Past history–especially if attempts were serious
Family history–increased risk in twin and adoption studies
Possible biologic markers: Decreased CSF 5-HIAA, increased CSF MHPG,
    nonsuppressing DST, low platelet MAO, low platelet serotonin, high platelet
    serotonin-2 receptor responsivity
Poor physical health–renal dialysis patients have a suicide rate 400 × higher than
    the general population

Psychologic

History of recent loss
History of parental loss during childhood
Important dates–anniversaries, holidays, etc.
Family instability
Social isolation–loss of social supports

Social

Sex–male 3 × females
Race–Whites 2 × nonwhites, except urban areas where rate is the same; Native
    Americans have higher rates
Age–in men rates rise with age above age 45; in women the peak risk is about age
    55, then the rate declines
Religion–Protestants and atheists have higher rates than Jews and Catholics
Geography–urban rates higher
Marital status–divorced > single > widowed > married
Socioeconomic–high rates at both ends of spectrum, retired and unemployed at
    higher risk

Note. From *Concise Guide to Consultation Psychiatry* (p. 154) by M. G. Wise and J. R. Rundell, 1988, Washington, DC: American Psychiatric Press. Copyright 1988 by American Psychiatric Press. Reprinted by permission.

Appendix D.2
SAD PERSONS Scale

A positive factor counts one point.
Scores: 0–2 = Little risk
        3–4 = Follow closely
        5–6 = Strongly consider psychiatric hospitalization
        7–10 = Very high risk, hospitalize or commit

Sex
Age
Depression

Previous attempt
Ethanol abuse
Rational thinking loss
Social support deficit
Organized plan
No spouse
Sickness

Note. From *Concise Guide to Consultation Psychiatry* (p. 44) by M. G. Wise and J. R. Rundell, 1988, Washington, DC: American Psychiatric Press. Copyright 1988 by American Psychiatric Press. Reprinted with permission. Adapted from "Evaluation of suicidal patients: the SAD PERSONS scale" by W. M. Patterson, H. H. Dohn, J. Bird, et al., 1983, *Psychosomatics, 24,* 343–349.

Appendix D.3
Mnemonic for Diagnostic
Criteria for Depression

SIG: E CAPS (Prescribe Energy Capsules)		
S	Sleep	Insomnia or hypersomnia
I	Interests	Loss of interest or pleasure in activities
G	Guilt	Excessive guilt, worthlessness, hopelessness, helplessness
E	Energy	Fatigue or loss of energy
C	Concentration	Diminished concentration ability, indecisive
A	Appetite	Decreased appetite, > 5% weight loss or gain
P	Psychomotor	Psychomotor retardation or agitation
S	Suicidality	Suicidal ideation, plan, or attempt

Note. From *Concise Guide to Consultation Psychiatry* (p. 44) by M. G. Wise and J. R. Rundell, 1988, Washington, DC: American Psychiatric Press. Copyright 1988 by American Psychiatric Press. Reprinted by permission.

Appendix D.4
Examination of a
Potentially Suicidal Patient

Is there a wish to die?
Is there a plan?
What is the method planned?
What epidemiologic risk factors are present?
Is there a history of recent substance use?
What medical illnesses are present?
What psychiatric diagnoses are present?
Is there a past or family history of suicide attempts?
Is there a history of impulsivity?
What is the level of psychological defensive functioning?
Has there been a will made recently?
Is there a history of recent losses, and how do they relate to past history of losses?
Is there talk of plans for the future?
What is the nature of the patient's social support system?

Note. From *Concise Guide to Consultation Psychiatry* (p. 155) by M. G. Wise and J. R. Rundell, 1988, Washington, DC: American Psychiatric Press. Copyright 1988 by American Psychiatric Press. Reprinted by permission.

Appendix E
Action Guidelines:
Legal Issues in
Emergency Psychiatry

Legal Issues in Emergency Psychiatry

A. General Principles
1. *Document* data, source, reliability, reasoning, and rationale in developing plan, interventions.
2. *Decide* recommendations explicitly and record them, together with availability of resources.
3. *Obtain* consultations freely as needed to determine course of action.
4. *Determine* whether specific intervention is necessary.

B. Dangerousness to Others
1. *Check for* history of impulsivity, threats, violence, assault record, short temper, grudges, ownership of weapons, substance abuse.
2. *Obtain* data from widest possible number of sources with patient's permission; if permission refused, weigh risk/benefit of breach of confidentiality against danger.
3. *Assess for* toxic states, obsessional thoughts of violence, grudge or revenge, persecutory delusions fixed on specific persons, anger, tension, violence of speech or action on examination.

C. Dangerousness to Self
1. Suicidality
   a. *Check for* history of affective illness, especially depression; history of psychosis or suicide attempts in patient or family; substance abuse and alcoholism; recent losses; marital status; availability of resources.
   b. *Assess for* toxic states, clinical depression, command suicidal hallucinations, advanced age, acuteness of suicidal press, risk/rescue factors.
   c. *Locate* patient on continuum of suicidal ideation, intent, plan, means, attempt.
   d. *Distinguish* true suicidality from specious, feigned, or chronic suicidality.
2. Inability to care for self
   a. *Check for* degree of illness versus degree of functioning by history, availability of resources (residence, family, others).
   b. *Assess* present functioning, remediable problems.
   c. *Attempt* return to self-care state or *provide* caretaking environment.

D. Therapeutic Interventions
1. Crisis intervention
   a. Verbal: *allow* abreaction, ventilation; *define* problem; *validate* difficulty; *attempt* to reestablish perspective.
   b. Chemical: *treat* acute states with appropriate psychoparmacologic agents; *begin* long-term antidepressants if safe and indicated.
2. Consultation to existing relationships
   a. *Assess* point or issue of breakdown of preexisting relationship.
   b. *Attempt* to restore relationship, recruit assistance of objects, facilities, family, community resources.

(continued)

   c. *Return* the patient if possible to previous supportive relationship.
3. Environmental manipulation
   a. *Remove* patient from noxious environment (to friends, family, emergency shelter).
   b. *Place* patient in protected environment: "asylum" concept. (This may be a hospital.)
4. Hospitalization Indications
Patient:
   a. requires immediate intensive psychiatric observation and monitoring;
   b. requires specific psychiatric treatments best delivered in an inpatient setting (e.g., pharmacologic equilibration, introduction to new therapist).
   c. requires protection of containment in hospital because of dangerousness due to mental illness.
   d. requires asylum from deteriorating, chaotic, overburdened, or overwhelmed extra hospital support structures.
   e. requires intensive support during stressful interval (e.g., parents' vacation, loss of therapist).
5. Hospitalization: Contraindications
Patient:
   a. presents serious danger of nonconstructive regression.
   b. presents history of persistent failure to use appropriately or to benefit from hospitalization.
   c. desires to use hospital for nontherapeutic purposes (escape law, avoid final exams, as a place to sleep).

Index

Index

About the Author

The author of *The Suicidal Patient,* Bruce Bongar, Ph.D., is an associate professor in the doctoral program in clinical psychology at the Pacific Graduate School of Psychology in Palo Alto, California. Dr. Bongar has also taught clinical psychology at Holy Cross College and conducted research on the suicidal and difficult patient at the Department of Psychiatry, University of Massachusetts Medical School. His past clinical appointments include service as a senior clinical psychologist with the Division of Psychiatry, Childrens Hospital of Los Angeles, and work as a clinical/community mental health psychologist on the psychiatric emergency team of the Los Angeles County Department of Mental Health. For the past 12 years, Dr. Bongar has maintained a small private practice specializing in psychotherapy, consultation and supervision in working with the difficult and life-threatening patient. He is a fellow of the Academy of Psychosomatic Medicine, a member of the board of directors of the American Association of Suicidology (AAS), the chair of the AAS training committee, and a consulting editor for the AAS journal *Suicide and Life-Threatening Behavior.* Recently, he was appointed to the Education and Training Committee of the American Psychological Association's Division of Psychotherapy (Division 29). In addition to his published research on suicide and life-threatening behavior, Dr. Bongar's published work reflects his long-standing interest in the wide-ranging complexities of therapeutic interventions with difficult patients in general.

The legal consultant for this book is Eric A. Harris, Ed.D., J.D., a national authority on law and psychology, as well as special consultant to the Practice Directorate of the American Psychological Association. Dr. Harris holds appointments as a clinical instructor of psychology in the Department of Psychiatry at Harvard Medical School and is a faculty member of the Massachusetts School of Professional Psychology.